BEYOND COLLEGE FOR ALL

BEYOND COLLEGE FOR ALL
CAREER PATHS FOR THE
FORGOTTEN HALF

JAMES E. ROSENBAUM

A Volume in the American Sociological Association's
Rose Series in Sociology

Russell Sage Foundation • New York

The Russell Sage Foundation

The Russell Sage Foundation, one of the oldest of America's general purpose foundations, was established in 1907 by Mrs. Margaret Olivia Sage for "the improvement of social and living conditions in the United States." The Foundation seeks to fulfill this mandate by fostering the development and dissemination of knowledge about the country's political, social, and economic problems. While the Foundation endeavors to assure the accuracy and objectivity of each book it publishes, the conclusions and interpretations in Russell Sage Foundation publications are those of the authors and not of the Foundation, its Trustees, or its staff. Publication by Russell Sage, therefore, does not imply Foundation endorsement.

Library of Congress Cataloging-in-Publication Data

Rosenbaum, James E., 1943—
    Beyond college for all : career paths for the forgotten half / James Rosenbaum.
       p. cm. — (American Sociological Association Rose series in sociology)
    Includes bibliographical references and index.
    ISBN 0-87154-727-9 (cloth)   ISBN 0-87154-753-8 (paper)
    1. School-to-work transition—United States.   2. Vocational education—United States.   3. High school graduates—Employment—United States.   4. Youth—Employment—United States.   5. Occupational training—United States.   6. Labor market—United States.   I. Title.   II. Series.

    LC1045 .R77 2001
    331.11'423—dc21   2001041783

Text design by Suzanne Nichols

RUSSELL SAGE FOUNDATION
112 East 64th Street, New York, New York 10021
10 9 8 7 6 5 4 3 2 1

The Rose Series in Sociology

The American Sociological Association's Rose Series in Sociology publishes books that integrate knowledge and address controversies from a sociological perspective. Books in the Rose Series are at the forefront of sociological knowledge. They are lively and often involve timely and fundamental issues on significant social concerns. The series is intended for broad dissemination throughout sociology, across social science and other professional communities, and to policy audiences. The series was established in 1967 by a bequest to ASA from Arnold and Caroline Rose to support innovations in scholarly publishing.

= Contents =

About the Author

James E. Rosenbaum is professor of sociology, education, and social policy at the Institute for Policy Research at Northwestern University.

═ Preface ═

We assume that we already know the basic processes by which American society operates. As participants, we have lived through it ourselves, and, as scholars, we have read many studies. Yet, although we do not realize it, we have blinders. Comparative research can help us see beyond our blinders, to see processes that we never imagined.

This project began as a vague set of ideas and questions about whether school-to-work practices in Japan and Germany had any counterparts in the United States, and, if not, then how various actors perceived the process. In this inquiry, prior research on Japan and Germany raised questions about the United States which led us to discover unmet needs, unexplored resources, unconsidered options, and even promising initiatives, which do not work out because the other people do not understand and do not respond. Employers, students, and teachers take actions that all three find unsatisfactory because they do not see alternatives, or they do not realize how to make them work.

Besides bringing some interesting ideas to the project, and convincing three foundations to provide support, my primary accomplishment was to interest some very talented graduate students into the enterprise. This book is very much a joint project. Graduate students have been involved in all phases of this project, and they have made important contributions. Several graduate students joined me in collecting and analyzing data and in joint authoring published papers from this project. These collaborative publications appeared in a diverse array of journals and books, and form the basis of several chapters in this volume. Related earlier publications are listed in the chapter notes at the end of the volume.

As graduate students and collaborators, Amy Binder, Stefanie De-Luca, Stephanie A. Jones, Takehiko Kariya, Melinda Krei, Shazia R. Miller, and Karen Nelson were influential in helping develop the ideas that pervade this book. The task of extending and integrating these diverse works and providing the missing pieces fell to me as my students went on to other projects. I hope that by updating the papers and integrating them with the other work in the project, this book shows the broader implications of each study and its relationships to the others.

Special mention must be made of one of my former students. In 1984, Takehiko Kariya, a recent college graduate from the University of Tokyo, came to the United States on a Fulbright fellowship to complete graduate studies. He had read my first book and wanted to do similar work. Since that time, we have worked together, continuously, while he finished his Ph.D., and nearly every summer since then. We have both learned a great deal from each other. We have learned about each other's nation, and we have learned to see our own nation's practices in new ways. This book is the result of that seventeen years of collaboration. I hope that it continues for many more.

As former editor of the Rose Series, George Farkas provided enormous support and thoughtful criticism to the development of this book. Additional comments and suggestions were provided by Tom Bailey, John Bishop, Regina Deil, Greg Duncan, Mark Granovetter, Maureen Hallinan, Christopher Jencks, Felice Levine, Aaron Pallas, Anne Pille, Michael Schwartz, David Stern, Burton Weisbrod, and Chris Winship.

Support for this work was provided by the Spencer Foundation, the W.T. Grant Foundation, and the Pew Charitable Trusts. A new grant from the Sloan Foundation permitted me to extend some of the information in chapter eleven. I am especially indebted to Professors Fay Cook and Burton Weisbrod, directors of the Institute for Policy Research at Northwestern University, who provided the seed-money support that fostered this project when it was an unfunded idea and who maintained support for writing of this book after the grants ended.

Finally, I am indebted to my wife Ginny and daughter Janet, who discussed these ideas, and provided the support that made this work possible. It is to them that I dedicate this book.

═ Chapter 1 ═

Pathways to Adulthood: Reversing the Downward Spiral of the Youth Labor Market

A CRISIS is emerging in the American labor market. Young people who do not get college degrees have been called the "forgotten half" because society offers them no way to enter adult roles (Howe 1988). They either experience enormous difficulty getting jobs or take dead-end jobs that offer low status, little training, and pay too low to support a family (Osterman 1980; Althauser and Kalleberg 1981; NAS 1984). Among new high school graduates, 26 percent of whites and 56 percent of blacks still had no job four months after graduating from high school (NCES 1993, 82). Moreover, another study found that most graduates who got jobs (58.3 percent) were only continuing the same dead-end jobs that they already held during high school (Nolfi 1978). Obviously, high school graduation does not give these students access to better jobs. Moreover, their difficulties do not end quickly, and their early problems may hurt their career many years later (D'Amico and Maxwell 1990; Lynch 1989). Even at age thirty, a large portion of high school graduates continue to hold low-paying, high-turnover jobs (Osterman 1995).[1]

College is often viewed as the solution. Like many political leaders, President Clinton urged all student to attend college, and high school officials in some communities have stressed college preparation, while dismantling vocational programs. This college-for-all approach has clearly had an impressive impact in raising students' plans. A national survey finds that nearly all seniors (95 percent) plan to attend college (National Educational Longitudinal Survey, NELS 1992). Unfortunately, school officials who embrace college-for-all programs,

1

rarely examine what happens to these students in subsequent years. Only 28 percent of young adults, age thirty to thirty-four, have a B.A. degree or higher, and another 8 percent have an associate's degree (NCES, 1999, table 8). What happens to students between high school and age thirty? Instead of bragging about students' high expectations, school officials should be considering the long-term effects of the college-for-all approach. We shall follow a cohort of high school seniors for ten years after their graduation to see which ones follow through on their educational plans and whether earnings benefits follow (see chapter 3, this volume).

The youth labor market also poses difficulties for employers. Employers complain that high school graduates have poor basic skills in reading, writing, and mathematics, and that as a result they are incapable of handling good jobs (CED 1985; Marshall and Tucker 1993; NCEE 1983). Many employers are so concerned that they are providing basic skills education programs for their workers (Eurich 1985). These problems will become more serious because demand is projected to increase, particularly in jobs requiring the higher skills that youths lack, but the number of young people is not increasing. As one analyst (Howe 1988, 30) described the double-edged nature of the problem: "Unless workforce basic skills are raised substantially, and quickly, we shall have more joblessness among the least skilled, accompanied by a chronic shortage of workers with advanced skills." Even in today's strong labor market, youths still have difficulty in getting jobs with advancement opportunities, and employers have great difficulty in hiring workers with good skills and work habits. Many business and labor groups foresee "labor market disruptions" for some sectors of the economy. The projected skill shortage suggests that we can no longer afford such serious educational failure, nor can we squander the potential labor force contributions of new high school graduates in long periods of unemployment and aimless job turnover.

Although the strong labor market reduces unemployment, it does not solve employers' skill shortages, and it does not give unskilled youths good jobs that pay enough to support a family. Moreover, a strong labor market will not last forever. Even low unemployment rates do not solve the underlying difficulties of employers and youths.

These problems are not inevitable; indeed, other nations have managed to avoid them. Germany and Japan have had dramatically lower youth unemployment rates than the United States over long periods of time (Hess, Petersen, and Mortimer 1994, 5; Hamilton and Hurrelmann 1994; U.S. Department of Education 1987). In addition, while

American youths were two and a half times more likely to be unemployed than adults in 1965, and four times more likely by 1979, this ratio was much lower and did not increase in Japan and Germany (Coleman 1994, 35). Even in the 1990s, youths' disadvantage in the labor market remained much lower in Japan and Germany than in the United States (Stern and Wagner 1999, 6). Moreover, Japanese and German employers even see advantages to hiring younger workers, who, besides being less expensive, are often more energetic and more easily taught, especially in new technologies. An American researcher noted that German eighteen-year-olds hold responsible jobs that Americans believe eighteen-year-olds cannot do (Hamilton 1990). Young people are seen as desirable and capable workers in Japan and Germany, but not in the United States.

Why do these differences occur? Are American young people inherently defective, or is there something about the way they are brought into work that creates their work-entry difficulties? Youth work-entry difficulties are not an inevitable feature of young people or of labor markets. They vary across different societies, and they seem to be affected by social contexts (Shavit and Muller 1998). As we describe later, Japan and Germany have clear systems for helping high school students enter work, and the resulting contacts have dramatic benefits for employers, students, and schools. These Japanese and German systems may explain their lower youth unemployment rates, youths' better preparation for employment, and employers' confidence in the value of youth.

In contrast, the U.S. labor market is highly decentralized and lacks a clear system. Every year schools turn out students, and employers hire some of these students, yet we know very little about the relationships that form between these institutions—how these institutions communicate information, how they respond to each other, and whether they use information from each other. We suspect that the relationships between employers and high schools vary a great deal, and that this variation in contacts may affect work-entry processes and outcomes (Granovetter 1974/1995).

This book explores the ways in which American students, employers, and teachers perceive each other, what information they receive about each other, and what actions they take to affect the youth work-entry process. Analyses of the youth labor market usually focus on either employers or youths, but we examine both, as well as high school influences. Moreover, while most analyses blame students for poor skills or blame employers for restricted job opportunities, this book considers whether the relationships between these parties contribute to the problems. We examine whether youths' work-entry problems arise because of poor interaction, poor information flow, or poor incentives for employers, students, and teachers.

Like neoclassical economic theory, I focus on employers' and students' incentives. That theory assumes that students and employers see incentives to respond to each other's needs, but I consider whether they actually do. Employers or students may not perceive incentives correctly, they may send inadequate information about their needs (or qualifications), or they may not use all of the information they receive. Unfortunately, research has rarely tested these assumptions. Instead of making assumptions about perceptions, we examine the incentives that students and employers actually perceive and the factors that affect their perceptions and actions. If employers and students do not perceive their presumed incentives, that could explain youths' work-entry problems.

The studies in this book arise from a new model, the linkage model. This model resembles mainstream labor market theories in some ways. Like signaling and network models, the linkage model focuses on information problems and on the ways in which social contacts convey information (Granovetter 1974/1995). Like the neoclassical economic model, our model emphasizes the importance of incentives. Like the structural model, it contends that social structures create and contribute to inequalities.

However, unlike the structural model, which emphasizes structural barriers and unequal resources, the linkage model suggests that institutional contacts influence not only resources but also incentives. The model contends that inequalities arise, not merely from initial differences among individuals, but also from the incentives, or lack of incentives, that society and schools offer to individuals. Because societal linkages tend to offer incentives to advantaged students but not to others, linkages often magnify preexisting differences in human capital.

The result is stratified incentives, which increase the motivation and human capital of some students while decreasing them for others. We show that American society offers stratified incentives: it offers strong linkages and incentives to high-achieving students and weak linkages and few incentives to other students, who consequently see no reason to exert effort in high school. Stratified incentives create a perverse situation in which lower-achieving students not only are at a disadvantage, but they also have no incentives to improve their achievement. In contrast, higher-achieving students not only are at an advantage, but they also have clear incentives to keep improving. Contrary to a common assumption, we find that many low-achieving students plan high career goals but obtain poor information about the requirements for their goals and about actions they could take to achieve desirable career payoffs. This situation is not inevitable, and as we show, some other nations do not stratify incentives, and they give work-bound students clear incentives for school effort. These societies provide a linkage structure that offers incentives to all students, regardless of career goal or prior achievement.

The linkage model considers additional questions that are usually ignored by other theories. While signaling theory contends that actors need more information and network theory contends that contacts affect the amount of information (Raider and Burt 1996), the linkage model contends that actors also need better information—that is, information with the right qualities. Often actors have the problem of deciding how to select information to use and how to get information that is relevant and trustworthy. We examine the ways in which long-term, repeated contacts affect the amount, relevance, and credibility of information, as well as the factors that influence who gets better information, including stratification influences on the quality of information. Some students may get better information about their incentives than others.

This book explores new questions about American work-entry practices and makes new discoveries about students, employers, and high schools. We show that poor information leads students to make unrealistic plans and to fail to make some efforts that could help them achieve their goals. We discover that students are far more confused than is generally realized, and that some groups of students have predictably high failure rates, yet counselors do not provide the career advising that we had assumed is part of their job.

Of course, work-bound students' incentives are affected by employers' reactions to their efforts. We examine how employers get information about recent high school graduates, how high schools help students get jobs, and how institutional relationships affect these processes. Although informal personal networks have been studied, studies usually ignore institutional contacts, repeated contacts, and the ways in which high school–employer interactions may influence youths' labor market outcomes. Some critics have noted that employers use invalid and biased information in hiring; we examine employers' reasons for using information about which they have misgivings. The nature of contacts may affect whether employers use school information in making hiring decisions; whether or not they do, in turn, affects students' incentives for school effort.

We also examine high schools' effects on the work-entry process and on work-bound students' incentives. High school is the main societal institution that could help students enter society. It is the last institution that serves nearly all youths. High schools could influence employers' perceptions of students, students' perceptions of the labor market, and students' incentives. Our research examines whether high schools provide information to employers about students that corresponds to employers' needs, that predicts students' labor market success, and that creates incentives for students. We also examine whether high schools help students get better jobs, and if so, how this happens in the absence of formal procedures. We discover deficiencies in current practices and describe circumstances that might address those deficiencies.

These studies also point to actions that could remedy these problems. These studies discover that some employers have found ways to use high schools to meet their needs, and that some teachers have found ways to create incentives for students. We also discover actions that students can take in high school to get desirable jobs, including some of which many students are unaware. For instance, we discover that high schools give evaluations that signal students' value in the workplace and predict their eventual career success, yet most employers, students, and teachers are not aware of the predictive power of these indicators. We also discover that some students benefit from hidden school job-placement practices that lead to large earnings payoffs, and that, surprisingly, these school job placements help minorities and women more than white men. (White men rely more on family contacts, which we find actually have lower long-term earnings payoffs than school contacts.) Indeed, though the American system lacks formal linkages, we discover that some American teachers create informal networks with employers that are similar to the formal school-to-work institutional contacts in Japan and Germany. These informal linkages enable teachers to guide youths toward actions that enhance their labor market value, and they provide employers with trusted signals of youths' productive value.

The linkage model contends that an appropriate infrastructure of strong-tie contacts can convey relevant and trusted information about the positive value of lower-achieving students. Such linkages show students and employers each other's needs and show them incentives to respond to each other. Just as the College Board infrastructure creates incentives for college-bound students, school-employer linkages can create strong incentives for work-bound students.

The linkage model concurs with network theory that contacts are important; however, we explore the conditions necessary to make contacts effective. We show that some reforms that tried to improve labor market access without creating appropriate contacts have inadvertently stigmatized participants and failed to convey their positive value. We explore the theoretical basis for creating effective contacts—information channels, normative sanctions, and reciprocity. We examine how some teachers create effective contacts that give meaning and value to the actions of students, particularly disadvantaged students who otherwise would have difficulty showing their positive qualities in the labor market.

The rest of this chapter has three tasks. First, we review the findings of prior research that suggest that the interactions between employers, students, and teachers sometimes make youths' work-entry problems worse. These results indicate the need for a new view of these interactions.

Second, to get a fresh perspective on interaction, we look at a system in which labor market interactions are very different from ours. Like fish not noticing the water, people have difficulty seeing customary interactions because they take them for granted. It is particularly difficult to notice missing elements—aspects of interaction that could occur but do not. This new perspective raises questions that we ordinarily do not think to ask, challenges our implicit assumptions, and points to what our society is lacking that may be contributing to the difficulties of employers and students. This suggests new research issues for our study of the American labor market. Third, this chapter outlines the agenda for the rest of the book.

Mutual Responsiveness or Downward Spiral?

Do interactions between employers, students, and teachers reduce youths' work-entry problems, or do they sometimes make these problems worse? It would be nice to assume that problems will easily fix themselves. Neoclassical economic theory suggests a plausible way in which problems create pressures for constructive change. If employers cannot get suitable workers, they will create incentives for students to prepare themselves adequately, and students will respond. If work-bound students lack skills for getting good jobs, they will anticipate their problem and increase their efforts and preparation. This theory predicts an upward spiral—employers and students responding to each other's needs so that they can benefit from each other.

Unfortunately, that positive scenario may not happen. Instead of an upward spiral, there are indications that a downward spiral sometimes occurs. As we note later in the chapter, employers do not always create clear incentives for students to increase their efforts, and they sometimes inadvertently contribute to the problems they decry.

Nor do students necessarily respond to employers' needs. Research indicates that some students not only are low-achieving, but they also lack the motivation to improve their achievement or to exert any effort in school. Far from responding to each other's needs, employers and students seem to be strikingly *un*responsive to each other's needs. Economic theory did not foresee this downward spiral.

Employers and the Downward Spiral

Are employers at fault for the poor school-to-work transition? Do employers really care about academic skills, or are they complaining only to justify the poor jobs that they offer to young workers? In particular, if employers care about youths' academic skills, why don't they pay attention to school performance in their hiring practices?

Judging from their public statements, employers care a great deal, and they see youths' poor academic skills as causing serious productivity problems. The heads of major corporations often give speeches on highly visible occasions about the poor academic skills of young people and the resulting problems for national productivity (Ray and Mickelson 1993). Many national blue-ribbon panels have issued reports decrying youths' poor skills (CED 1985; NAS 1984; NCEE 1983).

Yet there are reasons for doubting these claims. Some critics have wondered whether these Sunday speeches are merely a smoke screen to justify offering poor jobs and poor pay to youths (Ray and Mickelson 1993). Employers have many undemanding jobs, and they often restrict youths to "youth jobs" that demand little skill or responsibility and offer no training or advancement. Researchers have found that job tasks often do not really need the amount of education stated in formal job descriptions (Berg 1971; Attewell 1987: Levin and Rumberger 1987). Looking over the jobs that employers need to fill, it is easy to infer that they do not necessarily need workers with academic skills or any other skills to fill them (Borman 1991).

Moreover, despite employers' claims of needing workers with academic skills, few employers use students' high school performance in their hiring decisions. Although an employer survey in five cities found that over 70 percent of employers require a high school diploma, employers most often ask for this information in applicants' self-reports. Fewer than one-third of employers check applicants' education, and fewer than 5 percent recruit directly from schools (Holzer 1995, 52, 55). In the 1997 National Employer Survey, employers asked to rank the relative importance of various potential criteria in the hiring process on a five-point scale (from "essential" to "not at all important") put "tests and academic performance" near the bottom of all criteria (2.3 and 2.5), just above "teacher recommendations" (2.0), and far below "applicants' attitude" and "employer references" (4.6 and 3.9, respectively) (Shapiro and Iannozzi 1999, table 2). Employers rarely make efforts to obtain valid information from schools. As John Bishop (1993, 343) notes, "Many employers were remarkably casual about their hiring selections." In fact, longitudinal surveys of new high school graduates consistently find that grades, test scores, and other school information have little effect on unemployment, earnings, or the jobs that graduates get after high school (Griffin, Kalleberg, and Alexander 1981; Meyer and Wise 1982; Willis and Rosen 1979).

Why do grades and test scores have so little influence on hiring? Sometimes the fault is with high schools, which fail to send transcripts to employers (Bishop 1993). However, high schools generally respond to strong needs by local interest groups (Useem and Useem 1974), especially when they are asked to do something as simple as providing transcripts. Thus, if schools are not providing transcripts, we must wonder whether employers have asked them to do so. Indeed, research indicates that many employers do not care about school information. In a large survey, employers report that grades are important for hiring college graduates, but not for hiring high school graduates (Crain 1984), and another study found that most employers do not even request school transcripts (Bills 1988). Even when employers consider school experience, they do not necessarily focus on academics. A bank personnel officer reported that he sought people with social skills, and that extracurricular activities were thus more important than grades (Bills 1988).

Employers' neglect of school performance in their hiring decisions seems to cast doubt on their claims about the importance of academic skills. High schools devote enormous efforts to evaluating students repeatedly over the year and to compiling a record of students' cumulative achievements. Nonetheless, employers ignore these evaluations. Without any awareness of the irony of their statements, employers complain about their workers' poor academic skills and poor work habits, and yet, in the same interviews, they report that they ignore applicants' records of academic achievements and school efforts (chapter 6).

This book examines whether employers really want youths to have stronger academic skills or are complaining for some other reason, perhaps to justify confining youths to jobs with poor pay and career prospects (chapter 5). It also examines whether school information has any value in predicting which youths will do well in the workplace (chapter 8). It looks at employers' perceptions of school information and their reasons for not using such information (chapter 6). It also considers the effect of the larger context in which employers receive school information on their reluctance to use it, and some circumstances in which employers are willing to use school information (chapters 6 and 10).

Students and the Downward Spiral

Do work-bound students perceive incentives to improve their school achievement? Economic theory assumes that students do perceive such incentives, and that these incentives lead them to work hard in school to improve the skills they bring to the labor market.

Although some blue-ribbon commissions have blamed teachers, there are many indications that students are not responding to teachers' efforts. In every Gallup poll over the past three decades, parents identified student disinterest, misbehavior, and drug and alcohol use as among the greatest high school problems. Many kinds of motivation and discipline problems are widespread: absenteeism, class cutting, tardiness, disruptive behavior, verbal abuse, failure to do homework assignments, and substance abuse (Birman and Natriello 1978; Chabot and Garibaldi 1982; Cusick 1983; DeLeonibus 1978; DiPrete 1981). Students are inattentive in class, look out of windows, talk to each other, groom themselves, and even sleep in class (Sedlak et al. 1986). In the National Educational Longitudinal Survey(NELS), 31 percent of high school sophomores do only one hour of homework a week or less, and teachers report that 10 percent of students rarely do homework (DeLuca and Rosenbaum, forthcoming). Before we can improve students' achievement, we must understand why students exert so little effort in school.

These are not just problems for schools; they are problems for society. One of the fundamental challenges for any society is to engage each new generation of youth. To persist for another generation, society must engage youths' efforts to achieve societal goals (Durkheim 1956 [1912]). Schools have the primary responsibility in this process, and school disengagement is probably a precursor of societal disengagement. The disengagement of large portions of students is a real threat to society and to youths' own prospects. Indeed, many working-class and black youths have great difficulty becoming engaged in school and society (Willis 1977; Fordham and Ogbu 1986).

Moreover, the disengagement of a few individuals has far-reaching implications for the entire schooling process. Even if only a few students are absent in a day, different students are absent each day, so teachers must keep backtracking to help the prior day's absentees catch up. Passive student disinterest can force teachers to adjust their instruction to keep most students following along, and active disruption by just one or two individuals can bring instruction to a standstill. In addition, teachers have difficulty improving students' effort if they are met by a uniform lack of effort by students (Sedlak et al. 1986). Thus, work-bound students' poor motivation undermines the overall sense of purpose in classrooms.

Motivation problems may be more serious than achievement problems, and they are hard to explain. Although economic theory assumes that youths see incentives for school effort, and employers call for reforms to improve students' poor academic achievement, few studies have examined whether students see any incentives for school effort. Do students lack motivational capacity, do they fail to perceive incentives for school effort, or are they unresponsive to those incentives, perhaps because they do not see any actions they can take in high school that will help them attain their career goals?

Teachers and the Downward Spiral

Although employers urge teachers to raise academic demands, it is not clear that students would respond. Just as it is not clear that students see incentives to exert effort in school, it is not clear that they see teachers as possessing authority over any rewards that matter to them. Grades are the main direct sanction that teachers control. When employers do not use grades for hiring, students see that grades do not affect the jobs they will get and teacher authority is severely crippled. Employers often ask why teachers do not exert their authority, but by ignoring grades, employers may unwittingly be undermining teachers' authority over work-bound students.

With their authority undermined, teachers still must come to terms with students. How do teachers respond? As long as they are in the same classroom, they must reach an accommodation, and with limited bargaining power, teachers compromise their expectations. "In most high schools there exists a complex, tacit conspiracy to avoid sustained, rigorous, demanding basic inquiry" (Sedlak et al. 1986, 83). Teachers make an implicit bargain with students: they will demand little of students if students will demand little of them. As a high school senior reported, "As long as I do not cause too many hassles for teachers, they will let me get by and graduate" (Rosenbaum 1976, 109).

External constraints can limit this bargain, so it is not likely to affect students who aspire to selective colleges. Students who aspire to selective colleges cannot press for lower standards, because selective colleges penalize schools and students with low achievement. These colleges also give teachers authority to evaluate students and give schools incentives to devote resources (better books, teachers, and laboratories) to college-bound students.

However, similar constraints may not apply for other students. Do students who aspire to open-admissions colleges, which are designed to open access, see incentives for effort in high school? This book examines how these policies affect students' views of payoffs to high school effort (chapter 3).

Of course, students know that colleges and employers demand diplomas, which teachers still control. However, all-or-nothing rewards like diplomas encourage students only to satisfy minimum requirements, and failure is not a credible threat against what Theodore Sizer (1984, 158) has described as a "common front of [student] uninterest," since teachers cannot fail *all* students if performances are "uniformly shoddy." Moreover, teachers are unlikely to fight to maintain standards for work-bound students when employers do not care enough to use grades for hiring.

Incremental rewards like grades are far more effective at motivating people than all-or-nothing rewards, but they are not effective if they do not influence valued outcomes. The motivation and discipline problems of work-bound students may indicate that grades have become ineffective and that teachers may not have authority over any incentives that students value.

Are teachers crippled by a lack of authority to influence important outcomes for most students? Or do teachers have ways to buttress their authority and provide meaningful incentives? Do teacher evaluations predict the educational outcomes of students, even in an era when many students attend open-admissions colleges and seek two-year degrees? Can teachers give any evaluations that affect job outcomes? Are there any circumstances in which employers value teacher evaluations and give teachers authority to influence job outcomes?

The Dilemmas of the Downward Spiral and an Alternative System

It is dismaying to discover that we are in a perverse situation: employers contribute to the problems they decry, and students respond by becoming increasingly unsuited for college or jobs. Employers ignore students' school achievement, and students respond with just the behaviors that employers deplore—doing the minimum required to pass and developing habits of poor attendance, poor discipline, and low engagement. Teachers are blamed for students' shortcomings, but it is not clear that they have authority to influence outcomes that students value, so they may dilute standards and bargain with students about assignments. Instead of problems fixing themselves, as economists assume, we have the opposite—employers, students, and schools may sometimes make their problems worse.

Is this downward spiral inevitable or do alternatives exist? We can gain some perspective on the American situation by comparing it with a radically different system. Japan has an explicit system to coordinate the behaviors and expectations of employers, students, and teachers. Japan's system creates an upward spiral in which employers and students are mutually responsive. We use the Japanese example to pose new issues and to suggest studies of American practices that have not been examined. Our aim is not to urge that we emulate Japan, but to gain a better understanding of American practices by contrasting them with Japan's. These studies allow us to discover new aspects of American practices, and they suggest a way for the United States to escape the downward spiral.

The System That Helped Japan Escape Its Downward Spiral

Like the United States today, Japan in the 1920s had a serious shortage of skilled workers while unskilled workers had high unemployment rates. A series of policies was tried to create a better-trained workforce over the next several decades, but each one failed, and employers became increasingly dissatisfied with youths' preparation and productivity. Even in the 1950s, "Made in Japan" signified inferior production. Yet today there is widespread respect for the high quality of Japanese products, and Japanese youths excel in academic achievement and productivity. Some attribute Japan's success to its culture, which the United States cannot easily duplicate. But Japan's culture has not greatly changed over this period. Its practices have changed, however, so its practices, not its culture, are the most likely explanation for Japan's great success at training work-bound youths.

Japan implemented a system in which high schools are much more involved in allocating students into the labor force than American schools are. The United States and Japan have similar proportions of high school graduates who directly enter the workforce (about 40 percent). While American high schools help only 10 percent of these students find jobs, Japanese high schools help over 75 percent.

Japanese high schools do not just give advice—they provide access to jobs. Schools have long-standing relationships with certain employers who offer the same number of jobs to a school each year and expect schools to nominate seniors of dependable quality for those jobs. These employers expect schools to nominate students with better grades for better jobs.

Homeroom teachers advise students on their choices and allow them to apply for the school's nomination if their choices are appropriate. A committee of teachers then nominates and ranks students for job openings; it is that process that permits students to apply to these employers. The employers cannot choose among all interested students, only among those selected by teachers, and students cannot apply to these employers without the school's nomination. Thus, youths compete for jobs before entering the labor market, and teachers make the first selections.[2]

Does this system actually work, as the policy claims? Like U.S. employers, Japanese employers are uncomfortable relinquishing their influence over hiring. Indeed, 99.7 percent conduct job interviews for high school graduates, and 48.6 percent expressed reservations about letting schools restrict their choices for hiring students. Therefore, we must wonder how often employers ignore teachers' nominations.

Similarly, the policy directs teachers to base selections entirely on students' achievement. Like American teachers, however, Japanese teachers are ambivalent about relying heavily on grades. They know their students as whole people, and they want to take account of all aspects of students' capabilities and character. We must wonder to what extent teachers nominate students based on academic achievement and to what extent they select favored students or reward cooperative behavior.

Research findings are reassuring on both points. Despite their qualms, Japanese employers do accept teachers' nominations to a very large extent. Even in recessions, when they do not need new workers, employers still try to maintain their linkages with schools by hiring some graduates from these schools (although they may reduce the numbers hired). These unneeded hirings are a price that employers pay to preserve stable sources of recruits of dependable quality. These temporary costs are regarded as investments in the relationship, not as expenses. Of course, in these periods they stop recruiting from nonlinked schools entirely (Amano 1982).

The amount of control that Japanese employers delegate is considerable. Employers hire over 81 percent of applicants when they are first nominated, and of those rejected, over 84 percent are hired by the second firm to which they are nominated. Fewer than 3 percent of all students have to apply to three or more employers. Since some students apply with weak ratings, schools' influence is probably even stronger than these numbers imply.

Similarly, despite their qualms about grades, teachers use them as the primary criterion for nominating students. Teachers report that they feel constrained to use grades in order to maintain their relations with employers. Indeed, 47.5 percent of schools do not recommend students with substandard grades, even if that means they do not fill their quota of jobs. Moreover, analyzing the jobs that students actually get after graduation, we find that grades are the strongest determinant of who gets desirable jobs, while deportment, attendance, tardiness, and even socioeconomic background have little influence.[3]

Although human capital theory assumes that institutional linkages are unresponsive to market demand, schools' commitment to standards is reinforced by an implicit threat of sanctions. If schools fail to send qualified workers, employers stop giving job offers to them in later years. Although the actual frequency of such sanctions is not known, teachers perceive the loss of jobs as real risks, and they feel compelled to recommend qualified students to maintain relations with contract employers.

Skeptics might wonder whether linkages let schools abuse their special influence to relax meritocratic standards and recommend favored students with lower grades. Our results find the opposite. Grades are *more* important for getting good jobs with *linked* employers than they are with nonlinked employers. Rather than lowering requirements, schools hold youths to more stringent achievement standards for the desirable jobs in linked firms.

Maintaining these relationships is crucial to a school's success in placing its graduates in jobs and to an employer's success in recruiting capable employees on a continuing basis. As a teacher said, "Getting jobs is only a onetime experience for individual students, but it is repeated year after year for schools" (Rosenbaum and Kariya 1989, 1363). Every hiring decision reaffirms the mutual commitment of the school and employer to each other. Schools must select students who satisfy employers in order to continue receiving job allocations in the future, and employers must continue hiring a school's graduates in order to maintain a stable source of employees of dependable quality. Deviations from agreed standards would jeopardize their relationship, so these standards are stable, dependable, and difficult to circumvent.

In comparisons of different societies, it is hard to know which factors cause outcomes. For instance, it is clear that Japanese students work harder than Americans, but it is not clear why. In *More Like Us*, James Fallows (1989) argues that cultural differences are responsible:

Japanese strive for effort for its own sake, while Americans exert effort for the sake of rewards. The cultural view, however, ignores the rewards that Japanese high schools offer: Japanese students might work hard if they did not have incentives, but they do not have to make that choice, since their efforts are well rewarded.

The strong incentives in the Japanese system surely contribute to the greater efforts by Japanese students. Moreover, if one accepts the cultural view that Americans are more motivated by rewards, incentives like those in Japan would have even greater effects on American students' motivation compared with the current American system, which offers no incentives to work-bound students.

The superior efforts of Japanese students pay off in higher achievement. At a time when American achievement scores have declined and rank poorly in international comparisons, Japanese scores are at or near the top in most comparisons (Cummings 1979, 1980, 1986; Crosswhite 1984; Bishop 1989; Dore and Sako 1988). The Japanese advantage is not among top-achieving students; they do about as well as their American peers. The Japanese advantage is especially large for students in the bottom half of the class; the bottom of the achievement distribution is much higher in Japan than in the United States (Stevenson and Stigler 1992). Japan's incentives for work-bound students, which are stronger than in any other developed country, undoubtedly affect the achievement of these students.

The Japanese system also contributes to more realistic aspirations. It tells work-bound students what they must do to get better jobs and how well they are doing. Every year students can look at their grades, and if their grades are too low, they can either revise their job aspirations or increase their efforts. One consequence is that Japanese students' job aspirations become more realistic over the course of junior and senior high school and are highly realistic by senior year, while American high school seniors often have unrealistic aspirations (Kariya and Rosenbaum 1987; Rosenbaum 1980b).

Finally, since Japanese linkages produce such high-achieving youths and give employers dependable information about applicants, they may contribute to employers' willingness to invest in young employees and to give them training for more skilled positions.

Americans are suspicious of linkages between public schools and employers. Employers worry that exclusive linkages will prevent them from getting the best applicants from the entire labor market. School staff often worry that linkages give employers excessive influence over public schools. Neither has been a problem in Japan. Indeed, the opposite has occurred. Although linkages with a few schools limit employers' access to other schools' graduates, they get vastly better information about applicants because teachers are committed to making it trustworthy. Schools maintain their emphasis on academic achievement, and employers express dissatisfaction only if teachers depart from these criteria, owing to favoritism or social class background, to reward lower-achieving youths.

Implications of the Japanese Model for American Practices

The Japanese system is much more effective than American practices. Linkages make work entry much easier in Japan than in the United States. Of high school graduates not attending college, almost all Japanese students (99.5 percent) start working immediately after graduation. In contrast, as we have noted, only about half of American work-bound graduates have jobs by graduation, and most of these are only continuing the part-time jobs they had in high school (Nolfi 1978).

Not only does the Japanese model produce desired outcomes for employers, teachers, and students, but it also provides conditions to encourage the right behaviors to improve responsiveness, encouraging each party to make short-term sacrifices to meet their obligations to each other. Thus, Japanese employers hire students even when they do not need workers; teachers do not recommend a student who does not meet employers' expectations even if they want to help the student; and students exert themselves in school even if they hate schoolwork. This system provides conditions that help everyone pursue long-term benefits in spite of short-term sacrifices.

Not only are these behaviors missing from the U.S. system, but Americans do not even think about them, and our theories do not focus on them. Neoclassical economic theory assumes that these conditions occur in ordinary labor markets, but it does not examine whether they actually do occur, or the conditions that would encourage them to occur. For instance, when researchers find that school achievement predicts earnings outcomes (Jencks et al. 1972), they assume that students see those relationships and see incentives for school achievement, and that employers realize that school grades can predict an applicant's productivity. However, research has not examined whether students and employers do indeed perceive these relationships.

The Japanese model extends signaling and network theories by considering the qualities of information that encourage its use and the nature of networks that communicate effective information and ensure its trustworthiness. It encourages research to examine the specific ways in which employers, teachers, and students receive useful information from each other and what qualities make information trusted; the incentives to encourage these parties to respond to each other's needs; and the social conditions of a relationship that allow each actor to trust that others will respond to his needs. Do employers use the information they receive about applicants, and do they send usable information to them? Do teachers know what attributes employers value, and do they provide candid information, even if it hurts a likable student? Although teachers may give candid evaluations, how do employers know they are candid and trustworthy? Do students see incentives for school effort, and do they know how to get jobs? This book examines these issues.

Besides suggesting neglected issues in signaling and network theories, Japan's system suggests a practical way to escape the downward spiral and youths' labor market problems. Japan's system gives employers trustworthy information about job applicants, it tells teachers what information employers need and gives them authority to influence hiring decisions, and consequently, it creates strong incentives to encourage work-bound youths to be motivated and improve their achievement. Moreover, Japan's system creates incentives that allow each party to trust that the others will respond to his needs. This encourages and maintains these favorable outcomes in what might be termed an "upward spiral" of continued improvement.

While Americans generally blame youths' labor market difficulties on poor school preparation or poor employer practices and focus on reforms inside schools or workplaces, a look at the Japanese work-entry systems suggests that these problems may arise, not in schools or in employers, but in their interaction. Specifically, the Japanese system shows that institutional transition mechanisms can create positive incentives and mutual responsiveness. It suggests the possibility that in the United States the lack of relationships between employers, teachers, and students deprives them of both dependable information about each other and incentives to respond to each other. This leads to a downward spiral of unresponsiveness that is inefficient and goes against the best interests of employers, teachers, and students. While the United States cannot and should not simply imitate Japan's system, we must ask whether Japan's procedures for helping youths enter work offer any lessons for reducing work-entry problems for American students and for encouraging employers, teachers, and students to interact differently.

The Japanese system also inspires us to look at American practices in a new way, and it raises new questions that we might not have considered otherwise. Japan's system provides explicit selection criteria, which students can use to assess realistic career plans and to decide what efforts will help them achieve their career plans. For employers, Japan's system provides explicit hiring criteria. Although employers are not compelled to use these criteria, most choose to do so, and they are pleased with the workers they get. Teachers in Japan's system have great influence over students' future jobs, and employers largely defer to teachers' evaluations.

We may also wonder what actions American schools take to help work-bound students, if any, and how these actions compare with those in Japan. Do the grades that teachers assign to students have any relevance to employers' needs? Could the teachers who prepare work-bound students have relationships with employers, and if so, how would these relationships affect hiring? Are these relationships meritocratic, as they are in Japan, or are they based on petty academic trivia, favoritism, or bias?

This book presents new studies that examine these questions about American practices. These questions are of fundamental importance to the operation of schools and the labor market, but until now no one has asked some of them. The radically different way in which Japan handles the school-to-work transition points to the need to investigate these issues in the United States. These studies reveal new processes in the United States that we did not realize existed, and they give us new insights about how American practices operate and how they could work more effectively.

The Purpose of This Book

This book seeks to understand how American students and employers act, the reasons they act as they do, and the variations and alternatives that may sometimes help them escape the downward spiral in which they are caught. All of these studies are about the United States, not Japan, but we use the lessons from our studies of Japan to see U.S. practices in a new way. The Japanese model prompts us to ask new questions about the United States, and we discover new aspects of American practices that have not been noticed before. These findings suggest a new approach to dealing with youth motivation and work-entry problems.

Chapter 2 puts these issues in the context of four competing theories of the school-to-work problem, and it identifies some crucial issues that have been ignored by these theories and by research. Human capital theory and structural theory are the two most common ways in which work-entry problems have been viewed. Human capital theory sees students as the primary cause of these problems, and structural theory sees employers as the cause. However, two other theories offer different explanations and suggest other remedies that have rarely been considered. Signaling theory points to poor information as a cause of the downward spiral, and network theory points to the lack of social contacts as a cause of poor information. Our review notes several sources of poor information that lead students and employers into inappropriate and self-defeating actions. A review of practices in Japan, Germany, and the United Kingdom indicates that the quality of information and the context in which it is communicated are important features that the four theories have overlooked. We examine whether social linkages that convey signals of youths' value to employers are a potential solution to these problems.

Chapter 3 examines American students' perceptions, plans, and disappointments. Unlike employers, who repeatedly encounter hiring problems and develop ways of responding, students face career decisions as novices and may be confused. They may not know whether they are college-bound or work-bound, or what actions will prepare them for their goals. Indeed, in an era when open-admissions policies allow anyone to enter college, today's students may see high school's role in career preparation differently, old notions about how and when students decide between college and work may no longer be correct, and researchers may not know how to identify which students are work-bound.

This chapter examines several issues. We look first at students' beliefs about how high school is related to their future career plans, and how these beliefs affect their school efforts. Second, we examine the relation between students' stated college plans and their actual outcomes, and whether students who think they are college-bound are really work-bound—that is, likely to drop out of college and enter the labor market with a high school diploma as their highest degree. We examine whether discrepancies between students' plans and their actual long-term outcomes are predictable from information that students and their counselors already know. We find that American high schools systematically fail to help some kinds of students to anticipate their predictable outcomes, and that students' mistaken beliefs undercut their school efforts and their preparation. Administrators are encouraging college enrollment so they can brag about students' "high expectations," but they are not trying to find out how many of their students drop out of college—perhaps without earning any college credits and in worse shape for entering jobs than if their high schools had offered better information.

Chapter 4 examines how counselors advise students who hold unrealistic plans. Although most people think of guidance counselors as "gatekeepers," and this view is supported by old studies (compare, Cicourel and Kitsuse 1963; Rosenbaum 1976), our recent interviews with guidance counselors find that they take a new hands-off approach in advising students about their plans. We explore the reasons for their actions. As a result of counselors' well-intentioned "college-for-all" advice, students have higher plans, but many students with little chance of completing college are prevented from making realistic backup plans and from using high school to help them prepare for an alternative career.

We also find that high school counselors do not give labor market advice. Of course, high school counselors may be right to avoid giving labor market advice if employers do not value the skills that high schools teach and the evaluations they give. The next two chapters look at these issues.

Chapter 5 examines whether employers really need academic skills from high school graduates. Employers do not use academic grades or test scores to determine which high school graduates they hire or what they pay them, so there is reason to doubt employers' speeches about their need for academic skills from high school graduates. However, analyzing detailed interviews with fifty-one employers, we discover other hard-to-see employer actions that indicate that employers really do need academic skills. We also discover that they hire and retain youths with these skills through special efforts, including informal social contacts with high schools, which have been unnoticed in previous research.

Chapter 6 explores the question of why employers use invalid and biased information for their hiring decisions. While sociologists have criticized employers for using biased and invalid information and economists have denied that employers would be so irrational as to do so, no one has asked employers why they use some kinds of information and not others, or how they view the information they use. Surprisingly, we discover that many employers concur with critics that their most commonly used procedure, the employment interview, is seriously flawed, but they have a variety of reasons for believing that the alternatives are even worse. Moreover, we discover that employers avoid some of these problems by using two forms of social networks, and we consider whether such networks raise concerns of cronyism.

Why are school-employer linkages so rarely made? Although chapter 6 finds that school contacts provide benefits to employers, employers rarely use such contacts. Following the suggestions of the new institutional economics (Granovetter 1974/1995), chapter 7 looks at why many employers do not hire through school contacts. Our interviews with fifty-one employers find several social elements that prevent school-employer contacts from occurring and thus impede youths' entry into the labor market. These results, which suggest the sociological foundations of economic transactions, have policy implications for improving the school-to-work transition.

The final five chapters focus on high schools: how can they meet employers' needs and help students get jobs? Chapter 8 asks whether students' noncognitive behaviors in high school are related to their later life attainments. Teachers, colleges, and employers give mixed messages about the importance of the noncognitive behaviors that students exhibit in school. This study uses the ten-year follow-up of the High School and Beyond (HSB) national survey to determine whether students' attendance, discipline, effort, and participation are related to their grades, their later college attainments, and their earnings many years after high school. Using multivariate analyses on a national sample of more than six thousand students, we find that some noncognitive behaviors in senior year of high school strongly predict later educational and earnings outcomes at age twenty-eight, and that these relationships are partially signaled by high school grades, even though employers and students may not realize it.

Chapter 9 reports a new discovery. Although Americans assume that high schools do not help youths get jobs, we discover that the United States has a hidden school-to-work system that helps about 8 percent of high school graduates get jobs, helps females and minorities more than white males, and leads to jobs with better advancement, even better than the jobs that students get through relatives. We also find evidence for this system in other studies, although the researchers did not remark on their findings.

Chapter 10 finds one source for the job help that students receive from high schools. Some vocational teachers help students get jobs through socially constructed linkages with employers. Interviewing 110 vocational teachers in twelve diverse high schools, we discover that some teachers take informal actions to foster trusted linkages with employers, and that they use these linkages to learn employers' needs and to place their students in jobs. Their actions are not required by their jobs, nor are they recognized by administrators or policymakers, but the informal linkages these teachers make have some similarities to the formal job-placement linkages in Japan and Germany, and they raise doubts about our stereotyped notion that social contacts are always unmeritocratic.

Chapter 11 considers implications for theory. Recent social theory has noted that individuals' capabilities are affected not only by their own human capital but also by societal contexts—their social capital

(Coleman 1994). Just as eyeglasses transform one's capabilities, so can social capital. However, social capital has usually been noted in static traditional settings, such as ethnic social networks, and there has been little indication that institutional practices might create social capital. This chapter examines how linkage practices increase students' capabilities—by helping them to see incentives that they otherwise would not see, motivating them to work more fully to their potential, informing them about the actions they can take to improve their value, and conveying trusted signals of their value—so that employers will give them jobs that reflect their potential.

Finally, chapter 12 considers policy implications. Contrary to laissez-faire social policies, the "invisible hand" needs a helping hand. The invisible hand of the market is not sufficient to make the youth labor market operate. It provides incentives, but an infrastructure is also needed to convey information so that students and employers will see their incentives. Thus, we have seen that, without an infrastructure, many perverse outcomes arise because incentives are not seen. In contrast, we have discovered that some employers and teachers take steps to create informal linkages that help market processes to work. The linkage model indicates that students' motivation and work-entry problems arise because the labor market fails to give many of them clear information about incentives, about the actions they can take, and about signals of their productive value that employers will trust and value. Informal linkages can provide this kind of information.

This model leads to a new policy agenda. The United States may not need Japanese employment agencies or German-style apprenticeships, which are expensive and hard to implement. Rather, the practices of some American schools already incorporate the basic prerequisites of what is needed, but these practices have been informal and unrecognized. By identifying the networks that already exist, and by encouraging them and making them explicit, society can give students incentives for school effort and give employers ways to identify the valuable skills and work habits in high school graduates. After an infrastructure is in place and formally recognized, the market can operate, and students and employers will see incentives to be mutually responsive to each other's needs.

=== Chapter 2 ===

Market and Network Theories of the High School–to–Work Transition

THE TRANSITION from high school to work has attracted concern because of youths' great difficulties in making this transition.[1] Many high school graduates spend their first years after school unemployed or job hopping, with consequent loss of training and productivity. Work-bound youths also have great problems in school that may be related to their anticipated problems entering work.

The problem is hard to conceptualize because it involves many complexities. Is the problem due to shortcomings in one or more of the parties (youths, schools, or employers)? Is it due to problems of information flow between them? Or is it due to problems in their relationships? Sorting out essential elements and causal mechanisms is difficult. We need some way to gain conceptual clarity about these complex phenomena.

This chapter reviews four theories of the school-to-work transition. Each theory provides a coherent perspective, supported by a body of research. Each theory has strengths and weaknesses for explaining the school-to-work transition—that is, each explains some aspects well and other aspects poorly. This chapter reviews the strengths and weaknesses of each one.

First, *segmented labor market theory* shows how these problems arise from the structure of labor markets, although the theory is vague about the transition and the way in which individuals are selected and respond. Second, *human capital theory* contends that youths' work-entry problems arise because of their own deficiencies, yet several features of the school-to-work transition do not fit this interpretation and suggest that poor information prevents human capital from being identified and developed. Third, *signaling theory* explains the

24

economic constraints on the use of information, but it ignores non-economic constraints. Fourth, *network theory* explains how personal and institutional networks improve information flow and affect the hiring process. Since institutional networks between high schools and employers are rare in the United States, we review how such networks operate in other nations (Japan, Germany, and the United Kingdom), and how they aid youths' work entry by improving both signals to employers and incentives for youth.

This review considers only the transition from high school to work. Although transitions from higher education and from other levels of education are important, and some similarities apply across various levels, they are not considered here.

Segmented Labor Market Theory

Segmented labor market theory points to some barriers, particularly discrimination, that prevent individuals from entering certain industries, sectors, or firms (Katz 1986; Tolbert 1982; Dickens and Lang 1985; Gordon 1972; England and Farkas 1986). Such structural barriers may restrict females, minorities, and youth from access to better-paid industries, sectors, or firms. Moreover, internal labor markets within firms limit and channel career advancement opportunities (Doeringer and Piore 1971; Rosenbaum 1984). In addition, individuals are not paid for their human capital value but rather are placed in a labor "queue," ranked by their value and other attributes, and this is the sequence in which they are allocated jobs, which pay predetermined amounts (Thurow 1975). Thus, if youth are always placed at the back of the queue because of their age and lack of experience, then employers never even try to examine other aspects of their value.

Segmented labor market theory contends that labor markets are highly stratified. Research has shown that labor markets are segmented (Althauser and Kalleberg 1981; Osterman 1980; Sørensen 1977; Stolzenberg 1975) and that access to these segments is constrained by discrimination and credentials (Bills 1983; Bowles and Gintis 1976; Collins 1979; Crain 1984; Meyer 1977; Ornstein 1976; Rosenbaum 1984; Rosenthal and Hearn 1982; Spenner and Otto 1982).

Segmented labor market theory contends that the segmented nature of the labor market secures the organizational control system and perpetuates a system of credentialism and inequality (Baron 1984; Cain 1976; Carline 1985; Collins 1975, 1979; Kanter 1977; Raffe 1981; Spenner 1995). For example, James Baron (1984, 55) notes that "Marxists argue that employers are motivated by a need to control the work force and use schooling to determine whether workers' values and traits are appropriate for the organizational control system." Similarly, Rosabeth Kanter (1977, 48) argues that "homosocial reproduction" occurs in organizations to "carefully guard power and privilege for those who fit in, for those they see as 'their kind.'" Randall Collins (1979) also discusses the use of credentials and social background to ensure "normative control" in the organization and to dictate the nature of one's interactions with other members of the organization. These notions suggest that the real goal served by a segmented market is not to find individuals with better skills but rather to keep social advancement in the hands of those who have such power.

Extending the notion of social control, one version of segmented labor market theory hypothesizes which school criteria employers would use for hiring. Samuel Bowles and Herbert Gintis (1976, 59, 132) propose a correspondence between the social relations in schools and work, in which employers determine the selection criteria in schools. "Cognitive attributes are not central to the determination of social stratification. . . . Different levels of education feed workers into different levels within the occupational structure." Extending the work of Kohn and Schooler (1983), Bowles and Gintis propose that while colleges stress the internalization of norms and self-direction, teachers and employers of noncollege youth ignore academic achievement and emphasize non-academic behaviors of rule obedience, attendance, punctuality, and effort. However, these hypotheses were not supported in several empirical tests (Jencks et al. 1979, 255; Olneck and Bills 1980; Kariya and Rosenbaum 1988; Rosenbaum and Kariya 1989).

Despite its clear description of market segments and the Bowles-Gintis speculations about the correspondence between school and work, segmented labor market theory does not explain the school-to-work transition very well. First, although segmented labor market theory describes outcomes, it does not describe processes. The theory describes labor market segments (Dunlop 1957; Doeringer and Piore 1971; Gordon 1971), but it does not explain why these segments exist, and some approaches make arbitrary distinctions between segments, as critics have noted (Zucker and Rosenstein 1981; Hodson and Kaufman 1982). Nor does the theory explain the processes by which segmented labor markets interact with other institutions (like schools), although some work has speculated about processes (Bowles and Gintis 1976; Osterman 1988).

Second, by focusing only on the employer side of the transition, the theory says very little about individuals. The theory lists which kinds of people are assigned to which jobs, but it does not say much about why these groups were chosen, how they respond, how they could alter these circumstances, or why and how often exceptions occur.

Third, the theory does not explain why youth are treated differently or how the selection process changes as youth become adults. The theory identifies youth as one of the groups relegated to worse jobs, along with women and blacks. However, unlike other statuses, "youth" changes with time. Although segmented theory indicates that people get better jobs after they become adults, it does not explain why or how this happens. Youth are assigned to secondary jobs that offer no advancement, but somehow they advance as they age and become adults (Andrisani 1973, 1976; D'Amico and Brown 1982). The theory does not explain how aging allows them to gain access to better jobs from jobs that offer no advancement.

Finally, since segmented labor market theory does not focus on the use of information, it does not explain why employers choose the particular selection criteria they do. If employers received good information about employee productivity, would they ignore it and continue using age, sex, and race?

No theory can explain everything. Although this is a good theory for many purposes, segmented labor market theory is particular weak at explaining transitions from school to work because of its one-sided focus on the structure of employment. We next turn to a theory with the opposite focus—a one-sided focus on individuals.

Human Capital Theory

Human capital theory contends that youths' work-entry problems arise from their own deficiencies. This theory contends that individuals' productive capability comes from their abilities and skills—their "human capital." Human capital is analogous to the physical capital (such as machinery) in factories: people invest in improving their stock of capital, and they make those investments (effort, tuition payments, and so on) based on their estimates of their likely returns.

Human capital theory is based on the market model, which assumes that people compete in free markets and that people who are worth more are paid more. Unlike network theory (considered later), market models are critical of institutional linkages between schools and employers. According to market models, preferential relations between employers and certain schools would limit competition, reduce employee quality, and raise labor costs. Without such linkages, employers must rely on pure market forces, and applicants' value alone determines their selection. This market view underlies the high school–to–work transition in the United States.

Human capital theory suggests that work-entry problems arise because youth are defective. Taking this view, numerous reports have identified the poor academic skills of American youth as the cause of their work-entry problems (NCEE 1983; NAS 1984; CED 1985; NAEP 1985).

Yet three aspects of work-entry problems suggest that human capital is not the whole problem. First, school achievement is partly determined by motivation, which is strongly affected by external incentives. Second, although employers complain about youths' poor human capital, they do not use selection criteria that would help them select applicants with better human capital. Third, although work-entry problems are so pervasive in the United States that they seem intrinsic to youth, Japan eliminated such problems with reforms that improved the information flow between schools and employers.

School Achievement, Motivation, and External Incentives

Although human capital theory blames poor school achievement on poor ability or instruction, motivation and discipline are critical influences as well. They are also important problems in schools: in every Gallup poll over the past thirty years, parents have identified discipline as one of the top problems facing public schools (Rose and Gallup 1999). More intensive studies reach similar conclusions (Goodlad 1984). Students' poor motivation is manifest in a variety of ways. Absenteeism, class cutting, tardiness, disruptive behavior, verbal abuse, failure to do homework, and drug or alcohol abuse (Meyer 1971; Birman and Natriello 1978; Hollingsworth et al. 1984; Cusick 1983; DiPrete 1981; Chabot and Garibaldi 1982; DeLeonibus 1978; Thompson and Stanard 1975; Sedlak et al. 1986).

These behaviors seriously detract from the development of youths' human capital, but human capital theory cannot explain them. They are less influenced by ability and training than by motivation. Motivation is caused by many factors, including personality and socialization, but one important determinant is the incentive structure in schools. Incentives are critical influences on motivation, as is widely recognized by psychologists, sociologists, and economists. Since incentives are easier to change than ability or personality, human capital may be most effectively improved by changing the incentive structure of schools.

This conceptual distinction can be seen in practical terms. Policies based on human capital theory have called for longer school days, longer school years, and increased standards. However, if motivation is the problem, then such policies would be inadequate. Like pushing on string, increased hours and demands will be ineffective if students lack motivation and ignore their assignments. Reforms that compel students to spend more hours in school cannot compel them to exert effort and may only increase the school dropout rate (McPartland and McDill 1977). Human capital theory is not sufficient to understand these problems.

Employers and Selection Criteria

National panels (NCEE 1983; CED 1985) indicate that employers want applicants to have greater human capital, particularly basic skills in reading, writing, and math. However, employers do not take the actions we would expect if that were their main concern. Employers do not respond to the selection criteria that theory, national panels, and teachers expect them to value. Grades and test scores have little effect on which youth get jobs, which ones get the better jobs, or which ones earn the better wages. Using national survey data (National Longitudinal Survey of the Class of 1972, NLS72), Larry Griffin, Arne Kalleberg, and Karl Alexander (1981, 212) found that aptitude, class rank, and other school information have small and often insignificant effects on the unemployment and job attainments of high school graduates who directly enter the workforce. They conclude that "none of the variables included in these equations . . . has substantial impact on positioning persons in either the primary or secondary sector or even on employment/unemployment."

Using the same data, Robert Meyer and David A. Wise (1982, 312) found that class rank in school has insignificant effects on wage rates two years after graduation (1974), and only barely significant effects four years after graduation (1976). Robert Willis and Sherwin Rosen (1979) found that a one-standard-deviation increase in math and reading scores of high school graduates lowered the wage of their first job by 3.5 percent. John Bishop (1987a) found that, although basic achievement raises productivity, it has relatively small effects on youths' wages. In analyses of seniors in the High School and Beyond survey, grades have large effects on youths' ability to get white-collar and skilled jobs in Japan, but grades have small effects in the United States (Rosenbaum and Kariya 1991). The small effects of grades on early jobs in the United States have been extensively documented.

This lack of influence of grades and test scores on hiring is puzzling. Human capital theory suggests that employers would give better jobs and higher pay to youths with better grades, because such youth will be more productive. Human capital theory cannot explain why grades and test scores do not influence hiring decisions.

Eliminating Work-Entry Problems in Japan

Work-entry problems are so pervasive in the United States that they seem intrinsic to youth. Such an assumption supports human capital theory. However, these problems are largely absent in Japan. Of high school graduates who do not attend college, virtually all Japanese students (99.5 percent) start working immediately after graduation (Ministry of Labor 1982). In contrast, only half (49.4 percent) of American noncollege graduates have obtained jobs by graduation, and many will not have a job until three or six months later (Nolfi 1978, 53). Even then, an American high school graduate's first few jobs may only be dead-end jobs that offer low pay, little training, and no advancement opportunity. It is not surprising that American students question whether school will help their job chances.

Of course, it is possible that American youth delay work entry to find more appropriate jobs. However, even after they find a job, American youth have a higher turnover rate than Japanese youth when they first leave school (under age twenty) and in later years (age twenty to twenty-four), during both rapid and slow economic growth periods (Rosenbaum and Kariya 1991). Moreover, of high school graduates who changed jobs within two years after graduation, 15 percent of American youths were fired or laid off (NCES 1982), while only 3.2 percent of their Japanese counterparts left a job for that reason (NSK 1984).

For American youth who get jobs right after graduation, most of those jobs (58.3 percent) are the same part-time job they had in high school (Nolfi 1978, 53). These students, and others who view their experiences, must have serious doubts about the value of the high school diploma when it only permits them to continue jobs they were already doing. Although the strongest incentive for work-bound students is a better job, youth receive no information communicating such incentives.[2]

Youth work-entry problems, which seem to be inherent in youths' human capital, are absent in Japan, so they are not inevitable. Indeed, Japan had similar work-entry problems earlier in this century and ended them with policy reforms. While these reforms had many aspects, they included changes in information transfer between schools and employers (Inoue 1986; Rosenbaum and Kariya 1989). Therefore, youths' work-entry problems may not be inevitable, they may not be inherent deficiencies in youths' human capital, and they may be reduced by improved information flow.

In a review of various theories, George Farkas, Paula England, and Margaret Barton (1986, 109) conclude that many studies

> profoundly undermine the older neoclassical view in which "market forces" constantly erode net wage differentials between sectors. . . . In combination, discrimination, search costs, personal networks and the contractual features of internal labor markets explain the imperfect sorting of workers posited by structural sociologists.

Although human capital theory is a plausible explanation of youth work-entry problems, other explanations, each related to information problems, are possible, including: youths' poor motivation suggests that they do not get information about incentives to work in school; employers' disregard of grades and tests suggests that poor information about human capital, rather than poor human capital itself, may account for their difficulty in finding good workers; and work-entry problems are not due to inherent deficiencies in youths' human capital. Japan eliminated youths' work-entry problems, not by trying to fix their personal deficiencies but through reforms that improved information flow between schools and employers.

Signaling Theory

Whereas human capital theory does not recognize the practical costs of information or limits on its availability and usefulness, signaling theory does address such questions. How do employers discern human capital and choose which signals to use to select appropriate applicants? How do youth know which skills to develop, how to present themselves, and to which employers? Signaling theory describes the economics of these questions. Because of the importance of these questions for the school-to-work transition, for which information is problematic, we devote considerable space to reviewing signaling theory.

As George Stigler (1961, 213) reminds us: "Information is a valuable resource: knowledge *is* power." Labor markets are an example of Stigler's insight. When making hiring decisions, employers find value in any information about job applicants' abilities. Yet obtaining information about applicants' true abilities is costly, so employers often hire employees based on available "signals": limited information about job applicants (see, for example, Arrow 1973; Spence 1974; Stigler 1961). Therefore, instead of fully assessing applicants' "human capital," employers interpret the information that they can obtain easily—such as age, sex, race, school prestige, and educational credentials—and apply what they have learned from past experience to infer an individual's "conditional probability of competence" (Blaug 1976, 846).

Signaling theory considers the economic aspects of signals. It notes that information has costs, and that the central dilemma in many decisions is how to get adequate information at low cost. Signaling theory explains why easily measured indicators like educational credentials have such great influence. Employers can often get better information by giving more realistic and more expensive tests, but they may not do so if they decide that increased information is not worth the cost (Spence 1974).

However, signaling theory does not discuss or predict which signals employers use, which signals have the greatest impact on hiring decisions, or whether the same signals are used equally to screen all applicants. Signaling theory also ignores the information process and the structure of the market itself; that is, signaling theory does not consider how information is gathered, coordinated, transmitted, and finally evaluated. As Kenneth Arrow (1973, 144) notes, it is "hard to define the process by which a signal gets to be recognized as such and how the receiver learns to discriminate among them." In addition, signaling theory fails "to distinguish signals from the underlying attributes about which one is really concerned" (Spence 1974, 105).

Signaling theory relies on market mechanisms. Market outcomes are the vehicle to transmit information, and markets do not effectively communicate subtle information about applicants. Employers receive only crude signals to differentiate job applicants (age, sex, race, and education are the most common), and they interpret these signals, relying on their past experiences, through a process that Lester Thurow (1975) calls "statistical discrimination." On the other hand, applicants receive even worse information about employers' preferences: the results of employers' hiring decisions as they appear in the "market." Signaling theory does not examine the ways that the market communicates information about hiring criteria or job candidates, or which information it communicates poorly.

Signaling theory also ignores normative constraints on signaling use. Are some kinds of signals considered "fair" and others "unfair"? Are some types of signals trusted more than others? Is this normative system explicit or implicit? How do employers deal with conflicting norms about signals, for example, when informal stereotypes about classes of people conflict with laws against discrimination? Although the use of age, sex, and race as signals is illegal, these signals have traditionally been influential in hiring decisions. Similarly, the use of educational signals is "legally permitted and generally approved" (Blaug 1985, 22); more normatively ambiguous are preferences for graduates of some colleges over others, but such preferences are commonly used (Rosenbaum 1984). Finally, when employers violate norms, what sanctions exist and under what circumstances are they exercised? Signaling theory ignores these questions.

According to signaling theory, individual employers decide which signals are important. If each employer makes these choices in isolation, with no guidance from general normative consensus, as market theories assume, then how can youth get a coherent view of the full array of preferences? Moreover, if employers act in isolation from school staff, then how are their needs communicated to schools, and how do schools provide meaningful information so that students will know employers' needs? Such one-sided decisions would not necessarily become usable information to schools or youth. In contrast, while employers acting in isolation can be idiosyncratic, employers interacting with other employers or with school staff would create and encourage meaningful signals.

Signaling theory helps to frame some relevant conceptual issues in the school-to-work transition. What skills do employers want to have signals about? Does youthfulness itself serve as a negative signal to employers? Do employers consider youth inherently inferior, or do they ignore youths' talent because they think that less information is available on youths? Why don't employers use school-generated signals? We consider each of these questions.

The Skills That Employers Seek from Youth Labor

Before considering what criteria employers choose as signals, we must know what personal attributes they want to select. Contrary to popular assumptions, several researchers find that when selecting non-college-bound youth, most employers are not looking for labor with specific vocational or occupational skills and training (Blaug 1985; Hamilton 1986; Newitt 1987; Wilms 1984). Instead, these researchers argue, most employers of youth labor want employees with essential reading, writing, and mathematics skills (see also CED 1985; NCEE 1983) and employees who can "follow the rules," work hard, and be in attendance and on time.

Mark Blaug (1985, 20) concludes that the "vast bulk of jobs in an industrial economy involve competences that are acquired on the job in a few weeks and require, not a given stock of knowledge . . . [about a specific vocational area], but the capacity to learn by doing." Blaug finds that, in addition, most employers, whether public or private, "care less about what workers know than about how they will behave," and that "few workers ever make specific use of the [specific] cognitive knowledge acquired in schools" (19). Employers therefore seem to be looking not for applicants with specific vocational training, but for applicants who have the essential basic skills and can demonstrate a potential for training.

Youthfulness as a Potentially Negative Signal

The pervasiveness of youth work-entry problems suggests that employers may consider youthfulness itself a negative signal. Age is an important influence on life events in many societies. In traditional societies, normative expectations create the basis for age stratification, defining the social roles associated with an age (Riley and Waring 1976; Neugarten and Hagestad 1976).

In modern society, norms about age stratification are often defined by institutional practices. Schools define the ages of entry and exit into the various levels of education, and these norms have become more uniform in recent years (Kaestle and Vinovskis 1978). In turn, the various levels of school—elementary, junior high, senior high—affect norms about individual behavior, while isolating students from other age groups (Coleman 1974). Workplaces, though less age-segregated than schools, often cause employees' careers to be strongly affected by age norms (Lawrence 1987; Rosenbaum 1984). Apprentice programs for craft positions often select people within narrow age limits (Hogan and Astone 1986, 115). Some of these practices—such as compulsory school attendance laws and minimum work ages—are determined by the state (Mayer and Muller 1986; Modell, Furstenberg, and Hershberg 1976; Coleman 1974). These norms may also be changed by historical events like depressions (Elder 1980) and the size of birth cohorts (Ryder 1965; Riley et al. 1972). Thus, sociologists regard age norms as not necessarily rational or consciously decided.

In contrast, economic signaling theory might consider age an economically rational selection criterion. When employers do not hire new high school graduates into the primary labor market (jobs offering training, advancement, job security, and better wages), this might occur because employers think recent graduates are too young and too unreliable. "Well established firms with a sizeable investment in plant and equipment . . . prefer to hire men twenty-five to thirty years of age, who are married and ready to settle down, after they have, so to speak, sowed their industrial wild oats in other plants" (Lester

1954, 53). Other studies have also found that younger workers are hired by smaller firms, construction firms, and firms that hire many clerical workers, while older workers are preferred by manufacturing firms with skilled blue-collar jobs (Malm 1954; Hill and Nixon 1984). Similarly, a study of thirty-five Massachusetts firms found that primary labor market firms, those providing the best-paid, most desirable jobs, "generally prefer not to hire young men just out of high school" (Osterman 1980, 26). These preferences are sometimes company policies. Several Fortune 100 corporations have policies against hiring applicants under age twenty-five for full-time jobs (Hamilton 1987; Rosenbaum 1989a). Employers turn to the "less desirable younger workers" only when "the more preferred workers are in short supply" (Nardone 1987, 40).

Stephen Hamilton (1986, 240) suggests that "employers consider young people—especially males under the age of 22—to be inherently irresponsible and thus poor risks for positions that require responsibility and entail an investment in training." Employers may avoid hiring youth because they want employees who are likely to stay in the firm, and they see age as an indicator of stability. Thus, employers may avoid hiring young employees not because of their lack of skills, which employers feel they could provide, but because of their inferences about youths' propensity to stay with the firm (Osterman 1980).

As signaling theory indicates, employers choose selection criteria that not only help them get better employees but are based on easily obtained information. Age is easily obtained and may predict stability, responsibility, and other aspects of productivity, so it seems to be a useful signal.

Is youth an accurate signal of poor productivity? Remarkably, signaling theorists do not investigate the validity of signals. They assume that employers do that. Signaling theory relies on a functionalist inference: if employers use a signal, they must have a good reason to do so. Of course, this may not be true. Selections can be irrational or unwarranted by empirical evidence, especially if employers rely on stereotyped preconceptions and do not gather that evidence systematically.

Despite many stereotypes about youths' unreliable productivity and attendance, high turnover, and unstable attachment to the labor force, the body of empirical work addressing these questions has produced mixed and ambiguous findings regarding age-related differences in productivity, turnover, attendance, commitment, and attachment. The general finding of this research is that youth is a poor signal of productivity (Rhodes 1983; Waldman and Avolio 1986).

Less noted by signaling theory are questions about the long-term effects of selection practices. First, early selections may have long-term effects on careers. Screening mechanisms used early in a career may continue to shape an individual's entire career trajectory, especially within internal labor markets (Blaug 1976 1985; Granick 1973; Rosenbaum 1984; Holsinger and Fernandez 1987). Early signals therefore become incorporated into firms' career systems and indirectly affect later career outcomes.

Second, even if youthfulness accurately signals poor productivity, the use of this signal could have future negative effects by reducing incentives to acquire basic skills and work habits. If employers offer high school graduates only unskilled jobs that do not use basic skills and are not rewarding, then high school students will not see incentives to acquire basic skills or work habits. Then, even if employers offer good jobs to twenty-five-year olds with basic skills, this delayed incentive seven years after graduation may come too late to motivate high school students to acquire the skills that employers want. While employers can get more mature workers by hiring twenty-five-year-olds, they also acquire the products of this poor incentive system—an outcome not considered by the signaling paradigm.

In addition, by waiting until applicants reach age twenty-five, employers have more difficulty assessing their basic skills. This may explain why grades (earned seven years earlier) do not affect hiring for better jobs, since this information is pretty old by the time employers hire twenty-five-year-olds.

Although existing research does not settle the question of whether employers avoid giving youth good jobs because of irrational norms or rational signals, research indicates that age is a poor signal of productivity. The use of such a weak signal also raises questions about why other signals are not used.

School-Generated Signals Used by Employers

Although youth entering the workforce have little work experience, their many years of school experience signal their ability, academic skills, and work habits. Employers' use of such a weak signal as age makes us wonder why they do not use more promising signals, such as those conveyed by schools.

Credentials   One aspect of high school that clearly affects jobs is the diploma (Jencks et al. 1979; Faia 1981). Over 85 percent of American youth obtain diplomas, and the diploma is a prerequisite for a decent job and even for many low-skill jobs in many developed and less developed nations (Dore 1976). However, it is not clear why diplomas are used. Does the diploma improve job prospects because it signals greater skills, or is it merely a credential—a symbol of status that signals little about achievement? Researchers are split on this issue; economists generally take the former position (Spence 1974; Kane and Rouse 1995), and sociologists the latter (Collins 1971; Meyer 1977; Dougherty 1994), but the evidence is not sufficient to resolve the issue (for further discussion of this issue, see chapter 3, note 7).

However, besides credentials, schools also create signals by evaluations and categories. Schools grade students in each course and rank and differentiate courses by ability and curriculum grouping. How do employers respond to schools' evaluations and categories?

Ability and Curriculum Tracks   Schools attach so much importance to ability and curriculum tracks that we might expect employers to use them as signals. High schools create tracks to influence students' future paths and the preparation they are to receive. The college track aims to prepare youth for college, vocational tracks aim to prepare youth for specific occupational careers, and the general track aims to offer general preparation for both. Within curriculum tracks, high-ability groups present a higher level or faster-paced curricula than lower-ability groups. Indeed, research has shown that college plans and admissions are strongly influenced by students' ability and curriculum tracks (Alexander, Cook, and McDill 1978; Heyns 1974; Rosenbaum 1976, 1978, 1980a).

However, the benefits of noncollege tracks are less clear. The general track is the largest noncollege track. It seems to be a residual category that promises very little to students. While college tracks and vocational tracks promise preparation for specific goals, the general track is more vaguely defined. In some schools, general tracks make vague promises of preparation for "further education" or basic skills for work, without offering any specific preparation or goals (Oakes 1985; Rosenbaum 1976; Sedlak et al. 1986).

Even when schools are committed to preparing youth for jobs, they are not necessarily effective. Vocational tracks offer clear goals, but they often deliver less than promised. The evidence on the benefits of vocational tracks is mixed. Although, some studies find no difference between vocational and general track graduates in job level, salaries, or work performance (Kaufman and Schaefer 1967; Garbin 1970; Grasso 1972; Oakes 1985, 152), other studies find that vocational programs give some advantage in obtaining a high-status job and in raising wages if the job is related to one's training (Daymont and Rumberger 1982; Hotchkiss and Dorsten 1987; Meyer 1982). Moreover, there is great variability in the quality and effectiveness of programs both across and within schools. Although vocational tracks improve employment and earnings if students get jobs related to their training, it is uncertain from the evidence why some students get relevant jobs and others do not. (This issue is explored in greater detail in chapters 5, 9, and 10.)

Grades   As noted, employers do not use the readily available signals of the skills they need: they ignore grades, transcripts, and referrals (Bills 1988; Bishop 1988a; Collins 1974; Crain 1984; Kariya and Rosenbaum 1988), and they seldom consult schools and school counselors (Kariya and Rosenbaum 1988). These school evaluations would provide very inexpensive signals of youths' work habits and their skills in reading, writing, and math—the personal qualities that employers say they need.

Why don't grades, test scores, and tracks influence the jobs that students get? Part of the reason may be that schools do not try to influence youths' jobs. High schools originally were for only a small elite. As late as 1890, high school students accounted for 1.6 percent of all elementary and secondary enrollments, and only a small proportion of these students succeeded in graduating (Labaree 1988). Although high schools have broadened their mission (Trow 1961), the stress on college is still evident in many school practices. College preparatory classes get better teachers, new textbooks, better science laboratories, and more special programs (Rosenbaum 1978, 1980a; Oakes 1985). Teachers and guidance counselors allocate more time to helping college-bound students (Heyns 1974). Counselors build rapport with college recruiters and help them select appropriate students to admit, but they rarely contact employers to help them select students to hire (Borman and Hopkins 1987). Thus, while high schools focus a great deal of effort on helping students apply to college, fewer than 10 percent of high school seniors entering work report that their high school helped them get their job (NCES 1983).

Bishop (1989) also believes that schools are responsible for the fact that grades do not affect jobs. He notes the experience of Nationwide Insurance Company, which sent applicant-signed transcript requests to twelve hundred high schools and received only ninety-three responses.

However, schools may not be the only reason grades are not used. Employers tend to be well represented on school boards, and schools usually respond when employers are unhappy with a specific aspect of schools (Useem and Useem 1974). If many employers wanted transcripts or wanted schools to help in job placements, schools would probably respond to their requests. We must wonder how many employers care about getting transcripts and whether they would respond if they knew students' grades.

Research suggests that employers choose not to use grades. A national survey of nineteen hundred personnel officers found that few considered grades important for hiring high school graduates (Crain 1984). A strong personal impression in an interview and a recommendation from a manager were rated "very important" by 76 percent and 56 percent, respectively, of personnel officers, while grades and tests were so rated by only 18 percent and 12 percent. Daniel Diamond's (1970) survey of employers in New York and St. Louis also found that fewer than half used tests even for the most demanding jobs, and the main hiring criterion for these jobs was impressions in an interview. David Bills (personal communication, May 27, 1988) found that none of the employers he interviewed were concerned with grades. Employers rarely obtained school transcripts, and some employers did not even request them. One employer actually refused to consider applicants with high grades because of a belief that these individuals would lack social skills. Even employers who considered school experience did not necessarily focus on academic experience. To a bank personnel officer who reported seeking people with social skills, extracurricular activities were more important than grades. Crain and Bills both found that employers care about grades for college graduates, but not for high school graduates.

Why don't employers use information from schools? Perhaps they do not care about academic skills, despite their claims. Chapter 5 explores this question and finds strong evidence that employers go to great lengths to recruit and retain employees with strong academic skills, even though they are reluctant to start them off at higher pay grades. However, we may wonder whether employers' opinions of school-provided information make them reluctant to use these signals. As we shall see in chapter 7, employers report that course titles, abbreviations, and grades on school transcripts are hard to interpret. Course titles are often designed to attract students' interest, so it is hard to know what skills they teach. (Does "Literature of Self-Exploration" teach reading competence?) Grades are also difficult to interpret. Courses are graded on a curve, but it is not always clear whether the norm is the school, a particular track, or a single classroom. Nor is it clear how much achievement a grade indicates. The difficulty of interpreting and comparing transcripts probably deters many employers from using them.

We may also wonder whether employers trust grades and references. Employers may not trust reference letters that youth can see and even contest with lawsuits. Employers may also doubt that grades and test scores indicate the kinds of skills needed in jobs. Like Americans generally, they may mistrust tests (Jencks and Crouse 1982). These problems of interpretation and trust could explain employers' reluctance to use grades, tests, and references as signals.

Signaling theory ignores some important factors that affect employers' choice of signals. Cost and predictiveness are not the only factors that determine which signals are used. Signals must also be understood and trusted. Signaling theory does not help us know the conditions under which information is meaningful and trusted by recipients.

Youths' Use of Signals in Deciding How to Prepare for Jobs

Signaling theory focuses on employers' use of signals to select employees, usually ignoring the other half of the labor market transaction: youth themselves may use signals in choosing an area in which to gain training and in choosing where to apply (Granovetter 1985, 481). We know very little about how youth gather information and make decisions about the employment process and employment opportunities. These crucial decisions that affect youths' motivation and incentives are generally ignored by signaling theory.

How do young people find and choose jobs? Most young Americans find jobs "through friends and relatives and through the direct application to employers" (Meyer and Wise 1984, 123; see also Granovetter 1974/1995), and the state "plays little role in placement of youths or . . . adults into jobs" (Layard 1982, 500; Osterman 1988).

Many young people searching for jobs do not know how to fill out applications or how to dress for job interviews, and they lack personal contacts (Rees 1986). Many youths do not have enough information about jobs or about work life in general (West and Newton 1983), and school counselors seldom provide such assistance for noncollege-bound youths (Dunham 1980; Rosenbaum 1976). Similarly, Blaug (1985, 26) indicates that youth need to know the "techniques of interviewing and presentation of biographical information."

Youth from low-income or minority backgrounds may lack this kind of information more than other youth. Youth from higher social backgrounds have better information about employment opportunities (Parnes and Kohen 1975, 44), and they have access to such "superior family resources" as "personal contacts" for jobs and "capital to make a start toward independent enterprise" (Kett 1977, 152). Social class also affects socialization and social conceptions of the workplace (Haaken and Korschgen 1988; Kohn 1979).[3]

Perhaps work-bound youths' most important choices are deciding how much and which kinds of training to get to prepare themselves for work. They must use signals from the labor market to make these decisions. Signals tell youth what they can gain from working hard in school, what courses they should take, or whether they are better off spending their time in after-school jobs or having fun. These signals are likely to be important determinants of youths' school motivation, and consequently of how much they learn in school.

Although young children believe their parents and teachers when they say that good grades will help their future career—despite social class differences (Kahl 1953)—work-bound students over age fourteen are less swayed by this incentive. In part, this may be because school counselors and teachers spend little time helping work-bound students (Heyns 1974). Counselors report that they lack time to help all students, and that they feel work-bound youth can find jobs without their help (Rosenbaum 1976).

Another reason may be that work-bound students get signals directly from the labor market by observing the experiences of their older peers. The evidence that employers ignore grades suggests a strong pattern that youth could not miss seeing.

Certainly, work-bound students' behaviors imply that they realize that grades do not matter. Although research is lacking on students' perceptions, many studies report that work-bound students do not take grades seriously, except to get the minimum grades needed for a diploma (Cicourel and Kitsuse 1963; Oakes 1985; Rosenbaum 1976; Sedlak et al. 1986). As a student reported, "I'm just here to get the diploma, waiting until they give me the diploma" (Rosenbaum 1976, 163). A teacher reported a similar view: "These kids do not want to learn. You can't teach them anything. They are just sitting in these seats until they get their working paper—a diploma." As a result, students do not work in school, and teachers know they can't make them work (Sedlak et al. 1986).[4]

The experience of college-bound students illustrates the importance of a different set of signals. Since students' grades and tracks affect college admissions, college-bound students see incentives to work hard in school, while work-bound students do not. Obviously, there are other differences between these two groups, so this may not be the entire explanation, but the different incentive structure cannot be ignored.

Thus, work-bound students shift from accepting the general statements of parents and teachers to observing the experiences of their older peers. Meanwhile, school staff seem to be making less effort to inform and guide their choices than those of college-bound students. As a result, work-bound youth increasingly disregard grades as signals of the kinds of jobs they can get. However, it is not clear that any signals are substituted, so work-bound youth are increasingly deprived of signals to help them decide in what areas to gain training and how hard to work.

Problems in Signaling Theory

Market theory and human capital theory assume that information is sent, that incentives operate, and that individuals acquire the right training to fit employers' needs. But without dependable information, markets cannot work effectively. Signaling theory specifies some determinants of information use.

However, signaling theory does not explain why employers ignore the signals they get from schools and why schools do not give youth incentives to work in school. These findings are particularly baffling if grades are reasonably good signals of employees' productivity, as we explore in chapter 8.

While signaling theory focuses on information and its economic value, our analysis suggests that social context influences whether signals are accepted, trusted, and used. Schools do not try to influence jobs very much, they do not try to make their evaluations important to employers, and they do not try to explain their tracks, course titles, or grades to employers. Nor do employers try to contact schools. As a result, employers do not understand or trust schools' rankings, and they do not use tracks and grades as signals—despite their claim that they need employees with better academic skills.

We turned to signaling theory because information is an important influence on the school-to-work transition. However, non-economic constraints also affect employers' and youths' decisions to use available information. The next section considers some conditions that may affect these features of signals.

Network Theory

The market model, which is the basis of human capital theory, contends that linkages between schools and employers interfere with the efficiency of markets. In contrast, network theory suggests that such linkages can improve market processes. The new institutional economics considers the efficiencies of institutional relationships (Lazear 1979; Rosen 1982; Williamson 1975, 1981). In Mark Granovetter's (1985, 502) model, market relations are embedded in, and responsive to, social relations: "A high level of order can often be found in the 'market'—that is, across firm boundaries . . . [that level of order] depends on the nature of personal relations and the network of relations between and within firms." Many examples illustrate the point: exchanges between diamond brokers (Ben-Porath 1980), corporations (Useem 1979), salesmen and purchasing agents (Macaulay 1963, 63), contractors and subcontractors (Eccles 1981, 339), and job applicants and employers (Bridges and Villemez 1986; Granovetter 1974/1995). Unlike the market model, this view posits that institutional linkages could raise efficiency and strengthen the relationships between achievement and jobs by increasing information and trust (Stinchcombe 1985; Zucker 1986).

Signaling theory assumes that information is trusted, but this is not always the case. Economic actors may be "opportunistic, . . . and agents who are skilled at dissembling realize transactional advantages" (Williamson 1975, 255). Giving inflated recommendations is one way to dump a disliked subordinate on another employer.

Network theory describes some ways in which information is given meaning and trust in transactions, and how information is transmitted not only through market results but also through social networks. Despite the potential rewards for deception, trust arises because transactions are embedded in "personal relations and structures (or 'networks') . . . generating trust and discouraging malfeasance. . . . People prefer to deal with individuals of known reputation, or, even better, with individuals they have dealt with before, so social relations . . . are mainly responsible for the production of trust in economic life" (Granovetter 1985, 490–91). For example, purchasing agents know salesmen personally, and disputes are settled in discussions, without legal recourse. "You do not read legalistic contract clauses at each other if you ever want to do business again" (Macaulay 1963, 61). Thus, trust arises because transactions occur in networks of personal relationships.

In earlier work (Rosenbaum and Kariya 1989), we have indicated that Granovetter's analysis applies not only to personal contacts but also to institutional contacts, which arise from regular patterns of interactions. Trust develops in long-term, interdependent role-relationships, and new occupants of these roles make sacrifices (investments) to maintain the history of trust. For instance, the relationship between a salesman and a purchasing agent is likely to be maintained even when a new person takes one of those jobs. Admittedly, the relationship is problematic at first, but the new role occupant has strong incentives to maintain the existing relationship because of the trust and dependability that has been built.

The transition between high school and work illustrates how mistrust creates inefficiencies in markets. High schools and employers are interdependent: employers depend on schools to supply trained workers, and schools depend on employers to hire their graduates. However, this interdependence has not jelled in the United States. Employers avoid relying on schools by hiring adults over age twenty-five for good jobs, they do not use school rankings, and they do not understand or trust information from schools. They do not know how to interpret grades, course titles, or tracks, and they do not know if they can trust reference letters that youth can see and even contest with lawsuits. Similarly, school staff doubt that employers care about education, and so they see little reason to stress education for work-bound students (Useem 1986). They report that they are not responsible for placing youth in jobs, and that youth can do that themselves. Mutual mistrust has prevented this interdependence between schools and work from flourishing.

Information by itself is not enough to make a market operate, so this market failure cannot be explained by signaling theory. Understanding and trust are important considerations in evaluating signals. They are not necessarily properties of signals per se, but of the context in which signaling takes place. Markets need ways in which to guarantee that information is understood and trusted.

One way to increase understanding and trust of signals may be to embed them in the context of ongoing social or institutional relationships. Trust arises in social interactions, and social norms give meaning and dependability to exchanges (Granovetter 1985). These contextual features offer performance guarantees that would not emerge from simple market mechanisms.

One problem with these labor market theories is that they are based on observations in the United States. U.S. labor markets generally follow the market model: the ideal market relation is assumed to be between individual job applicants and employers, with schools having no role in the transaction. Schools are not supposed to be involved in helping youth get jobs, and employers are supposed to wait for youth to apply for jobs (Timpane 1984). Youth must navigate the school-to-work transition by themselves.

Therefore, while the United States provides good examples of market processes, the institutional linkages between its high schools and employers are less common and less studied. Because American social scientists take this system and its outcomes for granted, theories about institutional linkages have not been applied to the school-to-work transition. Would the high school–to–work transition create fewer problems if high schools had direct linkages with employers, as network theory suggests? Or would such linkages create greater inefficiencies, as market theory suggests? Studying alternative systems may increase our understanding of market and network systems and may help us detect previously ignored processes in the United States (see chapters 5, 9, 10, this volume).

Social Networks Linking High Schools and Employers: Japan

As noted in chapter 1, Japan has strong linkages between high schools and employers, so it illustrates the issues raised by network theory, particularly the ways in which networks address the issues of understanding and trust. Japan's institutional system is a striking contrast to the U.S. market system. Since we have already described Japan's system in chapter 1, here we will only summarize the key points and their implications for understanding how institutional contacts affect market processes.

First, while Americans assume and hope that students respect teachers' authority and see incentives for school effort, Japan does not leave this to chance. Many firms have long-term arrangements in which they authorize certain high schools to nominate students to fill their job openings. Schools influence a student's job search and ultimate job placement, and most youth find their first job without entering the labor market (for details, see Rosenbaum and Kariya 1989). This semiformal system gives teachers clear authority for affecting important student outcomes, and it creates clear incentives for students to exert effort in school. In contrast to the unclear institutional linkages in the American labor market, which may cause ambiguous incentives, Japanese institutional contacts create very clear authority and very clear incentives. Students know how the system works, and they see clear incentives to work in school (see Rosenbaum and Kariya 1989).

Second, like their American counterparts, Japanese employers insist on interviewing applicants on their own, but they usually end up endorsing the students recommended by schools. Employers hire over 81 percent of nominees on their first job application, and 85 percent of nominees for their second job. Fewer than 3 percent of all students had to apply to three or more employers.

Third, while there are many temptations to deviate from the system, actors also have very strong incentives to continue taking appropriate actions. These linkages impose obligations on both schools and employers to satisfy one another. Although teachers may sometimes be tempted to help a likable but lower-achieving student, they keep using grades and selecting the assigned number of students because they do not want to endanger their relations with an employer or to have their job allocations reduced.[5] Although employers may be tempted to reduce their hiring from a school in a particular year, they know that they must continue hiring a school's graduates to keep on receiving a stable source of employees of dependable quality. Several employers mentioned cases in which they had hired students they ordinarily would not have selected because they did not want to hurt their relationships with the schools (Rosenbaum and Kariya 1989). These undesired hirings are the price that employers pay to get the benefits of linkages.

Fourth, these linkages provide information that would be difficult for employers to get otherwise. Employers prefer to recruit from the same high schools continually so that they know what to expect from the school's graduates (Hida 1982; Iwanaga 1984). Moreover, Japanese employers expect schools to nominate the best students for their best jobs. They want youth with good work habits and good basic skills, and they do not expect vocational skills, which they feel are easily acquired at work. Employers feel that these linkages are a good way to get information about students' capabilities and effort, and they rely very heavily on schools' nominations. As a result, employers get better-achieving students for their more demanding jobs.

This system is clearly not a market. Employers choose not among all interested students but only among those nominated by school staff, and students cannot apply to an employer without the school's nomination. Thus, students compete for jobs before they enter the labor market.[6]

Japan's system illustrates the ways in which institutional networks can create useful and trusted information. Employer misunderstanding and mistrust of school rankings, a risk of ordinary market relations, are reduced by institutional networks that ensure that information is dependable and that provide institutional penalties for bad information.

It might be noted that institutional linkages do not exist in the same sense between Japanese universities and employers. As a result, the same employers who trust high schools to nominate employees do not extend this privilege to university officials. Instead, employers must make these selections themselves, based on signals.

Germany and Britain

The German system, one of the most effective in Europe, is another example of a school-to-work transition that relies on "institutional" linkages. It "offers a comprehensive list of services, organizes the transition from the national government down, [supervises schools' efforts] to initiate and carry out activities without outside supervision, uses bridging agencies that strongly involve the labor market authorities, and integrates youth services with those for adults" (Reubens 1974, 50). It provides clear incentives for students, since students with better educational backgrounds—that is, better and higher-ranked academic diplomas and/or academic achievements—get into better vocational schools, get apprenticeships in better occupations, and ultimately get better jobs.

It also provides clear linkages between school and work. German schools provide clear vocational preparation; 88 percent of workbound students receive a recognized vocational qualification, and few fall between the cracks (Osterman 1988, 114). Moreover, in contrast with the uncertain preparation of the general and vocational tracks in the United States, employers trust vocational graduates to have a dependably high level of skill, and youths' first jobs tend to be related to their preparation. The German Federal Employment Office also enhances the linkage by providing vocational services to schools and individual counseling to those leaving school, of whom 60 to 80 percent participate (Arnow 1968, 142). Employers also contribute to the linkage. "Employers have social obligations to fulfill by training apprentices," and the federal government can levy a payroll tax if a firm fails to provide its share of apprenticeships (Hamilton 1987, 322). The German apprentice system enables youths "to move directly into primary-labor-market careers at a time when their counterparts in the U.S. . . . begin a period of low-skill and low-paid work" (314).

In the German system, school-employer linkages are weaker than in Japan, but stronger than in the United States. German apprenticeships are influenced by educational attainments, that is, educational levels, school types, educational certificates, and academic achievements (Heinz 1986, 1999; Prais 1995; Soskice 1994). In addition, after regular school ends, the "dual system" combines apprenticeships and part-time vocational education through age eighteen. However, secondary schools are not necessarily involved in placing graduates into apprenticeships, and part-time vocational school achievement does not affect jobs after the apprenticeship (Cantor 1989). Although schools have become more involved in placement in recent years, the main role of guidance and placement has been played by public employment offices (Cantor 1989). In the 1981–82 school year, 60 percent of prospective graduates came to local offices, and two-thirds of apprenticeships were filled by the public employment service. Thus, while educational achievement affects placement into apprenticeships and schools' influence has increased in recent years, the allocation process relies more on cooperation between government agencies, employers, and trade unions than on schools (Cantor 1989).

On the other hand, the linkages between school and work are stronger in Germany than in the United States. Instead of wandering around in the labor market after graduation, graduates move directly into primary jobs as apprentices through institutional agreements between states, employers, and trade unions, although females and foreign youth (mostly Turkish) are less likely to get such positions (Herget 1986).

Examinations also create an institutional incentive for learning in this system. An examination given at the end of apprenticeship measures a student's occupational competence and affects that individual's next job (Cantor 1989).

Regarding information flow, the German example shows how institutional linkages help employers learn about the competence of potential employees. During the apprenticeship period, employers can obtain information about their trainees' job competence in face-to-face situations. Based on this information and the apprenticeship examination, employers make their hiring decisions with considerable confidence about job applicants' productivity. On the other hand, trainees learn from apprenticeships the level of competence needed for a job and the prevailing job conditions. The apprenticeship is an institutional arrangement that provides relevant information to both employers and trainees.

Thus, unlike the Japanese system, in which schools and employers are directly linked, the German system creates new institutions to bridge the gap. Government employment offices, which have linkages with schools, employers, and unions, provide counseling and placement. Apprenticeships and examinations also provide institutional linkages that facilitate information flow.

Britain, like the United States, once had a very loose transition from secondary school to work based on market mechanisms. Facing serious youth employment problems, however, including high unemployment and turnover, Britain is now moving toward a system similar to Germany's (Raffe 1981). After thorough study of European practices, Britain began in the late 1970s to adopt new policies that offer part-time vocational training to work-bound youth leaving secondary schools. In programs such as Youth Opportunities Programs (YOP) (starting in 1978) and its replacement, the Youth Training Scheme (YTS) (starting in 1983), Colleges of Further Education have been established to provide part-time vocational education to unemployed youth who left school (Cantor 1989). Some educational programs are combined with apprenticeships, as in the German "dual system." These recent policy changes indicate that the United Kingdom has shifted away from free market approaches and toward institutional linkages.

British researchers credit the value of institutional linkages not only to training but also to the smoother information flow through such linkages. YOP serves "a screening function . . . by providing prospective employers with a criterion for selection that is complementary or even alternative to educational credentials, and by giving employers a cheap way to gain direct information about potential recruits" (Raffe 1981, 219). By this interpretation, the shift from market to institutional linkages has occurred because better information is created and conveyed through institutional linkages than by market mechanisms.

Institutional Networks in the United States

Do such linkages exist in the United States? Some recent educational reforms are similar in some ways to Japanese linkages, although we are not aware of any U.S. programs that have linkages as strong as those in Japan. A number of reformers have proposed "partnerships" between schools and employers (Jobs for the Future 1993; Neubauser 1986; Seeley 1984; Timpane 1984), and several public school systems have sought to foster such linkages (including Atlanta, Chicago, and Boston). Accounts of "industry-school partnerships" indicate that businesses offer instructional resources, but the accounts are not clear about whether programs offer job assurances, authorize schools to nominate students, or rely strongly on grades (Spring 1986).

The school-to-work transition in small towns in the United States may also resemble Japanese linkages. In small towns, regular interactions every year between a few employers and the schools may lead to linkages. Unfortunately, we know of no systematic evidence to indicate where and to what extent such linkages exist or how they operate (compare, Nelson-Rowe 1991).

More generally, similar linkages may also occur in American higher education, and in its relationships with other institutions. Some colleges regularly recruit the same number of students from certain high schools every year, while not recruiting from other high schools of comparable quality. Guidance counselors in these high schools know the college recruiters, and these relationships may resemble Japan's "semiformal contracts." Similarly, some MBA programs regularly send the same number of graduates to certain major employers every year. The two institutions may have close interdependencies: MBA programs seek to improve their graduates' success in getting jobs, while employers seek the benefits of having employees with prestigious degrees (Burke 1984). Grades also affect which MBA students get the best jobs (Burke 1984), just as grades affect college graduates' jobs (Crain 1984). These are often long-standing relationships, and schools and employers may make investments (sacrifices) to maintain these relationships. Little is known about how much long-term investing in such institutional linkages occurs in the United States, what forms it takes, or how much it interferes with labor-market processes.

The Boston Compact   The Boston Compact, a reform effort that consciously tries to strengthen linkages between high schools and employers, may demonstrate how institutional networks could work in the United States. In 1982, Boston businesses, trade unions, and colleges signed agreements with the Boston public schools to increase youth employment and access to college, while the schools promised to improve student achievement, attendance, and graduation rates (Farrar and Cipollone 1988).

Although the Boston Compact did not state incentives for students to improve their achievement, some Boston high schools have used jobs as incentives for work-bound students, reserving highly prized jobs (white-collar jobs with better pay, better training, advancement, and job security) for students with the best school records. Grades, teacher evaluations, and attendance are used to determine who is nominated for the best jobs (Rosenbaum 1989a).

We must caution that the practices of the Boston Compact may not apply to all Boston schools or to all students in the schools. A single career specialist probably affects only a few juniors and seniors, and even fewer young students. Indeed, there is little way that the compact could motivate elementary and junior high students. By the time students become aware of the compact in high school, they may feel they are already too far behind the schools' achievement standards to catch up. These questions require more detailed study.

Judging the overall success of the program, the Boston Compact has not lived up to all of its goals. Although employers offer jobs, the schools have failed to raise achievement, attendance, and graduation rates (Farrar and Cipollone 1988). Some observers have concluded that the program is a failure. However, it is possible that the Boston Compact does not go far enough to implement its ideals: although it creates incentives for employers and schools, it does not create incentives for students.

Nor does the compact bring teachers into the process. In Japan, grade-based job selections give teachers authority over students. If teachers and students knew that grades affected jobs, teacher authority could be increased and discipline problems greatly reduced (Sedlak et al. 1986).

Unlike the Japanese system, which creates incentives all the way through the school system, the Boston system has done little to show elementary students, junior high school students, and all students in the high school that grades matter. The Boston Compact is an effort in the direction of increasing linkages, but it is only a weak approximation.

Conclusions

This chapter reviewed four labor market theories. Each has strengths and weaknesses in explaining the school-to-work transition. Each imposes a conceptual structure that helps us understand some aspects of the transition but also imposes blinders that prevent us from clearly seeing other aspects. We have not proven that one theory is better than the others: each has some strengths and some utility. Segmented labor market theory shows features of labor markets that constrain markets' responses to individuals. Human capital theory shows how individuals invest in themselves for anticipated returns. Signaling theory indicates the economic factors limiting the use of information. Network theory stresses the ways in which context influences the use of information.

Because it is a new theory, we have stressed the strengths of network theory and the shortcomings of the others, which are well established. We have extended this new theory beyond personal networks to include institutional networks, and we have described Japanese and other systems as examples.

This is not to say, however, that network theory is superior to the other three. Human capital theory is better able to describe individuals' investments in themselves under conditions in which they clearly understand and trust information about the contingencies of various investments. Signaling theory provides a better explanation of employers' hiring decisions under these same conditions, including the hiring of college graduates in Japan. However, when information is not understood and trusted, these theories are less applicable.

Network theory is less parsimonious and less elegant than these theories, for it broadens our focus to a larger context. It raises questions about how information acquires meaning and trust from the social context of personal and institutional relationships. When these matters are not at issue, network theory is unnecessary, but the theory contends that these matters are in fact often at issue and must be considered before segmented market, human capital, or signaling theories can be applied.

Moreover, network theory can explain some aspects of the school-to-work transition that are not easily explained by other theories. It explains why U.S. employers do not use grades in their hiring decisions but Japanese employers do; why youthfulness is a negative signal in the United States but not in Japan; and why work-bound youth have few incentives to do well in their schoolwork in the United States but not in Japan.

Network theory also shows a large gap in our knowledge of how employers choose signals (Spence 1974). Signaling theory explains why selection criteria are chosen, but not which attributes are used. Although educational certificates are nearly universal signals, other criteria, like grades, school tracks, or age, are not necessarily used as signals. Their use depends on institutional decisions or social beliefs about ability, and perhaps on the relative influence of schools on selections (Rosenbaum 1980a, 1986). The fact that high school grades are important in Japan but not in the United States suggests that the selection of signals is not a simple function of technology or capitalism. Apparently, specific institutional arrangements in capitalist societies can differ considerably on the selection criteria used, and they may be affected by features of networks.

We believe that institutional networks represent an important extension of network theory. Economic models rarely consider how schools and employers invest in stable relationships to maintain their labor supply and demand, although Oliver Williamson's (1979) "transaction-specific investments" suggest the possibility of such investments. Moreover, economic models rarely consider schools to be part of the hiring transaction. In part, this omission reflects U.S. reality, for these features are less true in the United States than in Japan. However, reliance on the U.S. experience has prevented researchers from developing models that are applicable to institutional linkages.

Such relationships are governed by institutional agreements, not by temporary market conditions, and the goals transcend current circumstances. A Japanese teacher posed the issue clearly: "Getting jobs is only a one-time experience for individual students, but it is repeated year after year for schools." Schools seek dependable *future* demand for students, and employers seek dependable *future* supply of employees. When employers accept most school nominees and hire when they do not need new employees, these actions are viewed as *investments* in the future continuity of their labor supply. Schools' strict adherence to standards hurts their job placement records in some years, but it is also an investment in their relationships with employers. Though inefficient in the short run, these practices are seen as investments with long-run benefits. This system also shows how labor market competition can occur before youth enter the labor market, while they are still in school, and it shows the consequences for labor market functioning.

The institutional networks in Japan show just how much signaling theory incorrectly takes for granted. In Japan, linkages make grades trusted selection criteria that give employers good indications of youths' human capital and notify youth of their relative positions in the "labor queue" (Thurow 1975). They make it easy for youth to anticipate their probable career options, to interpret how they are doing, and to increase their efforts or lower their sights accordingly. This delegated job selection also reinforces schools' control over students, and it may also avert motivation crises for those students eliminated from higher education, since grades still have an important impact on job attainment. The continuing incentive to get good grades may keep students working harder, increasing their basic skills and making their work attitudes more compliant (Kariya and Rosenbaum 1987; Kariya 1988).

In contrast, the lack of linkages in the United States creates serious signaling failures. American employers do not understand or trust information from schools, and students do not get signals about their career options and how they are doing. As a result, because employers do not know how to select youth with the best human capital, they rely on discriminatory criteria or avoid youth entirely, while youth do not know whether to invest in their human capital. Since school performance has little payoff for jobs, such poor articulation may reduce youths' school motivation (Stinchcombe 1965). Peter Bullock (1972) also finds that American work-bound youth lack motivation to study hard, since they think these efforts are rarely rewarded in the labor market. Thus, the absence of networks between schools and employers may interfere with American youth acquiring marketable skills (Kariya and Rosenbaum 1987).

These theories also raise practical issues of great policy importance. As Kurt Lewin said, there is nothing as practical as a good theory. Theories help us think clearly about causality and to have a coherent view of social processes. Network theory points to faulty assumptions in human capital and signaling theories. Since these theories are the basis for much current policy, faults in the theories would lead to practices with unanticipated and undesired outcomes—employer discrimination and avoidance of youth, youth motivation and discipline problems, schools' lack of authority, and the failure of educational reforms that increase instructional hours. These are not predicted by human capital or signaling theories, but they do occur. Segmented labor market theory does predict them, but it does not adequately explain them. Network theory is a useful extension because it explains these phenomena and suggests possible policy efforts that might successfully address these problems, as we examine further in later chapters.

══ Chapter 3 ══

College for All:
Do Students Understand
What College Demands?

I N BEGINNING a study of the high school–to–work transition, we
must first establish whether high school is still an important institution for affecting work entry. For much of this century, most
people entered the labor market directly after high school, but there
has been an astounding growth in college enrollment in recent decades. If nearly all students are planning to attend college, then high
school may no longer be an important influence on work entry.

Community colleges have enormously increased college access in
just one generation. While four-year-college enrollment roughly doubled between 1960 and 1990, public community college enrollment
increased fivefold in the same period, from 200,000 to more than
1,000,000 (NCES 1992, table 169). In turn, college opportunities have
dramatically increased. While 45.1 percent of high school graduates
entered some postsecondary institution in 1960, over 62 percent did
in 1993. Moreover, community colleges initiated open-admissions policies and remedial courses to reduce the academic barriers to college.
The value of the associate of arts (A.A.) degree has increased in the
labor market, so that students no longer need a B.A. to gain an economic benefit from attending community college (Brint and Karabel
1989; Grubb 1992, 1993, 1996). Community colleges have increased
access to an economically valued degree.

Have these changes created an easy route to college success, or do
they merely confuse students so that they fail to prepare themselves
appropriately? In an early study, Burton Clark (1960) showed the am-
biguity of the mission of community colleges: they seemed to offer
access to four-year colleges but in fact these institutions "cooled out"
aspirations as students gradually realized that college was not appro-

55

priate for their abilities. Studies since Clark's have continued to find substantial college attrition (Grubb 1989; see also, Clark 1985), and they have focused on the factors that redirect students' plans (Karabel 1972, 1986).

Clark took the term "cooling out" from Erving Goffman's (1952) analysis of confidence swindles. The key to a swindle is to give "marks" confidence that they will gain a valuable reward at very little cost, and then lure them into an "easy success" strategy. That is why a mark willingly hands over something of value to a swindler, and why people pay for "snake oil" remedies that offer high expectations for a small price. Marks do not realize that their expectations were mistaken until a later time, after the swindler who encouraged the expectation is no longer present.

This chapter contends that the high level of community college dropout arises because high schools offer vague promises of open opportunity for college without specifying the requirements for degree completion. Like Goffman's confidence schemes, students are promised college for very little effort. Lured by the prospect of easy success, students choose easy curricula and make little effort. Just as some high schools implicitly offer students an undemanding curriculum in return for nondisruptive behavior (Sedlak et al. 1986), many high schools enlist students' cooperation by telling them that college is the only respectable goal and that it is easily attainable by all. Failure in community colleges may stem not from any overt barrier in those institutions but from seeds planted much earlier—when youths are still in high school. Because students usually do not realize that their expectations were mistaken until long after they have left high school, high schools are rarely blamed for their graduates' failures in community college.

Today many high schools encourage the "college-for-all" norm, which states that all students can and should attend college but fails to tell students what they must do to attain a college degree (Rosenbaum, Miller, and Krei 1996). A variant of the so-called contest mobility norm, which says that opportunity for upward mobility should always stay open (Turner 1960), the college-for-all norm encourages youths to retain ambitions of advancement as long as possible, but it ignores the barriers that limit their careers (Rosenbaum 1975, 1976, 1986). Noting the change in students' aspirations, Barbara Schneider and David Stevenson (1999) have called them *The Ambitious Generation.*

Americans are rightly proud of the college-for-all norm. It discourages schools from tracking students prematurely, and it encourages high expectations in youths. It argues for better instruction in schools, especially schools serving low-income youths. Without this norm, society might give up on raising the educational achievement of the most disadvantaged youths.

Although it is not meant to be deceptive, the college-for-all norm can inadvertently encourage a deception that hurts many youths, including the disadvantaged youths it is meant to help. The college-for-all norm encourages all students to plan on college, regardless of their past achievement. So as not to discourage students, the college-for-all norm avoids focusing on requirements, but in the process it fails to tell students what steps they should take to be successful in college, and it does not warn them when their low achievements make their college plans unlikely to be attained. Such encouragement helps younger children, but it may mislead students in their later years of high school.

Thus, while 95 percent of high school seniors in the class of 1992 planned to attend college (up from 80 percent of the seniors in 1982), half of twelfth-grade students lacked basic ninth-grade math and verbal skills (Murnane and Levy 1996), and only 36 percent of high school graduates age thirty to thirty-four had a college degree.[1] Indeed, only about half of college entrants complete a college degree (Resnick and Wirt 1996). This has not always been true. The dropout rate from public two-year colleges increased sharply after 1972: 36.0 percent in 1972 versus 49.6 percent in 1980 (Grubb 1989, table 2).

While Jerome Karabel (1986) blames community colleges for misleading students, Goffman's model suggests that the deception occurs earlier, often in a different location, and is more subtle. Indeed, marks go along with a swindle because their hopes are initially "heated up" to unrealistic expectations, and they "cool out" only late in the process. Thus, rather than focus on the cooling-out process, we need to examine why youths' expectations are so unrealistically high that "cooling out" is required.

This chapter asserts that information is central to this process. If high school students were informed that they are poorly prepared for community college, they could either increase their efforts to prepare themselves or revise their plans to make them more realistic. In either case, cooling out would not be needed, and youths' plans would be less likely to fail.

High schools probably do not intentionally deceive students. Indeed, schools have good intentions when they encourage students to hold high expectations, but schools' actions may have unintended consequences. High schools encourage all students to make college plans, even students whose subsequent failure is highly predictable in high school. These students do not anticipate their probable failure, and they do not take actions to prepare themselves for their goals.

Such a mechanism is more subtle than the one Karabel describes. Poor information allows many students to have high hopes but to use their high school experiences poorly, and thus they seem to be personally responsible for their failures (Rosenbaum 1980b, 1989b). By the time students enter community college, their eventual outcomes are largely determined. Community colleges themselves cannot be blamed for the poor preparation of their entrants. Yet the high schools that poorly convey information about requirements are not a visible target. Indeed, they are praised for encouraging students to have "high expectations." Like the mark who realizes that his expectations are mistaken only after the swindler who encouraged those expectations is no longer present, students realize their failure some time after they leave high school, and they may not even blame high schools for their loss.

This description suggests that students' perceptions of college requirements are key to their efforts in high school and to their college attainments. We can pose a model with several elements, which can be tested empirically.

1. Many low-achieving high school seniors believe that they can attain a college degree.

2. Students who believe they can attain a college degree in spite of low achievement, including college-bound students, exert little effort in high school.

3. Such a belief is partly correct—students can enter college even if they have been low-achieving in high school.

4. High school achievement predicts degree completion, but students' plans do not anticipate this relationship.

5. High school achievement predicts much of the lower attainment and disappointed plans of disadvantaged students.

6. Students whose high school achievement was low get less economic payoff from a college degree.

This chapter makes three sets of discoveries. First, we discover that many youths believe that high school achievement is not relevant to their future career, and that youths with such a belief exert less effort in school. Second, we discover that many students who think they are college-bound are really work-bound—that is, they are likely to enter the labor market with their high school diploma as their highest degree. Third, we discover that students' "no penalty" beliefs are wrong: high school grades have a strong impact on their educational attainment and earnings, and grades explain students' failure to attain their educational plans. We discover that large numbers of college-bound high school seniors are very likely to fail to attain a college degree, and that these failures are highly predictable from their high school grades, information that students and their counselors already know. High schools are not making a practice of informing them about the importance of grades and their actual career prospects, and so students hold mistaken beliefs. Administrators brag about students' "high expectations," but they do not examine how many students drop out of college, many with few college credits. High expectations are not an unmitigated good if students do not know how to attain their goals, do not anticipate their predictable failure, and do not have backup plans and preparation.

Data and Methods

This study is based on three kinds of data. First, students' perceptions are described using detailed interviews with a nonrandom sample of high school seniors in two high schools. Second, students' views are systematically analyzed using a survey of 2,091 seniors, administered to a random sample of classes at twelve high schools across the Chicago metropolitan area from 1992 through 1994. The schools and sample are diverse in ethnicity and socioeconomic backgrounds and are described in detail elsewhere (Rosenbaum and Roy 1996).

Third, students' outcomes are assessed using the twelve-year follow-up of the High School and Beyond (HSB) 1980 sophomores (NCES 1983). This national sample was first surveyed in 1980 (as sophomores) and subsequently surveyed in 1982, 1984, 1986, and 1992. Of the original 14,825 sophomores in 1980, the survey obtained responses from 95.1 percent in 1982 (14,102), and 85.3 percent in 1992 (12,640). This survey provides a unique opportunity for a long-term study of the determinants of educational attainments. This chapter studies the outcomes for the individuals responding in both the 1982 and 1992 surveys.[2]

Many Low-Achieving High School Seniors Believe That They Can Earn a College Degree

Economic theory is a good model of our rational, commonsense assumptions. For instance, human capital theory explains students' achievement using two factors: students' inherent capabilities and their efforts to invest in themselves. The theory says that students invest in themselves and exert effort in school because they know there is a societal payoff.

Although it is widely assumed that students believe that school efforts have a payoff, this assumption is rarely examined. Do students believe that school effort and achievement are relevant and helpful in improving their future career? Of course, teachers tell students this, but it is clearly in teachers' self-interest to convince students of their own importance. As parents and teachers often notice, one of the less convenient aspects of adolescence is the cognitive capacity that enables them to doubt what they are told.

Arthur Stinchcombe (1965) hypothesized that many students believe that school is not relevant to their future career, and that students' school efforts are determined not only by their internal motivation but also by their perceptions of school's future relevance. Economists assume that incentives exist and are seen, but Stinchcombe suggests that this may not be true for work-bound students. Unfortunately, while Stinchcombe provided an intriguing model, his small sample and simple bivariate analyses (on a card-sorter in the precomputer age) were too simple for a convincing test.

To examine these ideas, we asked a nonrandom sample of fifty students about the relevance of school. Consistent with the dictum "The more things change, the more they stay the same," these interviews in 1993 found sentiments similar to those that Stinchcombe had found thirty years before. Many students reported that school was not relevant to their future career. Yet something had changed. While Stinchcombe found that only work-bound students expressed this belief in 1960, it was expressed by college-bound students as well in 1993. Many students who planned to attend college reported that high school achievement was not relevant to their future career. Their comments suggest that the vast expansion of community colleges over the past thirty years contributed to their views. One student noted: "High school doesn't really matter, . . . because . . . junior college is not such a big deal to get into." Said another: "If you could apply yourself [in junior college], you'd get better grades [regardless of high school grades]." Many students agreed with the student who saw the "two-year college as another chance for someone who's messed up in high school." This second chance was also viewed as making high school effort less relevant. As one student said in explaining why he did not try hard in high school, "I think college is much more important than high school."

To examine Stinchcombe's hypotheses more systematically, we constructed survey items that reflect two aspects of individuals' perceptions of schools' relevance: whether they believed that high school education had relevance for their future success (hereafter "future relevance"), and whether they believed that there was no penalty for poor school performance (hereafter "no penalty" attitude). The first variable refers to students' belief that high school could help their future career; the second refers to the belief that bad school performance (even if possibly relevant) is not necessarily a barrier to attaining their future career.[3]

As noted earlier, surveys were administered to 2,091 high school seniors enrolled in twelve city and suburban high schools in the Chicago metropolitan area. Just as Stinchcombe found, the survey finds that many students doubt school's future relevance. This belief is held not only by work-bound students but also by almost as many college-bound students. On five-point scales ranging from "strongly agree" to "strongly disagree," analyses find that 28 to 40 percent of students do not agree with such statements as, "My courses give me useful preparation I'll need in life" (39.3 percent for the whole sample, 37.2 percent for college-bound respondents), "School teaches me valuable skills" (29.7 percent; 28.2 percent of college-bound), and "Getting a good job depends on how well you do at school" (36.6 percent; 36.5 percent of college-bound). These items are summed to create a scale for "future relevance."

For the items in our "no penalty" scale, similar patterns are evident. Almost 46 percent of students agree with the item "Even if I do not work hard in high school, I can still make my future plans come true" (45.9 percent; 44.3 percent of college-bound). Although educators want students to believe that students with bad grades rarely get a college degree or good jobs, many students disagree with the first point with regard to graduation from a two-year college (40.7 percent; 41.2 percent of college-bound), and almost as many disagree with the second when it comes to getting good jobs after high school (37.9 percent; 32.9 percent of college-bound). Most surprisingly, despite many campaigns against dropping out of high school, over 40 percent of seniors do not disagree with the statement "People can do okay even if they drop out of high school" (43.7 percent; 40.8 percent of college-bound). Apparently, many students see no penalty to their planned career if they do not work hard in school and fail to earn a high school diploma or good grades. These items are summed to create a scale for "no penalty."

The two scales of "future relevance" and "no penalty" hang together fairly well. Although their alpha coefficients are weaker than those for our other scales, they indicate reasonable levels of reliability

(.567 and .622; see table 3.A1). The two scales are correlated, but the correlation is far from perfect ($r = .30$). Students who plan to get a college degree have a somewhat higher sense of school's future relevance, and a lesser sense that there is no penalty if they do poorly in high school, than students without college plans, but the difference is not large (about one-third of a standard deviation). Moreover, these beliefs vary substantially within these groups, and the variation is similar within both groups (standard deviations of .61 to .65).

Students Who Believe They Can Earn a College Degree in Spite of Low Achievement Exert Little Effort in High School

Although there is nothing wrong with students having optimistic hopes, we would be concerned if they responded to those hopes by reducing their efforts. This section examines the factors that may determine "future relevance" and "no penalty" beliefs, the factors that may determine students' school efforts, and whether these beliefs mediate the potential influence of other factors on students' school efforts and have independent influences on students' school efforts.

We look first at the antecedents of "future relevance" and "no penalty" beliefs. The survey included three or more items relating to locus of control, parent support, teacher help, school help, peer pro-school influences, and peer anti-school (rebellion) influences. These items were factor-analyzed, and scales were constructed (see appendix to this chapter). All items had alpha coefficients over .70 (ranging from .736 for "locus of control" to .859 for "rebellious peers"; see table 3.A1). The survey also asked about race, ethnicity, parents' education and occupation, and gender (for details, see Rosenbaum and Roy 1996).

First, regressions (ordinary least squares) find that both "future relevance" and "no penalty" beliefs are strongly explained by parent support for school, teacher help, and personal locus of control. Peers and low socioeconomic status also have significant coefficients, but gender and being black do not (table 3.1, columns 1 and 2).

Second, we examine the antecedents of students' school effort. Effort is measured by a scale combining students' reports of their behaviors: how much time they spend on homework, and three other items—"I just do enough to pass my classes," "I try to do my best in school," and "I only work in school if I'm worried about failing" (on a five-point scale from "strongly agree" to "strongly disagree").

Like previous research (Kandel and Lesser 1972), these analyses

Table 3.1   Determinants of "Future Relevance" and "No Penalty" Beliefs and Effort (Standardized Coefficients)

	"Future Relevance" Belief	"No Penalty" Belief	Effort (step 1)	Effort (step 2)
Parental support for school	.1702**	−.2786**	.2795**	.2128**
Rebellious peers	−.0576*	.0943**	−.1369**	−.1143**
Pro-school peers	.0949**	−.0217	.1157**	.0979**
Locus of control	.1253**	−.1655**	.2060**	.1627**
Female	−.0411	−.0149	.1051**	.1094**
Low SES	−.0439*	.0828**	−.0554*	−.0366
Black	.0344	−.0202	.0006	−.0076
Hispanic	.0526*	−.0391	−.0370	−.0510*
Asian	.0660**	−.0030	−.0043	−.0149
Teacher help	.2822**	.0510*	.0893**	.0530*
School help	.1310**	−.0441	.0564**	.0300
"Future relevance" belief	—	—	—	.1550**
"No penalty" belief	—	—	—	−.1448**
R-squared (adjusted)	.2446	.1710	.2947	.3393

Source: Author's compilation.
Note: N = 2,091.
* = p < .05
** = p < .01

find that students' school efforts are explained by parent, peer, and school variables (see table 3.1, column 3). Being male and of a low socioeconomic status have negative coefficients, but ethnicity has no influence. Students' locus of control has a large significant coefficient.

Third, when "future relevance" and "no penalty" are added, they mediate much of the potential influence of parents, school help, teacher help, and locus of control, but relatively little of the potential influence of the two peer variables (column 4). They also reduce the negative coefficient of socioeconomic status (SES) to insignificance, suggesting that they mediate much of the SES effect on effort. After controlling for other factors, "future relevance" and "no penalty" have strong and significant independent coefficients, suggesting that they have strong effects on students' school efforts (column 4).

These findings have implications for theory and practice. Theoretically, they support Stinchcombe's hypothesis. Students vary in whether they see school as relevant to their future lives, and this variable is strongly associated with their school efforts. This chapter identifies a second measure as well, the "no penalty" belief, and shows that both sets of beliefs have significant, independent relationships with school effort.

These results imply that some youths have misread the American emphasis on opportunity. Although Americans may believe that society should provide youths who need them with "second chances," youths might misinterpret this belief, as Stevenson and Stigler (1992) warn, to mean that school failures never matter and their efforts are unnecessary. This chapter finds that many youths see very little penalty to avoiding school work and little payoff to high school, and that these attitudes may justify their poor effort in high school.

Of course, it is possible that causality goes in the other direction, that individuals rationalize their poor effort by denying its future relevance. However, the view that there is little payoff to high school effort, whether a belief or a rationalization, is held by 40 percent of students, so this view is not just the problem of a few individuals. Indeed, since guidance counselors do not challenge this belief, part of the problem arises from school practices (see chapter 4). Even if this view arises as a rationalization, it is not effectively challenged by schools and it may represent a misconception that encourages an ongoing cycle of low effort.

Students Can Enter College Even if They Have Been Low-Achieving in High School

Are students wrong when they say school achievement is not relevant to their future? Community colleges are frequently seen as "second-chance" institutions for those who have done poorly before. They offer open admissions, low tuition, and remedial courses. In some community college departments, remedial courses may be 40 percent of the courses offered (Deil and Rosenbaum 2000). Over 40 percent of freshmen at public two-year colleges take one or more years of remedial course work, just to acquire the skills they did not learn in high school (NCES 1995).

Although sociologists have produced extensive research showing that grades are strongly related to college attendance (see, for example, Kerckhoff and Campbell 1977; Porter 1974), much of this research is based on studies from the 1960s and 1970s. Yet college admission practices have changed a great deal since 1960. As noted, the fivefold growth of community colleges has dramatically increased opportunities to go to college, and fewer students are likely to face barriers to access to college.

Moreover, community colleges have initiated open-admissions policies and remedial courses to reduce the academic barriers to college. In the past, college admission standards compelled lower-achieving students to confront their unrealistic college plans. College admission standards were a severe barrier to college for low-achieving students in 1960, but admission standards are now practically nonexistent in community colleges. For example, Illinois high school graduates can attend a community college even if they have D-average grades and no college prep courses. (Applicants over the age of twenty-one are not even required to have a diploma.) In addition, a full array of remedial courses has been devised to provide high-school-level curricula in the community colleges in order to improve students' chances of success (Brint and Karabel 1989; Dougherty 1994; Grubb and Kalman 1994). Open-admissions policies and remedial courses have removed some academic barriers to college entrance.

Are students correct in the belief that high school performance is not relevant to their educational outcomes? The HSB data indicate that poor high school performance does not prevent college attendance. Even students with low grades (Cs or lower) can attend college. Indeed, 27 percent of students enrolling in two-year colleges had low grades in high school. That is only slightly less than the proportion of students with low grades who did not enroll in any postsecondary education (30 percent). Obviously, low grades are not a barrier to enrolling in two-year colleges. College-bound students who think high school effort is irrelevant to their future plans are partly correct—high school grades are not an obstacle to enrollment at two-year colleges.

High School Achievement Predicts Degree Completion, but Students' Plans Do Not Anticipate This Relationship

Having found that many students believe high school achievement is not relevant and, indeed, that many students with low grades can enter two-year colleges, one must wonder whether these students are correct that high school achievement is not relevant to college attainment. This section addresses this question with simple percentages, and the next section uses multivariate analyses.

These analyses emphasize grades because all students know their grades, so students can use this information if they choose to do so. But do they choose to do so? Grades are often dismissed as erroneous and irrelevant, perhaps because most people have had a few teachers who gave arbitrary or unfair grades. Yet averaging grades should eliminate random idiosyncrasies and might make grade averages a meaningful indicator. This section examines whether students' cumulative grade point averages in high school predict college outcomes.

The analyses find that many students with college plans fail to attain a college degree, and that high school grades strongly predict which students will fail at their college plans. Of the 12,475 seniors (in the class of 1982) with complete information on plans, grades, and educational attainment, 8,857 (71.0 percent) planned to get a college degree (A.A. or higher) in their senior year of high school.[4] Many seniors (4,103 of the 12,475) had low grades (Cs or lower), yet 51.5 percent of those with low grades (2,112) still planned to get a college degree.

However, low grades have a strong impact on actual educational attainment. Among all seniors with college plans, 37.7 percent succeed in getting a college degree (A.A. or higher) in the ten years after high school, as shown in the first panel of table 3.2. Low high school grades cut students' chances markedly—only 13.9 percent of seniors with low grades attained their college plans. Of seniors planning to get a B.A. or higher, 44.5 percent succeed in getting that degree (table 3.2, panel 2). Students with As have a 65.8 percent chance of getting a B.A. degree or higher, those with Bs have a 41.5 percent chance, and students with a C average or less have only a 16.1 percent chance of getting a B.A. degree.

Since the A.A. is a shorter and perhaps easier degree than a B.A., we might expect that students planning to get an A.A. degree are more likely to be successful. That is not the case. Seniors who plan to get an A.A. degree succeed less often than those planning to earn a B.A. Of the seniors who plan to get an A.A. degree, only 18.7 percent succeed in getting a college degree (A.A. or higher) in the next ten years, and only 8.0 percent of those with low grades (Cs or lower) do so (table 3.2, panel 3). Recall that these tables are explaining students' college-degree outcomes, based only on their high school grades, giving youths ten years to attain any college degree (A.A. or higher).

Ironically, although the colleges offering A.A. degrees are more accessible than four-year institutions to students with low grades, the A.A. degree is not necessarily more available to them. Students with A.A. plans have lower success rates than students with B.A. plans, both because students with A.A. plans are twice as likely to have low grades and because their chances of getting the degree are very slim if they have low grades (8.0 percent). Multivariate analyses indicate that grades explain most of this differential success rate between those with B.A. and A.A. plans (Rosenbaum and Miller 1998).

Why do over half of seniors with low grades believe they can have

Table 3.2   Seniors with College Plans Who Complete College Degrees Within Ten Years

1992 Degree Attainment of HSB 1982 Seniors Using College Transcript File

Seniors with College Plans (A.A. or Higher) Who Complete an A.A. Degree or Higher

Average high school grades	As	Bs	Cs or Lower	Total
Percentage attaining A.A. or higher	63.9	37.1	13.9	37.7
Percentage not attaining any degree	36.1	62.9	86.1	62.3
Number of students	2020	4725	2112	8857

Seniors with College Plans (B.A. or Higher) Who Complete a B.A. Degree or Higher

Average high school grades	As	Bs	Cs or Lower	Total
Percentage attaining B.A. or higher	65.8	41.5	16.1	44.5
Percentage not attaining B.A. degree	32.2	58.5	83.9	55.5
Number of students	1674	2959	928	5561

Seniors with A.A. Plans Who Complete an A.A. Degree or Higher

Average high school grades				
Percentage attaining A.A. or higher	39.0	21.8	8.0	18.7
Percentage not attaining any degree	61.0	78.2	92.0	81.3
Number of students	346	1766	1184	3296

Source: Author's compilation.

college plans? Perhaps to students the open-admissions policies in colleges resemble the "social promotion" practices in high schools: automatically promoting students each year to the next grade regardless of their achievement. Students may infer that college degrees are an award for putting in time, regardless of academic achievement. Students may view school as a credentialing process rather than a human-capital-building process.

Newspaper stories sometimes report that students who got As in high school actually lack the academic skills to do well in college. This may explain our findings that more than one-third (36.0 percent) of the students with As in high school do not complete their plans to earn an A.A. degree or higher. Yet newspapers rarely consider another issue—that students with Cs in high school have very little chance of completing a college degree, and their plans do not seem to recognize these risks.

In sum, many students report that they plan to get a college degree even though their academic achievement in high school has been poor, yet in fact low grades predict much lower chances of attaining a degree. Over 86 percent of students with low grades who planned to get a college degree failed to do so, and the failures were even greater for those planning to get an A.A. degree. Even without making any causal inferences, the strong predictive power of high school grades is important—it tells seniors how to place their bets. Although students are correct in believing that they can enter a college with low grades, they are usually mistaken in thinking that they can complete the degree. Their poor success rates make that outcome a real long shot, not something students should be counting on.

High School Achievement Predicts Much of the Lower Attainment and Disappointed Plans of Disadvantaged Students

The strong predictive power of high school grades may tell seniors how to place their bets, but do grades really predict educational attainment after controlling for other factors? If students want to raise their chances, they need to know whether to focus on improving their grades, homework time, or track placement, and they may be worried that their future attainment is predestined by their social background (socioeconomic status, ethnicity, gender) or intelligence (as test scores are sometimes interpreted). Policymakers also need to know to what extent grades or other factors predict the lower outcomes and disappointed plans of disadvantaged students.

Regression analysis is an ideal way to examine these issues. It allows researchers to look at simple gross associations between background characteristics and attainment, and then to examine the mediating and independent predicting power of other factors, such as high school achievement. We ran a series of OLS regressions on the HSB cohort who graduated in 1982 and were followed through 1992. The survey had 9,100 respondents, with information on all variables in our model.

As shown in table 3.3, these analyses use five dependent variables: students' cumulative grade point averages ("Grades"), tested achievement ("Test"), homework time ("HW"), educational plans ("EdPlan"), and educational attainment ("EdYears"). The first four are information gathered in students' senior year (1982); educational attainment is students' years of educational attainment in 1992, taken from college transcripts. The independent variables include social background variables (black, Hispanic, female, and a cumulative index of parents' socioeconomic status computed in the HSB file), region of the United States (the South, West, and Northeast, with the Midwest as the comparison), and school variables (private school, general and vocational tracks, with college track as the comparison). Regressions on educational plans and educational attainment add grade point average, tested achievement, and homework time as independent variables.

The first finding is that blacks, Hispanics, and low-SES students have much lower grades and achievement test scores (table 3.3, columns 1 and 3). If these coefficients indicate influences, the SES effects are partly mediated by track and private schools (columns 2 and 4). Even after controls, blacks, Hispanics, and low-SES youths have much lower grades and test scores.

Second, high-SES youths and blacks report higher homework time (column 5), and the SES relationship is only partly diminished after controls (column 6). While low-SES youths spend much less time on homework than high-SES youths, blacks spend significantly more time on homework than whites. (Hispanics spend the same amount of time as whites.) Despite potential concerns about this finding because homework time is self-reported, Signithia Fordham and John Ogbu's (1986) findings would predict that blacks will underreport school effort (to avoid being seen as "acting white"), but these analyses find the opposite.[5] If homework time turns out to be an important predictor of educational attainment, then it may account for the lower attainment of low-SES students, but it is not likely to do so for blacks.

Third, low-SES youths have much lower educational plans, but blacks have higher plans than whites (column 7). These results remain after controls for track and private school (column 8). The SES relationship declines considerably after controlling for grades, tests, and homework time, but the positive association for blacks increases (column 9). Blacks have even higher plans than others with similar achievement, as previous research has noted (Jencks et al. 1972).

Fourth, black, Hispanic, and low-SES youths have much lower educational attainment (column 10). Although these relationships are somewhat altered after controls for track and private schools (column 11), they are even more strongly mediated by grades, test scores, and homework time. Indeed, when grades, test scores, and homework time are added, the SES relationship declines substantially (from .870 to .530), although it remains strong, and the black and Hispanic coef-

Table 3.3 Regression Analyses for the Predictions of Grades, Test Scores, Homework Time, Educational Plans, and Educational Attainment

	1 Grades	2 Grades	3 Test	4 Test	5 HW	6 HW	7 EdPlan	8 EdPlan	9 EdPlan	10 EdYears	11 EdYears	12 EdYears
SES	.370* (.018)	.292* (.019)	4.448* (.114)	3.575* (.114)	.424* (.020)	.314* (.021)	1.446* (.032)	1.217* (.032)	.770* (.030)	1.026* (.025)	.870* (.026)	.530* (.024)
Black	-.600* (.042)	-.636* (.042)	-6.129* (.264)	-5.865* (.259)	.241* (.047)	.267* (.047)	.707* (.074)	.694* (.073)	1.204* (.067)	-.195* (.059)	-.208* (.058)	.279* (.053)
Hispanic	-.464* (.041)	-.483* (.040)	-5.814* (.254)	-5.421* (.246)	-.055* (.045)	-.011 (.045)	-.131 (.071)	-.093 (.069)	.438* (.063)	-.416* (.057)	-.330* (.055)	.125* (.050)
Female	.449* (.026)	.445* (.025)	-.644* (.160)	-.704* (.153)	.500* (.028)	.489* (.028)	.176* (.045)	.156* (.043)	-.063 (.040)	.139* (.036)	.122* (.034)	-.068* (.032)
South	—	.062 (.033)	—	-.949* (.199)	—	-.177* (.036)	—	-.043 (.056)	.072 (.050)	—	-.088 (.045)	-.030 (.040)
West	—	.166* (.040)	—	-.080 (.244)	—	-.075 (.044)	—	.114 (.069)	.104 (.061)	—	-.352* (.055)	-.392* (.048)
Northeast	—	-.224* (.035)	—	.850* (.215)	—	.009 (.039)	—	-.069 (.061)	-.081 (.054)	—	.048 (.048)	.076 (.043)
Private	—	-.057 (.041)	—	1.797* (.253)	—	.415* (.046)	—	.498* (.071)	.237* (.064)	—	.468* (.057)	.324* (.051)

Vocational	—	−.542*	−5.145*	—	−.450*	—	−1.258*	−.586*	—	−.911*	−.380*	
		(.037)	(.226)		(.041)		(.064)	(.058)		(.051)	(.046)	
General	—	−.445*	−3.155*	—	−.475*	—	−.990*	−.484*	—	−.682*	−.287*	
		(.028)	(.173)		(.031)		(.049)	(.044)		(.039)	(.035)	
Test	—	—	—	—	—	—	—	.076*	—	—	.054*	
								(.003)			(.002)	
GPA	—	—	—	—	—	—	—	.245*	—	—	.336*	
								(.018)			(.015)	
HW	—	—	—	—	—	—	—	.335*	—	—	.159*	
								(.015)			(.012)	
Constant	4.177	4.466	53.205	55.203	4.425	4.734	14.775	15.344	8.492	13.599	14.043	8.820
	(.020)	(.032)	(.124)	(.195)	(.022)	(.035)	(.035)	(.055)	(.157)	(.028)	(.044)	(.125)
R-squared (adjusted)	12.4	16.0	27.7	33.8	7.9	12.0	19.6	25.1	41.2	18.5	23.9	40.5

Source: Author's compilation.
Note: Unstandardized coefficients are presented.
N = 9,100.
* = p < .05.

ficients actually reverse and become significantly positive (column 12). Thus, students' grades, homework time, and tested achievement explain a large part of the lower attainment of low-SES students, and black and Hispanic students have higher attainments than whites with similar achievement.

Finally, by adding seniors' plans to the regression, the analyses can discover which high school information predicts the disappointing attainments of disadvantaged students many years later (table 3.4). Since some students (11.8 percent) attain more than they planned, they are removed from the analyses in table 3.4, leaving 8,027 students in the analyses.[6] The discrepancies between students' plans and their attainments ranges between zero and eight years (since M.D., L.L.B., or Ph.D. is coded as 20). Table 3.4 shows the factors predicting how much students' attainments will fall short of their plans. The analyses find that low-SES, black, and Hispanic students have significantly lower attainments than they had planned (column 1). However, when variables for school achievement and effort are added, the ethnic variables become insignificant and the SES coefficient becomes smaller (column 3). Apparently, the disappointments of black and Hispanic students are entirely predictable from their lower achievement and effort in high school.

Indeed, students' plans do not take sufficient account of their achievement. Over 58 percent (.029/.050) of the relationship between test scores and attainment, and 75 percent (.221/.296) of the relationship between grades and attainment, remain after controlling for plans (table 3.4, columns 2 and 3). Less than half of these relationships are mediated by plans. Thus, consistent with the cross-tabular analyses (table 3.2), we conclude that, even after controls, seniors' college plans vastly misestimate their attainments, and their grades, test scores, and homework time account for a significant amount of the discrepancy. In making their college plans, students do not fully realize how much their grades, test scores, and efforts predict their ultimate educational outcomes.

It is noteworthy that the female coefficient on educational attainment, which is positive in the early regressions (table 3.3, column 10), becomes significantly negative after controlling for achievement (column 12). Apparently, women have higher educational attainments than males, but their attainments are still below what they would be if their previous achievement were the only determinant. Females have higher grades and homework time than males (but lower test scores; see table 3.3, columns 1 through 6), so there should be some concern about why their attainments are lower than their achievements would predict.

Table 3.4   Regression Analyses for the Predictions of Educational Attainment: All Students, Whites, and Blacks

	All 1	All 2	All 3	Whites 4	Whites 5	Blacks 6	Blacks 7
SES	.372*	.523*	.302*	.614*	.326*	.361*	.284*
	(.022)	(.022)	(.021)	(.030)	(.029)	(.049)	(.049)
Black	−.379*	.315*	−.030	—	—	—	—
	(.046)	(.049)	(.046)				
Hispanic	−.191*	.188*	.053	—	—	—	—
	(.044)	(.046)	(.043)				
Female	.078*	−.033	−.013	−.088*	−.026	.209*	.113
	(.028)	(.030)	(.027)	(.040)	(.036)	(.067)	(.066)
South	−.004	.021	.006	−.008	−.009	.010	−.008
	(.036)	(.037)	(.034)	(.049)	(.044)	(.091)	(.088)
West	−.255*	−.266*	−.290*	−.344*	−.346*	−.207	−.221
	(.043)	(.045)	(.041)	(.060)	(.055)	(.154)	(.149)
Northeast	.119*	.096*	.118*	.115*	.141*	.123	.122
	(.039)	(.040)	(.037)	(.051)	(.047)	(.107)	(.104)
Private	.268*	.353*	.257*	.361*	.273*	.329*	.251
	(.046)	(.048)	(.044)	(.060)	(.055)	(.159)	(.154)
Vocational	−.300*	−.306*	−.135*	−.350*	−.149*	−.075	−.030
	(.041)	(.043)	(.040)	(.060)	(.055)	(.082)	(.079)
General	−.226*	−.258*	−.110*	−.246*	−.086*	−.171*	−.106
	(.032)	(.033)	(.031)	(.044)	(.040)	(.076)	(.074)
Test	—	.050*	.029*	.051*	.026*	.044*	.034*
		(.002)	(.002)	(.003)	(.003)	(.005)	(.005)
GPA	—	.296*	.221*	.309*	.233*	.262*	.222*
		(.014)	(.013)	(.018)	(.017)	(.029)	(.028)
HW	—	.153*	.063*	.154*	.054*	.072*	.040
		(.011)	(.010)	(.015)	(.014)	(.026)	(.026)
Plans	.368*	—	.274*	—	.306*	—	.134*
	(.007)		(.007)		(.010)		(.016)
Constant	7.951	8.885	6.560	8.789	6.195	9.680	8.415
	(.109)	(.116)	(.123)	(.156)	(.165)	(.257)	(.292)
R-squared (adjusted)	46.1	42.6	51.5	42.8	52.3	33.2	37.5
N	8,027	8,027	8,027	4,898	4,898	1,000	1,000

Source: Author's compilation.
Notes: Unstandardized coefficients are presented. Analyses are based on cases in which a student's educational attainment is less than or equal to educational plans.

Finally, while these analyses look at simple additive effects of ethnicity, we might still wonder whether some of the factors in our model have different coefficients for blacks and whites. One indication of bias is when blacks get less benefit from their achievements than whites get from theirs. In the 1970s, James Porter (1974) found that blacks received less gain in educational attainment from their high school grades than whites did. After repeating the prior regressions on educational attainment separately for whites and blacks, we find that grades, test scores, and homework time have somewhat smaller coefficients for blacks than for whites (table 3.4, columns 4 and 6). Apparently, the old pattern of discrimination still holds true—blacks get lower attainment benefits for increasing their grades—but its impact appears to be smaller than in older research. Indeed, test scores are somewhat stronger for blacks than for whites in prediciting which students will attain their plans (table 3.4, columns 5 and 7).

In sum, socioeconomic status, ethnicity, private schools, and track are related to attainment, but grades, test scores, and homework time mediate much of the relationship between disadvantaged backgrounds and attainment. The plans that many students make suggest that they do not realize how much high school achievement predicts future attainment. Although all students know their grades, their plans underestimate the extent to which their grades predict their later attainment, and this is true for both black and white students. Indeed, grades are the single best predictor of the ways in which attainment will fall short of a student's plans. If a student improved performance by one standard deviation on a single variable, the greatest benefit in educational attainment would come from an improvement in grades, and this is true for both blacks and whites. If students could focus on changing one aspect of their high school experience to make their plans come true, they should improve their grades.[7]

Thus, these analyses suggest that students are overly complacent about the ease of getting a college degree. The plans of many students have little chance of succeeding because they underestimate the relationship between high school achievement and later attainment. It seems likely that these students would have worked harder if they had realized the future relevance of high school achievement.

Students Whose High School Achievement Was Low Get Less Economic Payoff from a College Degree

Despite these odds, some students with low high school grades get a college degree. Do they get the same earnings payoff from college as students with better grades? While Richard Murnane, John Willett, and Frank Levy (1995) have shown additive wage payoffs of educational attainment and achievement (measured by test scores), our analyses examine whether college degrees have lower payoffs for those

Table 3.5   Earnings Payoff to College Degrees for Youths with Low High School Grades (Unstandardized Coefficients)

	Ln(Earnings)	Ln(Earnings)
SES	.101*	.101*
Black	.040	.041
Hispanic	.026	.025
Female	−.299*	−.299*
South	−.032*	−.032*
West	−.036	−.036
Northeast	.097*	.099*
Private	.043*	.045*
Vocational	−.030	−.031
General	−.027	−.026
Test	.003*	.003*
Grades	.034*	.025*
HW	−.004	−.004
A.A.	.101*	.155*
B.A.	.145*	.166*
M.A.	.096*	.112*
AALoGPA	—	−.227*
BALoGPA	—	−.123*
MALoGPA	—	−.022
Constant	9.657	9.695
R-squared (adjusted)	13.2	13.5

Source: Author's compilation.
Note: Annual earnings (log) explained by degrees (A.A., B.A., M.A.) and degrees for youths with low high school grades (AALoGPA, BALoGPA, MALoGPA). N = 8,413.
* = $p < .05$

with lower achievement, which is operationalized by high school grades since it more clearly indicates achievement (rather than ability) and is known by all students. The model already outlined is used to explain the 1991 earnings of the same HSB cohort, adding dummy variables for educational attainment (A.A. degree, B.A. degree, M.A. degree or higher). By taking the log of annual earnings as the dependent variable, unstandardized coefficients can be interpreted as percentage increases in earnings. In the first step, the OLS regression indicates that youths who get A.A. and B.A. degrees receive 10.1 percent and 14.5 percent higher earnings, respectively, than those without a degree (table 3.5, column 1).

To see whether students with low grades get the same benefits from degrees, these analyses create a new dummy variable, AALoGPA, for people who got an A.A. degree and had low grades (C or lower) in high school (AALoGPA equals one if a person had an A.A. degree and low grades, and zero otherwise), and similar variables for BALo-GPA and MALoGPA. Adding these three variables into the regression, the analyses find that youths who had low high school grades get less of an earnings advantage for their college degree (table 3.5, column 2). To figure the payoff to B.A. degrees for students with low grades, the coefficients for a B.A. and BALoGPA are added, so the payoff to a B.A. degree is 4.3 percent (.166 − .123 = .043), and the payoff to an A.A. degree is −7.2 percent—less than if the student had not obtained the degree (.155 − .227 = −.072). While the average student gets strong earnings benefits from getting B.A. and A.A. degrees, students with low grades get much smaller earnings benefits from a B.A. degree, and lower earnings from an A.A. degree than from no degree at all.[8] Previous studies have found that poor grades predict lower earnings for young adults who have only a high school diploma (Miller 1997; Rosenbaum, Miller, and Roy 1996). These results indicate that low grades also substantially reduce the payoffs to college degrees.

Do Students with Bad Grades Get Any College Credits?

Our analyses ignore the value of isolated course credits. Kane and Rouse (1995) find that students get some economic benefit from the college credits they earn, even if they do not complete a college degree. Although critics have noted some ambiguities about this finding,[9] if valid, it raises some doubts about our emphasis on degree completion.

However, even if isolated credits have payoffs, there is one group of students who gain little benefit from attending college: those who get few or no college credits. Kane and Rouse (1995, 602) find that 40 percent of two-year college dropouts "completed fewer than a semester's worth of credits," and a large number completed no credits (Kane and Rouse 1995, figure 1).

No one believes there are payoffs to zero college credits, so it is worth examining whether high school grades predict which students will get zero college credits. In our HSB sample of 14,700, 11,223 students entered college or other postsecondary schools. Of these college entrants, 1,822 students got zero credits, and another 1,669 had no transcript; the latter group probably lacked a transcript because they did not stay in college long enough to have one created (Grubb 1995a).[10] Merging these two groups of students who leave college with zero credits, we find that 16.2 percent (1,822 out of 11,223) of the

Table 3.6   College Entrants with Zero Credits Ten Years After High
School Graduation

College Entrants	N
Leave college with zero credits	1,822 (16.2%)
Leave college with no transcript	1,669 (14.9)
Total with zero credits	3,491 (31.1)
Total	11,223

Source: Author's compilation.

students entering college obtained no college credits on their transcripts, and another 14.9 percent (1,669 out of 11,223) had no transcript, which may mean that they got no credits either (table 3.6).
Thus, perhaps as many as 31.1 percent of college entrants got no
credits. Moreover, while only 11.7 percent of students with As in high
school got zero credits, 52.4 percent of students with Cs did so.

If we restrict our sample just to the high school seniors who
planned to a complete B.A. degree or higher, we find that 3.5 percent
of these students never entered college, 7.3 percent got zero credits,
and 4.7 percent had no transcript (table 3.7). Thus, 84.6 percent of
students with B.A. plans got one credit or more. But this outcome was
strongly related to grades. Although only 7.6 percent (100.0 − 92.4)
of college-planning seniors with As failed to get even one credit, 14.8
percent of those with Bs got zero credits, and 31.6 percent of those
with Cs did so.

Finally, multivariate analyses confirm the influence of grades. Run-
ning logistic regression to examine which students get one or more
credits, we find that even after controlling for socioeconomic status,
race, gender, region, track, homework time, and educational plans,
grades are a strong significant predictor of which students will get
one credit or more (table 3.8, column 1). This remains true for an-

Table 3.7   Seniors with B.A. Plans Who Complete One Credit or More, by
Grades

Number of Credits	As	Bs	Cs or Lower	Total
One credit or more	92.4%	85.2%	68.4%	84.6
Zero credits	4.4	7.2	12.6	7.3
No transcript	2.0	4.4	10.6	4.7
Did not enter college	1.1	3.2	8.4	3.5
N	1,674	2,959	927	5,560

Source: Author's compilation.

Table 3.8   Logistic Regression for Predicting Which Students Will Earn at Least One College Credit

	All Students		Students with College Plans	
	B	Exp(B)	B	Exp(B)
SES	.421*	1.524	.340*	1.401
	(.041)		(.066)	
Black	.063	1.065	−.182	.834
	(.082)		(.123)	
Hispanic	.043	1.044	−.075	.928
	(.067)		(.118)	
Female	.223*	1.250	.338*	1.402
	(.053)		(.092)	
South	−.168*	.846	−.311*	.732
	(.069)		(.126)	
West	−.160*	.853	−.468*	.626
	(.079)		(.139)	
Northeast	−.222*	.801	−.380*	.684
	(.072)		(.129)	
Private	.070	1.072	.141	1.151
	(.064)		(.100)	
Vocational	−.363*	.695	−.446*	.640
	(.075)		(.146)	
General	−.307*	.735	−.219*	.804
	(.058)		(.098)	
Test	.051*	1.052	.052*	1.053
	(.004)		(.007)	
Grades	.253*	1.288	.275*	1.317
	(.025)		(.042)	
HW	.063*	1.065	.019	1.019
	(.020)		(.034)	
Plans	.351*	1.421	—	—
	(.015)			
Constant	−8.354*	—	−2.126*	—
	(.263)		(.395)	
Chi square	3475.580	—	403.714	—
			.0000	
Significance	.0000	—	.0000	—
N	10,014	—	5,031	—

Source: Author's compilation.
* = p < .05

alyses of just those seniors who plan to get a college degree, A.A. or higher (table 3.8, column 2).

This chapter has implied that many students enter college for naught. This section has studied students who literally got "naught" from the experience. Even if isolated college credits yield economic benefits, such benefits will not occur for students who get no credits. Students who get no credits surely derive much less academic and economic benefit from college than they anticipated, and we suspect that they experience relatively large psychological costs. However, this failure could have been predicted. Even at the end of high school, students could foresee their chances of getting zero college credits merely by looking at their high school grades.

Conclusions

These analyses help elucidate the school-to-work problems of disadvantaged youths. Simple gross analyses find that low-SES, black, and Hispanic students have much lower educational attainment. However, the SES coefficient declines when achievement variables are entered, and the ethnic disadvantages actually reverse and become significant advantages: blacks and Hispanics have significantly higher educational attainment than whites with the same high school achievement. In addition, high school grades and test scores predict many of the cases in which the attainments of disadvantaged youths are lower than they had planned.

Looking at these results, some might blame disadvantaged youths for their own failures, but another interpretation is more plausible. Students plan what they think they can expect in the future, and their plans are likely to influence their high school efforts. In finding that students' plans do not take sufficient account of the influence of grades on their ultimate educational attainment, we can infer that students do not realize how much high school achievement affects their actual prospects. This is consistent with the "future relevance" and "no penalty" beliefs noted earlier. These results may indicate that schools fail to provide clear information to students. That finding would be consistent with what we learn about counselors' advising practices in the next chapter.

What could be wrong with letting students have "high expectations"? Perhaps such plans are just dreams that make students a little happier and do them little harm. Consistent with this outlook, Charles Manski (1989) has proposed that many youths begin community college as an "experiment"—a low-cost way to discover whether they can make it in college. He analyzes the process from the viewpoint of a student who is already in a community college, noting that his analysis does not consider students before they enter college. But is it really low-cost to enroll in a community college?

There are opportunity costs to any decision, and this "experiment" has some large opportunity costs to students while they are still in high school. Should students with an 86 percent chance of failing at college place *all* their bets on their college "experiment"? Or would it be prudent for such students to hedge their college bets and make backup plans?

The first opportunity cost of the college-for-all norm is that students' high expectations may inadvertently encourage them to see high school as irrelevant and thus to make poor use of it. Our interviews and survey of high school seniors indicate that 40 percent of students with college plans believe that high school is irrelevant. Postponing the key test for determining whether one is college-bound until after high school may inadvertently reinforce the notion that high school achievement is not important.

As a result, the college-for-all norm may lead to a lack of effort. Human capital theory posits that people invest effort in improving their capabilities if they believe that better outcomes will result. If students believe that they can get the same outcomes without effort in high school, they will not make the effort. If students realized that their low high school grades will block their college plans, they would probably increase their efforts. Yet a large majority (78.0 percent) of poorly achieving students with college plans do less than an hour a day of homework, and many (25.3 percent) do less than an hour in a whole week. These HSB students exert little effort even though they have low grades. Moreover, as we will see in the next chapter, guidance counselors do not tell students what level of high school achievement is needed to succeed in community college, so students are lulled into a complacency that leaves them unprepared for getting a college degree.

The second opportunity cost of the college-for-all norm is that students with little prospect for getting a college degree will fail to get vocational training. Encouraging poorly achieving students to delay their work preparation until they see the results of their college "experiment" makes it likely that they will make poor use of vocational preparation in high school, which has been shown to improve earnings (Campbell et al. 1986; Kang and Bishop 1986; Rosenbaum 1996a). Indeed, students with poor grades are less likely to be in vocational courses if they have college plans than if they are not planning college (Rosenbaum 1996c), and many students who are unlikely to succeed in college have no backup plans or training. Similarly, many public schools (such as those in Chicago) have reduced or ended their vocational programs because they expect all students to delay their vocational decisions until they get to college.

Although it was not part of Manski's analysis, a much less expensive experiment to help students determine their readiness for college is available—high school. If the college-for-all norm did not focus so much on getting everyone into college, high schools could tell students their realistic chances of attaining a college degree. If students realized that high school achievement is the first "experiment" that has strong predictive power, then students with poor grades would either revise their plans down or would spend more than an hour a week on homework.

Failing to challenge students to examine the plausibility of their college plans has serious opportunity costs—it prevents them from seeing the importance of high school, it prevents them from making the additional efforts that might help their plans come true, and it prevents them from preparing for alternative outcomes. Some seniors have high school records that make their college plans highly likely to fail, but their school's practice is to continue to protect their "high expectations." Far from being kind, that practice looks a lot more like the confidence scheme that Goffman describes—distracting the mark from taking other constructive actions.

Unfortunately, students understand very well that the *short-term* consequences of their high school efforts are minor. But they assume that this means that high school achievement and effort are generally irrelevant, and that there will be no penalty if they do badly in high school. They believe they can postpone their efforts until they get into college, and that their plans will work out fine.

Students' misperceptions may arise from their limited knowledge about older cohorts. High school students can see the college enrollment of last year's seniors more easily than the college completion of much older students, and they can more easily identify with the students a year older than themselves who enter college than with the twenty-eight-year-olds who never finished the degree. As a result, their perceptions are likely to be distorted. Students easily see college enrollment, for which high school achievements are irrelevant, but they have difficulty seeing college completion, for which high school achievements are highly relevant. Under such circumstances, students' perceptions will not improve unless policy action is taken.

Policy Implications

The community college system and open-admissions policies are rightfully sources of pride. They have created new opportunities for large numbers of youths. For the 14 percent of students with low grades who get a degree, open admissions was an extremely helpful second chance. However, an 86 percent failure rate suggests that the college-for-all approach is usually an unrealistic policy for these students. They need to be told how hard they must work to overcome these odds, and they need to consider fall-back options.

Good reforms can also have unintended consequences that are less positive. While policy has focused on opening college admissions, it has not devoted similar efforts to providing clear information about community colleges (Orfield 1997; Paul 1997; Rosenbaum, Miller, and Krei 1997). The college-for-all norm pushed by many schools lulls students into a complacency, which ultimately is unwarranted. Their high school grades could inform students about their likelihood of attaining a college degree, but this fact is hidden from students' awareness, and perhaps even from teachers' and counselors' awareness.

To return to Goffman's model, the college-for-all norm is highly misleading and does great harm to youths. It offers big promises to students without warning that few low-achieving students will get a college degree. Indeed, it leaves many youths worse off than before: kept in the dark about actual requirements, they fail to take suitable actions to prepare themselves to accomplish their plans. It also harms youths as they waste time, energy, and money on a college experience that they are ill prepared to handle and that is likely to lead to failure, low self-esteem, and misused opportunities in high school. While high school counselors brag about their college enrollment rates, students will blame themselves for the failure that they did not anticipate but which was highly predictable.

Policymakers have also misperceived this situation and underestimated the number of work-bound students. The question of the number of work-bound students turns out to be complex. If "work-bound" is only those who do not plan to pursue a college degree, then only 30 percent of high school seniors are work-bound. However, this is a gross underestimate. About 60 percent of seniors who plan to get a postsecondary degree fail to get *any* degree in the next ten years, and the failure rate is much higher for those with poor grades. These "college-planning" seniors are effectively work-bound—they will ultimately have only their high school diploma when they enter the labor market. If we define work-bound students to include those who actually end their schooling with no degree above a high school diploma, then a substantial majority of high school graduates are work-bound, in that they will enter the labor market with no degree above their high school diploma.[11] Even if we consider the value of isolated college credits, 31.1 percent of all students who enter postsecondary schools obtained *zero college credits* in the next ten years, and this too can be highly predicted from students' high school grades.

Large numbers of students who think they are college-bound will end up getting little or no benefit from postsecondary education and will enter the labor market with only a high school diploma. Although it is highly predictable, high school students do not anticipate that this will happen, so these work-bound students are "unidentified" to policymakers and to school staff. As a result, they do not prepare these students for their subsequent risk of failure, they do not advise them to have backup plans and to make backup preparations, and high schools do not help them find jobs.

The college-for-all norm also has a great impact on other school policies. For example, in the Chicago public schools in the early 1990s, Superintendent Argie Johnson urged all the city's high schools to stress college goals, and she closed or withdrew resources from many vocational programs. Even the famous Chicago Vocational School began stressing that its goal was college preparation, not vocational preparation. Meanwhile, the Chicago schools had achievement levels far below those of the rest of the state, many graduates lacked the academic skills needed to take college credit courses in the city college, and the degree completion rates at some of the city colleges were under 15 percent (Orfield 1984). It was politically popular for the superintendent to urge more students to attend college, because that message fit the college-for-all norm. This policy stressed "high expectations" but probably led to increased failure.

This is not to urge that our schools abandon "high expectations" entirely or scrap open-admissions policies. But three other reforms are warranted.

First, high schools should provide more complete information on community college success rates as a function of students' grades, test scores, and homework time. This could be aided by a universally recognized test of achievement (not aptitude or intelligence), either statewide (like the IGAP achievement test in Illinois) or national (like the proposal for national proficiency examinations). Even if such tests are not available, grades can be used. Even though grades from individual teachers are highly imperfect, grade point averages have strong predictive power (stronger than test scores in some of these analyses). Schools and society should be stressing their importance to students. Students need to realize that "open admissions" does not mean that high school achievement is irrelevant.

Second, linkages between high schools and colleges may help improve high school students' understanding of college requirements.

By seeing that many college students must repeat high school classes, high school students will learn that they can either work hard now or repeat the same class in college and pay tuition for it. Several recent reforms seek to improve the coordination of high school and college programs—for example, tech-prep, two-plus-two programs, and career academies—and that linkage may help students see the future relevance of their current courses (see Berryman and Bailey 1992; Stern et al. 1995).

Finally, students must prepare backup career options if their college plans are unlikely to succeed. Although schools can encourage all students to aim for college, this should not be an excuse to cut vocational programs. Research indicates that after controls for test scores, vocational education graduates are 10 to 15 percent more likely to be in the labor force, and are paid 8 to 9 percent more, than graduates of academic programs (Campbell et al. 1986; Kang and Bishop 1986; Rosenbaum 1996a). Even if students plan to attend community college, the low success rates at these colleges suggest that backup plans would be prudent, particularly for students with low grades. Over 86 percent of such students fail to get a degree, and they lose time, tuition, and self-confidence in the process. After they drop out of college, they enter the labor market without the vocational skills or preparation that they might have obtained if they had not been taken in by the college-for-all rhetoric.

Appendix: Scales

To test quantitatively for perceptions of relevance, we used scales for "future relevance" and "no penalty" measures were used. "Future relevance" was measured by the following statements:

- My courses give me useful preparation I will need in life.
- School teaches me valuable skills.
- Getting a job depends on how well you do in school.
- I need more schooling to avoid dead-end jobs.
- Nothing I learn in school is relevant to my future [reverse-coded].

"No penalty" perceptions were measured by the following statements:

- Even if I do not work hard in school, I can make my future plans come true.
- What I do not learn in school, I can always pick up later.

- People can do okay even if they drop out of high school.
- Students with bad grades often get good jobs after high school.
- Without a good education, it is likely that I will still end up with the kind of job I want.

Both scales, which emerged from factor analyses, showed high intercorrelations and strong reliability of items (reported in Rosenbaum and Nelson 1994). The scales are highly correlated to each other, but not identical (correlation = $-.3035$). High scores in "future relevance" do not always result in low scores for "even if" perception. In fact, sizable numbers of students exhibited high scores in both measures.

Other scales were constructed for these analyses:

Teacher Help

- My teachers have contacts with local employers.
- Employers respect my teacher's recommendations.
- My teachers can help students get careers they want.
- My teachers will help me get the career I want.

School Help

How much could these people help you get your plans after high school if they tried?

- Your favorite vocational teacher?
- Your favorite academic teacher?
- Your school counselor?

Effort

How much time do you spend on homework?
How much do you agree with each of these statements about your school?

- I do just enough to pass my classes.
- I only work in school if I'm worried about failing.
- I try to do my best in school.

Locus of Control

- How do you feel about each of the following statements?
- When I make plans, I am almost certain I can make them work.

- My plans hardly ever work out, so planning only makes me unhappy.
- I do not have enough control over the direction my life is taking.
- Every time I try to get ahead, something or somebody stops me.
- Chance and luck are very important for what happens in my life.
- In my life, good luck is more important than hard work for success.

Rebellious Peers

How many of your friends:

- Drink alcohol?
- Use drugs?
- Have sex?

Pro-School Peers

How many of your friends:

- Get good grades?
- Work hard in school?
- Attend class regularly?

Parental Support of School

How much do you agree with each of these statements about your school?

- My parents do not pay attention to my grades.
- My parents do not care if I behave in school.
- As long as I graduate, my parents do not care what I do in high school.
- My parents feel it is important for me to get As.

Table 3A.1   Descriptives for Regression Variables

Variable	Alpha	Mean	Standard Deviation
"Future relevance" belief	.5672	−.003	.635
"No penalty" belief	.6218	.010	.650
Locus of control	.7363	−.004	.660
Parental support	.8006	−.004	.793
Rebellious peers	.8590	.000	.885
Pro-school peers	.7677	−.001	.829
School help	.7985	.002	.846
Teacher help	.7788	.000	.777
Female	—	.545	.498
Low SES	—	.199	.400
Black	—	.336	.473
Hispanic	—	.253	.435
Asian	—	.062	.241

Source: Author's compilation.

== Chapter 4 ==

Gatekeeping in an Era of More Open Gates: High School Counselors' Views of Their Influence on Students' College Plans

SOCIOLOGICAL research has provided a clear picture of the ways in which counselors channel students' educational destinies.[1] Focusing on the ways in which counselors influence which students attend college (Cicourel and Kitsuse 1963; Schafer and Olexa 1971; Rosenbaum 1976), studies have given sociology the model of counselors as active "social selectors" for colleges, a role in which they screen out those students who they feel are poorly prepared, often exhibiting biases against low socioeconomic status, minorities, and (sometimes) women (Heyns 1974; Erickson 1975). However, much of this research is based on fieldwork from the 1960s and early 1970s.

Three major changes since the early 1970s may have radically changed counselors' job. First, sociological studies of counselors and tracking have raised public awareness of these issues. Aaron Cicourel and John Kitsuse's (1963) work was extensively reprinted in counseling textbooks, and its influence spread beyond educators. Some documentary movies, such as *High School* (Frederick Wiseman) and *Growing up in Webster Grove*, which depicted the heavy-handed efforts of counselors to steer students' futures, were widely seen and reviewed in national media. Greater public awareness may have increased parent resistance to counselors' steering and may have dissuaded counselors from engaging in it. It is possible that a version of Heisenberg's principle took hold, that sociology's measures (and reports) of the phenomenon of counseling changed the way counselors act.

Second, the growth of community colleges has dramatically increased opportunities to go to college, and many more students attend some form of college now. In 1960, about the time when Cicourel and Kitsuse (1963) were gathering their data, 45.1 percent of high school graduates attended some postsecondary institution. By 1993 over 63 percent did. The change is particularly dramatic for two-year colleges. While enrollment at four-year colleges roughly doubled between 1960 and 1990, public community college enrollment increased fivefold, from less than 200,000 in 1960 to over 1,000,000 in 1990 (NCES 1992, table 169). Therefore, as more students have attended college, counselors have needed to dissuade fewer students from planning on it.

Third, the open-admissions policies of community colleges have greatly reduced the need for high school counselors to advise students that they are unsuited for college. In the past, college admission standards compelled counselors to confront students' unrealistic college plans. Now, however, admission standards are practically nonexistent. In Illinois, for example, high school graduates can attend a community college regardless of grades or course enrollments (and nongraduates can attend if they are older than twenty-one). Sociologists have noted that community colleges have taken on the "cooling-out" function (Clark 1960), but less noted has been the consequences for high schools. To the extent that counselors' jobs have traditionally included making students face up to college entrance requirements, open-admissions colleges may have removed this burden.

In light of these dramatic changes, this chapter investigates how counselors view their influence in guiding students' college plans and the strategies they employ in advising students as they make choices. Although caution is required in accepting counselors' views, we note some aspects of their reports that suggest their validity. Sociological research from before 1972 found that counselors had a powerful influence on students' future destinies; we present evidence indicating that their influence, how they see their job, and the strategies they use for counseling students are now quite different from this widely held view. These results raise questions about the role of counselors, not just for helping students enter college but also for helping them complete it successfully. These concerns are particularly great for low-income students.

Previous Research

Historically, the job definition of a school counselor has shifted with the times. By the early 1960s, an earlier emphasis on vocational counseling had been displaced by college counseling as the major activity of these professionals, followed by a growing trend toward more personal (therapeutic) counseling (Armor 1971, 115).

Although counselors have long espoused the "contest mobility norm"—that is, the norm that opportunity always remains open (Turner 1960)—counselors of the 1960s were not reluctant to close off some students' college opportunities and were clear about their responsibilities in selecting students for higher education. Counselors reported many ways in which they identified students who were not suited for college (Cicourel and Kitsuse 1963). Although such methods included the use of test scores, counselors were equally confident about making personal assessments based on a variety of subjective inferences, including "adjustment, motivation, realistic goals, overachievement, or participation." As Cicourel and Kitsuse noted, these kinds of statements constitute significant qualifications of the folk norm of contest mobility: "Decisions are made by professionals who are guided not by folk norms but by explicit and implicit educational doctrines and practices" (137). Counselors' "judgments about the student's maturity, emotional stability, character, and personal appearance are often important determinants of his social mobility" (136). Counselors were not shy about influencing students' college decisions and would even convince some parents that their child should not apply to college (120).

Similarly, in earlier work in 1971 (Rosenbaum 1976), we observed counselors' interactions with students and parents in a working-class high school. These counselors were no less aggressive about imposing their judgments on students' careers. Counselors had strong opinions about which students should be in the college preparatory track and sometimes prevented students from moving up to this track because of minor blemishes on their record (for example, Cs in typing). Similarly, counselors had strong opinions about which students should apply to college, and they were quite assertive in discouraging some students from applying. Counselors would often tell students that they lacked the ability, skills, or work habits to handle college. They would enforce their assessments by guarding access to college recruiters and would not jeopardize their relationships with recruiters by recommending a student about whom they had doubts.

However, counselors were not always candid about the social selection process. When students or parents refused to abide by a counselor's advice, some counselors responded by providing vague and inadequate information that would give the student the impression that college was a possibility when actually it was not. We described cases of students who in the spring of their senior year believed that they would be attending a four-year college in the fall, but who had not taken any of the necessary steps for application and lacked crucial prerequisites (Rosenbaum 1976, chapter 6).

These counseling strategies may be described as "cooling out" in that counselors "sidetrack unpromising students rather than let them fail" (Clark 1960, 573). Clark described "cooling out" in community colleges: "This is the 'soft' response: never to dismiss a student but to provide him with an alternative. One form of it . . . is to detour to an extension division or a general college, which has the advantage of appearing not very different from the main road" (573). Similarly, we found that high school counselors sometimes resorted to "cooling out," telling students they could plan on "further education," which students thought was college (Rosenbaum 1971). In fact, these students would be qualified only for vocational institutes.

If counselors overtly directed some students away from college in the 1960s and 1970s, recent studies imply that their behavior has changed. The literature of the 1990s finds that counselors are primarily suppliers of information and personal help whose actions influence students' careers only in minor ways (DeLany 1991, 201). The counselors in five Maryland high schools indicated that academic programs are now largely set by new state and local requirements and that departments in the school often make most of the decisions about student placement in classes (Wilson and Rossman 1993; see also Useem 1992). Counselors also say that parents are increasingly active in academic decisions, and they describe their own role as now little more than scheduling, monitoring, and paper pushing (Wilson and Rossman 1993, 153).

In addition, Brian DeLany (1991) found that the financial squeeze experienced by many school districts in the 1980s often left counselors and schedulers overwhelmed with the basic tasks of checking student records and finding adequate spaces in classes. Academic placements were frequently made with limited knowledge of students' backgrounds, interests, or plans, and counselors often did not even know students' names; clearly selection was not a central task.

Gary Orfield and Faith Paul (1994) found that counselors may not be presenting the information that students and parents need to make good choices about postsecondary options. Students and parents were uninformed about the influence of tracks, the requirements for selective colleges, or the possibilities of financial aid. Orfield and Paul speculated that large caseloads and a preference for handling personal problems may prevent counselors from providing the kinds of information that could help students and parents make more realistic decisions about the future.

These studies are informative, but their observations about counselors were made incidentally in the course of studying other issues. Unlike those studies, the research reported in this chapter focused explicitly on counselors' views of their influence on students' college plans and the strategies they use.

Methods and Sample

This chapter examines the self-reported practices of twenty-seven counselors in eight large midwestern high schools—two mostly white, two mostly black, and four racially mixed. The schools were evenly split between urban and suburban. Three urban high schools were racially mixed, and one was predominantly African American. Only one suburban high school fit the traditional stereotype of white middle-class; the other three had high proportions of working-class students: one was mostly white, one mostly black, and one racially mixed. Respondents, whose racial composition reflected their school's enrollments, included sixteen males and eleven females.

During face-to-face structured interviews lasting about one hour, we asked counselors to describe their responsibilities; the types of students (college-bound or work-bound) they see most often; how they recognize that students may have unrealistic college plans; the advice they give to students who they believe have unrealistic plans; the advice they give regarding vocational training; and the reactions they have received from parents and others as a consequence of their advice. In addition, we asked counselors about the effects of the open-admission policies of community colleges on student plans and about the advice they give students on enrolling in a community college or making plans to work full-time after high school.

Counselors' Views of Their Influence on Students' College Plans

Studies of occupations often find that role occupants exaggerate their own influence and importance. Managers brag about their own importance in keeping their organization operating (Dalton 1951), and lawyers boast of their contributions to the firm (Smigel 1965). Consistent with that finding, 1960s counselors spoke of their powerful influence on students' future destinies (Cicourel and Kitsuse 1963) and described such acts of influence as the primary component of their job (Armor 1971).

However, counselors in the 1990s draw a very different picture. On the topic of college advising, which was their central task two decades ago, counselors now emphatically belittle their influence. They play down any role they may play in influencing either students' choices or their lives. Counselors even downplay their ability to help students make wise choices, making arguments like, "I don't give advice; I give information." In many ways, they minimize their role in helping students make the transition from high school, presenting themselves as having no influence on a student's selection of a job or a college.

Moreover, as we listened to counselors' accounts of their jobs, it became clear that they see their jobs as constrained by other factors. In their view, a variety of powerful factors prevent them from taking a broad view of the guidance they offer. They see clear limits to their job duties. Despite holding the title "guidance counselor," they do not interpret "guidance" to include guidance about jobs. Although they see college counseling as one of their responsibilities, they see clear limits in what they should do. In regard to the task of dissuading students from making unrealistic college plans, counselors report that they do not *want* to do it, they cannot make students do it, parents will not let them do it, and they do not have the authority.

Counselors Do Not Advise Students About Jobs

Although U.S. high schools used to provide access to jobs (U.S. Bureau of Education 1916; Lazerson and Grubb 1974), they no longer do so. Neither schools nor society at large have defined what counselors should do to assist work-bound students (Armor 1971). Counselors receive no training in job counseling, and there are no standard procedures to help them advise students as they make school/work choices or fill out job applications. Since employers rarely state academic prerequisites or use grades or counselor recommendations when making hiring decisions, employers provide no structure that would help counselors give job advice. In addition, counselors typically have little knowledge of the specific skills or training needed for the jobs available to high school graduates, and they generally lack contacts with employers.

Thus, by the 1970s, guidance counselors rarely provided career guidance (Ginzberg 1971). In a national survey of guidance counselors in the mid-1980s (conducted in schools included in the High School and Beyond (HSB) survey), few guidance counselors reported that career counseling was a high priority, and few counselors spent much time on career planning (Krei and Rosenbaum 1998).

In our sample of counselors, when asked whether their school does anything to help students get jobs, many counselors replied, "No, I don't think it's our responsibility to do that." Said another, "I am an educator; it's not my job to find jobs for students."

Because counselors do not know much about the labor market, the advice they give is not very helpful. Few counselors in our study advise students to take jobs or apprenticeships. The most common suggestion of those few who do advise some students to take a job is to tell them to look at want ads, but this advice is unlikely to be very helpful to students who know little about the work world. Recognizing this, a few counselors said that they go through the want-ad listings with some students, pointing out promising jobs for them, but even they do not have enough time to help more than a few students in this way. Almost none of the guidance counselors know any employers who regularly hire high school graduates.

The main exceptions were counselors who hold the job title "employment counselor." We were told that there are few guidance counselors in the state of Illinois who are licensed as employment counselors. There were only four in our sample. They have contacts with some employers, but most of their contacts are offering only poor jobs in fast-food restaurants or small retail shops. Only the two employment counselors in the regional vocational school have ongoing contacts with employers with good jobs. With the exception of these two, the other counselors do not help students directly in obtaining good jobs.

The counselors we surveyed usually frame postsecondary plans as a choice between college and work, and they give strong priority to the former. Nearly all of our counselors say they view college as a necessity in the current job market, and many encourage work-bound students to enroll in community college evening classes. Some counselors say that the only jobs students can get after graduating from high school are in fast-food restaurants or small retail shops. Few counselors are aware of the skilled jobs in manufacturing, services, or business in which vocational teachers regularly place students— sometimes in their own schools—through their contacts with employers (see chapter 10). Although a few counselors refer students to vocational teachers for advice, many do not, either because they do not realize that vocational teachers can help place students or because they think that all students should try to go to college.

Most counselors urge students to defer their job plans until they have had some college experience. A counselor in a predominantly African American suburban school explains that he tries to convince all of his students that attending city college "would enhance their marketability."

Counselors Do Not Want to Discourage Students' College Plans

Besides their ignorance of jobs and their belief that all students should attend college, counselors do not want the responsibility of discouraging students' plans; it is an unpleasant task that they have no desire to perform. Counselors worry that the students will not be able to handle such rejection or that they themselves will appear mean in the eyes of the students. Counselors do not want to be the person who tells students who have completed no science classes that they cannot become doctors. Many counselors express the fear that if they try to bring students' aspirations into line, the students will feel bad. Counselors take great pains to not be seen as ogres. As one counselor said, "I don't want to be remembered as one of those counselors who said that a student could never make it, because I heard that when I was young." When they do offer students discouraging information, counselors are very careful to do so in a way that's not "devastating to them."

Counselors Cannot Make Students Listen to Their Advice

Just as psychotherapists maintain that patients are not receptive to good advice until they are "ready," many counselors believe that candid advice would be a waste of time. Even when counselors feel the need to provide students with some sort of guidance, they often do not, or do so halfheartedly, because they believe that "some kids don't think past next weekend's date," that students are "too short-sighted to see beyond graduation," and that most students "just want to get out . . . [and] try to take the minimum number of classes that they need to." Students' present-orientation discourages counselors from talking realistically about the future. One of the most poignant stories was told by a counselor who had taught night school classes so that people in their twenties could get the remedial class credits they had failed to complete in their teenage years. He asked them to explain "what happened when they were sixteen, seventeen, and almost everyone said, 'Everybody tried to tell me, I wasn't listening.' A lot of them volunteered to come back to school and talk to the kids and I said, 'I don't think the kids would listen to you any more than you listened to the adults of your time.' Their interests are elsewhere."

Although the comments of the returning students suggest that counselors are right in believing that students often do not listen, this counselor appears utterly resigned to the notion that students will never hear him when he is trying to guide them. Such resignation provides further justification for counselors to refrain from providing good information and advice to students about their futures.

This resignation tends to encourage counselors to give the vague advice we have associated with cooling out. Believing that "children only wake up to reality after they leave the protected nest of Mom and Dad," some counselors maintain that students cannot be convinced to make realistic plans until after they leave high school. In the words of another counselor, many students "haven't come to grips with the fact that they're probably not going to ever be successful in college. That's something that has to be a self-realization. You can't walk up to someone and say to them, 'You have to come to grips with yourself.' Sometimes the only way to learn something is to go and try it."

However, counselors' conviction that they cannot make students listen leads them to deny students the opportunity to learn from the wisdom of others and to force them to learn by trial and error.

Parents Prevent Counselors from Discouraging College Plans

Perhaps the greatest barrier to the ability of counselors to provide students with realistic advice is the power of parents to override counselors' advice and make counselors' lives more difficult if they disagree. More than two decades ago (Rosenbaum 1976), we showed that middle-class counselors could manipulate working-class parents, and Cicourel and Kitsuse (1963) showed that middle-class counselors could manipulate even middle-class and upper-middle-class parents. Now it seems that the situation is sometimes reversed. Many counselors speak of the power of parents to push their children in a certain direction, in opposition to the advice of counselors and often regardless of the child's abilities or wishes. One way in which parents exercise their power is by pushing their child into a higher-level class. "Parents want their student's schedule upgraded to a more difficult level when previous test scores, rating in junior high, and faculty say, 'No way,'" according to one counselor. "It usually ends up to be disastrous, but I have no choice." Even in regard to decisions within the high school itself, counselors are forced to yield to parental wishes.

The situation is similar when parents push their child toward college, regardless of the child's achievement or interest. "Parents make it hard to tell kids their plans are unrealistic," says one counselor, "because they see their children through rose-colored glasses, not really acknowledging their child's low level of performance." Many parents hold positive views of their children that are not always accurate. Although this is the nature of parenthood, the result is that parents make it difficult for counselors to present more appropriate options.

The same problem can occur when a student is deciding on an occupation. Parents, according to one counselor,

> make it difficult, because some of them are not willing to accept the fact that maybe their child is not going to go on and follow in their particular footsteps. . . . We can talk to the kids and I'll say, "What are your plans?" "My father wants me to be this." . . . Not so much what *he* wants to do. And some of our kids who say their parents want them to do certain things don't have the English [or] . . . math background that's necessary to go into engineering or medicine or something like that.

Unlike the parents of the studies in the 1960s, 1990s parents are often aware that they have veto power over counselors' recommendations and decisions, and they are not afraid to use that power. Most counselors report that parents have the final say over students' course selections and their future plans. Although some parents agree, overtly or tacitly, with counselors' advice, those who disagree are able to reverse counselors' decisions.

Moreover, if parents disagree with counselors' advice, they can exert considerable pressure and enlist the help of school administrators. Parents can put unpleasant pressures on counselors. As one counselor notes, "You try to be as realistic and honest as you can, but if it doesn't fit into the parent's plan, you have trouble." Some counselors take actions to avoid such trouble. One counselor notes that some counselors "would be concerned that the parent would call the principal and say, 'Do you know what that counselor said about my kid?'" Counselors fear that they may have to pay for clearly explaining a student's future options, so they back away from doing so.

The result of the increase in parental power and authority has been a decrease in counselors' authority. Not only do counselors often feel that they must yield to parental wishes, but they sometimes change their initial advice to avoid trouble before it starts. As one counselor says:

> We've had a number of times that we've told a kid that they are not going to a certain college, and the parents get very upset. . . . So now we send their application in.

Then, when the student does not get in, "we try to get them to look at alternatives."

Counselors remove themselves from providing disappointing news by simply not giving it and then waiting for an outside force to do the job.

Counselors Feel They Lack Authority to Discourage Students' Unrealistic Plans

Given counselors' belief that students always have the opportunity to attend college (the contest mobility norm), and their belief that parents have the right to overturn and complain about their advice, some counselors begin to question their own authority. Many believe that it would be an abuse of power for them to suggest that a student should not shoot for the moon. "When you're eighteen or seventeen and you have a whole life in front of you, who am I to say what is realistic and what is not? So I always say, 'The sky's the limit.'" Several counselors expressed a similar view, put well by one suburban high school counselor: "Who am I to burst their bubble?"

To support this position, counselors note examples of unpromising students who did very well. As one says, "I can't tell [students] they can't do something, because some long-shots do make it." Instead, counselors rely on students coming to terms with their own abilities on their own, after they leave high school and after they are no longer the counselors' responsibility.

Although no one wants to return to the days when parents quaked in awe before the mighty school counselor who determined students' destinies, counselors say that now they sometimes withhold good advice out of concern for parents' reactions and doubts about their own authority. This concern limits counselors' willingness to take on the role of providing career information and guidance. Indeed, when counselors ask, "Who am I to burst their bubble?" one gets the feeling that the pendulum has swung very far since 1960. If counselors lack the authority to advise students realistically, surely no other school staff has that authority. High school staff have largely left this domain to parents, regardless of whether the parents have adequate information with which to advise their children on making plans for the future.

Counselors' Strategies

If counselors did not shy away from telling students they were unsuited for college in the 1960s but now they avoid discouraging students' unrealistic college plans, how have their jobs changed to allow them to avoid this task? We find that counselors have adopted two strategies: urging college for all, and stressing personal-growth counseling. However, as we note later in the chapter, some counselors harbor private doubts about these strategies.

College for All

The easy access to community college presents counselors with a much easier task in helping students make educational plans than they faced in the past. Unlike their counterparts in the 1960s, when college access was limited, students' decisions were difficult, and counselors had to persuade some students to lower their aspirations, counselors in the 1990s do not have to force students to make tough decisions; they can encourage everyone to attend college. The sentiment that anyone who wants to can go to college is optimistic and encouraging. Counselors take great comfort in the fact that community colleges allow students' opportunities to remain open after high school. One counselor explains:

> I'm really glad that no matter how badly you do in high school, you've got the second chance to go to community college and start all over again. I love that. The teenage years are the toughest years in life, as far as I'm concerned, so are we going to condemn the kids who got Fs at seventeen to [have terrible lives]? That would be very unfair. This gives kids a chance to grow, get away from the teenage years, get away from [the high school] . . . and try again.

Echoing a sentiment out of Ralph Turner's (1960) contest mobility norm, this counselor is pleased that open admissions policies in community colleges give everyone a second chance. Of course, this is what open admissions is supposed to accomplish.

Yet it is still remarkable how widespread this belief has become. When counselors say they encourage college for all, they really mean it. They urge virtually *all* students to attend college, under almost any circumstances. Students are urged to enroll in college even if they have bad grades. One counselor speaks of dealing with students whose performance in high school has been very poor:

> You have to be honest and tell them, "You have a 1.6 [C-minus] average. Where do you think you're gonna go with this? And why don't you consider starting at maybe a junior college and getting yourself involved in school and seeing whether or not this is something you really want to do? Would you really like this? And if you can maintain a certain grade point average, then by all means [transfer to a four-year college]."

This counselor would encourage even students who cannot muster a C average to continue their schooling to see whether they like it. By sending all students to college, counselors can avoid the task of encouraging students to make unpleasant decisions.

Counselors also urge college attendance on students who are not interested in college and do not like school. At one school, the counselor tells students "who feel they should go right into the world of work" that they may have "more options" if they also go to a community college while working. At an all-black urban school, every student is required to fill out college applications whether they plan to go or not. Even individuals who do not want to go to college are pushed toward it. Thus, the vast majority of students take the ACT exams, yet the school's average score is 15. (The state average is 21.) Since black parents have become much more insistent that their high schools have high expectations for their children, this practice protects the counselors from parental complaints, although some counselors (and students) say it is a waste of time.

Even when students present an impossible situation, counselors do not entirely discourage their plans to attend college. One counselor reports: "I've got seniors who come to me with maybe a 1.0 [D] cumulative grade point average now and say, 'How can I get this to a 3.0?'" These are students preparing too late to apply to the state university, and this counselor's inevitable response to their question is, "Not in this life." Nevertheless, after "show[ing] them where they went wrong," even this counselor then reassures the student: "A lot of . . . the community colleges, they have what is known as a transfer program that allows access to four-year colleges."

Counselors also sometimes advise college for students whom the counselors believe are incapable of benefiting from the experience. One counselor reports having

> an EMH boy right now, which means his IQ is somewhere around 70 or below, and this particular kid wants to be a doctor. He wants to go to a four-year college. Bringing him down softly is sort of hard, because he just doesn't hear what we're saying when we suggest . . . that he doesn't have the classes that he should have to really be even in a two-year college. But in many cases we recommend for students who are unrealistic and don't have the background that they go to a two-year college first and see how it goes.

When students refuse to listen to advice, counselors feel they have no choice but to help them go on to college.

Indeed, counselors do not discourage even students with poor grades who want to attend an elite college, although they may redirect these students. One counselor remembers telling a student: "You have a grade point average of .777 [D-minus]. Now, Harvard may not be the place to send your money to, because they're not gonna look at this, you know. But let's look at Harvard in two years and see after you finish at community college or whatever." Through this approach, the counselor uses the community college to keep the goal of going to a top-tier college open to a student who has no chance of getting admitted directly from high school. Moreover, while the counselor probably knows that Harvard is unlikely to take such a transfer student, he is operating on the belief that students like this one lower their expectations to a more realistic level while in community college. Similarly, another counselor tells us that although he thinks that a certain student is "not academically qualified, . . . I've urged him to send in the application anyway. You know, there's no harm." Rather than trying to prepare the student to be more realistic, this counselor sees no harm in letting him base his plans for life after high school on an extremely unlikely college acceptance.

Those who are concerned that counselors have too much power to steer students away from college will be reassured by these results. Today's high school counselors are not letting anything limit students' opportunity to go to college. They are simply herding all students—regardless of their grades, abilities, or interest—toward additional schooling.

Stressing Personal Growth

When counselors recommend college for all, college counseling becomes less important as a job duty. In its place, counselors have focused a great deal of attention on personal growth. Even in the 1960s, as David Armor (1971) noted, counselors had begun to use their additional psychological training to put more emphasis in their work on personal counseling. In our interviews, many counselors rank personal growth counseling as the most important activity in which they engage. Many of the counselors we interviewed would agree with the one who says: "My responsibilities as a counselor are, first of all, to make school work for the kids, to help them develop, and to make the most out of school as possible."

However, the emphasis on personal counseling has implications for college counseling. When students approach counselors with unrealistic college plans, counselors convert the encounter into an opportunity to build self-esteem rather than provide objective information about the world. When students' college plans are unrealistic, most counselors cannot avoid providing them with some advice about the future. However, many couch their advice in motivational platitudes that provide little or no information to the student. These counselors take a warm, fuzzy approach. As one says: "I just try to be soft and gentle with most people. . . . It's not really up to me what these kids could become." Counselors who take the "soft and gentle" approach, however, avoid difficult issues. In the words of another counselor: "I counsel them all to believe in themselves." Others take a harder line but still provide no real information, telling students that getting into college or finding a good job will require that they "put forth more effort" or "establish themselves a little more as a person."

Even very concrete opportunities to teach youth about the criteria for success turn into self-esteem-building sessions or occasions on which to dispense more platitudes. "I also tell kids that now they're going into an age where you're gonna be rejected, and I try to have them look at rejection as not as something wrong with them, but [as] a loss on the [rejecting] university's part for not having an opportunity to work with them."

Rather than deal with the unpleasant task of redirecting students' plans or explaining the need for meeting expectations and criteria for success, counselors turn the discussion into a session on personal growth, vaguely soothing the student's ego. Another counselor reports that some seniors "tell me they are going to be a doctor or a lawyer, and their grades in high school have been Cs and Ds. They don't seem to feel that there's any correlation between the two." Nonetheless, this counselor does not alter her advice to tell them about the strict standards of most law and medical schools. "I just tell them that they have to change the way that they've been doing things if they are going to be . . . a college student." Again, a concrete situation is turned into an opportunity to offer vague motivational advice, to urge students toward "personal growth." Students get no concrete information about their best options from their current situation or about the levels of achievement needed to reach their goals.

This focus on personal growth is similar to Clark's (1960) description of "cooling out" in community colleges. High school counselors allow students to retain their plans, but they "sidetrack unpromising students rather than let them fail" (Clark 1960, 573). These counselors never tell students that they are being unrealistic; they support even the most unrealistic plans, assuming that students will eventually realize their futility.

However, it would be misleading to say that counselors are consciously trying to be deceptive. They believe they are acting according to good professional practice in responding to students' needs and helping them achieve "personal growth." As Clark (1960) rightly noted, it is the community college system that creates the cooling-out experience, and individual actors only need to allow youth to proceed through the system and let its effects take hold, regardless of the costs to those students in lost time, money and effort. Indeed, as noted, counselors seem to feel that they have no alternative: they cannot make students confront difficult choices because students will not listen, parents will complain, and counselors themselves lack the authority to influence students' plans.

Nevertheless, counselors could do more in the way of providing specific information. Although we cannot be sure what counselors say to students, in their interviews with us few counselors mentioned that transfer programs have higher entrance requirements than other programs in community colleges, or that students with a D-minus average from high school often need an extra year or two of noncredit remedial courses to qualify for college credit courses. Of course, these are facts that students discover for themselves, but only after they leave high school, by which time they are no longer the responsibility of the high school counselor.

Counselors' Private Doubts

Although counselors avoid discouraging students' college plans, some of them have their doubts about their actions. They worry that "college for all" may simply be encouraging denial, both their own and the students', of students' true options. One counselor directly told us that "just because I don't confront them doesn't mean that I don't think I should." Counselors seem to wonder whether they ought to be doing more to prepare kids for the future, or even standing up to parents. "I still feel I'm doing a disservice to the kid when she gets out of here, but I can't fight the parents."

Other counselors wonder whether giving vague advice and subduing overly ambitious plans are effective strategies, as this counselor so ambivalently expresses: "I *think* I don't want to say, 'You cannot do this.' That is *their* choice." But this counselor also has misgivings about letting students make these choices when they have a poor record.

Another counselor suggests that the whole notion of "career exploration" gets lost because all students know they can enter college. It is hard to persuade students to make serious choices when college offers such an easy route to postponing such choices. As one counselor says, "I'm not so sure that [career exploration] takes hold, and I think that's an area that we need to do more of." She wonders whether counselors give enough guidance to students, especially students who think that they can choose any career regardless of their preparation.

Yet it is clear that this counselor is uncertain about whether the choice entirely belongs to students. If students need firmer guidance, she is not certain that it's her place to provide it, particularly given the risks of parent complaints.

Unlike the counselor who feels that there is no harm in urging all students to go to community college, other counselors are disturbed by sending students to college if they have no chance of completion. Fewer than half of students at local city colleges obtain the two-year associate degree, and only 13 percent transfer to a four-year college. Some counselors feel that community college is likely to be a highly disappointing experience for students and a serious economic sacrifice for families who can ill afford it.

Other counselors worry that the community college system discourages students from working hard while still in high school. Although community colleges offer the opportunity for counselors to promote college for all, many counselors are aware that the academic requirements in community college can be more stringent than they appear; these counselors know that students often do not realize they need to do more to prepare themselves while still in high school. "Kids are going to get into community college no matter what their grades are," as one counselor notes. "Second chances are good, but not needing transcripts cuts down their motivation [in high school]." These counselors worry about a system that does not warn students that they are headed for academic trouble. "Some kids think they do not have to work because they are going to a community college, but that comes back to haunt them when they are unprepared." As another counselor reports: "A number of the students have the feeling that they can always go to the local community college, and I don't think that they really understand . . . the colleges . . . will accept you into certain parts of their program, but you've got to prove yourself if you want to get into the [four-year transfer] program."

Some counselors fear that students will take lenient admissions to community college as a sign that they are still on the right track and that because the community colleges have few entrance requirements, the requirements to complete their desired program or even pass their courses will be equally minimal. These counselors are unsure that students understand the system and that they themselves are doing what is best for students.

Limitations of This Study

Before concluding this chapter, we must note some limitations of this study. Although we have studied a larger sample than was used in previous in-depth case studies, and our sample includes a variety of high schools and several counselors in each school, the sample is nevertheless relatively small and not necessarily representative. Yet this approach has permitted this research to avoid prescribing the types of answers that respondents can give, as surveys must do, and to allow counselors to explain their views in their own words. This chapter offers some new observations of counselors' practices, and it has identified new issues for subsequent research.

We must also caution that this chapter reports counselors' self-reports of their behaviors. Counselors' self-presentations of their roles may be distorted from a desire to make themselves look good. Yet there are several reasons to accept these self-reports.

First, these reports are so detailed that they seem convincing, and many different counselors offer cases to illustrate the same points. These are not just vague assertions.

Second, these self-presentations are very different from the self-presentations reported by Cicourel and Kitsuse (1963). The 1960s counselors felt no need to deemphasize their college advising and selecting role, and they expressed assurance of their authority to influence which students attended college. In contrast, our counselors avoid discouraging students' college plans and doubt their own authority if students do not listen or if parents disagree.

Third, the counselors we interviewed stress, not any great influence, but rather their small influence on students' lives. When people state that their impact is low, then stress it, even stating their desire that their impact be low, they may be making an important statement about how they feel their community wants them to act. People typically exaggerate their self-importance, but these counselors are doing the opposite. Of course, we cannot be certain that their reports fully describe their work behaviors, but we also cannot ignore their obvious concerns about discouraging students' plans.

Fourth, these counselors report actions that are not socially desirable. For instance, when counselors do not brag about their strong influence, or when they report that they are not taking some actions that might be construed as part of their job (for example, advising weak students against college), they are reporting responses that are not socially desirable. Indeed, these reports could be seen as reflecting dereliction of duty. Counselors who report their reluctance to confront students' unrealistic educational plans often seem to be admitting a shortcoming in their actions, and the private doubts expressed by some seemed to confirm this view.

Conclusions

There is much here to cheer sociologists. Sociologists' critique of counselors as gatekeepers may have helped to reduce this barrier, but the victory may be illusory. Even when counselors stop being gatekeepers, other barriers can arise. Indeed, counselors' avoidance of gatekeeping may sow the seeds for their students' later problems in community college by preventing them from getting needed information, advice, and preparation. Moreover, when counselors say, "Who am I to burst their bubble?" they indicate a loss of authority and suggest that they are encouraging students to postpone addressing important problems for another year or more, when they may have less access to good advice.

Counselors undoubtedly are under less pressure today to be social selectors or even wise advisers. With open college admissions, counselors no longer need to act as intermediaries, screening students for colleges or preparing them to go directly to work. Rather than confront a student with bad news and risk confronting an angry parent, counselors can take the easy alternative of avoiding college advising almost entirely and urging college for every student. The current system transfers much of the cooling-out process from counselors to community colleges, and in so doing it has relieved counselors of an unpleasant task.

While counselors have probably never enjoyed being the bearers of bad news, counselors in the 1960s had the responsibility and authority to influence who applied to college. Channeling students to proper post–high school experiences was a major part of their jobs. In the 1990s, however, the open admissions policies of community colleges allow every student to be admitted. As we have seen, counselors do not feel that they have to warn students about unrealistic college plans. Counselors report that they do not like giving students bad news about their future prospects, do not want the responsibility, and feel that they do not have the authority to do it, especially in opposing parents. Instead, we see a strong emphasis on encouraging college for all while avoiding unpleasant realities until after high school, when school counselors will not be involved. Counselors' role in channeling students into different futures has been greatly altered.

Of course, counselors are still important in the status attainment process. First, roughly 25 percent of the youth cohort do not graduate from their high school, and about 40 percent of high school graduates do not attend a postsecondary institution. How these students choose their life course remains a very important issue and may be influenced by counselors. Second, the process of sorting students into various kinds of postsecondary institutions may still be influenced by counselors through the course selection process and their college advising role.

But our research points to a third way in which counselors are affecting the status-attainment process. By avoiding the advising that they once did, counselors are allowing some students to pursue a course for which they are unprepared and allowing them to leave high school unaware of their likely prospects. Rather than committing sins of *commission* (keeping deserving students out of college), today's counselors may be committing sins of *omission* (sending unprepared students to college). Moreover, counselors are not warning students that they are unprepared to complete college, and they are inadvertently giving students the impression that they do not need to exert greater effort in high school to prepare for college. In interviews with students, we heard comments like, "High school doesn't matter, only college achievement matters." Students may be getting a mistaken view that because community colleges have low entry requirements, there is no reason to work in high school. These students are unaware of the 50 percent dropout rate in many community colleges.

Lastly, the near-axiom in sociology that "low-income people always get hurt" is no less true here. Even if low-income students in the 1960s were hurt by counselors' advice, the reluctance of today's counselors to give advice may also hurt low-income students. It is especially important for low-income students to gain such information from counselors because they are unlikely to get the information at home or anywhere else. Moreover, even if college offers great benefits for low-income students, the costs of tuition and forgone wages are also greater sacrifices to them. In the current era, when college entrance is easy but college retention is hard, information about the requirements needed to finish college is crucial. Moreover, poor advice from counselors prevents students from choosing to take advantage of job training and placement help from their high school.

If heavy-handed gatekeeping by counselors has indeed become less common, no one will grieve its loss. But if counselors are not giving students the information they need about the requirements for completing college, then many students may be aimlessly drifting through high school and community colleges without any notion of what requirements they will ultimately be expected to satisfy. In that case, gatekeeping has not ended but only been deferred, and many students may be haplessly failing out of college without any forewarning that such an outcome was likely.

═ Chapter 5 ═

Do Employers Need More Educated Youth?

O NE OF the great policy questions of the 1990s is how to increase youths' skills to meet the needs of today's workplaces.[1] National blue-ribbon panels write about the academic skill needs of the workplace while complaining of youths' poor academic skills (CED 1985; NAS 1984; NCEE 1990). Business leaders give well-publicized speeches in which they place much of the blame for inadequate skills at the school doorstep. Yet critics have been skeptical about whether students really need academic skills for the jobs they obtain (Ray and Mickelson 1993).

Economists and sociologists offer conflicting views of employers' needs. Neoclassical economists assume that employers seek to maximize productivity, that they shop around for the best workers, and that they pay workers according to their skills and productivity (Becker 1964; Heckman 1994). In contrast, sociologists contend that employment structures constrain job access and wages. In a well-known study, Ivar Berg (1971) showed that job access is constrained by educational credentials, and that employers often do not need or use the amount of education that they formally require. Subsequent research supports this argument (Attewell 1987; Levin and Rumberger 1987; Shaiken 1984; Squires 1979).

This dispute remains unresolved partly because of difficulties in providing suitable evidence. Economists say that "employers need skills," but "needs" and "skills" are not easily measured, so empirical studies tend to examine indirect proxies. "Years of education" is the usual measure of academic skills, yet it is clearly a poor indicator when many high school graduates lack eighth-grade math and reading skills (NAEP 1985).

Economists measure employers' "needs" by the wages they pay for employee qualifications—for example, years of education or test scores (Murnane et al. 1995). However, by this definition, employers do not seem to need any academic achievements from those who fill the early jobs taken by high school graduates, for they neither offer higher pay nor have a greater propensity to hire based on academic achievements—that is, grades, test scores, or teacher evaluations (Griffin et al. 1981). Employers state that they require academic skills, but their actions do not support these statements.

Moreover, employers rarely distinguish between stated requirements and actual needs. Sociologists like Berg stress this distinction: when they measure "needs" by rating the skills needed to do job tasks, they find that employers pay excessive wages for "unneeded education." Although some sociologists concede that wages bear some relation to employers' needs, the relationship is far from perfect, since wages are also affected by pay hierarchies, compensation systems, and norms about age, gender, status, and so on (Althauser and Kalleberg 1981; Jacobs 1989; Rosenbaum 1984), including job evaluation systems that explicitly constrain pay levels by the imputed value of particular credentials (Bellak 1984; Cappelli 1991; Rosenbaum 1984). If wage is a poor indicator of employers' needs, and years of education is a poor indicator of skill, then studies of the relationship between wages and years of education are not good tests of the economic contention that employers need skills, or conversely, of the sociological contention that educational needs are overstated.

This chapter takes an alternative approach: using qualitative evidence to examine the concepts of skills and needs in greater detail. First, rather than quantitatively measuring academic skills by the usual crude proxy (years of education), we qualitatively describe employers' reports of the specific academic skills they say they have difficulty getting and the conditions under which these needs arise. *If employers are able to identify specific academic skills that they need and to indicate their relevance to job conditions, then Berg's contention of employers' credential requirements are excessive would be unsupported.*

Second, rather than identifying employers' needs through wages, we examine two other indicators of needs: whether some employers take costly actions to recruit or retain workers with skills, or conversely, to adapt to workers' low skill levels; and whether employers who claim to have high academic skill needs are more likely to take such costly actions than other employers. We are particularly interested in those employer actions that are discretionary and taken at the employer's own initiative, for we expect that such actions are a less ambiguous indication than wages that the employer actually needs these skills. *If employers take costly actions to recruit, retain, or adapt to workers' skills, and if these actions are taken by employers who have reported*

*difficulty in getting skilled workers, then Berg's contention that employers
do not actually need the academic skills they require would be unsupported.*

Third, regardless of whether analyses support these contentions,
sociologists may still be correct about labor market structures—that
employers limit access to jobs through restricted channels. If employers actually take special actions to recruit and retain skilled workers, those special actions may introduce labor market structures that
stratify workers and limit their job access. The free and unfettered
market assumed by economists ignores these realities.

Our findings contradict aspects of each model. Contrary to Berg's
model, we find that some employers do have clear needs for specific
academic skills, that these needs occur under relevant job conditions,
and that employers engage in costly actions to hire workers with
those skills. We also find that these costly actions are more common
among employers who express these skill needs. For instance, our
findings suggest that employers sometimes use unskilled entry-level
jobs to screen people for higher jobs ("on-the-job screening"). The
workers judged by Berg (1971) and Squires (1979) to be "overqualified" for their present job tasks may be in those jobs because employers are screening them for higher jobs that would actually use
these skills.

However, contrary to the economic model of unstructured labor
markets, we find that some employers' efforts to respond to their skill
needs create labor market structures: *Employers increase supervision, decrease job complexity, instigate special job accommodations, and construct
recruiting linkages with some schools.* In the process, labor markets become more stratified. Of particular interest, some employers create
school linkages that constrain hiring so that individuals outside those
networks have difficulty gaining access to jobs. Although our findings
support economists' premise that employers need academic skills, our
findings also support sociologists' contention that employers' actions
sometimes create labor market structures that channel job access.

While much sociological research has shown how *workers* use informal personal networks to learn about possible jobs, the use of networks by *employers* has received little attention (Granovetter 1974/
1995, 152). Some employers in our sample describe using networks
for recruitment. We discuss these networks and employers' reasons
for participating in them. The conclusion explores some distinctions
between personal and institutional networks.

In sum, this chapter seeks to discover elements of the hiring process through qualitative methods. Despite the many quantitative
studies of hiring outcomes (Bills 1992; Gamoran 1994), few studies
have examined the hiring process per se (Bills 1988). Some recent

studies have begun to study employers' reports about their hiring process, but these studies are not primarily concerned with the influence of academic achievement (Holzer 1995; Moss and Tilly 1996, 2000).

This chapter seeks to discover what actions, if any, employers take in pursuit of their stated skill needs and to assess whether they initiate actions (including nonpecuniary actions) that seem to be motivated by their stated skill needs. Open-ended interviews are a good way to gather such information, and they provide opportunities to discover employer actions that have not been previously identified in the answer sets asked in employer surveys.

Using these methods, we propose to examine the following propositions:

- Some employers report specific academic skills that they need, and they indicate job conditions that make these skills needed.

- Some employers take costly actions to recruit and/or retain young workers with academic skills, or they adapt to workers with low-level skills.

- Employers that state skill needs tend to take such costly actions.

- Some employers limit job access through social networks.

Existing research does not allow us to be specific about the skills, job conditions, actions, or social networks we may find, so these analyses must be seen as an exploration, not a test, of the four propositions.

Employers' Complaints and Their Behavior

Although there is little doubt that many high school graduates lack strong academic skills (NAEP 1990), sociologists have raised some doubts about whether employers really need better-educated workers. Berg (1971) contends that employers' reliance on education in making hiring decisions is not based on actual job needs. Rather, he argues, it fulfills an organizational desire for some kind of sorting criteria. Berg (1971), Squires (1979), and Collins (1971) review numerous studies that show that educational attainment is unrelated to job productivity, turnover, or absenteeism.[2] Expanding this argument, Collins (1971, 123) concludes that "employers tend to have quite imprecise conceptions of the skill requirements of most jobs."

More recent multivariate studies, however, do show relationships between academic achievement and productivity. Many studies in personnel psychology demonstrate that cognitive ability is the strongest predictor of job performance in many occupations (Hunter and Hunter 1984). Similarly, econometric analyses show associations between test scores and job performance (Bishop 1993; Barrett and Depinet 1991; National Research Council 1989; Gamoran 1994).

Yet it is not clear whether employers act on these relationships in hiring recent high school graduates for their early jobs. Research finds that employers fail to reward academic skills in recent high school graduates, whether in terms of hiring, better jobs, or better pay (Bills 1988b; Crain 1984; Griffin et al. 1981; Kang and Bishop 1986; Rosenbaum and Kariya 1991). Using national survey data (NLS72), Larry Griffin and his colleagues (1981) find that aptitude, class rank, and other school performance measures have small and often insignificant effects on the unemployment and job attainments of high school graduates who directly enter the workforce. Robert Meyer and David A. Wise (1982) show that high school class rank does not have significant effects on wage rates two years after graduation (1974), and Robert Willis and Sherwin Rosen (1979) find that increased math and reading scores of high school graduates slightly lower wages in their first jobs. Despite their claims of needing academic skills, and despite research suggesting that incumbents with academic skills tend to be productive workers (Bishop 1993), employers do not offer immediate rewards to high school students with better academic performance. Interestingly, although grades do not improve wages for new high school graduates in the High School and Beyond 1982 cohort, grades have a strong payoff for their earnings ten years later (Rosenbaum and Roy 1996; see also chapter 9).

Carol Ray and Roslyn Mickelson (1993) indicate that studies need to consider employers' actions, which sometimes convey a message that contradicts executives' speeches. As if responding to this point, some recent research looks at the actions that employers take to find better workers. Studies of employers' responses to school-to-work programs find that employers show limited commitment to such initiatives: they offer few positions to students, and they do not remain in such programs for very long (Bailey 1994; Lynn and Wills 1994; Pauly, Kopp, and Haimson 1995). Thomas Bailey (1994) concludes that employers' behaviors raise some doubts about their commitment to academic skills. But these are studies of employers' responses to special programs, not studies of the ordinary actions that employers routinely take to hire workers.

A recent survey found that although over 70 percent of employers require a high school diploma (self-reported), fewer than one-third of them check applicants' education, and fewer than 5 percent recruit directly from schools (Holzer 1995, 52, 55). Although Harry Holzer finds that tests other than physical ones are used "in roughly half of all non-college jobs" (55), the vagueness of this question allows employers to include almost any question they ask in an interview as a "test." In contrast, when employers are asked about the relative importance of various potential criteria in the hiring process on a five-point scale (from "essential" to "not at all important"), they rank tests and academic performance near the bottom of all criteria (2.3 and 2.5), just above teacher recommendations (2.0), and far below applicants' attitude and employer references (4.6 and 3.9) (Shapiro and Iannozzi 1999, table 2). Aside from requiring that applicants say that they have a diploma and requiring a brief interview, employers rarely take actions to ensure that they receive valid information from schools. As Bishop (1993, 343) notes, "Many employers were remarkably casual about their hiring selections."

Nor do employers respond to their purported skills problems by providing academic skills training. Robert Zemsky (1994) finds that employers express highly negative views of the academic skills of high school graduates, but they do not use training programs to redress these deficiencies. In a survey of twenty-eight-hundred employers, David Boesel and his colleagues (1994, table 2) discover that 71 percent provide training to their employees, but fewer than 3 percent provide basic academic skills training. Another survey of three thousand employers uncovers extensive employer complaints about academic skills but finds little indication that these employers use tuition benefits or remedial programs to address those academic shortcomings (NCEQW 1994). Commenting on these findings, Peter Cappelli (1992, 2) notes: "There has been a fair amount of noise in the business community about establishments having to provide remedial training. But it does not appear that they're doing it. It appears to be just noise." Cappelli is raising the same issue raised by Berg: Do employers really need academic skills, or are they complaining for other reasons?

These findings have been interpreted to mean that employers do not really have a need for better academic skills, and that employers' calls for academic skills are, at best, unwarranted and, at worst, a means of accomplishing some kind of social sorting, social control, or pay reduction (Bowles and Gintis 1976). Although empirical tests have not supported Bowles and Gintis's contention that employers need compliance, not academic skills (Cappelli 1992; Olneck and Bills 1980), these studies suffer from the same problems with measuring "needs" and "skills" noted earlier.

Methods

To discover whether employers actually value academic skills and act in accordance with that priority, researchers must go to the right informants, using methods sensitive to the task. Rather than rely on the views of corporate executives (as blue-ribbon panels do), we interviewed the plant and office managers who hire entry-level workers. In the less frequent cases in which human resources (HR) departments handled the hiring of high school graduates, we interviewed HR managers.

To get detailed information about the hiring process, we conducted one-hour interviews in employers' offices. Although observational methods would yield even better information, it is difficult to conduct observations over many organizations. Employers' detailed statements about their behaviors are a useful way to get at the intervening processes in a large number of organizations.

To get good qualitative data about the nature of job conditions and employers' behaviors, face-to-face interviews were required. Although the decision to interview reduced the number of respondents we could contact, our sample size of fifty-one is larger than those in some other qualitative studies (Bills 1988; Borman 1991), and larger than any single city in surveys by Lynn and Wills (1994) or Kirschenman, Moss, and Tilly (1995). Our sample was drawn from the roster of members of two local chambers of commerce, one in Chicago and one in Chicago's western suburbs. Although membership in these associations may introduce uncertain distortions on generalizability, the associations' support gave us a response rate of over 90 percent in both sites (better than the 65 percent and 55 percent in the Lynn and Wills (1994) and Boesel [1994] surveys, respectively).

Since we were interested in how employers' attitudes may limit youths' access to primary labor market jobs, we excluded industries that were likely to offer only "youth jobs" without advancement opportunities (for example, jobs in restaurants or small stores). The sample cannot be considered a random sample of all employers, so statistical analyses would be inappropriate. Yet this sample includes a wide variety of the kinds of entry-level jobs that are potentially available to high school graduates in manufacturing, graphics, the skilled trades, financial services, office work, and so on. These jobs also are of special interest because they may offer the possibility of access to the primary labor market. They are appropriate for our purposes of discovering the range of academic skills that employers may need and the job conditions and range of costly actions that may accompany skill needs.

Just under half (twenty-three) of the fifty-one employers in this sample are located in the city of Chicago, while twenty-eight are located in suburbs west of Chicago. The sample is composed of mostly small or medium-size firms, but it includes a few large ones; the companies range in size from fewer than ten employees to more than eighty thousand.

Findings

This section probes the sociological contention that employers overstate their skill needs. It investigates whether employers report a need for specific academic skills, and whether they indicate the relevance of specific academic skills to specific job requirements. It then examines whether managers take any costly actions to realize their stated needs, and if so, what strategies they use and whether these actions are taken by employers who report difficulty in getting academic skills.

Entry-Level Jobs That Require Math and English Skills

Although we should be skeptical about the needs voiced by the top executives on American blue-ribbon panels, our first-line supervisors expressed similar concerns. Of fifty-one urban and suburban managers interviewed, thirty-five state that basic academic skills in math and English are needed for the entry-level jobs they are seeking to fill.[3] Many employers describe specific job conditions or tasks that demand these skills. Employers are most certain about job requirements after they have hired workers with poor skills.

Thirteen of our thirty-five employers describe the tasks that require math skills in their entry-level jobs. Most report that their jobs require that workers have simple arithmetic skills, sometimes including the ability to add fractions. Some other jobs require algebra and trigonometry. The general manager of one Chicago steel manufacturing company reports that his general labor plant jobs require "the concept of adding, or reading a ruler or tape measure." He was frustrated by the difficulty of getting such skills in high school graduates, "We would like to hire people who know eighth-grade math, such as knowing the difference between a fraction and a decimal, but kids aren't getting that from high school, and we generally don't see that level of knowledge."

Another Chicago manufacturer complains that many workers have fallen short in very basic math. Asked about her experiences with young employees, she recounts the story of a young man she had just hired to work full-time in the shipping department:

> He came in my office and said, "You know, down in that shipping room you've got a lot of numbers out there." I said, "We've got a lot of numbers out there? Well, yes, I guess we do." And he said, "I don't know a lot about numbers," and I said, "Oh, do you want to learn?" He said, "Yeah, I think so." I said, "Have you noticed that there are periods between some of the numbers?" He said, "Yeah, what's that all about?" I said, "Where were you when they learned decimals in school?" He said, "I must have been absent."

Another ten of the thirty-five employers report that reading, writing, and communication skills are needed for their jobs. Their high school graduate employees are lacking, however, in even simple skills. One office manager in a small suburban graphics company tells of a secretary "who tried to spell *quick* with a *w*. She didn't know that . . . all words that have *q* need a *u!*" Echoing an oft-reported condition, a Chicago insurance company recruiter reports that applicants for data entry and claims adjustment jobs "can't understand some of the questions on the job application," and that some males bring a girlfriend to fill out the application. Another Chicago employer unhappily states that many of his applicants for unskilled labor jobs "can't read and write beyond, I suspect, a fifth- or sixth-grade level, and when they can read, they certainly can't comprehend what they have read." This is often a serious shortcoming: many employers report that their jobs require better than eighth-grade reading and writing skills. A suburban manufacturer states that "today's high school graduates don't comprehend as much. It takes them longer to catch on to instructions, and they can't read manuals for instructions as well as they used to, which are written at the twelfth-grade level." Another notes the need to find workers who can "put together two or three sentences in a complete thought."

Another twelve employers cite high school graduates' problems with both math and English, saying that both types of skills are needed in today's entry-level jobs. A Chicago metal-parts manufacturer complains that even though his entry-level jobs require only seventh-grade reading and math skills, he has a "terrible time getting even a 10 percent yield" for these skills in the applicants he interviews.

Of the sixteen employers who state that they have *no* need for academic skills, eleven say that their entry-level jobs simply require no skills, and three more say that their jobs require occupational skills but not academic skills. A suburban production manager says, "There aren't a lot of qualifications other than wanting to work." A suburban plant manager says that academic skills are actually counterproductive; people with such skills, "within a year or so, . . . get bored and move on." A Chicago custom-gearing manufacturer reports that his need is for people with "technical ability . . . [for] grasping the skills needed for machine jobs."

Secondary Jobs Attached to Internal Labor Markets: "Screening Jobs"

Some employers note that although academic skills are not needed in their entry-level jobs, these skills *are* needed for the higher-level jobs in their company that entry-level workers could move into. Even though these entry-level jobs are largely in the "secondary labor market," in that they offer minimal pay, benefits, and job security, they can sometimes lead to the bottom rung of a career ladder to better jobs. Doeringer and Piore (1971, 167) referred to such jobs as "secondary jobs . . . attached to internal labor markets."

Employers note that workers can move upward from such entry-level jobs only if they possess adequate basic skills at the time of entry. Of the thirty-five employers who state a need for academic skills, seventeen (48.6 percent) report that, although their entry-level jobs are undemanding, they allow some workers to move into higher-skilled jobs, and those jobs do require academic skills. Indeed, some employers prefer to recruit for their skilled jobs from their entry-level people, who can learn the firm's procedures and techniques by observation.

When asked whether entry-level unskilled employees may advance into higher-skilled jobs in the future, one Chicago manufacturer answers affirmatively, but adds that this is true only if workers have basic academic skills to begin with:

> They also have to have the ability, then, to understand math pretty well. Have to be able to add and subtract and multiply. They have to be able to subtract dimensions. . . . They have to be able to measure something like, .236 plus or minus .005. They have to understand what that means. They could be someone in the flame-cutting department, who would be cutting steel plate. In that case, they'd have to have the ability to run a small computer, and the readout on it, and so forth. . . . Some of that certainly can be learned by someone without a high school education, but a high school education is very helpful, in those areas.

But the ladder cannot always be climbed. When workers in the lowest-level jobs lack basic academic skills, as they often do, they are stuck in those jobs. In a Chicago commercial printing firm, workers with deficient skills do fine in the lower-level jobs, but they cannot rise into the better jobs:

> There are some [reading and math] deficiencies, but none that would probably keep them from performing their entry-level jobs. [But] it may affect them, you know, when it comes time to move up the ladder. . . . Once they get onto a piece of equipment, once they're performing a job that requires regular reading of customer job tickets . . . or written instructions from their supervisor, then it could become more of a problem.

As noted earlier, some employers report that they prefer to fill their more advanced jobs from within by promoting their entry-level workers. A Chicago manufacturer states that they have to recruit skilled workers from within since they need highly specific training, "and usually that training has to be in-house because it's specialized type of training." In effect, although few skills are required for the tasks in these entry-level jobs, these employers expect workers to be able to learn from the experience, since that is the main way they can fill their skilled jobs. On-the-job training is a central part of these jobs (see Doeringer and Piore 1971).

Other employers use their entry-level jobs for what might be called "on-the-job screening." A printer reports that his firm uses entry-level jobs as a way to discover whether workers have the ability to advance in the future:

> One of the questions I ask the pressman [the employee's supervisor] is, "Are they fast learners?" I ask, "How are they doing? Can they read and write? Are they picking up on the math and the instructions fine?" If that's true, there's no problem. I ask [their supervisors], "Hey, are these our future pressers?" They say, "Yeah." So that's the answer I'm looking for. That's what I'm looking for when we're hiring somebody: Are they going to be able to go up the ladder and become the feeder and the second man, then up to the first-man spot?

In entry-level jobs that offer on-the-job training or screening, if workers do only what is demanded by their simple daily tasks, they will not need academic skills. But if they can do only these daily tasks and they lack academic skills, then they will not advance to more demanding jobs, which employers expect to fill from these positions.

On-the-job-screening positions may illustrate Berg's findings on the artificially high premium placed on academic skills, but they also suggest a possible limitation of his study. Employers may be preparing the workers whom Berg finds to be "overqualified" for the task demands of their present jobs to advance into higher jobs, or they may be testing these workers' capabilities. To the extent that employers use some jobs to train or screen workers for higher jobs, their job requirements include skills needed for the higher jobs but not for the entry-level job itself. Indeed, if reformers want employers to offer more career ladders, then upgrading entry criteria may be required, even for entry-level jobs with simple tasks. Although we must be skeptical about employers' claims, and we cannot examine their actual rates of promotion from entry-level jobs, this chapter suggests that a complete test of Berg's contentions about excessive qualifications would require that researchers obtain measures of the probability of advancement and the academic skill requirements for higher-level jobs.

In sum, most employers (thirty-five of fifty-one) report a need for specific academic skills, and they can explain the relevance of specific academic skills to specific job requirements. They report that either their entry-level jobs need those skills or their entry-level jobs allow access to higher-level jobs that require those skills. Employers who state that they need academic skills tend to have jobs with specific academic-skill demands or to do on-the-job screening for advancement. The relationship of these skills and needs to advancement potential is of particular interest. Many of these entry-level jobs fit Doeringer and Piore's (1971) model of secondary labor market jobs attached to internal labor markets. Employers report that they seek to fill these jobs with workers who have adequate academic skills and the potential to be trained for more demanding positions in the future.

The Relationship Between Earnings and New High School Graduates' Academic Skills

One of the reasons for this study is to understand why some employers claim to need workers with academic skills even though their own behavior casts doubt on that claim. In particular, earnings, the most visible and easily measured indicator of value, seems to have no relationship to grades or academic achievement in the early career of high school graduates. If employers clearly stated their hiring requirements and then awarded jobs and higher earnings based on those requirements, researchers would not debate employers' needs, and students would not be uncertain about the payoffs to school efforts.

Why don't employers set earnings at levels that clearly signal their needs?

Employers gave several reasons why earnings are unrelated to new high school graduates' academic skills. First, employers are not willing to put youths into jobs that require much responsibility because they are reluctant to trust high school information. As we elaborate in chapter 6, employers do not know whether school tasks and teachers' evaluations have any relevance to their own needs, and they do not know whether they can trust teachers to give candid evaluations. They put all youths in a few entry-level jobs that do not demand much responsibility and are closely supervised. These screening jobs serve as a testing ground on which employers can observe how youths perform in actual work situations. Given their mistrust of the relevance of school tasks and evaluations, employers would prefer to evaluate performance themselves by seeing how youths perform in real work tasks that employers know are relevant.

Second, employers tend to pay people according to their jobs, not their personal qualifications. Strong labor market norms, union requirements, job evaluation practices, and "equal pay" legislation demand that employees get equal pay for equal work, regardless of their future value to the company (see Rosenbaum 1984).

Although economic theory is correct that earnings distinctions would have clear value in communicating employers' requirements to applicants, employers worry that earnings distinctions would also have dysfunctional consequences inside the workplace. Indeed, the fact that pay is a highly visible distinction makes it useful for research and as a signal to students but also makes employers reluctant to use it for differentiation, for it can be a source of jealousy and invidious comparisons. However, even if these considerations prevent them from offering pay distinctions, we find that employers can and do make informal, nonpecuniary distinctions, as we report later in this chapter.

Not Just Talk: Employers Demonstrate Their Need for Skills

Although most employers state a need for academic skills in their workers, we still do not know whether these needs remain merely at the level of discourse or whether they produce real changes in employers' recruitment activities and on-the-job procedures and policies. If employers loudly cite their needs but ultimately make no real effort to act on them, then we must be skeptical about their stated needs. We may assume that these employers are just sounding off about "needs" that pose no real problems to them. However, if employers actually take actions that entail extra effort or cost to ensure the selection of workers with better academic skills at the recruitment stage, or if they compensate for the skill shortcomings of present employees (for instance, through expensive redesigns or additional supervision), then we should be more inclined to believe that they have some commitment to these concerns.

In-depth data allow us to investigate these questions. The following sections explore whether such actual time-consuming or expensive recruitment and retention activities occur. We find that employers respond to skill needs by taking four kinds of actions not noted in previous research: they increase supervisors' responsibility to explain tasks; they adjust jobs to match workers' skills; they offer accommodations to hire and retain workers with valued skills; and they invest in linkages with potential sources of labor, like schools, in order to get prescreened workers. The last type of action—forming institutional linkages—is of particular interest, for it indicates that, in seeking to accomplish the productivity goals that economists describe, employers take actions that structure the labor market and limit access to jobs to individuals from certain institutions.

Retention: Increasing Supervisors' Responsibilities, Adapting Jobs, and Accommodating Good Workers

When faced with workers on the job whose academic skills fall beneath a certain level, do companies undertake expensive activities designed to compensate for their workers' poor skills? If so, we can infer that these companies are committed to their professed need for academic skills. We find that employers take three types of compensatory activities: increasing supervisors' responsibilities to assist and supervise less skilled workers, simplifying job tasks to match workers' poor skills, and accommodating good workers when they come along.

Increasing Supervisors' Responsibilities   First, we find that many employers increase supervisors' responsibilities to assist and supervise less skilled workers. They assign more experienced—and more expensive—workers the task of assisting less-skilled employees in performing their jobs by explaining the tasks in minute detail and supervising their performance more closely. Often this is an additional task for a supervisor or manager. This kind of strategy occurs in eleven companies in our sample. While nine of the thirty-five employers who state academic-skill needs increase supervisors' responsibilities to respond to entry-level workers' skill shortcomings (25.7 percent), only two of the sixteen who do not state such needs take such actions (12.5 percent). Apparently, those employers who claim to have academic skill needs are more likely to increase supervisors' responsibilities.

A Chicago manufacturer says that her firm compensates for high school graduates' lack of basic reading and math skills by repeatedly spelling out each task that must be done:

> We find if they can't understand the reading, they have to have an illustration, like we'll take a gauge and show them where it has to be. Instead of the worker being able to say to themselves, "This part has to be made within thousandths of an inch," and take the part and measure it to that thousandths, the foreman has to go over to the employee, pick up the part, pick up the gauge, set the gauge, and say, "If it does this, okay, and if it doesn't, not okay," and set up a scenario each and every time.

A plant manager of a small company succinctly sums up this strategy when he reports that he "basically just spend[s] time with them on the floor with a ruler and show[s] them the basic marks, and show[s] them how it works."

Simplifying Job Tasks to Match Workers' Poor Skills   When employers simplify job tasks to match workers' poor skills, additional costs are often incurred. Nearly half of the employers we interviewed (twenty-three of fifty-one, or 45.1 percent) report that they must adapt job tasks to make up for their entry-level employees' lack of basic academic skills. While more than half of the employers who claim to have academic skill needs (twenty of thirty-five, or 57.1 percent) adapt job tasks to respond to entry-level workers' skill shortcomings, only three of the sixteen who do not state such needs take such actions (18.8 percent). Employers who state academic skill needs are more likely to make these adaptations.

Many employers are matter-of-fact about needing to make jobs easier, as when one plant manager in a Chicago manufacturing firm says, "Yes, [simplifying] is a must. What I've done is gone all the way down to the grammar school level to get them to understand simple, simple math." The plant manager at a suburban metal fabricator says that his company has taken the ultimate step in bypassing workers' poor reading skills: "We have eliminated a need for math and reading skills altogether: every instruction we give workers is now verbal." A plant manager at a Chicago manufacturer agrees: "[We] only give people . . . a certain amount of instructions at a time. Spoon-feed them a little bit." Both of these employers are struggling with problems of poor skills in their workers and find such "spoon-feeding" to be an unanticipated and costly burden. There is much concern about the low-paid, low-skilled jobs in the work world, and much criticism of employers for not offering better jobs. In these examples, however, we see employers who feel compelled to reduce the skill demands of entry-level jobs because of workers' limitations.

Accommodating Good Workers   Third, some employers alter job conditions or rules to accommodate good applicants or workers. Such accommodations can occur either at the time of hiring—such as when employers change their own hiring schedules to meet the availability of a valued applicant—or as a way to retain a valued employee, such as when employers allow an employee to work at home rather than at the job site.

Of our fifty-one employers, sixteen try to accommodate valued employees in some way. While more than one-third of the employers who report needing academic skills try to accommodate valued employees (thirteen of thirty-five, or 37.1 percent), only three of the other sixteen employers take such actions (18.8 percent). Again, those employers who state a need for academic skills are more likely to take these actions.

To accommodate skilled employees, one Chicago printing employer says that he has sometimes created part-time positions in order to hire workers with good academic skills, even when he really needs someone for a full-time job and the part-time arrangement requires extra effort on his part during the uncovered hours. He has accommodated many high school seniors this way, giving them part-time jobs they can do during the school year and biding his time until May, when they graduate. "There have been times in February, March, April, when we may have a full-time position [open] but try to get by with a part-time, knowing that [the student] will be graduating in May and that we can then make the position full-time. We'll do that to accommodate a high school student with good academic skills." Similarly, the supervisor of the press room at a suburban print shop says that he tries to hire applicants with good academic skills even at times when the company has put a cap on full-time hiring. He does this by giving part-time jobs that turn into full-time jobs later under the guise of "summer help." He says he is willing to find "loopholes in the system" when he finds someone with good skills, because such applicants are rare.

Once a worker proves to be a valuable employee, supervisors are loath to lose them. To retain valued workers, some employers will accommodate them by allowing them to work flexible hours, at home, or in jobs they ordinarily would not hold. When an urban employer received a call from a valued former young worker who was moving back to Chicago, he reports that he enthusiastically asked, "How soon can you start?" Although it was a small firm that had no job vacancies, he added that the company would "reorganize" to have the employee back. A suburban metal shop manager explains that "when you see a guy or girl work out well, has a good work ethic, you hate to let them go. I'll find a place for them. Because somewhere down the line I'm going to need that person again, and I'll find some work for them." This employer indicates that even in periods of slack demand he will accommodate a skilled employee.

In sum, we find that employers use various methods to compensate for their workers' skill levels, such as assigning oversight and training responsibilities to supervisors or adapting job tasks to match their poor skills. Employers also accommodate employees whose capabilities they value. We find that thirty of our fifty-one employers (58.8 percent) use at least one of these methods.

Recruitment: Seeking Skills Through Linkages

Employers report that they participate in several types of contacts with schools and other institutions to seek out skilled high school graduates for their entry-level positions. Employers use some of these linkages to provide information about prospective workers. Some activities, like apprenticeship programs, do not involve schools but are sometimes related to a need for academic skills. School-related activities range from minimal involvements (job fairs) to high involvements (long-term linkages with teacher). Some of these linkage activities seem to be a form of investment in prescreening.

Apprenticeships have been praised as a form of training (Hamilton 1990), but they also have a screening function in Germany (Faist 1992; Rosenbaum 1992). Four of our employers use apprenticeships, and all four stress that apprenticeship programs are a dependable way to prescreen the academic skills of their applicant pool. Asked whether his company has trouble finding high school graduates with sufficient math and reading skills, one Chicago manufacturer refers to his use of an apprenticeship program for hiring young entry-level machinists-in-training: "They won't be in here if they don't have [academic skills]." Even before we asked about academic skills, this employer had explained that the apprenticeship test of academic skills and job skills creates an "up or out" situation. For entry-level workers to become apprentices at his firm, they must pass the test administered by the apprenticeship program. If they fail the test, they are out of a job.

When asked whether his company is willing to hire apprentices who have *not* passed the apprenticeship test, a different suburban manufacturer responds, "Oh yeah, we'll put them out here and give them the work experience. But of course, it would be a lesser-degree job." Both of these employers value basic skills, and both have found a way to ensure that their better entry-level positions are filled by high school graduates with these skills: they use apprenticeship linkages. Three of the four manufacturers that use apprenticeship referrals are among those who say they need academic skills. Nevertheless, apprenticeships as a means of selecting applicants with academic skills are not commonly used.

Employers' contacts with schools are far more common. Indeed, forty-two of our fifty-one employers (82.4 percent) participate in minimal forms of contact with schools—holding a job fair at a school, making a presentation to a class, or posting a notice for a part-time job opening. But employers see these activities as community services to help students learn about work; they rarely regard these activities as leading to full-time jobs.

Some employers, however, have long-term, close linkages with school staff. Employers with closer linkages frequently devote a substantial amount of time to these relationships; they serve on school advisory boards and try to hire recommended graduates of certain vocational programs. Unlike school-business partnerships, which are often short-lived (Lynn and Wills 1994), these contacts often carry long-term obligations and last many years. When these employers have job openings, they ask school staff to nominate students. Employers see these long-term linkages as a way to "get the straight scoop" about young graduates' skills. Of our employers, thirteen have long-term contacts with teachers and counselors. These linkages are particularly common among employers who say they need academic skills; twelve of thirty-five (34.3 percent) employers needing academic skills use a close form of school linkage, while only one of the others does (6.3 percent).

Despite the costs, several employers suggest that the time investment involved in the closer form of contact (trusted linkages with school staff) pays off in better academic skills. One executive at a family-owned printing company in Chicago says that his company is still able to get workers with good academic skills from a local high school based on the personal relationship that his father established with a teacher from that school more than ten years ago. Although this relationship is not without its costs (volunteered time on the school's advisory council), its benefits have been worth the sacrifices:

> I think we've had success because we have been able to reach inside the schools and talk specifically to certain teachers. . . . And the positive [aspect] of those contacts for us is that we're getting the straight scoop.

And there's many times where we've called, and the teachers, the instructors, have told us, "Look, I've got a classroom full of kids, but there's no way I would send any of them to you." So I don't know if the schools are doing a great job, but our success has been good because we've been handed, I think, a few of the better ones.

Asked to speculate on why these linkages with schools work, one suburban metal company supervisor says, "If someone is willing to put their name behind somebody and say, 'I think that this guy would work out good,' well, most people nowadays will not personally endorse anybody unless they're pretty confident they won't wind up with egg on their face." Because he expects the teachers he knows to care about their reputations, this employer trusts them to tell him the truth about applicants' skills. Through his teacher link, the employer can efficiently and effectively prescreen applicants and hire only those who come highly recommended.

But employers' actions to recruit through selected networks have adverse implications for alternative channels, even from the same school. Several employers who maintain long-term contacts with trusted teachers say that they are not willing to make an open channel of recruitment from the entire school, such as through co-op placement programs or the counseling office. When asked whether he would consider taking hiring recommendations from other school programs, a Chicago printer with strong teacher linkages reports:

We bypass the typical channels. . . . I think the placement office in . . . schools . . . they're out there, God bless them for it, but they're out there trying to get kids jobs, and I think they probably have less sensitivity to the workplace. I think the best of them probably have the idea that if they get the kid placed into a job, then they've done their job. And that's good [for their kids]. That probably is their role. But I don't know that it means that they fully understand what [the job requirements are], or whether they fully understand the student either. The teachers on the front line, I think they have their finger on the pulse a lot more.

Similarly, a suburban printer says that the principal of a local high school has done a laudable job in referring qualified applicants to him, but that, as we noted in chapter 4, the school staff members vested with that specific responsibility largely ignore employers:

You get a very strong distaste for working with high school counselors. I have very little use for high school counselors altogether, because, I don't know if their background is sociology with a specialty in psychology, or whatever it is, but the only applicants I've ever gotten from high school counselors have been absolutely worthless. . . . [They] have all just been really a waste of time.

In addition to distrusting recommendations from conventional school channels, employers who seek out teachers' assistance in hiring workers are also wary of putting too much stock in high school grades. Of our thirteen employers with strong teacher or counselor linkages, eight reject the idea of using grades to measure employability. When asked whether he thinks that school grades predict anything about work performance, one Chicago employer with linkages to teachers responds:

> Not in all cases. And that works both ways. There's a lot of people that come out of high school that have some great credentials and just never do anything; and then there are other young people who come out of high school with below-average grades that just have the will to succeed. For whatever reason, high school didn't grab them. So, actually, at this point in time, I wouldn't put too much weight on grades. The teacher comments I would put a lot of weight on if I know the teacher, but not typically the objective measures.

These comments help to clarify a puzzle in past research. Many employers, both in our sample and in society at large (see Crain 1984; Griffin et al. 1981; Rosenbaum and Kariya 1991), choose not to use grades as a hiring criterion, even while they complain about not getting skilled workers. These findings suggest that the skills that students learn in school are valued by some employers, but that the traditional ways of reporting those skills—grades—are perceived as untrustworthy, although employers may be mistaken as chapter 8 indicates. Given this situation, these employers believe their investments in long-term linkages may be their one way of getting trusted information instead of using a measure of skills that they do not trust.

These findings also indicate that although employers pursue the productivity goals that economists assume, some employers' means of obtaining trustworthy information about applicants' potential productivity actually restrict job access to only those students with the right contacts. Some employers will even mistrust applications from students who have good grades but who lack access to these contacts, and they will not consider these otherwise qualified applicants for employment.

Such linkages provide a good channel of access for students who have classes with linked teachers, and in inner-city schools these students' best chance of getting a job is through their teacher. But only a small proportion of teachers have such contacts (Rosenbaum and

Jones 1995), and these linkages can also pose structural barriers that prevent the labor market from operating in the unfettered way envisioned by economic theory, even though the linkages arise in pursuit of that theory's goals.

Conclusions

This chapter examines whether employers really need academic skills, as business panels claim. Despite our skepticism about the claims of top executives, we find that plant and office managers do take actions that indicate serious commitment to academic skills. Our findings confirm economists' assertions, although we find that employers' actions are different from the ones suggested by economists, and that they often occur through social structures. For instance, employers rarely hire based on school grades (Crain 1984), but some employers use similar information when it comes through trusted linkages.

We must note that our data come from employers' perceptions and may be distorted as a result. Yet the detail and specificity of these employers' stories make them highly credible. Moreover, we found that the employers who complain the most are not just whining. Their efforts to cope with skill deficiencies often involve significant effort and expense, suggesting a commitment to overcoming these difficulties. They screen people in entry-level jobs and through school linkages, they increase supervisors' responsibility to explain tasks when workers do not understand, they adjust jobs to match workers' skills, and they offer accommodations to retain workers with valued skills. These actions, which are often costly, are more common among employers who report a need for academic skills. In short, employers are generally putting their efforts where their complaints are. These employer actions have not been noted in previous research, and they warrant further study.

Although motivated by economic interests, employers' actions create social structures with important implications. They lead to changes in authority, preferential treatment, opportunities for hiring and advancement, and institutional networks. In particular, we find that some entry-level jobs with largely secondary labor market attributes (in that they offer minimal pay, benefits, and job security) are used as a form of screening to detect which workers are good bets for advancement.

Such "on-the-job screening" clarifies some theoretical puzzles. Although segmented labor market theory is correct in observing that youth are initially confined to secondary labor market jobs, it does not explain what keeps youth confined to segments (Granovetter 1981; Hodson and Kaufman 1982), or how the selection process changes as youth become adults (Hogan and Astone 1986; Parcel 1987). This chapter indicates that employers use some entry-level jobs to screen workers for access to the primary labor market. On-the-job screening helps explain the jump that some workers are able to make from the secondary labor market (where no skills are required) to the primary labor market (where academic skills are necessary). However, this jump depends on young employees having preexisting academic skills.

Moreover, these findings indicate that Berg may be partly correct about employers' overvaluation of educational credentials, but for different reasons than he supposed. When Berg (1971) and Squires (1979) found that employers require academic credentials that are unneeded for present jobs, it is possible that employers were using these jobs as screening mechanisms for higher-level jobs that did need academic skills. This chapter finds some cases illustrating this point, and these "screening jobs" deserve further study.

We also find that employers create institutional linkages to screen applicants. Sociologists have studied how workers use networks to learn about job openings (Granovetter 1974/1995), but research has not examined the other direction: how *employers* use networks to gain information about applicants (Granovetter 1985). Moreover, although research has focused on informal networks between individuals, it has rarely studied institutional networks. Many employers in our sample report having formed contacts with high schools, community colleges, and apprenticeships. Although these linkages are less formal than those in other nations (such as Japan and Germany), some are long-term networks, some transcend the original individuals who initiated them, and they perform some of the same screening functions as networks in other nations (Rosenbaum et al. 1999).

Like workers' search networks, employers' recruiting networks show the limits of neoclassical economic models, and both networks use nonmarket processes to improve information, an important prerequisite of market models. Indeed, although institutional networks seem inefficient to neoclassical economists, employers report that these networks improve their efficiency in selecting capable employees. Institutional networks are an important extension of sociological network theory, and they deserve further attention (Granovetter 1974/1995; Kariya and Rosenbaum 1995). I explore them further in later chapters.

After showing that "weak ties" have an advantage for workers' job searches, Granovetter (1974/1995, 163) has recently suggested that formal "strong ties" have an important role "where there is no easy way for job seekers and recruiters to assess one another's qualities, . . . for example, as students emerge from school, with no previous work experience and therefore no network of contacts from previous jobs." He develops this contention with illustrations of Japanese recruiting networks (Rosenbaum and Kariya 1989), German apprenticeships (Harhoff and Kane 1994), and some findings from the United States (Granovetter 1974/1995, 21, 162–65), including this study. Moreover, while weak ties have value in providing job leads to workers, our findings indicate that long-term strong ties give employers trustworthy information about applicants that reduces costly mistakes in hiring. Thus, *although employers participate in linkages for productivity-enhancing reasons identified by economic theory, the result of employers' actions is best described by sociological theory.* Employers' linkages create structures that put information in a trustworthy context, but they constrain job access to individuals in schools that have these linkages.

These results have important implications for social policy. Training programs for disadvantaged groups have often been ineffective (Betsey et al. 1985; Stern et al. 1995), but social policies that encourage school-employer linkages could help disadvantaged students and create a more systematic pathway from school to work, one similar to (though weaker than) the pathways in those nations that have formal linkages. Research indicates that high school graduates who find their jobs with assistance from their school get better jobs than those who rely on want ads or direct applications (Holzer 1995, table 3.4). Moreover, for students in vocational programs, school help raises wages both right after graduation and ten years later, and it raises wages even more than family contacts (Rosenbaum and Roy 1996; see also chapter 9).

Although teachers' biases are a potential concern, any procedure entails some bias, and the issue may be in choosing the lesser of evils. For instance, Kathryn Neckerman and Joleen Kirschenman (1991) find that employers who use employment tests are *more* likely to hire minorities than employers who lack such tests. Philip Moss and Chris Tilly (2000, chapter 6) confirm this finding for black women (but not black men). Testing may be biased, but the alternatives to testing may be worse.

Similarly, the alternatives to teachers' evaluations may be worse. For instance, employers may create more bias when they rely on their own snap judgments in brief interviews (Miller and Rosenbaum 1996) than when they rely on teachers' opinions, which are formed by viewing students' performances over an entire year (see chapter 10, this volume). Indeed, according to reports from some urban teachers, employers who are reluctant to hire females or minorities for skilled crafts jobs have done so when these youths are highly recommended by trusted teachers (Rosenbaum 1996b). Moreover, analyses of the High School and Beyond survey indicate that black males, black females, and Hispanic females are more likely to get their first jobs after graduation with assistance from their school than are white males—10.3 percent, 15.6 percent, and 10.1 percent, respectively, versus 7.2 percent (see chapter 9). Although research on the effects of linkages is still meager, preliminary indications suggest that school-employer linkages could create effective channels of access for disadvantaged students.

We find that economic theory adequately describes employers' motivations, but that it also predicts behaviors that do not happen (such as hiring based on grades) and ignores social processes that have important implications. We find that employers create social structures, selection mechanisms, and institutional linkages that affect hiring and promotions. These social mechanisms may improve information and efficiency, but they also affect whether youth gain access to better jobs, and which youth do so.

= Chapter 6 =

Hiring in a Hobbesian World: Social Infrastructure and Employers' Use of Information

H AVING shown that employers actually do need academic skills, we are still left with the puzzle of why they ignore school information in their hiring decisions.[1] Indeed, we know very little about how employers view various information sources and why they use some sources of information and not others.

According to signaling theory, the labor market problems may arise because employers do not have good information about job applicants' human capital (Spence 1974). This theory suggests that employers seek informational shortcuts, or signals, that indicate academic skill levels and work habits. For youth newly out of high school, these signals would presumably be school-based indicators such as grades, test scores, and other teacher ratings. Yet contrary to this theory, a large body of research indicates that employers do not use school information about applicants and fail to reward high school graduates' academic skills in terms of hiring them in the first place, hiring them for better jobs, or hiring them at better pay (Borman 1991; Gamoran 1994; Griffin et al. 1981; Kang and Bishop 1985; Rosenbaum and Kariya 1991). Moreover, they consciously choose not to do so (Bills 1992); they do not seek such information (Rosenbaum and Binder 1996); and they do not use it when it is offered (Crain 1984). Instead, they prefer to rely on their impressions in interviews. Given employers' stated needs for academic skills and good work habits in their workers, these findings are puzzling, yet existing research provides no explanation.

Sociological network theory provides a clue to this mystery. Granovetter (1995) contends that market transactions are embedded in a social infrastructure. He suggests that markets may fail to operate efficiently if the appropriate social infrastructure is absent. Even if information exists, if there are no conduits through which it can travel, it will not be received.

This chapter takes this analysis one step further. It examines why employers do not use all the information they receive and whether social context influences the ways in which employers view information and their willingness to use it. Having seen that employers do not use school information, we look at the conditions that cause employers to disregard some information.

Our findings indicate not only that social infrastructure is the means by which information is conveyed, but that it also influences the ways in which employers view information, and particularly whether they trust it. For some economic decisions, information is used only if it is trusted, and in these cases, social infrastructure can influence whether such trust exists. If the mechanisms through which information travels are suspect, the information will not be used.

In examining the circumstances that permit people to use information from others, we are addressing issues analogous to those considered by Thomas Hobbes. Hobbes asked how people could cooperate in the context of a competitive society in which information is potentially tainted by informants' selfish motives and by conflicts of interest. If people view all information as potentially tainted, then they will avoid using outside information and will rely on information they generate themselves. Human capital and signaling theories may be correct about the criteria that employers would *like* to use, but Hobbes asked: What information do they feel they can actually trust? Viewed through this Hobbesian lens, labor markets can operate only when employers receive information through trusted channels.

In interviews with our sample of fifty-one employers, we found that employers do see Hobbesian constraints on the information they receive. They receive many kinds of information, but they have reasons to mistrust much of it. They consequently rely a great deal on information they can collect personally by conducting brief interviews and trusting their "gut instincts." Although this strategy solves the problem of mistrust, research indicates that interviewing is a poor predictor of performance and is prone to racial and cultural bias, and some employers confess that it leads to bad choices.

However, we find that some employers have found ways to overcome the problem of mistrust—they use information from their own workers and from other long-term social networks. We find that employers trust and use information that is conveyed within the social context of an ongoing relationship. Although workers' use of networks in searching for jobs has been studied (Granovetter 1973; Manwaring 1984; Manwaring and Wood 1984), employers' use of networks in recruiting has not (Granovetter 1974/1995, 152). Our results support the contention of social network theory that social relations solve the Hobbesian problem (Granovetter 1974/1995). We conclude with implications for theory and policy.

Methods

Employers' own detailed descriptions of their behaviors are a useful way to learn about the hiring processes in a large number of organizations. It is difficult to get such detailed information with a survey, and observational methods are difficult to use over many organizations. To discover how the hiring process operates, we interviewed those who actually do the hiring—plant and office managers, and in a few cases, human resources managers.

This chapter uses the same interviews from the survey described in chapter 5. Although the sample cannot be considered a random sample of all employers, it includes a wide variety of entry-level jobs potentially available to high school graduates in diverse industries (manufacturing, graphics, skilled trades, financial services, office work, and so on). As noted, the sample is composed of mostly small and medium-size firms, but it does include a few large ones; the companies range in size from fewer than ten employees to more than eighty thousand.

Findings: Reconciling Employers' Stated Skill Needs with Their Hiring Behavior

Many of the qualities that employers want in their employees are reflected in school performance: academic skills, oral and written communication skills, dependable attendance, and good work habits. Many employers report that they need the academic skills of the school curriculum—math and verbal skills. Peter Cappelli and Nikolai Rogowsky (1993) find that employers (and employees) consider basic knowledge in math and English very important; Robert Hill and Regina Nixon's (1984) survey finds that employers overwhelmingly want schools to focus on making youth more employable by concentrating on basic reading, writing, and math skills, and Harry Holzer (1995) finds that 65 percent of employers need non-college-graduate employees who can perform basic arithmetic and that one-third need people who can write paragraphs. Moreover, employers' perceptions are supported by systematic studies of productivity; a research review found that cognitive skills are strong predictors of job performance, even after controlling for other attributes (Gamoran 1994).

Employers also express needs for workers with good work habits, including persistence, dependability, and a good attitude, all of which are also reflected in students' performance of school tasks. Robert Crohn's (1983) study finds that employers most want workers who are dependable and have a good attitude. A more detailed study finds that employers want workers who are dependable and can stay with a task until it is completed (Baxter and Young 1982).

Our study confirmed these employer preferences. Employers emphasized their need for workers with good academic skills, including reading comprehension and basic math. As one manufacturer says:

> I think it needs to go back to the reading and the writing and the arithmetic, the ability to communicate both in writing and vocally, and the ability to understand simple math: fractions, how to divide, add fractions, how to look at a ruler and come up with one and seven-sixteenths, you know, nothing beyond the simple math.

Another said: "They have to have a very solid grasp of reading and writing, the communication skills. From the reading aspect, reading instructions, writing directions, maybe writing simple correspondence. . . . I think they should have basic classes in problem solving."

Indeed, thirty-five of the fifty-one employers in this sample specifically state that their jobs require basic math and English, and many describe specific job conditions or tasks that demand such skills. Thus, many employers have an explicit need for the academic skills taught in school and reflected in school grades. Our study also confirms that employers need employees with good work habits that are likely to be related to the grades and attendance information in school transcripts and in teacher evaluations (Rosenbaum 1976).

Yet these reports pose a puzzling issue. Despite their stated needs, employers do not use information from schools. They do not ask schools to send them transcripts or teacher recommendations; they report that they do not use those sources of information in hiring, and that their hiring decisions are uncorrelated with teacher ratings or information in school transcripts. If, as human capital and signaling theories would lead us to expect, employers who need academic skills could use existing information from schools to identify which applicants meet their stated skill needs, why do they fail to do so when hiring?

Some have suggested that employers do not use grades because schools do not send them transcripts (Bishop 1987a). Yet employers tend to be well represented on school boards, and schools usually respond when employers are unhappy with some aspect of their local schools (Useem and Useem 1974). If many employers wanted transcripts or wanted schools to help in job placements, schools would probably respond to their requests. High schools readily respond to colleges' frequent requests for transcripts. We must wonder whether employers really care about getting transcripts and whether they would respond if they knew students' grades.

In fact, research suggests that employers consciously choose not to use high school information. A Census Bureau survey of four thousand employers also found that employers consider school measures, including grades, teachers' recommendations, and the prestige of the applicant's school, the three *least* important factors when hiring (NCEQW 1994), and that employers rarely obtained school transcripts. A national survey of nineteen hundred personnel officers found that many employers consider grades important for hiring *college* graduates, but few considered grades important for hiring high school graduates (Crain 1984). A strong personal impression in an interview was rated "very important" by 76 percent of personnel officers, while grades and tests were so rated by only 18 percent and 12 percent, respectively. Daniel Diamond's (1970) survey of employers in New York and St. Louis also found that fewer than half used tests even for the most demanding jobs, and that the main hiring criterion for these jobs was impressions in an interview. In his study of hiring practices, David Bills found that none of the employers he interviewed were concerned with grades (Bills 1988; David Bills, personal communication, May 27, 1988).

The research clearly indicates that employers do not use school information about applicants, that this is a deliberate choice, and that they choose instead to rely on their impressions in interviews. Given employers' stated needs for academic skills and good work habits, these findings defy the expectations of theory and common sense, yet existing research provides no explanation. We turn to our interviews to explore employers' explanations of their hiring practices.

All Outside Information Is Suspect

Employers report that they receive, or have the opportunity to receive, a great deal of information. The applicants' teachers, employment agencies, tests, and applicants' past employers can all provide information on applicants. However, employers avoid using most of this information because they do not consider it trustworthy.

Some Teachers Are Biased   Teachers spend large, regular amounts of time with students in an arena in which they can assess both skills and attitudes. Consequently, teachers would seem a promising source of information about applicants just out of high school. However, employers are often wary of getting information from teachers. Fifteen of the employers we interviewed simply do not trust teachers. Another eighteen say that they trust teachers, but then they explain why teachers would not provide accurate or valuable information.

Many employers believe that teachers are biased, although they disagree as to whether teachers are too harsh or too indulgent in their assessments. Some state that teachers give unduly glowing recommendations because they care too much about their students. These employers believe that teachers care more about helping their students than about providing honest assessments. One employer feels that teachers simply will not say negative things. Another comments: "I think subjective feelings probably get in the way with a teacher getting involved out of school. . . . They want to see [their students] do well. . . . They might tend to exaggerate skills and abilities."

Teachers are also seen as likely to give unduly good assessments based on qualities that are not important in the workplace. "Teachers are not realistic," claims one employer who feels that all teachers will make comments about their students like: "He was always nice to me," and, "I want you to meet this nice young lady. She can sew and make all her own clothes and she cooks."

Others express the opposite fear—that teachers are too harsh in assessing students because they use irrelevant criteria. "The teacher might say, 'Well, this child is very brilliant or not very brilliant,' and I don't know if that's a really accurate description of their work capabilities," says one employer. "You know, they might not be the greatest as far as textbook, but they might just be a good worker." Another employer points out that "teachers . . . might just go for the grades" and that they may focus on students' shortcomings. "They didn't go in for after-school activities," such teachers might offer, or, "They're really bad at English."

In sum, employers generally ignore information from teachers because they mistrust the validity and relevance of the information.

Employment Agencies and Tests Are Inadequate   Employment agencies are paid to find good workers for employers; they are a market solution to the need for information on applicants. Seven employers report using private placement or temporary agencies, yet they have been dissatisfied with the outcome; the procedure is "not very successful, and it's costly." Another employer complains: "We've had dismal success with employment agencies. . . . Very expensive, and they're not a lot better than just putting an ad in the paper and getting 80 to 90 percent unqualified people who they say are qualified." Such agencies can provide employers with applicants, but they provide no assurance that the applicants are qualified. One employer describes a search for a new receptionist: "I was working with two agencies. One lady, she sent me about twenty people, and I didn't find anybody out of all those, so then I called another agency who sent me twelve to fifteen . . . who just didn't have the skills. That's a lot of people to go through."

Although agencies purport to be a liaison between employers and applicants, they do not know enough about applicants' capabilities or employers' needs to play that role successfully. Using agencies, therefore, does not address employers' need for trusted information.

Tests are another possible source of information. Tests allow employers to determine whether a job candidate has the skills they need and provide a reliable basis for comparing candidates. Yet most firms in our sample do not use tests; only ten say that they use them, and thirty-one explicitly state that they do not. Mentioning the difficulty of creating valid tests, employers report that they find tests cumbersome to develop and administer under Equal Employment Opportunity (EEO) guidelines. "We just haven't spent the time and a lot of effort in that area to develop something that we feel would encompass what we need to know," says one. "It's too difficult to . . . validate the test," says another.

In addition, tests fail to tell employers what they need to know about applicants' work habits. When asked why he does not use tests, one employer replies: "I guess I go right back to the statement I've probably made too many times already. We're looking for someone . . . [who can] listen to instructions [and has] the ability to want to learn this type of thing." Another employer points out the lack of connection between tests and on-the-job performance:

I don't believe in them. Some people are very competent at taking tests. It doesn't necessarily mean they're any better at doing a job. Other people tend to have a difficult time taking tests, and I just don't [care about test-taking skills], you know. It kinda goes back to just because you're good at taking a test does not necessarily mean you're going to be very good at what you do.

Of the ten employers in our sample who give tests, most (six) use only typing tests, which are easy to administer and interpret. Only two of the four who have committed the resources to develop non-clerical tests are small businesses, and one of those uses a personality test to find introverts (who they believe perform better than extroverts). Overall, employers generally regard both agencies and tests as difficult to use and unreliable. Neither source provides information that employers trust.

Former Employers May Be Biased   Former employers are another source of hiring information because they have relevant knowledge about applicants, including work habits. But employers often do not turn to past employers either. Twenty-two employers express doubts about the validity of the information they can get from other employers, often for the same reasons they do not trust teachers: they are afraid that the former employer uses irrelevant criteria or has an ulterior motive. Many hiring employers do not trust other employers' recommendations because they believe they will be ill founded or self-serving. The employers we interviewed offer the same kinds of concerns that arise in a Hobbesian world.

One employer thinks that some past employers might give candidates bad recommendations because of personal animosity.

> I'm always afraid personal attitudes can become involved. I have had people work for me whom I haven't liked at all, but they worked very well, and I don't have to like them and they don't have to like me. That's something I've learned. . . . I've worked with a lot of foremen, and I've seen personality come into play, which it should not.

Another believes that a bad reference on a former worker is probably the result of bad management rather than poor performance:

> There's a lot of good employees that have worked in a situation where maybe they just didn't get along with their boss, or the boss wasn't a good communicator, or they weren't given the proper direction, so they come off looking not that great in a reference for those reasons. That doesn't mean they wouldn't perform extremely well here.

In other cases, employers believe that past employers may deliberately provide false information in order to get rid of bad workers or to avoid unemployment insurance payments.

> I don't put a lot into former employers' recommendations. Normally, when an employee leaves, and you're not really sure of the reason why

they left, and if they're collecting unemployment, the sooner the previous employer gets him off the unemployment, the better it is. So they'll tell you just about anything so that you'll hire [the applicant]. Your unemployment rates go up three times the minute somebody files for unemployment.

Another employer claims that "if somebody is collecting [unemployment] compensation," their former employer is likely to call that applicant the "greatest guy in the world," because if hired, the applicant will then be "off compensation."

In contrast, other employers seem to view former employers' recommendations as potentially trustworthy and relevant. However, few actually expect these recommendations to be useful. Twenty-one employers say they would *like* to use referrals from past employers, because employers share common standards and practices. As one employer says, "I would probably trust an employer who . . . saw things more through my eyes." Past employers are expected to be able to say more about how a worker functions in a work environment. "He's had firsthand experience looking at an employee's performance, absenteeism, and also their honesty." "I expect the employer to indicate how the person functioned in the work environment, whether they're courteous and punctual, whether they show up for work."

However, despite their hypothetical expectations, these employers doubt that they can actually get meaningful recommendations from other employers. For such information to be meaningful, the receiver must trust that the evaluating employer is being forthcoming, and unfortunately, few hiring employers believe that former employers are candid. Employers know that they themselves are wary about the information they provide when asked for recommendations, so they assume that other employers are equally wary.

Moreover, employers say that they cannot be sure that the information they give in recommendations will be used wisely, and they worry that they will be sued for giving an honest appraisal. As one says: "Everyone is too afraid to say too much. They're afraid of lawsuits. You don't want to get in trouble for saying something bad about someone, even if it is the truth." Another reports that "sometimes outsiders . . . don't want to say anything negative because, you know, the laws, you have to watch what you even say about people these days." Another claims that "no one gives out that kind of information anymore. They won't even, you know, tell you why they let someone go . . . 'cause they're afraid there'll be some kind of lawyer action taken. So I don't bother to call."

Employers have found that they cannot rely on getting more than a confirmation of an applicant's title and start date from former employers because they fear liability lawsuits. Moreover, these same liability concerns limit their own responses. Thus, although employers would like to get honest appraisals from other employers, they doubt that others will feel free to provide them.

Employers Trust Their Own Judgments in Interviews

Employers rarely trust information that they get from teachers, agencies, tests, or past employers. They believe that there is too high a risk that such suppliers will give bad information because they have ulterior motives or different standards. In effect, employers describe themselves as being in the Hobbesian world, unable to trust most outside information.

Their response is also Hobbesian—self-reliance. Employers rely on their own judgments. All fifty-one employers we interviewed lean heavily on the information that they can gather themselves by directly interviewing applicants; all of the employers we spoke with rely on interviews. They say, for example, "The only measure we have really is the interview. The way the person handles himself—communication skills." Nearly all of these employers express strong confidence in their ability to assess applicants in interviews. "I guess my own judgment in an interview would take precedence over an outside recommendation."

Despite their confidence in their ability to assess applicants in interviews, research indicates that their reliance on interviews is not warranted by outcomes. Decades of psychological studies suggest that the popularity of interviewing is not justified by its accuracy in predicting future performance (Wanous 1992). For example, John Hunter and Robert Hunter (1984) found that the validity correlation between interviewer ratings and subsequent job performance is only .14, and Richard Arvey and Robert Faley (1988) found interviews to be unfair to racial minorities. Yet employers overwhelmingly choose to make their decisions based on the five to sixty minutes they spend interviewing candidates.   •

Moreover, employers use only certain material from interviews. Even though employers gather specific facts in their interviews, they make only limited use of such information because they believe that applicants often lie. As one employer put it:

I have found a great number of younger people [are] willing to falsify their résumés as to where they went, what they did, and so forth, and older folk too, but especially newer applicants and younger people claiming that they're a graduate of a given college, and they attended one semester, that they've gone on to postgraduate studies and hadn't graduated.

Applicants may gain a job by inflating their credentials, and they have little to lose if they believe they will not even be considered without inflated credentials.

Consequently, rather than use the information provided by applicants, employers use interviews to gather clues about future work performance from applicants' demeanor and speaking style. They refer to this process as relying on "instincts" or "trusting my gut."

Other researchers have also noted the strong tendency of interviewers to make decisions based on superficial observations. For example, in one simulation, interviewers gave higher ratings to applicants who exhibited greater amounts of eye contact, head movement, smiling, and other nonverbal behaviors, and such movements accounted for 80 percent of the variance between candidate ratings (Arvey and Campion 1982). Tessler and Sushelsky (1978) similarly found statistically significant effects for eye contact and social status.

Although this literature seems to assume that employers would be surprised by these findings and might change their behaviors after learning about them, our interviews suggest that such findings would not be a surprise to them. Employers readily report such behaviors themselves and justify them as reasonable, and some are quite confident about the predictive powers of their observations. Indeed, employers state that interviews are primarily used for the physical cues they provide, and that these superficial cues provide the basis for their hiring decisions. Nearly all employers discuss interviewing in terms of the information gathered from the applicants' demeanor; they rarely discuss the content of applicants' statements about their qualifications or experience, explaining, "It's how they present themselves." When asked what might indicate that a person will not work out, one employer offers: "Their ability to be at ease or not at ease. Inability to look at you when they speak to you. Inability to explain what they've done, to verbalize that. And their appearance."

Most employers consider eye contact important, but some choose more unusual physical gestures to assess competence. One employer shuns individuals who slouch. Another says, "You can tell a lot by the way that they walk." One employer looks at facial expressions to decide whether the individual really wants the job. Some employers use these criteria even for manufacturing and other non-customer-oriented jobs.

Similarly, many employers judge applicants by their appearance. In describing the importance of appearance, one employer in the financial industry says, "Hair's important. It doesn't have to be totally conservative, but not wild and frizzy." Another employer, a manufacturer, explains the focus on appearance this way:

I was brought up that you never discussed business unless you were in a suit. Not even a sport coat. You were in a suit. Your pants matched your coat, and you had a tie on, and that was it. The first thirty seconds you spend with someone you have an opinion formed. A lot of that is [based] on the appearance of that person.

This employer proudly announces that he forms his opinion within the first thirty seconds, which is not enough time to hear what a person has to say but plenty of time to look them over. Although the suit criterion might be useful for assessing how well a person would fit into an office setting, this employer uses the suit test to hire for manufacturing jobs for which workers would never wear a suit.

Finally, although employers make few references to the information they gather during an interview, they often mention the need for candidates to converse with style. One employer "judge[s] someone not only on qualities, but also on communication—way of talking," and another says, "I pretty much get the feeling in dealing with people, asking the right questions, and seeing how the person reacts and how they answer." It is hard to overstate the importance that these employers give to conversational style when hiring, even though many of these jobs are in production, where speaking with style is not required.

When employers rely on their "gut" or their impressions in an interview rather than on more objective criteria, there is a strong risk that unintended biases will sneak into their assessments. For example, eye contact is demanded by most employers, but some Asian, Hispanic, and Native American cultures consider it disrespectful for a young person to stare an older person in the eye. Employers often think of a lack of eye contact as "shifty," but the applicant may only be trying to be polite. Moreover, the opposite risk was suggested in some employers' reports of some applicants staring at them in ways that seemed insolent or defiant. Even beyond cultural nuances, in a society in which race remains salient, it is hard for a white employer to know whether an uncomfortable feeling comes from an astute assessment or from racial bias (Arvey and Faley 1988). As Neckerman and Kirschenman (1991, 814) conclude, "However qualified they are for the job, inner-city black applicants are more likely to fail subjective 'tests' of productivity given during the interview."

In sum, interviews are the primary determinant of hiring. From interviews, employers believe that they can infer which applicants have the requisite attitude, interpersonal skills, and academic grounding to do the job. Employers believe that they can make broad inferences from interviews, even if they last only fifteen minutes. Moreover, employers base their inferences on applicants' most superficial traits, including posture, dress, and style of speaking. Although such observations may provide rough estimates about social skills, they are unlikely to provide much information about a person's diligence, attitude, or basic math and English skills—that is, the qualities in which employers say they are most interested. By not trusting outside sources of information, employers judge job applicants according to less fair and more superficial criteria.

The Results of "Trusting My Gut"   In the end, the proof should be in the results. If superficial traits allow employers to choose good employees, then their methods of choosing are adequate. As noted earlier, however, employers are not satisfied with their employees, and ten of them suggest that the hiring process is responsible for bad judgments and poor employees. They note that those who seem like promising candidates in an interview often turn out to be bad workers. As one reports, "Some of the few that I thought would be outstanding crashed and burned." Another notes, "I'll have an employee that really seemed upbeat and aggressive. Once they started work, they're very laid back, continually late or tardy, uninterested in the work." Another laments, "You know, it is more of a feel that you have. You never really know till you get somebody in. I've personally been duped both ways." Although these employers, like most of the others in our sample, say that they trust their own judgment and the power of their "gut" in making hiring decisions, they also confess that they have had many failures. Their confidence in their powers of assessment are often unsupported by their experiences. Some employers even directly complain about the failures of interviews.

> An interview is a bad game. It's a bad setup. We can't really learn much in an interview except the very obvious characteristics of a person. If a person has any skill at all, in being deceptive or a good actor, you can learn next to nothing in an interview.

"You really don't know how they're gonna turn out," admits another employer, "because you have to go with your feeling, but you really don't know for sure about anything." One employer even notes that one problem with hiring people based on their interviews is that the employer often ends up hiring good interviewers, not good workers: "I don't necessarily need somebody who's been polished and aired at the interview. We've hired people like that before too, of all age groups, and later found that the thing they do best is interview."

More often, however, employers retain faith in interviews, even as they note that the process is flawed. "I think I trust myself, but then you hire someone [who], in an interview, may seem fine, and on the job they just deteriorate. Or it could be the other way around too. But you know, with experience I think I've got to be a fairly good judge of who might work out." This employer still believes that he is a good judge of character, in spite of noting that he cannot reliably identify good workers. Similarly, when asked whether he trusts his judgment from an interview over recommendations, another employer would go with "my own judgment in an interview. It's hard to say; it's just how you went away feeling about the person after you talked, the impressions they made. But my judgments have been wrong in the past."

It is ironic that plant and office managers think of themselves as hardheaded and rational but make their hiring decisions based on feelings, not facts. Many employers who report trusting their own feelings after speaking with a candidate will admit that such decisions have been wrong before. This is the crux of the problem. Employers know that their methods frequently lead to bad hiring decisions, but their mistrust of other information often leaves them with no acceptable alternative.

Using Social Networks to Obtain Trusted Information

Employers could obtain abundant information from outside sources, but their mistrust leads them to ignore most forms of information and makes hiring much more difficult. This mistrust effectively discounts the value of available information on applicants' past history and thereby prevents employers from considering past performance; this mistrust is also likely to reduce the quality of employers' hiring decisions. We may speculate that employer mistrust of information sources may limit youths' motivation to prepare for future employment.

However, employers do use outside information when it is conveyed through a social network of trusted relationships. They trust those to whom they are connected, and there are some relationships in which sender and receiver share enough trust to be willing to pass on and use information. The most common of these is the relationship between employers and their employees.

Employers Trust Their Own Employees   Employers' favorite sources of information on potential employees are their current ones. Thirty-three employers say that they rely on employee referrals to get qualified workers. (The other eighteen do not mention either choosing to use employee referrals or choosing not to.) One employer proclaims, "Word of mouth is absolutely the best!" Because current workers know the employers' standards and expectations, employers believe that they will recommend only those able to do the work. Employers view the success of individual employees as evidence that they understand the skills and attitudes needed to do the job well, so employers trust their recommendations. One employer values the judgments of current employees because "they're comfortable with us, we're comfortable with them." The social relationship allows employers to trust information from employees.

Employers also believe that employees have self-interested reasons for not recommending low-quality individuals. First, they will have to work with the new employee and would not want to do extra work to compensate for that person's shortcomings. Second, they would not risk their reputation by bringing in someone who is not good: "Nobody wants to send someone in who's gonna make them look bad," notes one employer. Employers assume that workers take personal pride in their judgment: "When they recommend somebody, they understand that they're putting their name and character on the line." Employers also consider the relationship between the employee and the applicant beneficial, because they can rely on the employee to provide an accurate portrayal of the work to the applicant. The current employees, notes one employer,

> also understand what the job entails, so the person isn't coming in under any false hopes. I'm pretty sure that this person, whoever recommended them, has told them the good and the bad parts of the job, so I don't have to worry about letting them down and usually they don't let us down. It works out pretty good.

Because workers can explain the merits and drawbacks of the applicant to the employer, and of the job to the applicant, both parties can make informed decisions, thus reducing turnover: "They seem to stay longer," one employer observes. Many of these employers actively encourage employees to recommend people for employment, but two go so far as to have incentive programs: they pay a bonus to employees for bringing in new workers. For these two employers, employee referrals are valuable enough to pay for.

Only two employers express doubts about the value of employee referrals, but these two exceptions elucidate the mechanisms that give the process value. Both are large companies where human resources personnel rather than managers do the hiring; thus, at neither company is there a personal relationship between the employee making a referral and the person doing the hiring. One of these human resources managers tries to compensate for this lack of relationship by reminding recommending employees that she is counting on their judgment. "You'll also say, 'Hey, people have brought other people in and it hasn't worked out, you know. Are you sure that you would back this person up 100 percent?' And if you have a good rapport, your saying that . . . makes you feel better." Similarly, she tries to appeal to the "rapport" she has with that employee and assesses the strength of their personal connection when deciding how much to trust the employee's referral. The personal quality of relationships and the perceived sense of obligation form the basis for trust in employee referrals; when these are weakened, employee referrals work less well. However, even these two employers who are relatively less supportive of employee referrals than other employers still use and value them.

Although employee referrals allow employers to get better information than they usually obtain in interviews, the two methods share a common drawback—the likelihood of bias. Employees tend to refer people like themselves. If the workplace is already diverse, then employee referrals reflect that diversity. As one employer says, "We have a lot of minorities, so getting applications from people they know is not a problem." But for other companies, preexisting biases are merely replicated. As one employer explains: "Probably half the people we hire are through employee contacts. It's the people in the know, which is very unfortunate for those people who aren't in the know." One employer explicitly notes that his firm's hiring procedure conflicts with its efforts to meet Equal Employment Opportunity guidelines: "It hurts your EEO and AAP [affirmative action plan] type of plan because basically you're going to get referred similar people that they associate with, which creates a problem. But you tend to get very qualified people that way." Of course, employers who are less committed to such goals, especially those too small to be covered by EEO guidelines, may feel little conflict about this issue. Although employers choose their hiring procedures on their perceived merits, both employee referrals and employment interviews have implications for the ethnic composition of new hires.

Some Employers Trust Certain Teachers   Although many employers look to their internal relationships with workers for information on potential applicants, seven of the employers we interviewed have developed relationships that allow them to secure trusted information outside of their organization. These seven have developed long-term connections with vocational teachers at local high schools. The long-term nature of the relationship allows the employer to convey expectations to the teacher and to be sure that the teacher makes recommendations based on relevant standards.

Employers using such information are quite satisfied with the quality of the youths recommended by teachers. One employer explains:

> I think we've had good success because we have been able to reach inside the schools and talk specifically to certain . . . teachers . . . who handle these students. And they generally call us, and the positive [aspects] of those contacts for us are that we're getting straight students. . . . I don't know if the schools are doing a great job. . . . Our success has been good because we've been handed, I think, a few of the better ones.

This employer does not get quality applicants because the schools are turning out only high-quality students, but because he can rely on the ability of certain vocational teachers to identify good workers. The long-term nature of the relationship allows trust to develop. As one employer explains: "You get to know the teachers and get to know they pretty much tell the truth and they tell it pretty straight." Over time this employer has learned that the teachers he knows are honest, and their integrity allows him to trust their recommendations. Another who had a relationship with a high school for fifteen years notes: "I think there's a lot of guys like myself that would be more than glad to work with schools only because it's helped us [identify good workers]." Another notes: "They did a good evaluation of the student before he ever got here, so . . . you had a real good idea before they ever came in what type of students you were getting." A broader survey by Bishop (1993) suggests that such trust is well placed. He finds that new hires recommended by a vocational teacher are 15 percent more productive than those hired without such a referral.

Moreover, some employers report that if they had trusted relationships with teachers, they would be willing to use their recommendations. Several employers who lack such contacts and express reluctance to use outside sources note that if they had a long-term relationship with a teacher, they would have more faith in the teacher's fairness and they would use the teacher's information when choosing employees. One employer explains:

> I mean, obviously I'd put a lot of weight on what a high school teacher said too, if I felt I had somebody that [I knew]. . . . If I would just take a cold call from a high school teacher that I didn't know, I would worry about that. But if it was somebody that I knew, that would carry a lot more weight.

Although employers who find all school information irrelevant are unlikely to use outside sources, employers who simply doubt teachers' fairness and reliability might use schools if they knew the teachers well enough to believe that they agree on standards, or if they had developed a relationship with a particular teacher.

Conclusions

As the common wisdom claims, youth labor market problems arise when employers have difficulty getting workers with the skills they seek. Yet our findings indicate that the problem is not the one suggested by signaling theory—that employers do not get enough information—but that they have great difficulty identifying information that is trustworthy and useful. We find that employers have access to much information but they mistrust the dependability and usefulness of information from people with whom they do not have a relationship.

As we have noted, employers' mistrust of available information has several implications. First, *employers' mistrust prevents most of them from seeking or using information from schools and previous employers.* Employers are deprived of potentially valuable information, and the quality of their decisions is likely to suffer. Employers complain that they cannot find employees with good academic skills and work habits, yet they ignore pertinent information about these attributes because they feel they cannot trust it. Although their mistrust may be warranted at times, it clearly deprives them of information that is relevant to their stated needs and creates the circumstances for their own poor selections.

Second, these findings suggest that *for employers to act in the way human capital and signaling theory predict, not only must they receive information, but they must receive it in the context of a social infrastructure that reassures them of its trustworthiness and relevance.* Indeed, we find that some employers have found ways to overcome the problem of mistrust—they use information from their own workers and from long-term social networks. These sources create a social context that allows employers to trust information and to use it to make better selections. Although researchers have long recognized workers' use of casual networks (Granovetter 1973), Granovetter (1995, 162–65) has recently written about employers' use of more formal networks, reviewing research on Japanese recruiting networks (Rosenbaum and Kariya 1989), German apprenticeships (Harhoff and Kane 1994), and some findings from the United States (Rosenbaum and Binder 1997). This research suggests that such successful networks can provide information that employers trust.

Third, *employers' mistrust of school information makes youths' school performance irrelevant to their future employment.* In effect, employers' neglect of school information may remove the main incentive for work-bound students to learn academic skills and work habits in school. Students may infer that nothing they do in school will help them get better jobs. Consequently, employers' own actions may be contributing to the poor academic skills that they decry. Rather than blaming schools, they may have themselves to blame.

Fourth, *employers' mistrust of outside information forces them to rely on information they can gather in interviews.* Research findings that interviews select on superficial attributes are no surprise to employers, who explicitly state that their inferences are based on observations of posture, dress, hairstyle, eye contact, and style of speaking. Although plausibly relevant to customer service jobs, these attributes were used to assess candidates for manufacturing and other jobs in which customer contact is unlikely. Moreover, even for customer service jobs, employers' greatest complaints are often about workers' academic skills and work habits, so it is not difficult to see why their hiring procedures do not serve these ends. Our findings help explain why research has found that interviews are poor predictors of performance (Wanous 1992).

Fifth, *although employment discrimination is sometimes intentional, these results suggest another possibility—that discrimination may arise from the choice of hiring procedures.* Employers' mistrust of outside information, and their resulting choice to base hiring on interviews, may increase hiring discrimination, because employers' snap judgments are based on superficial appearances and "gut feelings." Research has shown that interviews are unfair to racial minorities (Arvey and Faley 1988). Similarly, worker referrals, which provide a dependable source of information, can have negative implications for the hiring of minorities. It is no wonder that employers deny discriminatory intent, while many minorities believe that employers are deliberately discriminatory (MacLeod 1987). Employers may choose hiring procedures on their perceived merits for providing trusted information, but these procedures have repercussions for discrimination that employers may not intend or consider. Other hiring procedures might reduce bias. Indeed, while it is recognized that employment tests are often biased against minorities, Neckerman and Kirschenman (1991) found that employers who use employment tests are *more* likely to hire minorities than employers who lack such tests. Testing may be biased, but the alternatives to testing may be worse.

Sixth, *by providing more dependable information, social networks may make hiring selections more meritocratic*. Social networks are often seen as arising from conscious intentions to create social preferences and biases. Although this may sometimes be true, as in ethnic social networks, employers describe social networks as meritocratic, motivated by the need to obtain dependable information. For employers, networks are a way to assess applicants more accurately and to hire people with stronger skills. The networks that employers have reported are not preexisting social connections that are used to give preferences to certain groups; rather, they use the networks created during the process of hiring to serve their need for trustworthy information. Of course, once formed, such networks do work to the advantage of some individuals and the disadvantage of others, but that is a consequence of this means of identifying merit, not the intent.

This leads to an awkward paradox: employers are using a system of preferential treatment in order to find meritorious applicants. Although some would argue that a more open system is preferable, open systems do not necessarily lead to more meritocratic or less discriminatory selections. As noted earlier, when employers lack trustworthy outside information on an applicant, they rely on the idiosyncratic and biased information they get from interviews. The evidence suggests that allowing applicants to plead their own cases in interviews does not lead to merit-based selections.

Free markets may open access to all applicants, but disadvantaged youth are less likely to have the personal connections used in employee referrals to give them knowledge of the job openings and trusted recommendations (Granovetter 1974/1995). In contrast, schools are among our most democratic institutions, and school-employer relationships can open jobs to a wider range of young people.

Social networks limit access to certain schools, but many of the schools that employers mention are low-income, predominantly minority, urban schools. Several employers say that their teacher contacts are a good way to identify well-qualified minority applicants and to get trusted information about them. Two different banks mention that they get minority employees through their high school contacts, who give them trusted information about their students' honesty and dependability. A manufacturer mentions one of the vocational teachers at a local urban school as a source of minority candidates. He reports that this teacher does a good job of teaching the skills and work habits required in his workplace and gives recommendations that he can trust. Disadvantaged youth in these schools may gain job access that would have been unlikely in "open markets."

Thus, employers can make hiring decisions based on merit criteria that they could not obtain outside of trusted relationships. Because they trust specific teachers to give them candid and relevant evaluations, particularly on hard-to-assess qualities like work habits, teachers can spread the advantage of connections to youth who lack personal connections and who would do poorly in the more "objective" system of hiring walk-ins. Our linked employers say that they do get minority workers through teachers' recommendations, and urban employers prefer urban workers because they believe that short commutes improve attendance. We urge further research to determine whether and to what extent such linkages create ethnic, gender, or social class preferences.

These results have important implications for social policy. Training programs for disadvantaged groups are often ineffective (Betsey et al. 1985; Stern et al. 1995), but social policies that encourage school-employer linkages could help disadvantaged students and create a more systematic pathway from school to work, one similar to (though weaker than) the pathways in nations that have formal linkages (Hamilton 1990; Rosenbaum and Kariya 1990). Our evidence suggests that these linkages improve employers' willingness to hire youth for responsible jobs, and other research indicates that high school graduates whose school helps them find a job get better jobs than those who rely on want ads or direct applications (Holzer 1995; Rosenbaum and Roy 1996).

This research is only a first step to understanding how employers make hiring decisions. Although "weak ties" may be sufficient for workers to get job leads, these findings indicate that employers need "strong ties" to get the kind of trustworthy information about applicants that would reduce costly hiring mistakes (see also Kariya and Rosenbaum 1995). Although economic theory describes employers' motives, social conditions affect their choice of information and their decision to participate in social infrastructures to obtain trusted information. These results indicate the need for further sociological research on the ways in which social conditions affect economic processes.

= Chapter 7 =

Ships Passing in the Night: The Sociological Foundations of Economic Transactions

F UNCTIONALIST theories assume that various parts of society interact to serve their mutual needs and the needs of society.[1] For instance, sociological functionalism assumes that schools socialize and select youth for employers, and consequently that employers will come to them for hiring youth. Even some critics who reject the conservative premises of functionalism concur that schools serve employers' needs, and that employers use schools' evaluations in their hiring decisions (Bowles and Gintis 1976). Some economists make similar assumptions. They assume that any good transaction that could happen will happen, that markets are efficient, and that therefore the best matches between producers and consumers generally do occur.

These views are rational and comfortable, but often wrong. In particular, the youth labor market poses a serious challenge to these views because it works so badly. Transactions often fail to occur: the unemployment rate of youth (age sixteen to nineteen) has been approximately double that of young adults (age twenty to twenty-four) for the last decade (NCES 1997a). The youth labor market also seems insensitive to the quality of matches: youth with the best high school records do not obtain better jobs or better wages, nor are they less likely to be unemployed (Bills 1992; Borman 1991; Crain 1984; Gamoran 1994; Griffin et al. 1981; Kang and Bishop 1986; Rosenbaum and Kariya 1991). Although many employers complain about the academic skills and work habits of their job applicants (Boesel 1994), fewer than 5 percent of employers use schools when hiring high school graduates (Bishop 1993; Holzer 1995), and few employers use schools' evaluations (Crain 1984; Rosenbaum and Kariya 1991).

Yet research suggests that schools could serve employers' needs. Employers who develop long-term linkages with teachers are more likely to trust the information they receive, to hire youth, and to be pleased with young workers (Miller and Rosenbaum 1997). Moreover, research finds that high school graduates who find their jobs through school placement get better occupations (Holzer 1995, table 3.4) and better pay even nine years after graduation (Rosenbaum, Miller, and Roy 1996).

Thus, although functionalist theories are correct in assuming that schools could help employers' hiring decisions, employers rarely take advantage of this potential. These findings present a challenge to functionalist theories. If these transactions are so good, then why are they so rare? This chapter examines this question.

Institutional Obstacles to the Operation of Economic and Functionalist Theories

Some economic theories suggest that a process that gives an actor an "edge" in the market should become widespread; those who use it should be more successful, and those who do not should be at a disadvantage and eventually fail. Thus, we would expect beneficial school-employer linkages to be more common. Although the failure of the market to provide expected, rational results is far from uncommon (Etzioni 1988), we sought to understand why this particular rational result does not occur, and more broadly, why markets sometimes fail to support efficient transactions.

Sociological theory similarly suggests that employers will interact with schools. Émile Durkheim (1912/1956) said that schools exist to prepare youth for society, including their role in economic production. Samuel Bowles and Herbert Gintis (1976) take this a step further and suggest that employers use schools to mold students to their needs and that vocational programs are designed to prepare students for working-class jobs and channel them toward those jobs. Thus, we have a rare circumstance in which classical economic theory and sociological theory agree: both predict that employers will make efforts to recruit workers from schools.

Unfortunately, this prediction is often wrong. Stephen Brint and Jerome Karabel (1989), seeking to verify the Bowles-Gintis (1976) hypothesis, found the opposite in their study of community colleges: employers were quite uninterested in using community colleges as a source of workers. Other researchers have also noted that employers are reluctant to work with high schools (Useem 1986), and that employers do not use high school grades in their hiring decisions (Crain 1994; Bills 1988a).

In response to the failed predictions of neoclassical economic and sociological theories, new theories have arisen in both fields. The new institutional economics considers the efficiencies of institutional relationships and calls for studies of actors in contexts (Williamson 1975; Lazear 1979; Rosen 1982; DiMaggio and Powell 1991). Sociological models contend that markets often "depend on the nature of personal relations and the network of relations between and within firms" (Granovetter 1985, 502; see also Dore 1983; Dalton 1959, 170–73). Instead of assuming that information is always trusted, these models describe some ways in which information is given meaning through social networks. "People prefer to deal with individuals of known reputation, or, even better, with individuals they have dealt with before. Social relations . . . are mainly responsible for the production of trust in economic life" (Granovetter 1985, 490–91). As this theory posits, if employers want to reduce information problems in hiring youth, they could establish relationships with teachers. Indeed, we have found that some employers do, and that it does indeed improve their hiring of youth (Miller and Rosenbaum 1996). Given the success of this method, this chapter asks the question: Why don't more employers establish relationships with teachers?

Within the specific context of school-employer transactions, we also seek to examine some of the institutional components required for market transactions to occur. The literature of the new institutional economics describes the underlying environments in which people interact. These institutional environments are described as "taken-for-granted scripts, rules and classifications" (DiMaggio and Powell 1991, 15), programmed actions or common responses to situations (Jepperson 1991), and "both supraorganizational patterns of activity through which humans conduct their material life in time and space, and symbolic systems through which they categorize that activity and infuse it with meaning" (Friedland and Alford 1991, 232). The new institutionalists seek to identify the underlying conditions in which people interact, beyond a simple focus on self-interest. Similarly, we seek to clarify these underlying concepts with two distinctions. First, rather than describing broad institutional conditions, we seek to describe the specific conditions required for market transactions to occur. Second, to find out how things do happen, sometimes it is useful to look at why they do not. We analyze why some beneficial transactions do *not* occur in order to understand elements of the institutions governing market transactions.

This examination suggests that a variety of social factors can prevent market transactions from occurring. The *lack of a social conception* that school linkages could be useful for hiring is the first stumbling block. Second, even if employers have such a conception, their *lack of knowledge* about whom to contact prevents linkages from being established. Third, even if employers contact the right person, their efforts are often ignored or ineffective because of the *lack of clear norms about procedures for establishing contacts.* Finally, the *lack of clear norms about responsibility* prevents employers from taking the actions needed to maintain linkages; as a result, incipient contacts often falter. We find that schools and employers take various initiatives to make contact with each other, but that these efforts are often neither recognized nor reciprocated and, like ships passing in the night, no transactions occur. We show that some employers overcome these social factors to create linkages. We find that transactions do not proceed automatically from functional needs or economic incentives, but rather that *social conceptions and norms are necessary preconditions if market transactions are to occur.* The results support new social network models in sociology as well as the new institutional economics.

Methodology

Since it is difficult to get detailed information about employers' behaviors on these issues using surveys, and it is difficult to conduct observations over many organizations, we conducted one-hour interviews in employers' offices to get their detailed descriptions of how they deal with these issues. To discover how employers relate to schools, researchers must go to those who actually do the hiring. Rather than rely on the views of corporate executives, we interviewed the plant, office, and (less frequently) human resources managers who hire entry-level workers. This chapter uses the interviews with the fifty-one firms described in chapter 5.

When Transactions Fail to Happen

Economic theories suggest that worthwhile transactions will occur, yet commonsense experience suggests that this is not always the case. Why do some transactions occur while others do not? We find that transactions related to school-employer linkages fail for a number of reasons. Employers do not know that high schools can be useful, whom to contact, how to initiate a contact (what to offer), or who is responsible for maintaining the contact.

Employers Do Not Know That Schools Can Be Useful to Them

The first step in a transaction is an awareness that it is possible and can provide something of value. Economic theories assume that, if a transaction is worthwhile, it will occur. If the actors do not understand that possibility, however, it will not occur. Hammacher-Schlemmer might have exactly the appliance you require, but if you do not know the store exists or what it offers, an exchange will not occur. Unknown choices are not real choices because they do not exist in the eyes of the choice maker. In business, most stores address this lack of information through advertising, but high schools do not advertise.

The lack of a social conception that school linkages are possible is the first stumbling block to the transaction. Some employers express surprise at the idea that schools can help them hire workers. Others do not consider working with schools because they do not realize that high schools have anything to offer them. They believe that performance in high school is indicative only of an ability to memorize trivial facts, a skill not generally useful on the job. What schools teach and evaluate is considered irrelevant to the work world. As one employer explains, "Students might not be the greatest as far as textbooks, but they might just be a good worker," and another agreed: "Some students can be just atrocious in school and be the best employee."

Employers assume that teachers base their judgments on unimportant criteria. For example, we were told that "teachers . . . sometimes lose touch with the real world, frankly. I don't mean to insult you or anyone else, but a different way of life and different qualities and considerations are involved in their work and their outlook." Many employers do not believe that teachers' evaluations are of any use to them.

Employers Do Not Know Whom to Contact

Even if employers have the social conception of an employer-school linkage, their lack of knowledge about whom they should contact prevents linkages from starting. A few employers have some notion that schools can be a source of workers, and they have taken the initiative to contact schools. Since most schools lack a job placement professional, however, employers do not know whom to contact.

Employers often decide to contact guidance counselors. Two considerations make this *seem* like an appropriate course of action. First, unlike most school staff, counselors have an office and are generally near a telephone. Second, counselors see many students, they know students' career plans, and they are nominally responsible for advising students about career plans.

But in fact, counselors are generally not good contacts for employers. Counselors place low priority on job counseling (Armor 1971; Rosenbaum, Miller, and Krei 1996). Indeed, since their major responsibility is college counseling, they often do not know very much about the requirements for the jobs that high school graduates could get.

As a result, employers generally report having had bad experiences when they contacted counselors. For instance, one employer reports that he learned about counselors when he tried to inform them about his occupational field. He discovered that counselors have been trained and socialized to help college-bound students but they have little grounding or interest in helping work-bound students. He was very disappointed with the result:

> Counselors are the worst bunch of bums. The counselors are trained to tell kids which college to go to. They've never come around here and said, "I'd like to learn about your industry." When I was president of TMA [Tooling Manufacturing Association], we invited the counselors in, and it was abominable, the low turnout. It was during their working hours, of course, but they wouldn't dream of coming after hours to visit a factory or anything. So counselors are a shameful group of people that America pays wages to.

Another employer told a similar story:

> I don't think that [the schools] are good role models in leadership. The reason I say that is I've been trying to get the counselors—I had a job fair a few years ago. I must have contacted about twenty different schools [and] found out who the education counselor or the development counselor was with work programs. I tried to get them to come to our location. We had one or two come. What that kind of told me is that all they're doing is just buying time. They're not really there helping the students out, I think.

It is easy to see why counselors would doubt the value of meeting with the Tooling Manufacturing Association when their job duties stress helping students get into college. Even if employers make all the outreach efforts, counselors are unlikely to respond if they see no relevant outcome.

Nonetheless, employers are right in believing that counselors should be concerned with the job market. Over 35 percent of high school graduates do not attend college, and the numbers are even larger in urban schools (Howe 1988). Moreover, since most students have jobs during college, a large proportion of high school graduates will need help understanding the job market (Stern et al. 1995). Employers are rightfully frustrated that their efforts to reach high schools with information about their needs are ignored by the school staff who are nominally responsible for career guidance.

When employers try to initiate a transaction with schools, they run up against a structural problem. While employers are focused primarily on hiring work-bound students, schools focus on college-bound students because college enrollments are perceived as a measure of a high school's success. The problem is exacerbated when employers, not knowing whom to contact, get in touch with counselors, whose major responsibility is promoting college admissions. As we note later, the few employers who contact vocational teachers find that they are much more responsive and helpful.

Employers Lack Clear Norms About Making Contact with Schools

Even if employers contact the right person, their efforts are often ignored or ineffective because of the lack of clear norms about procedures for establishing contacts. Economic theory assumes that good transactions will readily happen, but most transactions are governed by norms and established procedures. Although many transactions are straightforward (paying the cashier the price on the label), others are more complex and full of unwritten procedural rules. Restaurants do not list procedural rules, but if you fail to close your menu, you may wait a long time before the waiter takes your order. The black market announces no public rules, but if you request a transaction in a way that arouses suspicion, the transaction will not happen.

Similarly, the procedural rules for employer-school connections are neither well developed nor explicit. The initiator must guess how to proceed, and the respondent may or may not know what is expected in response. Like a transaction on the black market, both parties may be unclear on how to initiate a transaction. Without clear operating procedures, employers seeking to initiate a transaction must create their own procedures. We find that their initiatives are often not understood.

Frequently, their first gesture is to contact schools and offer something they think the school will value.[2] Although employers believe that school staff should help students find jobs because helping students is their duty, they also recognize that they themselves can sweeten the pot by providing something directly to the school, or even by helping a particular vocational teacher. Sometimes the gifts are tangible, such as printing ink for a graphics instructor, or scrap metal for a machining teacher. More frequently, employers offer field trips to tour their workplaces. This offer more pointedly meets employers' needs, because they believe that a teacher who understands their work is better able to identify students who would be appropriate job candidates, and that students might be more interested in joining the company after seeing the work in progress. In addition, both gifts and tours offer employers and teachers an opportunity to meet and perhaps develop into a relationship based on job referrals. Like an old-fashioned courtship ritual, employers offer gifts in exchange for time to get acquainted and decide whether a long-term relationship should ensue.

Teachers, however, often do not understand employers' intentions. They do not always recognize employers' overtures as efforts to build long-term relationships. Employers report that teachers often take these offers at face value: their response is based only on whether the offer is immediately beneficial to them—whether they need the particular supplies or want to take the tour—and they do not consider the pattern of give-and-take that could be established. Thus, many employers' efforts at outreach are dismissed by teachers as not of immediate use.

For example, one employer says that a teacher responded enthusiastically to a gift of graphics supplies but did not respond to a subsequent offer to give the class a tour of her printing firm. The employer feels that the teacher failed to "follow through" by not providing his students with an opportunity to make the class more relevant. She says, "I would think that they would, for sure, see how what those kids were doing pertains to real life." In spite of the initial rejection of an opportunity to develop the relationship further, this employer retains hope that the initial donation of printing ink will lead to a stronger relationship with the school in the future.

> Giving the ink to those two at [the school]—maybe now having come out here and talking a couple of times, I feel more that there could be a relationship between the school and here. That's really the first time. And whether or not I need to go to the schools and see them and introduce myself—but there's no time for that.

This employer seems to realize that she could make the effort of going to see teachers at *their* workplaces, but her comment that she does not have the time to do so ironically mirrors complaints that teachers do not make the time to help employers. Another employer hopes that the early connection will result in leads on good students that he can follow up according to the needs of his own schedule: "Usually, they initiate a contact, based on a student or a program that they are pushing for a while, and then our response is usually in time with filling our needs. If we get particularly busy in May, for example, then I might make a big push to see if in fact there are some outbound seniors."

Even when teachers understand that employers are looking for workers and they agree to participate in this effort, the two parties may still have different conceptions of the nature of the transaction. Teachers often see themselves as providing employers with simple information and access to a little-tapped labor market. In this role, they simply tell students about the potential job and send those who are interested to the employers—a fairly simple task. Employers, on the other hand, are often hoping teachers will prescreen students. Employers expect teachers to provide them with more detailed information about the work-readiness of the students they send along, or better yet, to send them only students who meet threshold qualifications.

With these contradictory understandings of the teacher's role, it is not surprising that employers who do manage to initiate a link with schools are often disappointed with the results. Employers are often unpleasantly surprised that teachers do not play an active role in placing students. They remark on the minimal help provided by the schools they have contacted. Says one:

> Some of the schools just put your name on the bulletin board, and the kids contact you. The teachers, to my surprise, are not good about finding their students work. I had one young boy come in one time, I think the teacher had given me his name, and it didn't go anywhere. And the teacher made no follow-up.

Teachers see bulletin board notices as the proper response to employers' requests, but employers are disappointed because putting up notices does not ensure that they will see only appropriate job applicants. Similarly, another employer complains that teachers do not consider his request a high priority. School staff, she says "don't respond unless you badger the teachers involved in a specific discipline. . . . They won't go through the effort of finding someone to send you."

Unlike the employers who approach counselors, this employer has learned to approach teachers in specific fields, but she still finds that most school staff do not make an effort to find candidates who will match her needs. As a result, teachers believe they have been responsive, while employers are disappointed.

In sum, employers and teachers have contradictory understandings of what is happening in their transactions. Without a clear conception of what the transaction will entail, one party can be dissatisfied without the other even knowing it.

Employees Do Not Know Who Is Responsible for Maintaining Linkages

Finally, the lack of clear norms about responsibility prevents employers from taking the actions necessary to maintain linkages, so incipient contacts falter. Even when employers successfully use linkages, they may not fully appreciate them, know how to maintain them, or know that they must maintain them. We found that many employers who find good workers through a teacher in a onetime transaction fail to develop the connection. In nine cases, employers called schools and had good luck finding teachers who recommended successful employees, but they never repeated the process. They did not see this interaction as the beginning of a long-term relationship, and they never called the school again. Two of these employers contacted schools that our research has shown to be especially conscientious about matching good students to good employers; if they had followed up, perhaps they would have developed a long-term supplier of good employees.

Even more remarkably, some employers who had steady, positive linkages with vocational teachers over several years let the connection fall apart when the teachers they worked with left the school. The linkages ended because the employers feel no responsibility to maintain the relationship and assume that good matches are normal and that maintaining linkages requires no special effort on their part.

At first, we suspected that linkages might have ended for economic reasons—perhaps they were not cost-effective—but employers who failed to maintain linkages never mention high costs or small benefits. Instead, their descriptions are couched in normative terms. Of the ten employers who discontinued long-term linkages, two are not hiring, one gives no reason, and six of the other seven present a normative argument that it is teachers' responsibility to maintain linkages. When teachers stop taking that responsibility, these employers believe that it is not their responsibility to do so.

Ironically, then, while neoclassical economists see the market model as an objective theory, employers see normative implications in the labor market and the laissez-faire ideal: employers who want to be efficient should encourage competition among suppliers and should not forge stable supplier preferences. Employers further see normative roles and responsibilities flowing from this view that economists would not see: employers should not play favorites with past suppliers since that discourages competition, and teachers should take the initiative to sell their students to employers. Employers do not take responsibility for maintaining linkages, not only because it is not their responsibility, but also because it would not be proper for employers to work with teachers who are not doing their duty. As one employer explains:

> I don't have any contacts anymore. I really haven't been approached by that many high schools, but if I was, I would be willing to work with them. I'm not going to seek the high schools, so the advice I would give them is that *they should contact employers* and find out if they would be willing to work with them to hire students, but [we] very rarely have anybody that calls.

This employer, who earlier described the good employees she has found through vocational teacher contacts, goes on to suggest that, since she is the "buyer," the teachers, as the "sellers," should reach out to her. Although she may gain from the transaction, she does not believe that it is her role to initiate or maintain the relationship.

Other employers make similar comments. Five years before, one told us, he hired students from the high school, and these students often became good employees, but he no longer uses the school because the teacher stopped calling him. This employer regrets the loss and sees it as having cost him a source of good workers, but he does not see himself as having any role in maintaining the relationship. He clearly sees this disintegration in normative terms; he blames the school: "The commitment is not there on the part of the schools." Similarly, another employer believes that it is the responsibility of teachers "to cultivate" [the relationship]."

These employers have a view of the labor market that puts the burden on teachers as sellers to approach them. They speak of the teachers' "lack of commitment" or their "failure to help their students" to get jobs. Not only do employers see schools as having the responsibility, but they also judge schools' nonresponse in normative terms. It is obvious to these employers that if schools are failing at their responsibilities, it is not their responsibility to devote their own time and energies to trying to work with schools, regardless of the benefits they might reap from doing so.

Thus, employers that have benefited from linkages with schools in the past do not maintain them because they assume that the responsibility lies with the schools; they take the previous teachers' actions for granted. Employers seem to believe that it is the market model's emphasis on competition that gives teachers the responsibility to maintain the contact. It is probably more the case that the emphasis on laissez-faire markets deprives both employers and teachers of clear norms specifying the responsibilities of each party. Regardless of the reason for employers' beliefs, they have normative, not economic, reasons for failing to maintain linkages with schools. When teachers stop maintaining the linkages, employers do not complain about costs; they lament the fact that vocational teachers are not reaching out to them, and they even blame the teachers for not doing so.

When Transactions *Do* Occur

In spite of the many ways in which market transactions can fail, they do sometimes occur. Some employers have various ways of overcoming the obstacles to transactions in their linkages with teachers. The seven employers who have ongoing relationships with teachers have different social conceptions than the unlinked employers do.

First, some employers recognize the potential value of teachers' recommendations. Unlinked employers believe that teachers' evaluations are narrowly academic and irrelevant to their needs, but all seven of the linked employers believe that vocational teachers' knowledge about students' work habits is related to the attributes they need in their workplaces. They also feel that teachers screen out clearly unacceptable students from their nominations.

Second, these seven employers acquired knowledge about whom to contact by meeting teachers in various contexts. Some are on advisory boards for vocational programs, some have employed students in co-op programs, and some know vocational teachers who have worked in their field. Although employers rarely approach schools with the intention of setting up a hiring relationship, they are generally involved with a school in some other way and are therefore in a position for such relationships to develop. Employers who have developed hiring linkages did so almost accidentally through other contacts with the school.

Third, employers develop procedures for working with teachers so that they can trust teachers' recommendations and teachers can see benefits for their students. Their relationship develops over time. Employers try out a student recommended by a teacher, perhaps in a co-op program or a summer job, and if they are satisfied, they may trust the relationship enough to make a full-time hire. Employers who develop hiring linkages expect teachers to recommend suitable youth, and they have formed relationships with teachers who will do so. With each transaction, these teachers gain a better understanding of employers' needs, and employers increasingly trust the teachers' judgment—often enough to rubber-stamp their acceptance of candidates sent to them by these teachers. As one employer says: "We probably weigh 90 percent, maybe 100 percent, of our decisions on whether or not to hire someone based on what the teachers who we work with recommend." Another notes that teachers "obviously work with these students all the time and should have some good handle on those who are most employable and have the best understanding of what they're doing."

Fourth, linked employers take responsibility for maintaining linkages when they realize how rare and valuable good linkages are. Most linked employers have not only had good relationships with schools but have also been burned by bad relationships, so they realize that teachers and schools vary in their ability to help them find good workers. Once they realize the value of good linkages, these employers take some responsibility for maintaining the link, and they try to make sure that transactions are mutually beneficial.

Although a lack of norms prevents most employers from taking responsibility for maintaining linkages, employers who realize the value of good ones make the extra effort regardless of norms. Employers who have seen the difference between good and bad contacts figure out that they will have to take responsibility to get the benefits of good linkages. Clear norms save Japanese employers from having to learn the value of good linkages from experience, but American employers must learn this lesson from experience. Of course, once they have seen good and bad relationships, no one has to explain to them what they have to do.

Conclusions

Contrary to functionalist theory and neoclassical economic theory, transactions do not automatically occur, even if they are useful for all parties. Although linkages are well suited to addressing employers' complaints and work well for some employers, we have found that a variety of social factors prevent such transactions from occurring. First, the lack of a social conception that school linkages can be useful for hiring is a stumbling block. Second, the lack of knowledge about who should be contacted prevents linkages from starting. Third, with no clear norms about procedures for establishing contacts, many employers find that their efforts are ignored and ineffective. Finally, the lack of clear norms about responsibility prevents employers from taking the actions needed to maintain linkages, so incipient contacts falter.

Just as functionalist and economic theories predict, we find that it is in the interest of schools and employers to interact, and we even find that they sometimes make various initiatives to contact each other. Yet the assumption that rational self-interest is enough to make transactions occur turns out to be too simple. The various efforts of employers and schools are neither recognized nor reciprocated, and like ships passing in the night, no transactions occur. Transactions do not seem to proceed automatically from functional needs or economic incentives but can be prevented from occurring by social conceptions and norms. The results support new social network models in sociology as well as the new institutional economics.

Although neoclassical economic theory suggests that desirable transactions tend to occur, economic sociology contends that social factors can prevent economically desirable transactions from happening or continuing. Our results point to some of the social factors that prevent desirable transactions from happening in the youth labor market.

We might explain the failure of these transactions by noting that public school teachers are not motivated to help students get jobs because they lack an economic incentive. However, teachers *are* motivated to help their students get jobs. In a study of 112 vocational teachers (see chapter 10), we found that all of these teachers try to help their students get jobs. Some teachers had left a previous job so that they could recommend students to particular employers in that industry. Other teachers do not know any employers and they do not know what to do, and their actions are largely ignored by employers (Rosenbaum et al. 1997). Just as one employer got no response from soliciting job nominees from guidance counselors at twenty different high schools, some teachers report getting no response from inquiries about job openings from local employers. If employers and teachers do not know how to initiate or respond to linkages, increasing "profit" incentives will not increase the number of transactions that occur.

Of course, the evidence from fifty-one employers is not adequate to disprove functionalist theories; these theories could provide other explanations for employers' behaviors that our study might not be able to rule out. However, while the theoretical explanations are plausible conjectures, they are only conjectures. They are not based on any empirical data.

In contrast, the evidence we present, although based on a small sample, is nonetheless real empirical evidence. We present employers' own explanations of what they do and why they do it. We find that economically rational actions can fail to occur because actors do not realize they are possible and desirable, and those actions can fail to be repeated because actors do not agree about the components of the transaction or about who is responsible for taking further action. The results support new social network models in sociology as well as the new institutional economics.

These results offer a new view of the value of German apprenticeships. Although apprenticeships are frequently cited as a model for reforming school-employer relationships in the twenty-first century, it should be noted that the German system evolved from the five-hundred-year-old guild system, which may not be quickly emulated in the United States. Moreover, the expense of this training has led even many German firms to reduce their commitments to apprenticeship training and may prevent any reform based on apprenticeships from spreading widely in this country. However, our results suggest that one of the primary benefits of apprenticeships is establishing norms that tell employers how to hire good students from schools and make schools responsible for sending good employees to employers.

It should therefore be possible to re-create some of the beneficial components of the German system without incurring its costs. One reason for the success of the German system that has largely been ignored is the social infrastructure that defines schools' and employers' responsibilities in helping youth enter the work world. Although parts of this infrastructure are expensive (apprenticeship training and the government employment service), the social norms that make schools and employers responsible to each other are not. The norms of German schools make them responsible for evaluating students as potential workers, and the norm among employers is to use schools' evaluations. These complementary norms do not create extra costs, yet employers believe that they greatly improve the quality of the workers they obtain, and youth believe that this system is a great help to them in entering the workforce (Rosenbaum et al. 1990).

Japan provides an example of a social infrastructure that requires teachers to evaluate students according to criteria that are valuable to employers, and requires employers to use teachers' evaluations to choose employers. In Japan the best jobs go to the work-bound students with the best school records, as determined by teachers. Employers are pleased with the dependable quality of the workers they get, and schools are pleased to be able to promise better jobs to students who work harder (Rosenbaum and Kariya 1989). The Japanese system is very inexpensive; it is largely implemented by a single teacher who does the grading and matching.

The U.S. market model directly discourages such an infrastructure and the kinds of linkages that have been useful in Germany and Japan. Because most American employers view the hiring process as a laissez-faire market, they expect market competition to result in the best outcomes and avoid stable social arrangements for hiring. Thus, even though a few employers have found such linkages to be of great value, the American market model discourages the spread of linkages.

There is some irony to this situation. The market model makes two separate contentions: competition tends to maximize efficiency, and employers do whatever is necessary to maximize efficiency. However, institutional analysts have shown that institutional arrangements may be more efficient than market transactions under some conditions— for instance, when it is important for employers to be assured of dependable future transactions, dependable types of specific preparation, and dependable quality of employees (Dore 1983; Kariya and Rosenbaum 1995; Williamson 1985). In these circumstances, employers' beliefs in competition may prevent them from creating stable relationships even when they are warranted and efficient. That is what we have seen: employers' beliefs in competition prevent them from creating the noncompetitive linkages that could increase efficiency.

This is not to say that employers are totally responsible for the lack of linkages or that linkages will necessarily happen if employers make more effort. This report has not looked at teachers' behaviors. Yet regardless of what teachers do, we find several social factors that prevent employers from forming linkages. Obviously, when employers do not consider making linkages, do not contact appropriate staff, do not know how to make linkages, and do not think they have any responsibility for maintaining them, linkages will not happen regardless of how teachers act. Employers may not be sufficient to make linkages happen, but they are necessary.

This chapter's findings provide clear examples of the inability of the market to make transactions occur if employers lack appropriate norms and conceptions. Rather than blame teachers or employers, however, we suspect that the actors' views of the market model provide the underlying conditions that discourage linkages. How American employers view the market model discourages them from considering, initiating, or maintaining linkages; this view also discourages stable supplier relationships with high schools, and it discourages both parties from knowing that linkages can be made, what benefits they can provide, and how to do them. Employers' views of the market model thus ultimately prevent all parties from taking appropriate actions.

The examples of Germany and Japan illustrate that a social infrastructure can improve the youth labor market, and this chapter has described some of the preconditions to improving that labor market that a social infrastructure can provide: a social conception about school linkages, a contact person in schools, contact procedures, and social norms that define responsibilities to maintain linkages. When these elements of a social infrastructure are in place, linkages are much more likely to occur. Perhaps the most serious problem with the American market model is the widespread view that the model itself makes such an infrastructure unnecessary.

= Chapter 8 =

Are Noncognitive Behaviors in School Related to Later Life Outcomes?

Aｓ ＷＥ have seen in the previous chapters, employers place a
high priority on noncognitive behaviors—such as work habits (NCEQW 1994)—that they have great difficulty inferring
from available information (Bishop 1993).[1] However, employers doubt
that students' behaviors in school are relevant to the work setting
(chapter 6). Many employers dismiss school grades as merely indicating that a student has learned academic trivia (like historical dates),
not the knowledge or work habits needed in the work world. Employers also mistrust the subjectivity of grades (although they often
base workers' pay on supervisors' opinions). Employers say that
workers' attendance, discipline, effort, and participation affect their
job performance, but they doubt the relevance of high school behaviors. Do students' attendance, discipline, effort, and participation in
high school predict their later job performance?

More generally, are students' noncognitive behaviors in high school
related to their later life attainments? Cognitive effects on attainments
have been studied extensively (Heyns 1974; Jencks et al. 1972; Murnane, Willett, and Levy 1995), but noncognitive effects are rarely studied. Indeed, the status-attainment models that incorporate social psychological factors do not include noncognitive behaviors (Sewell 1971;
Sewell and Hauser 1975). These models emphasize ability as a factor
limiting achievement, and only a few show any indication that noncognitive behaviors might vary across individuals or affect attainments (Buchmann 1989; Jencks et al. 1979; Smith 1967).

It is unclear how teachers, colleges, and employers respond to noncognitive behaviors in high school. Although teachers threaten to
penalize bad behavior, they often do not act on their threats, or do so

170

inconsistently (Sedlak et al. 1986). Nor is it clear how much students' noncognitive behaviors in school are related to later life outcomes. Some colleges consider noncognitive factors in college admissions, but many colleges are not selective, and some advocates of open admissions argue that poor behaviors arise from the low challenge in high schools and should not limit college access.

Not surprisingly, students are confused. They cannot tell whether their attendance, discipline, effort, and participation will affect their grades, college attainments, or earnings. This chapter examines these issues.

First, we examine whether noncognitive behaviors are related to grades. Although formally defined as academic achievement, grades may also have a noncognitive component if teachers penalize poor behavior. This study examines whether grades reflect the kinds of noncognitive behaviors that employers say they value.

Second, we examine whether noncognitive behaviors are related to educational attainments. Open-admissions policies and study skills courses may reduce the impact of high school behaviors.

Third, we examine whether noncognitive behaviors are related to earnings. Although employers are very disturbed by evidence of a poor work ethic, they see schools as setting boring and artificial tasks for students, and they do not believe that school behaviors provide any indication of how youth will perform at work.

From a sociological perspective, employers' disregard for high school behaviors and grades is puzzling. High school plays a central role in socializing youth, informing them about societal demands, teaching them how to succeed in meeting those demands, and letting them know how they are doing at mastering those demands. However, if high school behaviors are regarded as irrelevant by colleges and employers, and if they have no impact on students' college and work attainments, then high schools may not be making the right demands on students, and students may see no reasons to acquire good work habits in high school. This chapter examines these issues.

Previous Research on Noncognitive Effects

While many social scientists were studying IQ (and whether it was genetically determined), Bowles and Gintis (1976) made the radical proposal that IQ is less important than noncognitive behaviors. They proposed that schools' main function is to develop noncognitive characteristics to prepare individuals to fit into the work world. They argued that the same type of behaviors are rewarded in school and work. Their empirical research found that noncognitive behaviors outweigh achievement as predictors of grades, and that these behaviors mediate the influence of social class background.

Michael Olneck and David Bills (1980) partially supported Bowles and Gintis's contention that noncognitive factors have a significant impact on grades. They found that teachers' ratings of students' industriousness (hard work and effort) and cooperativeness (getting along with others and responsiveness to authority) had effects on grades, especially those of the children of blue-collar workers. Bowles and Gintis explained this impact in terms of social replication, and Olneck and Bills found some evidence to support this explanation. These studies, however, present only limited models of the factors that predict grades. Furthermore, these studies use data that are more than twenty-five years old. Cognitive and noncognitive characteristics might be differently valued in the post-industrial economy.

In this body of earlier work, I must note the important research by Christopher Jencks and colleagues (1979) who use multiple data sets from the 1960s and early 1970s to analyze personality and noncognitive effects on occupational status. They found that good study habits increase occupational status, but not earnings. Strangely, subsequent research over the past two decades has ignored their findings and not examined the long-term effects of high school noncognitive behavior.

Other studies of noncognitive factors have focused on the factors that motivate students to achieve and therefore may affect grades. Social responsibility, defined as adherence to social rules and role expectations, has been found to be instrumental in the acquisition of knowledge and development of cognitive ability (Lambert and Nicoll 1977; Parker and Asher 1987; Wentzel et al. 1990). The reason for this, Kathryn Wentzel (1991) argues, is that social responsibility may increase achievement both by promoting positive interactions with peers and by providing students with additional motivations to achieve. In studies in Hungary and Great Britain, Burt Kozeki and Nan Entwistle (1984) found that school motivation (which leads to achievement) is influenced by three kinds of factors: affective factors (warmth, identification, sociability), cognitive factors (independence, competence, interest), and moral factors (trust, compliance, responsibility). Although these studies address noncognitive factors that might affect grades, they do not compare behavioral to achievement factors (see Robinson, Shaver, and Wrightsman 1991).

In more recent research in junior high schools, Roger Shouse, Barbara Schneider, and Stephen Plank (1992) have shown that grades are related to completion of homework and inattentiveness in class among eighth-graders. George Farkas and his colleagues (1990) have shown that junior high grades are indicative of attendance, disruptiveness, work habits, and appearance, independent of basic skills and course mastery. At the junior high level, grades reflect not only students' academic achievement but also their school behaviors. A recent study at a large state university has shown that effort in college is related to college grades (Rau and Durand 2000).

Although we do not know of comparable research at the high school level, some observational research has suggested a similar finding. Michael Sedlak and his colleagues (1986) and Arthur Powell, Eleanor Farrar, and David Cohen (1985) have found that teachers strike a bargain with students: they offer better grades in exchange for peace in the classroom. These bargains make grades reflect school behaviors, independent of achievement. Teachers give somewhat better grades as a payoff for cooperation. These observations are suggestive, but they do not indicate to what extent grades reflect students' behaviors.

Turning to later outcomes, social theorists assert that schools' demands are relevant to the work world. Both conservative and radical theorists have proposed such relevance. On the conservative side, Talcott Parsons (1959) suggested that teachers have students perform tasks that are directly related to performance in society. On the radical side, Bowles and Gintis (1976) proposed a "correspondence principle," which contends that the social relations of schooling mirror the social relations of production. Both theories contend that schools' primary mission is to prepare youth to fit into society, and to this end, schools demand of students the behaviors and competencies needed by the work world.

Moreover, research on work demands has increasingly stressed the need for the kinds of behaviors that schools demand from students. Although employers who hire high school graduates seek workers with basic academic skills, they rarely demand advanced skills (Cappelli and Rogowsky 1993; Murnane and Levy 1996; Hill and Nixon 1984; Holzer 1995), and they are more concerned with noncognitive behaviors. Most notably, a survey of four thousand private employers by the National Center on the Educational Quality in the Workforce (NCEQW 1994) and a more intensive local study by Roslyn Mickelson and Matthew Walker (1997) find that employers place even more weight on noncognitive behaviors than on cognitive skills. Researchers find that employers say they are seeking workers with a wide variety of noncognitive behaviors, ranging from basic attendance, cooperativeness, and good attitudes to facility with social interaction, participation, leadership, effort, and preparation (Baxter and Young 1982; Cappelli 1992; Cappelli and Rogowsky 1993; Crohn 1983; Hazler and Latto 1987; Murnane and Levy 1996; NCEQW 1994;

SCANS 1991). Peter Cappelli and Nikolai Rogowsky (1993) suggest that, just as cognitive skills can lead to productivity benefits, noncognitive behaviors may also be important in predicting workplace productivity.

Surveys show that employers place high value on attitude and communication skills, but that research has not described what employers mean by these terms or why they are needed. Does attitude refer to *low*-level obedience, as Bowles and Gintis (1976) implied, or to *high*-level performances, as current reform literature implies? Moss and Tilly (1996, 2000) describe what employers mean by these terms, which they call "soft skills." Similarly, in our interviews with fifty-one small and medium-size employers, we found that employers' reports focus on three types of noncognitive skills:

- *Normative compliance:* Attendance, dependability, positive attitude, avoiding rule infractions, and handling social conflict

- *General work procedures:* Effort, persistence, problem solving, attention to quality, and preparing for next tasks

- *Social skills:* Communicating about work tasks with coworkers, leadership, and participating in activities beyond job tasks, such as maintaining operations and organizing the work group (Miller and Rosenbaum 1998)

Although some employers of the 1970s may have purposely deskilled jobs (Bowles and Gintis 1976), and there are doubts about whether employers are raising their hiring criteria (Osterman 1995), many of the employers we interviewed complain about the amount of time they put into supervising and providing instruction in noncognitive skills, including many of the "soft skills" noted by other researchers (Moss and Tilly 1996, 2000; Cappelli 1992; Olneck and Bills 1980).

The employers we interviewed give specific, highly credible stories of the costs they incur from poor noncognitive skills in their workers. Such costs are incurred when expensive supervisors need to use their judgment about work decisions, deal with discipline problems, and tell workers to anticipate and prepare for the next task. In contrast with a view that employers seek blind obedience, a public utility manager complains about a worker who returned after eight hours of visits to read gas meters in which every meter had already been read two days before. Blind obedience to the assigned task is not always productive behavior. Although employers' concern with social attitudes might seem arbitrary, employers' concern has been fueled by instances of young workers harassing women and minorities, getting in verbal or physical fights with peers or supervisors, and being careless with dangerous equipment.

Employers complain about workers whose poor attendance, discipline, effort, or participation interferes with the work process. However, even though these work behaviors are clearly similar to some of those that students exhibit in high school (for example, attendance, discipline, effort, and participation), employers do not think school is a good place to assess these behaviors. Employers believe that such behaviors in high school are based on arbitrary standards, irrelevant tasks, and regimented demands (Miller and Rosenbaum 1997). Many employers believe that school behaviors are irrelevant to their needs (perhaps because many employers in small firms did poorly in school themselves but are doing well at work). Moreover, studies of corporate recruiters find that they give some importance to college information in their hiring decisions, but little importance to similar information from high schools (Crain 1984).

Similarly, these behaviors may not be related to college attendance. Although college admissions have traditionally been partly based on school behavior, open admissions has made college attendance available to anyone with a high school diploma, regardless of grades or behavior. Moreover, the vast expansion of remedial programs, including study habit courses, is intended to overcome and diminish the influence of prior behaviors on college attainment. If students can learn study habits in college, poor high school efforts may have no relationship to college attainment. Despite the theoretical reasons for predicting a correspondence, employers (and open-admissions colleges) do not act in ways that would make these behaviors have an important influence.

Hypotheses

The research reviewed here poses contradictory expectations about the effects of school noncognitive behaviors. One view is that school behaviors have no relationship to grades, educational attainment, or earnings. The definition of grades as academic achievement leads to this expectation. For other outcomes, the beliefs of relevant actors, particularly students and employers, could make this lack of relationship occur.

The contrary expectation is suggested by teachers, who tell students that their school behaviors are important for their grades and for their college and earnings attainments. Although teachers have the authority to make school behaviors affect the grades they give, we do not know whether this is a general practice. In any case, teachers probably do not influence students' college persistence or employers' hiring decisions.

There is a third possibility—that school behaviors are counter-productive. The popular media sometimes suggest that successful school behaviors foretell societal failure: that is, the behaviors that help students do well in school are counterproductive in the real world. Everyone has their favorite story of the nerd who cannot tie his shoelaces, the obedient teacher's pet who lacks imagination and initiative, and the dropout who makes a billion dollars. Students who never cut a class may be seen as lacking imagination or initiative, especially by small-firm employers who did not excel in high school themselves (Rosenbaum and Binder 1997).

Finally, if school behaviors are important, do grades mediate this influence? Grades are the main evaluation by high schools. Do grades signal these noncognitive behaviors to colleges and employers?

These issues can be stated in four formal hypotheses. Although we have conflicting expectations for the first three, we pose null hypotheses of no effects to be tested.

1. School noncognitive behaviors are unrelated to grades.

2. School noncognitive behaviors are unrelated to later educational attainment.

3. School noncognitive behaviors are unrelated to later earnings.

4. If school noncognitive behaviors are related to educational attainment and earnings, the relationships are mediated by grades.

Methods

We examine these issues using an unusually good data set. As noted in chapter 3, the High School and Beyond survey followed students from their senior year (1982) to their outcomes in the ten-year (1992) follow-up. After missing data were eliminated (listwise), the sample for regression analyses was approximately 7,157 for whom we had information on all variables.[2] Ordinary least squares regressions are used to calculate our results. Variable definitions and means are listed in the appendix.

Our discussion of findings comes primarily from the twelve models presented in table 8.3. We first discuss the relationship to grades, using senior year school variables to explain students' grades. Then we examine whether senior year variables are related to educational attainment and earnings. These analyses examine long-term outcomes, over nine years after high school: educational attainment in

1992 and earnings in 1991 (the last full-year in the data). Nine years provide plenty of time for most students who are going to finish college to do so. Analysis after that period of time also gives a fairly good indication of labor market success.

Our aim is to address the question: Do high school noncognitive behaviors influence young people's long-term outcomes (at age twenty-eight)? Our aim is not to explain all the variance, so we do not include any independent variables that occur after high school. This is a model that shows the relationships of high school variables to long-term outcomes.[3] We would argue that years of education and annual earnings are good general measures of the career achievements of these young adults, without any controls for subsequent experiences.

Our independent variables are taken from the twelfth-grade survey. We selected every indicator of noncognitive behavior in the HSB survey. Some indicators seemed unlikely to be important because they were so minor (36 percent of students cut class once in a while; 78 percent report being interested in school). Other indicators seemed close to the key concerns of employers (attendance and discipline problems) and would be important if they indicated persistent behaviors (although employers believe that they do not; see Miller and Rosenbaum 1998).

Obviously, students' reports of noncognitive behaviors may underestimate problem behavior, so our findings may underestimate negative behaviors and potentially underestimate their effects. However, although these HSB data do not permit alternative sources of information for noncognitive behaviors, recent analyses of the NELS data indicate that students' self-reports for homework time, absences, and discipline problems correspond very strongly with teachers' assessments of the same students (DeLuca 2001).[4] It is noteworthy that our findings on high school grades correspond to those found by Farkas and his colleagues (1990) for junior high grades. That study used teachers' ratings of noncognitive behaviors, but unfortunately does not permit analyses of long-term outcomes.

Results

Do students differ in school behaviors, and are these differences related to school grades and later outcomes? We studied students who had made it through twelve years of school. Over this long period, they had surely figured out how to behave in school. Workplaces socialize employees to appropriate behavior, to a point where some observers worry about excessive conformity. Do we see such homogeneity among students?

Students were asked how many days they were absent in the fall of their senior year, perhaps the most important term in high school. About 1 percent of students were absent twenty-one days or more (one month in a term), 5 percent (465) were absent more than ten days (roughly 12 percent of a term), and 18 percent (1,606) were absent more than four days, more than once a month. (All percentages are cumulative of prior categories.) In contrast, almost 63 percent of students (5,481 of 8,893) were absent less than three days in the term. Obviously, there is great variation in absences.

Similarly, there is great variation in time spent on homework. No homework was done by 2.3 percent (185), 16.8 percent (1,348) do less than one hour per week, and 43.7 percent (3,495) do less than three hours per week. On the other end of the scale, 4.2 percent (336) do more than fifteen hours per week, 13.5 percent (1,080) do more than ten hours per week, and 35.8 percent (2,859 of 7,996) do more than five hours per week. Students' homework-related behaviors show great variation.[5]

Moreover, this variation is sometimes associated with variation in grades and later outcomes. For instance, although the average student in the sample attained 13.75 years of education, students absent more than ten days in a term averaged less than thirteen years of education (table 8.1). Although the average student earned $19,592 a year (antilog 9.8829), students absent more than ten days earned 9 percent less (9.8829 − 9.7931), and those absent more than twenty days earned 45 percent less. In contrast, while there are costs for bad attendance, the gains for good attendance are much smaller. Those who are never absent attain about .34 of a year more of education and 4 percent more earnings than the average student.

Homework time shows relationships at both ends of the scale (table 8.2). Students doing no homework average 1.2 years less education than the average, and 20 percent lower earnings. Students doing fifteen hours or more a week of homework attain about 1.48 more years of education and attain 16 percent higher earnings than average. This 2.7-year spread in educational attainment and 34 percent spread in earnings are both extremely large, especially considering that these outcomes are associated with variation in self-reported homework time in high school.

Regression Analyses

However, these are simple bivariate associations that may diminish or disappear after other controls. The next section investigates this possibility.

Table 8.1   High School Grades, Educational Attainment, and Earnings, 1991, by Attendance

Number of Days Absent Last Fall	High School Grades	Years of Education	Ln(Earn91)
Twenty-one or more days			
Mean	3.4605	12.6579	9.4287
N	76	76	49
Standard deviation	1.2695	1.1022	1.3017
Sixteen to twenty days			
Mean	3.7640	12.7303	9.5973
N	89	89	74
Standard deviation	1.0555	1.1458	1.1358
Eleven to fifteen days			
Mean	3.7037	12.9918	9.7931
N	243	243	175
Standard deviation	1.1547	1.4460	.7327
Five to ten days			
Mean	4.0261	13.2381	9.8361
N	1,033	1,033	781
Standard deviation	1.2398	1.6877	.7574
Three or four days			
Mean	4.2709	13.5326	9.8658
N	1,639	1,639	1,259
Standard deviation	1.2771	1.8648	.7428
One or two days			
Mean	4.5482	13.9255	9.9106
N	2,740	2,740	2,202
Standard deviation	1.2750	1.9755	.6977
None			
Mean	4.7275	14.0841	9.9154
N	2,176	2,176	1,728
Standard deviation	1.2483	2.0351	.6945
Total			
Mean	4.4280	13.7456	9.8829
N	7,996	7,996	6,268
Standard deviation	1.2908	1.9385	.7298

Source: Author's compilation.

Grades   Regressions were run on high school grades in a series of models. Since measures are concurrent with grades, we cannot infer the direction of causality, and this section is of less substantive interest than the following ones. However, these analyses can show the degree of correspondence between noncognitive behaviors and senior year grades.

Table 8.2   **High School Grades, Educational Attainment, and Earnings, 1991, by Homework Time**

Homework Time	High School Grades	Years of Education	Ln(Earn91)
No homework			
Mean	3.9243	12.5405	9.6967
N	185	185	133
Standard deviation	1.2000	.9723	.9081
Less than one hour per week			
Mean	3.9175	12.9622	9.8913
N	1,163	1,163	894
Standard deviation	1.2314	1.4774	.6820
One to three hours per week			
Mean	4.1905	13.3964	9.7886
N	2,147	2,147	1,669
Standard deviation	1.2202	1.7228	.7785
Three to five hours per week			
Mean	4.4202	13.7625	9.8723
N	1,642	1,642	1,297
Standard deviation	1.2466	1.8763	.7263
Five to ten hours per week			
Mean	4.6880	14.1737	9.9528
N	1,779	1,779	1,400
Standard deviation	1.2377	2.0524	.6953
Ten to fifteen hours per week			
Mean	4.9852	14.5470	9.9624
N	744	744	611
Standard deviation	1.2702	2.1031	.6686
Fifteen hours or more per week			
Mean	5.4167	15.2292	10.0416
N	336	336	264
Standard deviation	1.1916	2.2000	.7110
Total			
Mean	4.4280	13.7456	9.8829
N	7,996	7,996	6,268
Standard deviation	1.2908	1.9385	.7298

Source: Author's compilation.

Model 1 in table 8.3 shows that grades vary with demographic factors, socioeconomic status, ethnicity, and gender. It also indicates that social context has a substantial additional correspondence. Grades are lowest in the Northeast region of the United States, and then progressively higher in the Midwest (omitted reference category), the South, and then the West. In addition, students in private high schools have about the same grades as public high school students.

Turning to model 2, tested achievement is strongly related to grades. Clearly, grades are indicators of achievement, but social context factors remain large, significant, and with the same direction as in model 1. In particular, the regional factors have a somewhat stronger relation to grades after achievement is added, indicating, for instance, that students get slightly lower grades than their achievement would imply in the Northeast. Indeed, the more lenient grades in the South (b = .104) become even more lenient after controlling for tested achievement (.185). Similarly, after controls for tested achievement, the private school coefficient goes from insignificance to significantly negative (−.188), indicating that grading standards are stricter in these schools.

However, the demographic relationships are radically altered after tested achievement is controlled. The gender coefficient increases slightly, indicating that girls get better grades than their tested achievement would imply. (It is unclear whether girls' grades are inflated or their test scores deflated.) The previously large SES coefficient virtually disappears, and the black and Hispanic coefficients are cut enormously.

Turning to model 3, adding school behaviors adds 9 percent to the explained variance. Indeed, all but two of the school noncognitive behavior coefficients are significant and in the expected direction. For instance, each category increase in attendance (see appendix for categories) is associated with an increase of about 12 percent of a unit in grades. (Each grade unit is half a grade, for example, from "mostly Bs" to "Bs and As".) The greatest surprise is the insignificance of homework time, which is significant when test scores are removed, implying that homework time affects grades only by improving test scores.

These school behaviors explain a sizable portion of the variation in grades that is not explained by test scores. Apparently, teachers' grades do not just reflect students' academic achievement. In terms of the noncognitive dimensions that employers demand (Olneck and Bills 1980), better grades seem to be related to students' leadership, cooperativeness (participating in activities, not cutting class, being well disciplined, and showing interest), and industriousness (good attendance and preparation, but not homework time), but not to their sociability. Of course, we cannot reject the possibility that causality runs in the opposite direction, and that grades may influence these behaviors. In any case, the first null hypothesis is rejected.

Table 8.3 Determinants of Students' Grades, Educational Attainment, and 1991 Earnings, Including Work Habits–Noncognitive Indicators

	1 Grades	2 Grades	3 Grades	4 EdYrs	5 EdYrs	6 EdYrs	7 EdYrs	8 Earn91	9 Earn91	10 Earn91	11 Earn91	12 Earn91
SES	.367*	.014	−.009	1.042*	.643*	.579*	.581*	.174*	.120*	.097*	.099*	.080*
	(.021)	(.019)	(.018)	(.030)	(.029)	(.029)	(.028)	(.013)	(.014)	(.014)	(.014)	(.015)
Female	.461*	.545*	.369*	.139*	.234*	.048*	−.063	−.362*	−.352*	−.380*	−.405*	−.405*
	(.029)	(.025)	(.024)	(.041)	(.037)	(.038)	(.038)	(.018)	(.018)	(.019)	(.019)	(.019)
Black	−.528*	−.114*	−.259*	−.106	.363*	−.155*	.232*	.024	.089*	.059	.072*	.066*
	(.054)	(.047)	(.044)	(.076)	(.070)	(.069)	(.068)	(.035)	(.035)	(.035)	(.035)	(.035)
Hispanic	−.476*	−.028	−.068	−.284*	.225*	.144*	.164*	−.047	.024	.020	.025	.021
	(.049)	(.043)	(.040)	(.069)	(.064)	(.062)	(.061)	(.031)	(.031)	(.031)	(.031)	(.031)
Northeast	−.110*	−.213*	−.112*	.159*	.042	.112	.145*	.074*	.063*	.069*	.077*	.072*
	(.040)	(.034)	(.032)	(.056)	(.051)	(.050)	(.049)	(.025)	(.025)	(.025)	(.025)	(.025)
South	.104*	.185*	.172*	−.100	−.008	−.022	−.074	−.067*	−.053*	−.059*	−.071*	−.068*
	(.037)	(.032)	(.030)	(.052)	(.048)	(.046)	(.045)	(.023)	(.023)	(.023)	(.023)	(.023)
West	.217*	.209*	.331*	−.384*	−.393*	−.307*	−.406*	−.089*	−.087*	−.083*	−.104*	−.092*
	(.046)	(.039)	(.037)	(.065)	(.059)	(.057)	(.057)	(.029)	(.028)	(.029)	(.029)	(.029)
Private	−.049	−.188*	−.232*	−.513*	.356*	.279*	.348*	.097*	.074*	.074*	.089*	.079*
	(.046)	(.039)	(.037)	(.064)	(.058)	(.057)	(.056)	(.028)	(.028)	(.028)	(.028)	(.028)
Test	—	.085*	.073*	—	.096*	.079*	.057*	—	.013*	.012*	.007*	.006*
		(.002)	(.002)		(.002)	(.003)	(.003)		(.001)	(.001)	(.001)	(.001)
Preparedness	—	—	.129*	—	—	.015	−.024	—	—	.011	.003	.004
			(.013)			(.020)	(.019)			(.010)	(.010)	(.010)
Homework time	—	—	.013	—	—	.144*	.140*	—	—	.005	.005	.000
			(.009)			(.015)	(.014)			(.007)	(.007)	(.007)

	(1)	(2)	(3)	(4)	(5)	(6)	(7)	(8)	(9)	(10)	(11)	(12)
Attendance	—	—	.121*	—	—	.087*	.051*	—	—	.019*	.012	.010
			(.010)			(.016)	(.015)			(.008)	(.008)	(.008)
Interest in school	—	—	.191*	—	—	.276*	.219*	—	—	-.028	-.044	-.050*
			(.029)			(.046)	(.045)			(.023)	(.023)	(.023)
Cutting class	—	—	-.206*	—	—	-.079	-.017	—	—	.048*	.062*	.063*
			(.026)			(.041)	(.040)			(.020)	(.021)	(.020)
Discipline problems	—	—	-.088*	—	—	-.074*	-.048*	—	—	-.049*	-.044*	-.042*
			(.013)			(.020)	(.020)			(.010)	(.010)	(.010)
Unsocial	—	—	.011	—	—	.007	.004	—	—	-.055*	-.056*	-.056*
			(.012)			(.019)	(.019)			(.010)	(.010)	(.010)
Leadership	—	—	.231*	—	—	.200*	.131*	—	—	.054*	.038	.034
			(.027)			(.042)	(.041)			(.021)	(.021)	(.021)
Extracurricular activities	—	—	.046*	—	—	.052*	.038*	—	—	.005	.001	.000
			(.006)			(.009)	(.009)			(.004)	(.004)	(.004)
Grades	—	—	—	—	—	—	.298*	—	—	—	.064*	.054*
							(.018)				(.009)	(.009)
EdYrs	—	—	—	—	—	—	—	—	—	—	—	.031*
												(.006)
Constant	4.208	-.341	-.700	13.606	8.452	7.850	8.059	10.020	9.296	9.218	9.257	9.011
	(.031)	(.093)	(.105)	(.043)	(.139)	(.164)	(.161)	(.019)	(.068)	(.083)	(.082)	(.095)
F	14.78	430.70	314.44	218.77	402.57	244.39	254.66	86.40	91.96	52.27	52.37	51.31
R-squared (adjusted)	11.3	35.1	44.1	19.6	33.6	38.0	40.2	9.9	11.6	12.9	13.5	13.9
N	7,157	7,157	7,157	7,157	7,157	7,157	7,157	6,243	6,243	6,243	6,243	6,243

Source: Author's compilation.

Note: Standardized coefficients are used.

* = $p < .05$

Educational Attainment Regressions were run on students' highest educational attainment by 1992, ten years after high school. This was measured in terms of years, so that an associate's degree is fourteen, a B.A. degree is sixteen, and so on. Model 4 (table 8.3) shows that educational attainment varies with demographic factors, socioeconomic status, ethnicity, and gender. Educational attainment is also related to social context. Educational attainment is highest in the Northeast, and then progressively lower in the Midwest (omitted reference category), the South, and then the West. In addition, private high schools have much higher educational attainment than public high schools. It is noteworthy that these context factors' coefficients have the opposite signs for educational attainment than they had for grades, perhaps indicating that harder grading standards lead to higher educational attainment.

Turning to model 5, tested achievement is an important factor in predicting educational attainment. A one-standard-deviation increase in test scores (8.52) is associated with an increase of eight-tenths of a year in educational attainment (.096 × 8.52 = .82). Clearly, achievement affects educational attainment.

Social context and demographic effects on educational attainment are radically altered after tested achievement is controlled. The strong coefficients for the Northeast and for private schools decline considerably after achievement is added, but the negative coefficient for the West is unchanged. The demographic coefficients are radically altered after tested achievement is controlled. The gender coefficient increases, indicating that the educational attainment of girls is greater than their tested achievement would imply. The previously large SES coefficient declines a great deal (by 38 percent), and the negative coefficients of blacks and Hispanics are turned into significant positive coefficients. After controls for achievement, ethnic coefficients on educational attainment are positive, and these coefficients are large and significant.

Turning to model 6, school behaviors add to our explanation of educational attainment. They add almost 4 percent to the explained variance, and most school behaviors are significant. The SES coefficient declines again (by 10 percent), the test score coefficient declines (by almost 18 percent), and the positive coefficients of blacks and Hispanics decline a great deal (by 57 percent and 36 percent, respectively), indicating that minorities' advantages (net of test scores) largely arise because they have better noncognitive behaviors.

Overall, students' homework, participation in activities, interest, attendance, leadership, and discipline have significant coefficients. For instance, a one-standard-deviation increase in homework time (1.42) is associated with an increase of about one-fifth of a year in educational attainment. Apparently many, but not all, of the factors related to grades are also related to educational attainment. The second null hypothesis is rejected.

Earnings   Regressions were run on students' earnings in 1991, nine years after high school. (1992 earnings reflect only part of a year.) Model 8 shows that earnings are lower for low-SES individuals and females, but unrelated to ethnicity (not statistically significant coefficients). Earnings are highest in the Northeast and lower in the South and the West. In addition, private high school graduates have much higher earnings than public high school graduates.

Turning to model 9, tested achievement is strongly associated with later earnings. A one-standard-deviation increase in test scores is related to a 55 percent increase in earnings. The strong advantages for the Northeast and for private schools decline a little, and the coefficient of SES declines a great deal (31 percent), after achievement is added. After controlling for achievement, blacks actually get significantly higher earnings than whites, but females retain lower earnings than males.

Turning to model 10, adding school noncognitive behaviors affects the influence of some other factors on earnings. The SES effect declines by over 19 percent, and the black and Hispanic advantages (net of test scores) seems to be explained in part (about 33 percent and 17 percent, respectively) by their noncognitive behaviors. The reverse is true for females, who are even more underpaid after taking account of their noncognitive behaviors.

Most school noncognitive behaviors are significantly related to earnings. Sociability, discipline, leadership, attendance, and cutting class have significant coefficients. For instance, a one-standard-deviation (.97) increase in better discipline (fewer discipline problems; see appendix) is associated with a 5 percent increase in earnings. Thus, discipline problems in high school have a significant relationship with individuals' earnings nine years later, even after controlling for other factors. The third null hypothesis is rejected.

Turning to the fourth hypothesis, school behaviors' relationships with educational attainment and earnings are reduced after controlling for students' grades. Model 11 shows that after adding grades, substantial fractions of the coefficients of attendance, discipline, and leadership are reduced in the models for educational attainment and earnings. For instance, in the earnings model, the coefficient for attendance decreases by one-third and the coefficient for discipline decreases by 10 percent after grades are added to the model, suggesting that portions of the relationships of attendance and discipline to earnings may be mediated by grades. Even larger portions of these variables' relationships with educational attainment decline with the addition of the grades variable.

Although grades do not mediate all of the relationship of these school behaviors with the dependent variables, grades mediate enough to be useful to colleges and employers. Colleges and employers could use students' grades in high school to infer which youths show positive noncognitive behaviors and would do well in higher education and work nine years after graduation.

Conclusions

This chapter has explored the relationship between noncognitive school behaviors and educational and earnings attainments more than nine years after high school. Our contribution is both conceptual and substantive. Conceptually, sociologists have paid too little attention to grades. This chapter has stressed the importance of grades as perhaps the main societal evaluation of all youth in our society, particularly the theoretical contention that grades measure general attributes that society values. It has reviewed empirical research that shows the importance of high school grades to college completion and to earnings independent of years of education completed. This chapter has also noted the conceptual confusion about the meaning of grades and presented empirical analyses of the factors determining grades.

Grades are usually considered only an indication of cognitive achievement, but we find that grades are also related to noncognitive school behaviors. Since employers generally ignore high school grades in their hiring decisions because they believe that grades measure only "academic trivia," the relationship between grades and school behaviors is especially noteworthy—these are just the behaviors that employers value, and they could get indicators of them in students' grades (Rosenbaum and Binder 1997; NCEQW 1994).

Our results have largely contradicted the null hypotheses of no relationships. All three of the following null hypotheses are refuted:

1. School noncognitive behaviors are unrelated to grades.
2. School noncognitive behaviors are unrelated to later educational attainment.
3. School noncognitive behaviors are unrelated to later earnings.

Indeed, some school behaviors (attendance, discipline, and leadership) have strong significant relationships with all three dependent variables. Other variables are related to one or two outcomes. All but two of the noncognitive behavior variables are related to grades, and all but three are significantly related to educational attainment (and cutting class is nearly significant). For instance, school interest and school activities are significantly related to grades and educational attainment, but not earnings. On the other hand, sociability is strongly related to earnings but has little relationship with grades or educational attainment.

Interestingly, there is even some support for the counterproductivity of one school behavior. On the simple dichotomous question about whether the student cuts class once in a while, such minor infractions are related to lower grades but also to improved earnings. Perhaps employers are right that students who never commit such minor infractions lack imagination or initiative. However, we would not exaggerate this finding. This is a simple dichotomous variable, indicating whether students ever cut class. The coefficient is small and dwarfed by the large negative coefficient for poor discipline.

In contrast, some variables are associated with all three dependent variables. Students with discipline problems or poor attendance have significantly lower grades, educational attainment, and future earnings at age twenty-eight. Prior to this study, we might have suspected that these problem behaviors are transitory reactions to a bad school or poor teachers with no relationship with later outcomes, when the student gets into a job that seems more practical and real. Surely such reversals sometimes happen, but not always. Averaging over all students, school discipline problems and poor attendance have enduring significant relationships with educational and earnings attainments much later.

The final hypothesis is also supported. School behavior relationships with educational attainment and earnings decline after controls for grades. The declines in the coefficients for attendance, discipline, and leadership for both educational attainment and earnings when grades are added to the model imply that grades may mediate part of any possible influence (Alwin and Hauser 1975). These school behaviors are related to long-term outcomes, and a substantial portion of this relationship could be explained by grades. (Moreover, as shown in model 12, they are not altered by controls for educational attainment.) Grades do not mediate all of the relationship for these school behaviors, but grades mediate enough so that employers who care about these attributes could infer which youth with these behaviors would do well in work nine years after graduation merely by looking at their grades in high school.

As a methodological aside, it is noteworthy that we measure noncognitive behaviors by students' own reports. Students may not perceive some shortcomings in their behaviors, and their reports may be positively inflated compared to what teachers might have said. Nonetheless, even their reports have significant effects. We suspect that teachers' ratings might be more accurate and have stronger effects; this question is being investigated (DeLuca 2001).

While ten-year follow-up data are impressive, and our findings are probably fairly good indications of individuals' ultimate educational attainments, ten years may not be a sufficient amount of time to monitor individuals' earnings. This methodological limitation may cause us to underestimate earnings variation and to underestimate some of the influences on earnings variation. For instance, many of those who pursue graduate education have just gotten out of school at age twenty-eight, and some are still in school. For others, the first ten years of work are often a time to serve an apprenticeship, to find oneself, or to accumulate savings that may allow one to start a business. We might imagine that individuals with more persistence (homework), better work habits (preparation), and higher activity levels (activities) ultimately do better at their jobs, but these effects might not emerge until they are more than thirty or forty years old. Unfortunately, as impressive as these data are, they cannot address these speculations.

But regardless of the limitations of these data, they show remarkably strong findings. Moreover, as a practical matter, they indicate that employers are missing out on valuable information. The employers who complain about workers' poor attendance, discipline, effort, and participation could be using information about these noncognitive behaviors in high school. These school behaviors predict which youth ultimately do better at work. Employers believe that teachers impose arbitrary demands that are irrelevant to work; perhaps they are recalling the idiosyncratic demands of a few teachers they had themselves. However, students' school behaviors appear to be good indicators of who will do well in the workplace. Perhaps this means that most teachers demand the same behaviors that are relevant to employers, or perhaps that students who can respond well to teachers' "arbitrary" demands can also work well with supervisors, coworkers, and customers—all of whom can also make arbitrary demands.

Moreover, students are also missing out on valuable socialization experiences and potential signals of their capabilities. If employers used school behavior information in hiring decisions, students would see some reason to develop the noncognitive skills and work habits required to show these behaviors. Employers' neglect of this information undercuts teachers' authority to demand these noncognitive behaviors, preventing school from doing the socialization that employers demand from school. Unwittingly, employers' own hiring practices prevent schools from meeting employers' demands.

No one should be surprised that earnings are related to an individual's normative compliance, ability to follow work procedures, and social skills. However, what is surprising is that these behaviors and attitudes in high school affect earnings many years later. Most employers and students we interviewed doubt that school behaviors are relevant to current real-world performance, much less nine years later. Employers say that schools merely require rote memorization of academic trivia and that students are judged according to irrelevant criteria by out-of-touch teachers who play favorites with ingratiating, brown-nosing geeks. In turn, in our survey of two thousand students, over 40 percent doubt that high school has any relevance to their future lives (see also Steinberg 1996). Our HSB findings about the effects of high school behaviors on long-term earnings outcomes will come as a surprise to many employers and students.

The long-term effects of these school behaviors are remarkable. Like the initiation rites for testing youth in simpler societies, high school is a testing ground for the noncognitive skills that our society demands. Even though no one recognizes their efforts, and institutional structures do not encourage them, schools are demanding and rewarding some of the right noncognitive behaviors. These analyses indicate that schools are focused on exactly the noncognitive behaviors that employers desperately need. Only the lack of a suitable infrastructure prevents schools' efforts from being realized and fully utilized. We can only imagine how much more effectively teachers could help students acquire valued noncognitive skills if their activities were formally recognized and encouraged, and if they had authority to control incentives that would motivate students.

Appendix: Variables

Social Context

Personal Demographics

- *Female:* An HSB composite variable (SEX) redefined into a dummy variable
- *Race-ethnicity:* An HSB composite variable (RACE) redefined into two dummy variables, black and Hispanic; white is the reserve category and includes Native Americans and Asians
- *Socioeconomic status:* From an HSB composite (FUSES), which is composed of father's occupation, father's education, mother's education, family income, and material possessions in the household

Local Demographics

- *Region:* Region of the country in which the high school is located, broken into three dummies for the South, the Northeast, and the West, with the Midwest as the comparison category

- *Type of school:* Whether the school is public or private, the dummy is for private, which includes both Catholic and nondenominational private schools; the reserve category is public

Achievement

Achievement was measured by a test given to seniors as part of the HSB survey (FUTEST).

Behavioral Characteristics

Industriousness We use the term "industriousness" to describe a group of variables defined as follows:

- *Interest:* Does the student report being interested in school (yes/no)?

- *Preparedness:* The extent to which students come to class prepared to work. We expected teachers to reward students for showing up to their classes ready to work. This is a composite measure compiled from three questions:

1. How often do you show up to school without pen or pencil, or paper?

2. How often do you show up to school without homework?

3. How often do you show up to school without your books?

   The alpha for this variable = .70.

- *Work hard:* The average time the student spends on homework per week. We expected teachers to reward students who work hard, regardless of their success. This variable is scaled:

   2 = Doesn't do homework

   3 = Does less than one hour per week

   4 = Does one to three hours per week

   5 = Does more than three hours and less than five hours per week

   6 = Does more than five hours and less than ten hours per week

7 = Does more than ten hours per week and less than fifteen hours per week

8 = Does fifteen or more hours per week

- *Attendance:* How many days the student missed between the beginning of school and winter vacation. Teachers may reward students who simply show up to their classes regularly, regardless of the quality of the work they do. Values are:

1 = Absent twenty-one or more days

2 = Absent sixteen to twenty days

3 = Absent eleven to fifteen days

4 = Absent five to ten days

5 = Absent three to four days

6 = Absent one to two days

7 = No absences

Social Interaction   We use the term "social interaction" to describe these attributes:

- *Unsocial:* We expect teachers to reward students for popularity, that is, for being socially successful among their peers. This is a composite variable comprising three questions:

1. Do others see you as socially active?

2. How popular are you with other students?

3. Do others see you as part of the leading crowd?

The alpha for this variable is .67.

- *Leadership:* Measures the number of leadership positions students hold in extracurricular activities, including athletics; leadership is a valued skill that teachers may reward.

- *Participation in extracurricular activities:* A variable created by giving one point for each school-based extracurricular activity in which a student participates. It is restricted to activities run through school because those are the activities that teachers are most likely to know about and to oversee.

Discipline

- *Discipline problems:* This is a composite score based on three true-or-false questions used because teachers may penalize students who are known troublemakers, whether or not they do good work in the classroom. It includes the following questions (note that higher score means lower level of discipline problems):

Last year I had disciplinary problems for academic reasons.

Last year I was suspended or on probation for academic reasons.

Last year I was suspended or on probation for disciplinary reasons.

The alpha is .54.

- *Minor discipline problems:* Whether the student cuts class once in a while; this variable is used to measure lower-level misbehavior.

Table 8A.1   Means and Standard Deviations on All Variables, for All Students

	Mean	Standard Deviation
SES	.01	.74
Female	.53	.50
Black	.11	.31
Hispanic	.19	.40
Northeast	.25	.43
South	.28	.45
West	.18	.38
Private	.27	.44
Test	53.18	8.52
Preparedness	.002	.98
Homework time	4.91	1.42
Attendance	5.63	1.24
Interest in school	.78	.42
Cutting class	.36	.48
Discipline problems	.014	.97
Unsocial	.002	.99
Leadership	.42	.49
Extracurricular activities	2.12	.92
Grades	4.43	1.29
EdYrs	13.75	1.94
LogEarn91	9.88	.73

Source: Author's compilation.

═ Chapter 9 ═

Pathways into Work: Short- and Long-Term Effects of Personal and Institutional Ties

THE CENTRAL focus of this book has been to understand why students face great difficulties in gaining recognition of their value in the labor market.[1] New high school graduates have difficulty getting jobs that offer better pay or advancement, and their jobs and pay tend to be unrelated to their school achievements (Bills 1992; Crain 1984; Parcel 1987; Grubb 1992; Jencks et al. 1979, 117; Stern et al. 1995). These outcomes are not well explained by economic or sociological theories. For instance, human capital theory predicts that new high school graduates with higher achievement will get better jobs and pay, but that prediction is clearly contradicted by research (Griffin et al. 1981; Murnane et al. 1995; Gamoran 1994; Miller 1998). Sociological theories suggest that the problem resides in the labor market structure: the labor market is stratified and youth are confined to low-strata jobs that offer poor stability, low pay, and little advancement—in other words, the secondary labor market (Doeringer and Piore 1971). Stratified labor market theory explains these findings, but it overexplains youths' difficulties. It has two problems: it does not explain why some youth escape the secondary labor market at the outset, or why many individuals eventually are able to escape it later (Granovetter 1974/1995).

In response to the failures of traditional economic and sociological theories (Althauser and Kalleberg 1981; Dore 1983; Williamson 1975), new theories have arisen in both fields. The new institutional economics considers the efficiencies of institutional relationships, and it calls for studies of actors and social contexts (Lazear 1979; Rosen 1982). Similarly, new sociological models contend that markets often "depend on the nature of personal relations and the network of relations between and within firms" (Granovetter 1985, 502). Instead of assuming that information is always used and trusted, these models describe some ways in which information is given meaning through social contacts. "People prefer to deal with individuals of known reputation, or, even better, with individuals they have dealt with before, social relations . . . are mainly responsible for the production of trust in economic life" (Granovetter 1985, 490–91).

Some of our employers indicate that job contacts help them assess young job applicants (chapter 6), but our sample cannot say how many and which kinds of students would be affected. Job contacts might explain how some youth can evade the ordinary obstacles of the labor market structure and get jobs that lead to better immediate pay and to better career trajectories that increase their earnings over time. This chapter examines whether different kinds of youths use different ways to contact employers, and whether youths' ways of contacting employers affect their earnings right after high school and nine years later. Besides examining the effects of two kinds of personal contacts (relatives and friends), it also explores the influence of two kinds of institutional contacts (school job placement and employment services), which have rarely been considered in previous research.

Contact Influences: Personal Versus Institutional Contacts

In recent years, there has been increasing interest in the influence of social contacts on labor market outcomes. Granovetter's (1973) early study showed how the job search process is facilitated by personal ties, particularly weak ties (for example, casual acquaintances); these provide wide sources of information about jobs, from which the job seeker can choose the best. However, Granovetter's sample consisted of experienced, well-educated workers, and subsequent research has suggested that weak personal ties are "of most advantage to those higher up and least to those at the bottom" (Granovetter 1974/1995, 150; Lin, Ensel, and Vaughn 1981). For less-educated, inexperienced workers, weak personal ties may be less effective (Ericksen and Yancey 1980; Wegener 1991).

Moreover, there is an additional concern that "cross-sectional analyses may miss the role of personal contacts in building a career" (Granovetter 1974/1995, 149). Granovetter suggests that early contacts may have a greater impact on later jobs than on early jobs. This might occur because of the accumulation of advantages that comes from initial contacts: good initial contacts lead to more and better subsequent contacts. Alternatively, it might occur as the result of career ladders: youth with good contacts get early jobs that lead to better future career advancement, even though these jobs pay no better than others initially (Rosenbaum 1984). These contentions suggest the need for longitudinal studies.

Researchers have focused on personal contacts while largely neglecting institutional contacts in the United States, although the latter type of contact has been studied in other nations. In Germany and Japan, institutional contacts help youth get access to good jobs (Osterman 1988; Kariya and Rosenbaum 1995; Brinton 1993). In these nations, many youth, particularly youth with higher school achievement, gain access to jobs with better training and advancement because these nations have institutional contacts between schools and employers that communicate youths' value to employers. In Japan, high school teachers nominate appropriate youth for better job openings, and employers generally respond to teachers' nominations because they value teachers' evaluations as reliable signals of youths' abilities and work habits (Rosenbaum and Kariya 1989). Similarly, in Germany a national employment agency uses students' grades to determine which students are to be nominated to the better apprenticeships, and employers also use grades in hiring youth who apply directly (Hamilton 1989). Both nations have stratified labor markets, but institutional networks communicate youths' value to employers, and youth who do well in school gain access to jobs with better advancement opportunities.

The United States lacks a formal system like Japan's or Germany's, so institutional contacts may have weaker effects or none at all. Yet it is possible that informal institutional contacts exist in the United States, perform similar functions, and explain how some youth get jobs that lead to better pay.

With so little research interest in institutional contacts, it is not surprising that the information in popular data sets is often inadequate. The National Longitudinal Survey of Youth (NLSY) finds that 4.8 percent of unemployed youth get jobs through state employment agencies, and 14.3 percent from personal ties—friends or relatives (Holzer 1988, 10)—but the NLSY asks about only one type of institutional contact (state employment agencies). Although the NLSY ignores jobs through private employment services and high schools, Holzer's (1996, 52) survey of employers finds that more employers obtain their most recently hired workers from these two sources (4.4 percent and 4.6 percent, respectively) than from state employment agencies (3.3 percent).

Moreover, the NLSY ignores a potentially important distinction: it merges "friends and relatives" into a single category (Holzer 1988). Thus, the NLSY finds that 25.3 percent of new hires come from personal referrals, but these data cannot distinguish whether referrals were friends or relatives; we have found this to be an important distinction. Therefore, the NLSY cannot study the distinction between friends and relatives or between employment services and schools, nor can many other longitudinal surveys of youth.

This chapter examines two kinds of institutional contacts in the United States. *Employment services* inform job seekers about many job openings, but they provide meager information about those jobs. Although employment services provide listings of job openings and applicants, they rarely convey much information to either employers or applicants, they have weak relationships with employers (Holzer 1995), and their influence has declined in the past twenty years (Bishop 1993). Employers do not expect employment services to screen applicants, and they would not trust their screening even if they did (Osterman 1988). Moreover, applicants find that searches take longer if they use employment services (Wielgosz and Carpenter 1987, 159).

We also examine the effects of *high schools* as institutional contacts for job seekers. Holzer's (1996) study of employers finds that 4.6 percent of jobs are filled by school placements, and Bishop's (1992) study of employers reports that 7.9 percent are filled this way (for small and medium-size employers). Our analyses find that about 8.5 percent of students report that they obtained a job with the help of their school. School job placement is conceptually important because it represents a form of institutional help that may function in ways similar to the Japanese and German systems. Indeed, some American employers have developed strong ties with certain high school teachers, and they trust these teachers' recommendations of students (Rosenbaum and Binder 1997). Moreover, school job placement would have important policy implications if it were available to all youth who attend high school (Rosenbaum and Jones 2000). Yet because American society does not have a formal system of contacts between schools and employers, as Japan and Germany do (Hamilton 1990; Rosenbaum and Kariya 1989), and because job placement help is not a formal responsibility of American high schools, school job placement is generally unrecognized and unstudied.

Our research examines the effects of various kinds of contacts on youths' earnings. We look at two kinds of personal contact and two kinds of institutional contact. Although there are only a few studies that have examined hiring through institutional ties, those studies suggest that employers have weak relationships with employment services and strong relationships with vocational teachers (Osterman 1988; Rosenbaum and Jones 1995). We hypothesize that *youth receive better pay if they got their job through their high school, but not if they got their job through an employment service.*

The two kinds of personal contacts we look at in this chapter are *relatives* and *peers.* Many employers rely on recommendations by current workers, especially ones with seniority, and workers often recommend relatives (Manwaring 1984). Moreover, employers often consciously recruit within families, hiring the "lads of dads," in order to build on the social obligations and control that come with kinship ties (Grieco 1987, 37). Because they have less seniority and social control, youths' friends tend to have less influence with employers than relatives do (Borman 1991). Therefore, we hypothesize that *youth receive better pay if they got their job through a relative, but not if they got their job through a peer.*

In addition, following Granovetter's reasoning, we hypothesize that *contact effects may increase over time.* Consequently, we use a longitudinal survey that allows us to analyze the effects of various kinds of contacts right after high school and nine years later.

We also expect that different kinds of youths get jobs through different kinds of contacts. Since minority and low-SES youths' relatives are more likely to be unemployed (Wilson 1996), and since females, minorities, and low-SES youth tend to receive lower earnings (Jencks et al. 1979; Farkas 1996), this chapter considers them disadvantaged groups. We hypothesize that *these disadvantaged groups receive less job-seeking help from relatives.* The same may be true for friends, although research is less clear. Since societal institutions (high schools and especially employment services) are responsible for helping disadvantaged groups, we hypothesize that *disadvantaged groups get more help from institutional contacts than others do.* Although teachers often favor females and disfavor blacks and Hispanics in the classroom (Bossert 1979), research offers no indication of which groups are helped by school job placement. We also hypothesize that *jobs obtained though personal ties are unrelated to school achievement, but jobs obtained through school contacts may be related to school achievement.*

These hypotheses are based on little research, since few studies have been done. Indeed, as noted, some of the best longitudinal data sets do not permit analysis of some of these issues. If Granovetter (1995) is correct that longitudinal surveys are needed, the HSB data we are using are distinctively appropriate for studying the long-term effects of contacts.

The Model and Plan for Analysis

The hypotheses propose that different kinds of individuals get jobs through different kinds of job contacts, which have different effects on short-term and long-term earnings. The analysis is presented in two stages. First, we analyze who gets jobs through each type of job contact, in bivariate analyses and multivariate logistic analyses. Second, we analyze the effects of each type of contact on short-term and long-term earnings.

Our model examines who gets jobs through each type of contact, first in terms of individual background attributes (socioeconomic status, ethnicity, gender), and second by adding school variables (track and private schools) and individuals' test scores. In explaining earnings, our model examines the influence of individual background attributes (socioeconomic status, ethnicity, gender), school variables (track and private schools), test scores, and placement variables. Because earnings may vary by region, we add regional variables to the earnings regressions.

Data and Variables

The best test of the long-term effects of contacts would use longitudinal data because of the unreliability of retrospective reports of networks. Consequently, this chapter is based on the longitudinal survey High School and Beyond, using the cohort that graduated in 1982, followed through 1992.

For the job search variables, the survey asked students which job search method was most important in getting their first job. In studying the various kinds of job contacts, our analyses compare the effects of the various ways in which students get their jobs: school placement, relatives, friends, employment services, or other means (civil service, union, and so on), each represented by a dummy variable. The last category (civil service, union, or other) is included because it sometimes has strong effects, but it is not easily interpreted. Since the opposite of using contacts is making direct applications to employers in response to want ads or signs, direct application is in the constant. This question is clearly better than the NLSY item in allowing analyses to distinguish between many different types of help.

Since school tracking can have many effects on students' education (Gamoran 1994; Rosenbaum 1976), we include dummy variables for general and vocational tracks (with college track as the comparison). In the United States, the vocational track is the main institutional way in which public schools address work-entry issues, but nearly all students take some vocational classes (Wirt et al. 1989). Although some critics argue that the vocational track has a detrimental influence on students, research does not find that it hurts earnings, even compared to the higher-status college track (Kang and Bishop 1986; Rosenbaum 1996a). We also control for attending private schools.

The other independent variables are ones usually included in such analyses: socioeconomic status, ethnicity, gender, test scores, and region. Socioeconomic status is a continuous scale composite of parents' education and occupational status in the HSB data file. (Units are not comparable with Blau and Duncan's socioeconomic index [SEI] [1967] or other standard SES scales.) Black and Hispanic are dummy variables, with other races as the comparison (in the constant). Female is a dummy variable. Test scores are a composite from achievement tests in the HSB survey. Since wage rates often vary by region, variables are added for students' region—the Northeast, the South, or the West, with the Midwest being the comparison in these regressions.

To examine whether social contacts help youth evade secondary labor market jobs that offer low pay and little advancement in job status or earnings, we analyze earnings as the dependent variable. Early job contacts that lead to higher earnings, especially later earnings, would indicate escape from the secondary labor market (Althauser and Kalleberg 1981; Gamoran 1994). This chapter examines earnings in the first year after graduation and nine years later, in 1991. (1992 earnings are not for a full year.)[2]

Analyses: Use of Job Placement Help

This section describes the incidence of the various kinds of contact that high school graduates use to get jobs in the year after graduation. Most students get their first job directly, using no contacts (30.5 percent). Of those using contacts, most use friends (22.2 percent of all first jobs) or relatives (13.8 percent). School placement is a relatively infrequently used method of entry into the labor market (8.5 percent), and employment services are used even less (4.2 percent). A few youths use civil service, union, or other sources (11.0 percent).[3] If we take only this overview, then it is easy to dismiss school placement as an infrequently used method, and it is not surprising that previous studies with findings on school placement did not comment on them (Holzer 1996).

However, these averages conceal important variation among subgroups of youth (table 9.1). Women and blacks use school placement more frequently than do men and whites. Among high school graduates who had earnings in the year after graduation, black women use

Table 9.1   Job Search Method, by Gender and Ethnicity

	School	Relatives	Friends	Employment Service	Direct	Other	No Answer
Black women	15.6%	4.9%	19.6%	8.4%	36.4%	4.9%	10.2%
Hispanic women	10.1	12.3	21.4	6.5	33.5	6.3	9.9
White women	9.3	13.3	22.1	5.7	32.8	9.6	7.2
Black men	10.3	13.4	21.3	3.2	24.9	12.7	14.2
Hispanic men	5.1	15.4	23.4	2.4	29.4	11.6	12.7
White men	7.2	15.9	22.4	2.4	28.3	13.7	10.1

Source: Author's compilation.

school placement the most (15.6 percent), followed by black men (10.3 percent) and Hispanic and white women (10.1 percent and 9.3 percent, respectively). In contrast, fewer white and Hispanic men use school placement (7.2 percent and 5.1 percent, respectively). Relatives' job help runs in the reverse direction, with white and Hispanic males receiving the most job help from relatives, women receiving less help from relatives than males of all ethnic groups, and black women receiving the least such help. Although we would expect some inverse relationships since only one answer can be given, this particular relationship is striking, since the vast majority of students use other alternatives (especially friends and direct contacts). This finding suggests that schools help those groups that are less likely to get help from relatives.

It is also noteworthy that while only 8.5 percent of students get jobs through school placement, job placement is an activity at more than half of the 999 high schools in the HSB sample. About 46 percent of all high schools in the sample have no seniors getting jobs through school help. About half of the remaining high schools in the HSB sample place more than 12 percent of their students. Restricting our analysis to work-bound students in the HSB sample, we find that fewer than 5 percent of all schools place 25 percent or more of their work-bound students. Thus, school placement is widely distributed across American high schools, but only a small portion of work-bound students get such help in most schools.

Who Gets Which Kinds of Job Placement Help?

We now turn to multivariate analyses to examine which kinds of individuals get which kinds of job help. Unlike the preceding descriptions, these analyses control for other factors that may influence job help, such as achievement, private schooling, and track placement. Initial analyses included regions, but they are omitted here because they have no influence and do not alter other influences. Because each type of job help is a dichotomous dependent variable, logistic analyses are used.

We ran analyses in two stages, first using a simple demographic model (socioeconomic status, female, black, Hispanic), and then a full model that adds school variables and individual achievement. As is customary, we consider coefficients to be significant if they are twice their standard error.

We hypothesized that disadvantaged groups get little help from relatives and friends and more help from institutional contacts. Beginning with help from relatives, the short and long models both find that females and blacks are significantly less likely to get help from relatives, but Hispanic is not significant in either model (tables 9.2 and 9.3). Socioeconomic status has a significant influence on help from relatives in the full model (but not the short model). Students get relatives' help regardless of their track or school, and low-achieving students are more likely to get help from relatives.

In contrast, friends seem to be an equal opportunity provider. Females, blacks, and Hispanics get job help from their friends as often as white males do in both models. Moreover, in the larger model, none of the variables has a significant influence on getting jobs from friends. As we subsequently discover, friends' help does not lead to better-paid jobs.

School help also represents a contrast in the kinds of youth who are helped. In the short model, females, blacks, and high-SES youth are significantly *more* likely to get their jobs through school help, but Hispanics are not. In the full model, females and blacks are significantly more likely to get their jobs through school help, but the SES effect becomes insignificant, apparently mediated by test scores. In addition, higher-achieving students are significantly more likely to get their jobs through school help. Vocational-track students are as likely as college-track students to get school job help, perhaps because many college-track students take some vocational courses (Wirt et al. 1989).

In the short model, the employment service also offers significantly greater opportunity for females and low-SES youth, but not for blacks or Hispanics. In the larger model, the female and SES effects remain, and nothing else is significant. Just as its mission dictates, the employment service is more useful to low-SES youth.

To the right of each coefficient, the tables report the exponent of the coefficient (Exp [B]), which indicates how the variable changes the

Table 9.2 Logit Analyses of Kinds of Job Help (Reduced Form)

	1 School/Exp (B)		2 Relatives/Exp (B)		3 Friends/Exp (B)		4 Empl Service/Exp (B)	
SES	.275* (.075)	1.316	-.005 (.063)	.995	.065 (.052)	1.067	-.464* (.112)	.629
Female	.414* (.105)	1.512	-.278* (.086)	.757	-.024 (.071)	.976	.859* (.157)	2.361
Black	.525* (.158)	1.691	-.438* (.171)	.645	-.109 (.127)	.897	.206 (.232)	1.228
Hispanic	-.020 (.143)	.980	-.085 (.113)	.919	.004 (.093)	1.003	-.078 (.193)	.925
Constant	-2.589 (.089)		-1.654 (.064)		-1.204 (.055)		-3.675 (.141)	
Percentage correct	90.96		86.25		77.32		95.68	
Chi square	37.28		17.47		2.77		53.83	
Significance	.0000		.0016		.5972		.0000	

Source: Author's compilation.
* = p < .05

Table 9.3 Logit Analyses of Kinds of Job Help (full model)

	1 School / Exp (B)		2 Relatives / Exp (B)		3 Friends / Exp (B)		4 Empl Service / Exp (B)	
SES	.064 (.082)	1.066	.101* (.049)	1.107	.093 (.056)	1.097	-.333* (.121)	.717
Female	.435* (.108)	1.544	-.284* (.089)	.753	-.030 (.073)	.971	.898* (.163)	2.456
Black	.696* (.166)	2.006	-.486* (.176)	.615	-.116 (.132)	.891	.130 (.245)	1.139
Hispanic	.135 (.149)	1.145	-.140 (.118)	.869	-.024 (.097)	.976	-.143 (.203)	.867
General track	-.216 (.122)	.806	-.090 (.100)	.914	.109 (.081)	1.115	-.059 (.176)	.943
Vocational track	-.030 (.173)	.971	-.011 (.136)	.989	-.198 (.119)	.821	.361 (.210)	1.435
Private school	.089 (.122)	1.093	.008 (.108)	1.008	-.066 (.088)	.936	.048 (.186)	1.049
Achievement test	.056* (.008)	1.057	-.025* (.006)	.976	-.008 (.005)	.992	-.014 (.010)	.986
Constant	-5.587 (.464)		-.312 (.340)		-.773 (.284)		-2.987 (.593)	
Percentage correct	90.83		86.27		77.33		95.65	
Chi square	102.09		32.06		13.43		56.96	
Significance	.0000		.0001		.0978		.0000	

Source: Author's compilation.

* = p < .05

odds of the outcome. Thus, in the full model, being female increases the odds of getting school help by 54.4 percent and of getting employment service help by 145.6 percent, while decreasing the odds of getting relatives' help by 24.7 percent (1 − .753). Being black increases the odds of getting school help by 100.6 percent and decreases the odds of getting relatives' help by 38.5 percent. A one-standard-deviation increase in socioeconomic status (.66) increases the odds of receiving relatives' help by 7.1 percent but decreases the odds of employment service help by 18.7 percent. A one-standard-deviation increase in test scores (7.8) raises the odds of school job placement by 44.5.[4]

In sum, the hypothesis that disadvantaged youth get less help from relatives is supported for females, blacks, and socioeconomic status (long model), but not for Hispanics. The hypothesis that disadvantaged youth get more help from institutional contacts is supported for females and blacks in getting school help (but not for SES or Hispanics), and for low-SES and females for employment service help (but not for blacks or Hispanics). The SES effect on school help is the only significant relationship to contradict the disadvantaged hypothesis, but it disappears after test scores are controlled. As hypothesized, school help is meritocratic (based on school achievement), and relatives' help is unmeritocratic, helping low-achieving youth more.

To oversimplify, while relatives preserve social advantage and are anti-meritocratic (on test scores), school job placement helps many who are socially disadvantaged and is meritocratic. Employment services also serve many of those who are socially disadvantaged (females and low-SES), but they are not meritocratic. Friends are indiscriminate on most criteria.

Regression Analyses on Early and Later Earnings

The following analyses examine the influence of job contacts on youths' earnings. Because the policy literature considers the lack of a college degree the primary mark of disadvantage and labels this group "the Forgotten Half" (see Howe 1988), and some research suggests that college confers little earnings benefit unless one gets a degree (Jencks et al. 1979; Grubb 1993, 1995a; however, see Kane and Rouse 1995), our sample is youth who graduate from high school but get no college degrees (A.A. or higher).

We use multivariate analyses to examine the effect of the various kinds of contacts on youths' earnings. Since we have taken the natural logarithm of earnings, coefficients will indicate the *percentage* increases (not dollar increases) that each independent variable contributes to earnings. These analyses first examine the determinants of early earnings right after graduation. We then present analyses of youths' earnings nine years after graduation. For comparability, these analyses consider only the 3,245 youths who have earnings in both periods.

The Determinants of Earnings Immediately After High School

These analyses examine the factors affecting youths' first earnings after high school graduation. Many studies have examined the determinants of early earnings, and they typically explain small amounts of variance, just as we do. For instance, Richard Murnane, John Willett, and Frank Levy (1995, table 3) explain between 4 and 8 percent of wages six years after high school in the cohort of 1980 HSB seniors. Norton Grubb (1992, table 3) explains 3 to 11 percent of wages in the NLS72. Also analyzing the NLS72, Larry Griffin, Arne Kalleberg, and Karl Alexander (1981, 219) conclude: "Initial entry into labor market segments was almost a random process, at least for the pool of non-college-educated workers." In contrast, for youths who have been in the labor market for ten to fifteen years, analyses typically find an R-squared over 16 percent (see Farkas 1996, 47). Comparing several longitudinal and cross-sectional studies, Christopher Jencks and his colleagues (1979, 117) conclude that the effects of school factors increase steadily up to around the age of thirty-five.

In the first stage, the linear regression to explain early earnings finds that socioeconomic status has a strong positive influence, and that being female has a strong negative influence (table 9.4, column 1). Blacks' earnings are less than those of the comparison group (whites and Asians), but not quite significant. Hispanics' earnings are not significantly lower. Earnings are higher in the Northeast and West than in the Midwest.

In the next stage, adding school variables and individuals' test scores does not alter these influences (table 9.4, column 2). We find that the early earnings of vocational- and general-track students are not different from those of college-track students, and the earnings of private school graduates are not different from those of public school graduates. We find that individuals' test scores have no influence on their earnings right after high school, corroborating the findings of the many studies cited earlier.

Adding job search method (table 9.4, column 3), employment service help raises earnings by 6.6 percent, but since employment services focus on adults and help only 4 percent of these youths, this

Table 9.4   Determinants of Youths' 1983 Earnings (Ln) (Unstandardized Coefficient/Standard Error)

	Ln(Earnings 1983)	Ln(Earnings 1983) [adding school variables]	Ln(Earnings 1983) [adding placement variables]
All variables			
SES	.056*	.052*	.053*
	(.009)	(.009)	(.010)
Female	−.138*	−.140*	−.141*
	(.012)	(.012)	(.012)
Black	−.034	−.031	−.031
	(.019)	(.020)	(.020)
Hispanic	−.023	−.019	−.019
	(.017)	(.018)	(.018)
Northeast	.064*	.057*	.058*
	(.017)	(.018)	(.018)
South	.006	.003	.005
	(.015)	(.015)	(.015)
West	.087*	.089*	.089*
	(.017)	(.018)	(.018)
General track	—	.002	.002
		(.013)	(.014)
Vocational track	—	.011	−.014
		(.016)	(.017)
Private school	—	.035	.033
		(.023)	(.023)
Achievement test ($\times 10^{-2}$)	—	.058	.075
		(.085)	(.085)
Placement variables			
Relatives	—	—	.038*
			(.018)
Friends	—	—	.024
			(.016)
Employment service	—	—	.066*
			(.027)
Civil service, union, other	—	—	.029
			(.020)
School placement	—	—	.040
			(.027)
Constant	9.238	9.211	9.182
R-squared (adjusted)	6.8%	6.9%	7.0%
Significance (F-test)	.0000	.0000	.0000

Source: Author's compilation.
Note: N = 3,245.
* = p < .05

large effect is for relatively few individuals. The other methods have small and mostly insignificant effects. Relatives' contacts raise earnings by 3.8 percent (significant); school contacts raise earnings about the same, but the coefficient is not significant.

The Determinants of Earnings Nine Years After High School

Nine years later, when these youths are about twenty-eight years old, the linear regression to explain 1991 earnings (ln) finds that socioeconomic status continues to have a strong positive influence, and that being female continues to have strong negative influences on earnings (table 9.5, column 1). Hispanics and blacks do not have lower earnings net of SES. Earnings are higher in the Northeast than in the Midwest, but no other regional differences emerge.

In the next stage, adding school variables slightly alters these influences (table 9.5, column 2). We find that vocational- and general-track students have earnings that are no different than those of college-track students (who took jobs after high school). Private school graduates do not have significantly higher earnings than public school graduates. Test scores have a strong significant influence on youths' later earnings, in contrast with the earlier period. Apparently, although youths' achievements are not rewarded at the outset, they are rewarded later, as has been seen in other research (Murnane, Willett, and Levy 1995; Altonji and Pierret 1995).

Adding job search method (table 9.5, column 3), we find that school help has the largest influence, raising earnings by 17.0 percent. Relative contacts have smaller, but significant, benefits (8.6 percent), but the youths who got jobs through employment services no longer have significantly higher earnings. Youths who got their first jobs through friends have no earnings benefit.

Adding early earnings (table 9.5, column 4), we find that the influence of most variables (socioeconomic status, being female, and living in the Northeast) remain significant and at about the same level, although early earnings mediate some of the influences. Black and Hispanic remain insignificant. The achievement effect declines minimally and remains highly significant. Achievement has little influence on early earnings, and virtually all of its influence on later earnings is independent of early earnings. The placement variables decline after controlling for early earnings, but relatives and school placement remain strong and significant. School placement has a particularly large influence net of early earnings, suggesting that the jobs gained through this means offer better earnings trajectories.

Table 9.5   Determinants of Youths' 1991 Earnings (Ln) (Unstandardized Coefficient/Standard Error)

	Ln(Earnings 1991)	Ln(Earnings 1991) [Adding School Variables]	Ln(Earnings 1991) [Adding Placement Variables]	Ln(Earnings 1991) [Adding Prior Earnings]
All variables				
SES	.126*	.118*	.120*	.099*
	(.020)	(.021)	(.021)	(.021)
Female	−.379*	−.376*	−.372*	−.316*
	(.025)	(.026)	(.026)	(.026)
Black	−.017	.035	.030	.043
	(.042)	(.044)	(.044)	(.043)
Hispanic	.035	.030	.030	.036
	(.038)	(.040)	(.039)	(.039)
Northeast	.146*	.111*	.110*	.087*
	(.038)	(.038)	(.038)	(.038)
South	.057	.046	.048	.046
	(.033)	(.033)	(.033)	(.032)
West	.013	.011	.010	−.025
	(.038)	(.039)	(.039)	(.039)
General track	—	−.011	−.010	−.011
		(.030)	(.030)	(.029)
Vocational track	—	.017	.011	.017
		(.037)	(.037)	(.036)
Private school	—	.084	.075	.062
		(.050)	(.050)	(.049)
Achievement test ($\times 10^{-2}$)	—	.603*	.624*	.594*
		(.182)	(.182)	(.179)
Placement variables				
Relatives	—	—	.086*	.070*
			(.035)	(.034)
Friends	—	—	−.015	−.025
			(.033)	(.033)
Employment service	—	—	.084	.058
			(.058)	(.057)
Civil service, union, other	—	—	.115*	.103*
			(.043)	(.042)
School placement	—	—	.170*	.155*
			(.063)	(.062)
Ln (Earnings 83)	—	—		.401*
				(.037)
Constant	9.885	9.588	9.541	6.014
R-squared (adjusted)	7.7%	8.1%	8.5%	11.7%
Significance (F-test)	.0000	.0000	.0000	.0000

Source: Author's compilation.
Note: N = 3,245.
* = p < .05

These results confirm Granovetter's hypothesis: early contacts have a greater impact on later jobs than on early jobs. However, this is true only for certain kinds of contacts. Relatives and school placement have larger effects on later earnings than on early earnings. As hypothesized, relatives and school placement have significant effects, but friends and employment services do not. Most notably, school placement, which disproportionately helps females and minorities and is generally unrecognized in American society, has very strong effects on later earnings. School placement leads to vastly superior earnings trajectories over the first decade.

Conclusions

Just as institutionalized contacts allow Japanese and German teachers to help students get jobs, our findings indicate that American high schools sometimes help students enter work, and that blacks and females are more likely to get their first jobs through school job placement than white males are. Moreover, school contacts (and relatives) help youth to get jobs that lead to higher later earnings. School placement leads to vastly superior earnings trajectories. This is a degree of earnings advancement that is not consistent with secondary labor market jobs and may indicate that school contacts allow youth to escape the secondary labor market.

The results are different for personal and institutional ties. For personal ties, we find that both relatives and friends have little effect on early earnings. (The benefits of relatives, however, though not large, are significant.) The jobs obtained through relatives lead to large and significant earnings benefits nine years later, but the jobs obtained through friends do not. For institutional contacts, school contacts lead to jobs that result in higher earnings nine years later, while the benefit of getting a job through an employment service occurs largely at the outset and is not significant nine years later. This is consistent with findings from a study using a very different source of data—employer reports. Bishop (1992, table 7) finds that being referred by a public employment service has no effect on employees' longer-term profitability, but that being referred by a vocational teacher significantly increases profitability by about 15 percent. The results for long-term earnings generally support our hypotheses about institutional and personal ties: school placement and relatives' contacts have strong earnings benefits and employment services and friends' contacts do not.

These results confirm Granovetter's hypothesis: early contacts have less impact on early jobs than on later jobs. The effects increase over time. School and relatives' contacts have a significant influence on later earnings, but not on early earnings, and a significant influence on later earnings net of early earnings. Thus, one kind of contact that Granovetter did not study, school contacts, also supports his hypothesis. The idea that a factor could have a larger influence nine years later than it had at the outset is perhaps counterintuitive, but it is exactly what Granovetter predicted.

Our findings on school achievement fit the same pattern: twelfth-grade test scores have stronger effects on earnings over time. The increasing effect of test scores over time has been previously shown (Murnane, Willett, and Levy 1995; Altonji and Pierret 1995). In interpreting these findings, these economists assume that employers do not have information about test scores; the influence of achievement on workers' earnings emerges as its influence on their subsequent performance becomes manifest.[5]

In contrast, employers are aware of the contacts they use, so the signaling interpretation cannot be used. A structural interpretation seems plausible. Youths hired through relatives or school contacts may be assigned to jobs that offer better career trajectory possibilities and lead to higher later earnings, even though early earnings are not higher. In effect, contacts may allow youth to escape the customary dead-end "youth jobs" in the secondary labor market. This speculation warrants further study.

The small influence of most factors in explaining early earnings might be altered by adding new variables; however, our analyses are totally consistent with a large number of comparable studies (cited earlier) that control for various combinations of other variables and explain little variance in the early earnings of high school graduates. After analyzing many dependent and independent variables, Griffin, Kalleberg, and Alexander (1981, 213) state the finding succinctly: "The first job following high school termination . . . appears largely unaffected by a host of variables known to be important for later life achievement."

It is also possible that our early wage variable is unreliable. Of course, all national surveys of youth have the same problem of self-reported earnings and job attributes, which youth may misreport, misperceive, or misunderstand. Studies of firms' personnel records avoid the problem of reporting error; such studies suggest that new high school graduates are typically assigned to a limited set of entry jobs that offer fairly similar initial pay (Baron and Bielby 1980; Rosenbaum 1984). Moreover, employers report that even though they make special accommodations to hire youth with valued skills, they rarely differentiate their pay; they do, however, gradually advance these youth to more challenging jobs as they exhibit more potential (Rosenbaum and Binder 1996). Therefore, various sources of data support the inference that these earnings results reflect actual labor market processes, not just measurement error.

Are job contacts chosen by youth or determined by others? Youths with well-connected parents and teachers have choices. However, if youths' relatives are unemployed and their teachers lack job contacts, their choices are restricted to other kinds of contacts (especially friends) that do not lead to long-term earnings benefits in our analyses. William Julius Wilson (1996) has urged that high schools help disadvantaged groups get jobs, but schools rarely define this as a responsibility. Nonetheless, these results indicate that students do sometimes get jobs through school contacts, and that school contacts help females and blacks, the groups that get less help from relatives. Research needs to examine the question of why some schools or teachers offer job help while others do not. Research also needs to examine why youth choose one contact over another (for those who have several alternatives), and which youth have only poor alternatives. This chapter is a first step in addressing these issues.

We should not get lost in numbers and variable names. Job contacts are not merely variables. They represent potentially important social processes in youths' lives. In the United States, where formal job help systems are not available, the school contacts we have discovered appear to have a lasting impact on youths' first decade in the labor market, especially for some groups that cannot count on relatives.

From a practical viewpoint, these findings indicate that high schools can and do help youth get jobs, and that youth get better jobs this way. Students could benefit from knowing this information. School achievement and school contacts lead to jobs that ultimately result in much higher earnings, even if they have little or no early benefits. Because it is easier for high school seniors to see what happened to last year's graduates than to see how those who graduated ten years earlier are doing, they are more likely to be aware of early effects than later effects. This may explain why youth do not see incentives for doing well in school (Ray and Mickelson 1993; Bishop 1993) or for seeking help from their school in finding a job. Although teachers may tell students that school can help them, students tend to doubt such statements as self-serving (chapter 3). If work-bound students realized that school contacts and achievement could help them get better later earnings, they would see incentives to work in high school, as students who aspire to enroll in selective colleges now do.

In addition, although the United States does not give schools or teachers any responsibility for helping youth get jobs, we find that schools sometimes help students get jobs anyway, and that when this happens students gain substantial earnings benefits, especially in later years. Although few students are currently helped in finding jobs, it is possible that such help could be vastly expanded by encouraging teachers to provide it and giving them time and incentives to do so. Unlike the current policy focus on using job training programs to fix youths' labor market difficulties after they have become serious problems, policies that encourage school job contacts might prevent such problems from occurring in the first place. The next chapter explores how these school job contacts operate.

Appendix: The Effects of High School Grades

Employers rarely have access to test scores, which are expensive to administer and pose a threat of EEO litigation. Although our analyses have focused on test scores, as is customary in such research (Altonji and Pierret 1995), test scores may not affect employers' behavior if they do not have this information. In contrast, high school grades are readily available. Employers can ask job applicants to bring their transcripts to a job interview, or they can telephone teachers, who report that they are happy to evaluate students for employers (see Rosenbaum and Jones 2000).

As noted, employers complain about grades, but their complaints are perplexing. Employers say that grades reflect a student's grasp of narrow academic trivia, which is irrelevant to their practical needs, yet employers complain about workers' poor literacy and communication skills, which grades might signal. Employers also disparage grades as being distorted by teachers' biases and subjective impressions, yet employers are very concerned about their own foremen's subjective complaints, which are likely to be caused by the same kind of poor work habits and discipline that cause teachers' negative evaluations. Thus, although employers do not value grades, it is possible that they should. Grades may contain some information about students' potential productivity that employers should value. Some of this information will be about work habits and other behaviors that are not signaled by test scores, as we saw in chapter 8.

Like previous research (Altonji and Pierret 1995; Murnane, Willett, and Levy 1995), our prior analyses considered test scores and not grades. However, this appendix adds grades to the model, and we examine whether grades affect earnings independent of test scores. Unlike chapter 8, this chapter examines only noncollege youths, and it examines whether the grade effects are mediated by job placement variables.

Column 1 of table 9A.1 simply reproduces a previous finding (from table 9.5, column 2). Adding high school grades reduces the test score effects (column 2), and given employers' disdain for grades, it is surprising that grades have a clearly significant effect, while the test score effect is no longer significant. Adding job placement variables, we see that grades remain significant, and that little of their influence is mediated by job placement variables (column 3).

Grades have effects independent of test scores. Grades may reflect teachers' subjective judgments of student achievement, but it appears that these may be "judgments" that could be useful to employers—they pay a premium to students who had better high school grades, independent of their test scores. We might speculate that grades indicate achievement and work habits not signaled by test scores. In previous analyses of these data, Shazia Miller (1998) showed that grades have no effects on early earnings, but strong effects on later earnings. Our findings indicate that these grade effects occur even after controls for test scores, and they are independent of job placement effects. Although employers mistrust grades and think of them as biased, grades turn out to be good predictors of which youth will do well in the workplace. Employers could get a valuable indicator of youths' ultimate productivity by using grades in the hiring process. However, school placement continues to have an influence that is largely independent of test scores and grades.

Fixed-Effects

Although these results indicate effects at the individual level, students are in different high schools, and we might wonder whether the observed effects reflect schoolwide differences in which some schools offer more school placement and higher grading curves, rather than individual differences. Fixed-effects models, which look at the influence of each individual's deviation from his or her school-mean on that variable, allow us to examine whether individual differences in measured attributes have effects within schools.

Fixed effects are comparable to Hierarchical Linear Model (HLM) analysis. HLM has the advantage of producing estimates for the effects of various attributes at the aggregate level (for example, school size, resources, standards), while fixed-effects models do not produce such estimates. Fixed-effects models compare students within the same school, so any link between individual effort (deviation from the school mean) and success cannot be attributed to school charac-

Table 9A.1   Determinants of Youths' 1991 Earnings (Ln) (Unstandardized Coefficient/Standard Error)

	Ln(Earnings 1991)	Ln(Earnings 1991) [Adding Grades]	Ln(Earnings 1991) [Adding Placement Variables]
All variables			
SES	.118*	.121*	.123*
	(.021)	(.021)	(.021)
Female	−.376*	−.396*	−.391*
	(.026)	(.026)	(.027)
Black	.035	.043	.038
	(.044)	(.044)	(.044)
Hispanic	.030	.034	.033
	(.040)	(.039)	(.039)
Northeast	.111*	.119*	.118*
	(.038)	(.038)	(.038)
South	.046	.039	.042
	(.033)	(.033)	(.033)
West	.011	.001	.000
	(.039)	(.039)	(.039)
General track	−.011	−.004	−.004
	(.030)	(.030)	(.030)
Vocational track	.017	.022	.016
	(.037)	(.037)	(.037)
Private school	.084	.095	.086
	(.050)	(.050)	(.050)
Achievement test ($\times\ 10^{-2}$)	.603*	.369	.399*
	(.182)	(.196)	(.196)
High school variables		.041*	.039*
		(.013)	(.013)
Placement variables			
Relatives	—	—	.087*
			(.038)
Friends	—	—	−.011
			(.033)
Employment service	—	—	.092
			(.058)
Civil service, union, other	—	—	.116*
			(.043)
School placement	—	—	.161*
			(.063)
Constant	9.588	9.547	9.499
R-squared (adjusted)	8.1%	8.3%	8.7%
Significance (F-test)	.0000	.0000	.0000

Source: Author's compilation.
Note: N = 3,245.
* = p < .05

teristics. Some researchers consider fixed effects a more powerful technique for dealing with the unmeasured biasing characteristics of schools, since it does not depend on assuming that the research has controlled for all relevant school attributes. Since this research is concerned not with examining school attribute effects but only with removing school effects so that we can examine individual-level effects, fixed effects is an appropriate choice.

The models described earlier were run in fixed-effects tests, using the program STATA. Variables that are constant for a high school (like region and private school) drop out of the analysis. The fixed-effects analysis finds that most effects are somewhat smaller, but the grades effect appears to be larger. Most influences take virtually the same shape as in the regression analyses here (tables 9.5 and 9A.1). Even within schools, school placement continues to have a large influence on later earnings.

Table 9A.2   Fixed Effects Regression Analysis Predicting Earnings in 1991

	Ln(Earnings 1991)	Ln(Earnings 1991) [Adding Grades]	Ln(Earnings 1991) [Adding Prior Variables]
All variables			
SES	.090*	.091*	.051*
	(.019)	(.019)	(.022)
Female	− .366*	− .410*	− .358*
	(.023)	(.024)	(.028)
Black	.018	.032	.001
	(.042)	(.042)	(.050)
Hispanic	.005	.013	.031
	(.033)	(.033)	(.038)
General track	− .009	.003	.010
	(.027)	(.027)	(.030)
Vocational track	− .025	− .015	.006
	(.034)	(.037)	(.039)
Placement variables			
Relatives	.079*	.075*	.038
	(.034)	(.033)	(.038)
Friends	.012	.017	− .020
	(.029)	(.029)	(.033)
Employment service	.109*	.103	.026
	(.055)	(.055)	(.059)

(Table continues on p. 216.)

Table 9A.2 *Continued*

	Ln(Earnings 1991)	Ln(Earnings 1991) [Adding Grades]	Ln(Earnings 1991) [Adding Placement Variables]
Civil service, union, other	.117*	.114*	.102*
	(.038)	(.038)	(.043)
School placement	.170*	.138*	.119*
	(.049)	(.049)	(.055)
Achievement test ($\times 10^{-2}$)	.884*	.304	.299
	(.153)	(.174)	(.202)
Grades	—	.081*	.074*
		(.012)	(.014)
Log earnings 1983	—	—	.353*
			(.037)
Constant	9.478*	9.457*	6.252*
	(.088)	(.087)	(.355)
Overall R-squared	9.4%	9.3%	12.9%
N	5,204	5,203	3,739

Source: Author's compilation.
* = $p < .05$

= Chapter 10 =

Hidden Links: Teachers' Social Construction of Employer Linkages

C HAPTER 9 reported that high schools help students get jobs, and that this assistance leads to better long-term earnings outcomes. But the data behind this finding do not tell us how this happens.[1] Theory sometimes explains processes, but not in this case. Functionalist theories assume that schools and labor markets are mutually responsive by some automatic process, but these theories are vague about the specific mechanisms that make them responsive.

In contrast, network theory contends that market responsiveness often depends on social relationships. Unlike German and Japanese schools, however, most American high schools have no formal social relationships with employers for making job placements. High school career services do not provide job placement, guidance counselors rarely have job contacts, and schools do not specify any actions that staff should take to help students get jobs. School-business partnerships, co-op programs, and internships exist, but they do not involve placement into jobs after graduation.

Nor does it seem likely that employers would respond to schools' efforts. Unlike German and Japanese employers, who believe that high schools provide useful, relevant, and trustworthy information, American employers believe that high school information is irrelevant, not to be trusted, and not very useful (chapter 6). However, the employers we interviewed indicate that they have unmet information needs, and a few employers report that they have relationships with school staff, so we wonder whether some teachers help their students get jobs by meeting employers' needs.

Based on interviews with 110 vocational teachers in twelve diverse high schools, the central finding of this chapter is that some teachers take informal actions to foster trusted relationships with employers, and that they use these relationships to learn employers' needs and to place their students in jobs. These actions are not required by their jobs. Like the formal linkages in Japan and Germany, teachers act as informal intermediaries for conveying hard-to-assess, relevant, and trusted information between students and employers, and as a result, some employers hire applicants they might not have hired otherwise, including females, minorities, and youths with other disadvantages. These previously unnoticed linkage activities have theoretical implications for enabling schools to provide authoritative evaluations of students to employers and thereby to increase the social capital available to work-bound youths. These findings also have policy implications for creating dependable career pathways for disadvantaged youths.

Functionalist and Network Theories

According to functionalist theory, school "functions to allocate human resources within the role-structure of the adult society" (Parsons 1959, 130). While noting the influence of social background, Talcott Parsons contends that in recent decades

> selection . . . [largely] takes place on a single main axis of achievement . . . "earned" by differential performance of the tasks set by the teacher, who is acting as an agent of the community. . . . There is a relatively systematic process of evaluation of the pupils' performances . . . in the form of report card marks [which function both to provide incentives to students and to enable the] school system [to act] as an allocating agency . . . for future status in society. . . . Grades are based on skill attainments and "moral" qualities, like "deportment, . . . responsible citizenship, . . . work-habits, . . . leadership, and initiative." (135, 137)

Consequently, this educational process is highly beneficial to the operation of the economy for two reasons: it provides incentives for all students to gain appropriate skills and work habits, and it provides a selective mechanism for assigning youth to appropriate roles in society.

Similarly, human capital theory in economics contends that schools develop students' productive capabilities (human capital) in response to labor market needs, and even some Marxist writers contend that schools serve employers' needs (Bowles and Gintis 1976). Like sociological functionalism, economic functionalism portrays a smooth interface between schools and the economy that requires no special programs or efforts.

The functionalist view that markets work well on their own without intermediaries implies that no one needs to take actions to help students get jobs. Although students' work-entry problems suggest that these assumptions are wrong, these assumptions are widely held and often guide policy actions.

First, school staff are not encouraged to give information to employers. Teachers view their responsibilities as confined to the classroom (Lortie 1975). Teachers rarely know employers, they tend to mistrust employers, and they do not want to interact with them (Useem 1986). Similarly, guidance counselors, the school staff responsible for career guidance, unapologetically state that they do not help students with job placement because youth should be responsible for finding jobs on their own (chapter 4). Even vocational teachers, who are responsible for preparing youth for work, report that job placement is not one of their duties. They do not receive extra rewards or resources for providing job help, and most deny that there are incentives of any kind, aside from personal gratification (Rosenbaum and Jones 1998). If they take action (as we find they do), it is not because they are required or encouraged to do so.

Second, few American schools have formal procedures to help employers hire students or to help students get jobs. A survey of U.S. high schools finds that 56 percent offered counseling services, but only 37 percent offered any job placement services, and schools reported that they were increasing the former more than the latter (Stern et al. 1995, 54). Even when schools offer job services, they offer in-school training (reading want ads, filling out job applications, and interviewing skills), not outreach that identifies job openings. A review of hundreds of programs (Stern et al. 1994, 55) found one high school, Duncan Polytechnical in Fresno, California, that explicitly creates "a 'job developer' position . . . responsible for reviewing want ads, calling on local businesses, attending job fairs, and informing students of job opportunities." When this large report by the National Center for Research on Vocational Education can find only one such program, we must conclude that formal activities that identify job options are rare.

Third, while thousands of school-business partnerships have been initiated in the last two decades, these partnerships rarely identify job openings for students or help with job placement. Most partnerships are designed to provide mentoring or donations of money or equipment (Spring 1986; Timpane 1984). Apparently, teachers, counselors, school administrators, and employers adhere to the functionalist assumption that markets work smoothly on their own and that no action is required on their part.

Moreover, the evidence is mixed on whether employers use the vocational programs that schools create for them. Research indicates that, true to its mission, vocational education increases youths' employment and earnings after high school. Studying the 1983 National Longitudinal Survey on 6,953 youth, Paul Campbell and his colleagues (1986) found that vocational graduates were 8.2 percent more likely to be in the labor force, and that their pay was 5.6 percent higher than that of academic program graduates, after controlling for test scores and enrollment in higher education. Studying 6,098 youth in the HSB survey, Campbell et al. (1986) found that vocational graduates were 14.9 percent more likely to be in the labor force and were paid about 9 percent more than academic graduates, after controlling for test scores and college attendance. Another study found that male vocational graduates received 8 percent higher hourly wages, worked 10 to 12 percent more, and earned 21 to 35 percent more in the first calendar year following graduation. For females, vocational graduates received 8 percent higher hourly wages, worked 18 percent more, and earned 40 percent more than academic graduates (Kang and Bishop 1986). Similar benefits have been found for postsecondary vocational programs (Kerckhoff and Bell 1998; Wirt et al. 1989), and other recent analyses have confirmed the economic benefits (Lewis, Hearn, and Zilbert 1993).

However, these are average effects, and detailed analysis indicates very mixed outcomes. Although vocational education graduates receive significantly higher earnings on average, many of them gain little benefit because employers give them jobs unrelated to their training. Research indicates that the economic benefits of vocational education "are zero if a training-related job is not obtained. . . . Unfortunately, less than one-half of [vocational] graduates . . . work in occupations that match (very broadly defined) their training" (Bishop 1988b, 4). The National Assessment of Vocational Education (NAVE) concluded that the greatest influence on low payoff to vocational education "in most analyses was unrelated placements. In the first three years after graduation, unrelated placements . . . accounted for 25–31 percent of the underutilization [of vocational training] for men, and 37–44 percent for women" (Wirt et al. 1989, 73). Students with "low" amounts of job-matched vocational credits earn an average of $6.59 per hour, while similar students with a "high" number of credits matching their job earn $8.00 per hour (Wirt et al. 1989, 108). Both Bishop (1988a) and NAVE conclude that high schools should devote more attention to helping students with job placements and getting employers more involved.

Thus, even when schools provide vocational training, employers do not always respond. Many students do not get jobs relevant to their training, and they reap little benefit from their training. Apparently, the benefits of vocational training do not emerge automatically, as functionalist theory assumes.

Functional "need" may not be enough to make appropriate behaviors emerge. Network theory contends that the effectiveness of labor markets often "depend[s] on the nature of personal relations and the network of relations between and within firms" (Granovetter 1985, 502). Information is given meaning and credibility through social contacts. Unlike functionalist theory, which specifies vague labor market needs, network theory urges that we instead focus on the specific kinds of information that employers need, whether schools respond to these needs, and what social mechanisms enable this responsiveness to operate.

But this view only points us back to the mystery. How do high schools help students get jobs? What actions do they take, which school staff take actions, what social relations are created, and how do school staff overcome employers' mistrust and reluctance? To answer these questions, we must interview school staff. Since it has already become clear that guidance counselors do not provide this help, we turn to teachers, and we study the teachers who have the most contact with students who have declared that they are work-bound: vocational teachers.

What Kind of Information Is Conveyed in Good School-to-Work Systems?

As we begin to examine what school staff do, it is useful to have a model of what to look for. Since the United States has no explicit norms or official practices about job-seeking contacts, we suspect that such actions are informal and improvised, and perhaps unorganized and unplanned. The formal school-to-work systems in Germany and Japan may provide a good model for illustrating how enabling mechanisms can operate and for raising the questions that we should examine.

The Japanese and German job placement systems are effective because they provide information that is accepted by all parties (Hamilton 1990; Rosenbaum et al. 1990). We posit that effective school-to-work systems should provide information with three qualities. Teachers give employers hard-to-assess information, relevant information, and information in a context that ensures trust (see Kariya and Rosenbaum 1995).

First, teachers give employers *hard-to-assess* information about students. In both Germany and Japan, employers believe that teachers' ratings offer information about students' work habits and behavior that employers cannot easily assess for themselves. If employers could easily assess applicants, they would have no need for school information.

Second, teachers provide *relevant* information to employers. Japanese employers believe that school ratings are good indicators of youths' work habits, and teachers give ratings accordingly (Rosenbaum and Kariya 1989). German employers select workers based on their performance in relevant contexts (apprenticeship programs). Even though half of German apprentices get jobs in areas that do *not* use their specific apprenticeship skills, employers still pay a premium for out-of-area apprenticeships (Witte and Kalleberg 1994), presumably because apprentices learn competencies and work habits that have general value in other jobs (Berryman 1992). For instance, doing well in auto mechanic apprenticeships helps youth get jobs in other production jobs that require a knowledge of machinery and good work habits.

Third, teachers provide information in a context that ensures *trust*. In Germany, trust is developed through institutional bonds between the national employment agency, teachers, and employers (Hamilton 1989). In Japan, teachers build trust through their professional reputation, their history of transactions with certain employers, and their actions to preserve their reputation into the future (Kariya and Rosenbaum 1995).

Just as network theory posits, the formal mechanisms in Japan and Germany presume that employers have information needs and that schools can provide this information. Both nations have formal systems that give youth dependable pathways to good jobs by conveying information that employers need: information that is hard to assess, relevant, and available in a trusted context. If American teachers make informal contacts with employers, we may expect that their contacts will need to have similar features to be effective.

Do American Employers Have Unmet Information Needs and Do Teachers Create Informal Infrastructures?

In the absence of a formal system in the United States, do employers have difficulty getting appropriate information, and do teachers respond to these needs? Someone in schools must be taking such actions, since 5 percent of employers say that they hire new workers through schools (Holzer 1995), and 8.5 percent of graduating seniors get jobs with the help of their high school (chapter 9). We suspect that vocational teachers are the agents, since vocational students are twice as likely to get help from their high school in finding a job than other students looking for jobs, and many vocational teachers worked in a trade or business before becoming a teacher. Therefore, our inquiry focuses on vocational teachers.

Given the paucity of research on teachers' efforts at job placement after high school, we conducted a study of 110 vocational teachers in twelve diverse high schools (eight comprehensive high schools and four vocational high schools; for study design, see appendix). Following the earlier analysis of the information that is conveyed in school-employer systems, the following sections examine whether American employers have difficulty getting information that is hard to assess, relevant, and trustworthy, and whether teachers provide information with these properties.

Hard-to-Assess Information

In the popular stereotypes, confident employers know just what they want and know how to get it, and diffident teachers know little about the world and remain detached from it. Like all stereotypes, both are partly wrong. In hiring recent high school graduates, employers' highest priority is work habits, and they report that they have great difficulty inferring work habits from available information (Bishop 1993). Interviews are employers' primary method for assessing applicants (Wanous 1992), but research indicates that interviewing is not a very effective way for employers to find out whether job applicants will be honest, hardworking, cooperative, or trainable (Arvey and Faley 1988; Wanous 1992; Hunter and Hunter 1984), and some employers are aware of the problems of interviewing (chapter 6). Contrary to the functionalist assumption that employers automatically get the information they need, employers report that they actually have difficulty getting detailed, useful information about applicants (chapter 6).

In contrast to employers' lack of information, we find that some vocational teachers are confident that they know what information employers need, they believe they possess it, and they provide it in the references they give to employers. Teachers learn employers' needs through a variety of informal activities. Of our 110 vocational teachers, 95 percent entered teaching after having a career in their industry, and 86 percent have made special efforts to learn the specific needs of local employers. Many still have ties; they attend industry or union meetings and visit former colleagues at work or after work. Others build new contacts with employers by having advisory boards for their vocational program, by visiting students' co-op learning field sites, or just by visiting work sites to learn about employers' practices and needs. Some teachers say that when employers call seeking students to hire, they use these calls as a chance to learn the employers' specific needs and to build a relationship with them.

Most vocational teachers (82 percent) report that their recommendations give employers information about students' work capabilities that employers would have difficulty assessing by themselves. Indeed, some teachers assert that employers would be foolish to try to make selections without them. They report that they know better than employers do which students should be hired, and that their detailed knowledge about students gives them a special vantage point that can inform employers' hiring decisions. A teacher in an urban school notes:

> I've done the screening already. If they've gotta do the screening, employers have got some serious problems, because there's no way in an interview [that an employer] can come up with what's going on. I don't care how well you do this or how many years you do this, you can't call it that good. You don't know until you get the person under the gun how he's gonna handle it.

Another urban teacher believes that a teacher can give information about a job candidate's "quality . . . honesty, dependability, and helpfulness and that kind of thing. I think it would be very hard [for employers] to get that from another source."

Teachers get to know students over the course of a year or more, and this detailed knowledge is just what employers need for predicting youths' work performance. They cannot get it from other sources. As another urban teacher says: "My advantage is in knowing the student well. . . . I can give [employers] more specific measures of skills as well as attitudes." Another adds: "I can give [employers] some insight into the students' academic or personal [qualities] that they probably would have a hard time getting."

Teachers note that their evaluations are based on extensive information that employers cannot obtain on their own. A teacher at a suburban vocational school says: "I would have had the opportunity to see students in the classroom for at least a year. I would have evaluations from at least one or more employers based on the experiences that students have in the field. And I would make my recommendation based on that."

Thus, while employers realize the limitations of their hiring procedures, vocational teachers are confident that they possess detailed information about youths' work habits that is relevant to employers' needs. On their own, employers cannot get this kind of hard-to-assess information, which is exactly what these teachers' references provide.

Relevant Information

Second, contrary to the functionalist assumption that employers automatically get useful information from schools, we find that employers doubt that most school-provided information is relevant to their needs. However, consistent with network theory, some vocational teachers are aware of employers' needs, and they take actions to enhance the relevance of the information they provide to employers.

American employers doubt that most of the information they get about job applicants is relevant to their work demands (chapter 6). That is why employers were initially enthusiastic about apprenticeships (Lerman and Pouncy 1990), although their enthusiasm cooled once they realized the high cost of such programs (Harhoff and Kane 1994). A variety of school reforms try to make school instruction more relevant to work, but a survey of U.S. high schools estimates that few high schools offer tech-prep programs (7 percent), school-to-apprenticeship programs (6 percent), or youth apprenticeships (2 percent) (Stern et al. 1995, 7).

Vocational education was originally designed to provide relevant training and evaluations (Wirt et al. 1989). Although this is often interpreted to mean relevant skills, employers rarely stress specific job skills in hiring entry-level workers, and they often prefer to train workers in specific job skills themselves (Osterman 1980, 1994). Instead, employers stress work habits as the most relevant attributes in a job applicant—attendance, discipline, initiative, persistence, attention to quality, and ability to work with others (NCEQW 1994).

Vocational teachers believe that they are in a good position to assess students' work habits. In our sample of 110 vocational teachers, most felt that they could assess students' likely performance in work settings (65 percent), and this was even more true for the forty-six teachers in the four vocational schools (85 percent). In addition, vocational teachers increase the relevance of their evaluations in two ways: they create "quasi-apprenticeships" in their classrooms, and they make their student evaluations address attributes that are relevant to employers' needs.

Quasi-Apprenticeships Some vocational teachers design their classrooms to include work simulations that are relevant to employers' needs. With their industry experience and continuing contacts with employers, vocational teachers often know how the local employers in their field operate, and they have constructed classroom tasks to develop, monitor, and assess students' workplace capabilities. Although not as thorough as German apprenticeships, which last for several years in actual workplaces, classroom work-simulations do resemble apprenticeships in that they give students a chance to learn to perform joblike tasks, which teachers can monitor, evaluate, and certify. Teachers view their classroom work-simulations as quasi-apprenticeships (Rosenbaum and Jones 1995, 252; Jones and Rosenbaum 1995). One suburban teacher sees work-simulations in the classroom as very similar to the training provided in business or industry apprenticeships, especially "the hands-on experience. Most apprenticeship programs, be it for an electrician or a plumber, involve some classroom work. . . . So the academics is important, but the ability to perform, to do the work is even more important."

Another teacher expresses the same idea: "Our graduates really are like first- or second-year apprentices when they leave here." One teacher notes that the work-simulation includes responsibility: "We try and operate the on-board technology department as close as possible to a dealership. We use repair orders, we have a parts and service director, students are responsible for completing repairs. If the repair comes back, they are responsible for repairing it a second time, like a dealership would."

Teachers tell students that they must be able to see what tasks need to be done and to do them on their own. Teachers also monitor students' behaviors and help them progress to the point where they no longer need teacher supervision. While his students worked on their projects, a suburban drafting instructor remarked, "I give them confidence that they know that skill. . . . You can see now, a student is plotting a drawing by himself. I mean, I didn't give him any instructions. They know what to do, and that's important to me, because it's a simulation of what's in the real world." Thus, vocational teachers believe that their classes allow them to see behaviors that are relevant to work demands.

Conveying Relevant Information to Employers   Vocational teachers also make their recommendations relevant to employers' needs, and they match students with employers on a number of dimensions. Teachers see the particular needs of each employer, and they give employers information about relevant student attributes. In an urban vocational school, the broadcast media teacher states: "I send kids to the cable systems, my best kids. Not necessarily best, that's wrong. My most responsible kids. Kids who can work independently. . . . They're gonna be sent out with expensive [camera] equipment and told, 'Shoot this.' Well, they have to be able to work independently."

Because the quasi-apprenticeship structure of many vocational classes allows teachers to see student qualities that are relevant to employers' needs, many of these teachers feel that they can provide distinctively valuable evaluations. As one notes: "I have a better insight as to the work habits [than do teachers] in the traditional classroom. . . . Here, I can see the motivation and [self-direction]. . . . Will a student do something on their own? Will they think on their own? Will they problem-solve on their own, or are they asking me every two minutes how to do something?" A teacher at a suburban vocational center reports: "I think I can tell employers about those job transferable skills more than a regular high school teacher could, because I've seen 'em in action. I see how they work . . . their motivation, initiative, cooperation."

In turn, teachers' demands for worklike performances show students new dimensions of their own capabilities. As one teacher in an urban vocational school says: "The employer is really interested in what they can do, not just what they know." Focusing on work demands in academic classes also provides relevant information to employers, for, as one teacher notes, "I tell [students] that good academics indicates to an employer that you can show discipline, so even if they don't get stellar grades, students' efforts are important."

Tailoring evaluations to employers' needs shows students that their classroom behaviors are relevant to work. They realize that their class performance is an opportunity to show what they could do in a workplace. As one teacher reports: "I try to give them the self-evaluation thing—you know, such as, 'Do you really believe that you would want me to give a recommendation for you based on what you do in this class?' You tell the kid that they have to make you want to give them a job."

Indeed, many teachers let students know that their behavior is important and that there are incentives to demonstrate appropriate performances. Teachers say they cannot help students who perform poorly in class. Even if teachers want to help their students, they must report the truth about their class performance. "When I help a kid get a job, my reputation is at stake as well. If I put some dork in there who's going to screw up, then the next time the employer is looking for someone to fill a job, is he really going to call me again?" When students ask, "Do I have to do that? It's so difficult," one teacher responds: "Don't do it for me. But the employers I know who offer good jobs in this field require these skills, and I can't recommend you to those employers if you don't master these skills." Thus, students learn that their own performance is relevant and determines whether teachers can help them get a job.

Most vocational teachers believe that they are helping students and employers see alternative kinds of capabilities besides the academic ones evaluated in other classes. One teacher states this particularly clearly when he describes his grading scale: "An A student has a good attitude and works well with his mind and his hands. A B student works well with his hands and has a good attitude. . . . A C student maybe has just a good attitude." This teacher presents a range of student capabilities that are tailored to employers' needs.

Our classroom observations revealed how some teachers assess work-readiness. A graphics class was run like a print shop. Students were assigned a whole project, they solved problems themselves, and they kept busy and on task, even when the teacher was out of the room. In another school, business students dressed and acted as they would in an office. The machinist, sheet-metal, and carpentry programs were taught on a project basis with considerable autonomy and self-direction. Students performed lengthy, work-related tasks without teacher comments or close supervision, they solved problems that arose, they prepared equipment and materials for the next operation, and they organized the work site for the next person using it. Students stopped and talked occasionally, but the chats were brief and often work-related.

Having designed classes that simulate the demands of real workplaces, teachers can assess students in relevant contexts on relevant dimensions. Work-simulations permit teachers to assess how students work—their perseverance, initiative, responsibility, problem solving, and ability to learn—on tasks that resemble real work tasks. *This is the kind of information that employers desperately want and cannot get in job interviews* (chapter 6). Vocational teachers can certify students' work-readiness because they have seen them doing the same tasks that are done in workplaces.

Trusted Information

Trust is the most overlooked component of the labor market infrastructure. Although weak ties give job seekers more information about possible job openings (Granovetter 1995), employers report that they do not need *more* information, they need information they can *trust* (chapter 6). Consistent with network theory, research indicates that employers lack trusted information, and that vocational teachers take steps to make the information they provide trustworthy.

Employers' mistrust of information may explain why students benefit from co-op programs only if they are hired by their co-op employer (Stern and Stevens 1992), but not if they are hired by other employers (Stern et al. 1995; Lewis et al. 1993; Bishop, Blakemore, and Low 1985). Apparently, employers trust their own direct observations of co-op students, but they do not trust the evaluations of other co-op employers or teachers.

Many employers report that they do not trust teachers to be candid about students' shortcomings. In the words of one employer: "Teachers are trying to help their own students, heaven bless them . . . but that doesn't make them very useful to me." However, employer surveys indicate that about 5 percent of employers recruit new workers through school contacts, so some of them presumably have overcome this mistrust (Bishop 1993; Holzer 1995). How is this trust formed?

Japan provides a clue. Although Japan's system confers formal authority on teachers to nominate students for jobs, this does not force an employer to contact a particular school. Japanese teachers believe that their job placement effectiveness depends on building informal authority with employers, which comes from their school's reputation, the track record of their school's past interactions with employers, and the actions they take to preserve their reputation in the future (Kariya and Rosenbaum 1995). In effect, these teachers turn ordinary recommendations into trusted *certifications* of students' quality by building trust into their relationship with employers.

Some American vocational teachers also build trusted relationships with employers. In the study of 110 vocational teachers, more than one-third (38 percent) said they have a good reputation with employers, and the proportion was much higher in vocational schools (70 percent).

How do teachers build such a reputation? While Japanese teachers focus on their school's reputation and interactions with employers, American teachers build a trusted personal reputation by stressing their previous work experience in the trade, their track record in placing students with employers, and their activities to preserve their reputation in the future.

Experience in the Trade   In Japan, teachers' authority is conferred by society and the formal employment system. American teachers receive less respect than Japanese teachers (Stevenson and Stigler 1992), and U.S. employers do not value most teachers' recommendations (chapter 6), but some vocational teachers have built a reputation from their previous work in a trade. Of the 110 vocational teachers, 95 percent had some work experience in their field, and 32 percent had ten or more years of experience. Even after becoming teachers, most vocational teachers continue to identify with their trade, and 30 percent work in the same industry in the summer. Although a few have formal contacts through advisory boards or co-op programs, many keep up their informal contacts by visiting former workplaces, attending union meetings, and socializing.

Many vocational teachers are confident that they have a trusted reputation from their years in industry. As a teacher in an urban vocational school notes: "Being in the trade, I think they accept your recommendation, that you know what they're looking for." A suburban teacher reports: "My opinion of one of my students . . . would have more of an impact. . . . People would know me in the trade and know my level of performance and my expectations." Teachers' previous experience in the trade is a source of authority in recommending students for jobs.

Track Record of Placing Students with Employers   Many vocational teachers see their history of recommending students to employers as an additional basis for their reputation. An urban teacher notes: "They know from their past experience with me what they're getting." A suburban teacher adds that employers "trust me because I continuously try to work with them and give them . . . the kind of student that they want."

Many teachers feel that this history of references leads to trust. An urban business school teacher reports: "Based on the relationships that I've developed over the years, the employers have confidence in what I tell them." Trust comes from an implicit or explicit promise in the relationship. Another urban teacher notes that employers "get to know me, . . . and respect my position and who I'm gonna send them."

Vocational teachers see their relationships with employers as a valued "asset" that belongs to them personally, not to the school. Teachers were asked a hypothetical question: "If you took a job at a nearby school with a similar program, would the employers you've worked with in the past be more likely to deal with your *former school* or with *you* in hiring students?" Most teachers said that the employers they knew would keep working with them, not with their former school.

Trust is especially salient to new teachers, who are trying to build a reputation. Most already have job experience in their field, but as new teachers, they have not yet attained a reputation for placing qualified students. Building a reputation takes time. One teacher notes that his urban business high school "has a real good reputation, [but employers] didn't, of course, just trust me at the start." A new teacher at the same school has learned that employers see any student recommended by an older teacher as someone who is "gonna be a dynamite student." Asked whether employers automatically trust his own recommendations, he replies: "I don't know if I'm at that place yet."

In Japan, reputation resides with the high school, and teachers work to maintain the school's reputation. In the United States, reputation resides with individual teachers, and though a high school can enhance that reputation, teachers feel that they must build their own reputation by their history of transactions with employers.

Preserving Reputation: Prescreening and Candid References   In Japan, teachers take two kinds of actions to preserve their school's reputation. First, they prescreen students before nominating them for job openings, since they know that an employer who receives a poorly qualified student will not recruit from the school in the future. Second, teachers give candid references about students, even the likable but poor-achieving students they would like to help. Teachers feel that they must be candid if they are to be able to help capable students in the future. As one Japanese teacher states: "Getting a job is only a onetime experience for individual students, but it is repeated year after year for schools" (Rosenbaum and Kariya 1989, 1363). Teachers do not nominate a student if they think that student will not meet the employer's needs. Sometimes teachers do not fill all the job openings that employers offer because they do not have enough students who meet the employers' needs.

American vocational teachers boost their credibility with employers by using similar strategies—they prescreen students, and they give candid references. Many vocational teachers (32 percent) report that they prescreen students when they make nominations for a job opening even when the employer does not ask them to do so. Teachers see prescreening as necessary for maintaining their credibility with employers. As one teacher notes, nominating a student who is not likely to do good work "would make me look bad."

Teachers also give candid recommendations to maintain their reputation with employers. Most vocational teachers (85 percent) report that many students ask them for help in getting jobs, and virtually all of the vocational teachers want to help their students. However, teachers report that they must be candid with employers about students' shortcomings. Very few teachers (4 of 110) said they would send a student with poor work habits to an employer they knew. A business teacher in an urban vocational school reports: "I've always told [employers] the truth about all my students, including . . . a student's deficiencies." Similarly, a teacher in a suburban vocational school notes that if students lack skills, "I only feel it would be fair to tell the employer." Sometimes teachers sacrifice program enrollment and rapport with students to preserve their reputation with employers. One teacher notes: "There is even some hard feeling over it, but that's too bad. . . . Some [students] left the program, simply left, because they knew I wasn't going to recommend them for a job."

Teachers say that they can continue to help students from one year to the next only if they have credibility, and that requires candor about their students' shortcomings. Echoing the view of many others, an urban business school teacher notes: "It is very difficult for students to understand that we have a reputation to maintain." Another teacher points out that maintaining a good reputation requires ongoing efforts: "I've worked hard to build a good reputation, and . . . employers are aware of the caliber of students that we produce." Teachers are careful about their recommendations so as to preserve the integrity of their word. An urban business school teacher notes: "I go see [employers] all the time. My success is personal, face to face. . . . You're selling them *you*, not the kid."

Like Japanese teachers, many of these vocational teachers see themselves as effective only because they give employers what they need. Although there are no formal demands that they make such a commitment to employers' needs in the United States, these teachers feel that their credibility with employers is crucial to their ability to help future students.

Employers' Response to Teachers' Efforts

John Meyer and Brian Rowan (1977) contend that universities have "charters" that encourage employers to hire graduates because the university certifies their value. Similarly, management schools use specific strategies to build trusted relationships with employers (Burke 1984), and some vocational institutes have trusted charters for training technicians in certain fields (Mills 1977). Some high school vocational programs have developed strong programs (Stern, Raby, and Dayton 1992; Stern et al. 1995), but studies have not examined whether vocational teachers create "charters" that confer trusted certifications and ensure consistent placement of graduates.

As noted, national surveys indicate that some employers hire through schools (Bishop 1993; Holzer 1995); that "references from people who have recommended previous hires are . . . more profitable" (Bishop 1993, 369); and that students who get jobs with the help of their school receive higher earnings (chapter 9). However, many programs that try to help youth get jobs do not improve outcomes for them (Basi and Ashenfelter 1986; Lah 1983), so we need to examine what teachers do and ask why it has an impact.

This chapter permits analysis of vocational teachers' influence in the hiring relationship. A majority of the vocational teachers in our study (68 percent) say that some employers trust their recommendations. Many teachers make similar reports that employers trust their recommendations: "Some employers will even say, 'You just send me a student. You know what I want.'" "I have been here long enough that some [employers] have already said, 'Well, you know what I'm looking for,' . . . They take . . . my word, and it's worked out in the past." "[Some employers] say, 'Send me somebody, and I know who you send, they have always worked out.'" "Among my employers, they take my word for it. . . . Employers who keep calling back . . . know they can rely on my word."

Indeed, when asked, "What percent of your work-bound students can you place in good jobs that use students' skills?" most teachers report that they can consistently place large numbers of their students in jobs. Even during a weak labor market from 1991 to 1993, when large layoffs were common, 58 percent of the teachers said they could place three-quarters or more of their students in good jobs that would use their skills.[2] Although we might be skeptical about self-reports, these placement rates are credible, since the teachers who made these claims regularly attend professional association and union meetings, have employers on their program advisory boards, have former students who are workers and employers in the field, and could name five or more specific employer contacts in high-demand fields (such as administrative, clerical, sheet metal, heating, machining). As a check on teachers' reports, we interviewed fifty-one employers in the vicinity of three of these schools; over 20 percent report having contacts with one or more of these teachers, and over 13 percent have strong long-term contacts. Moreover, these employers consistently hire students who are highly recommended by these teachers (chapter 5).

Thus, some employers show confidence in teachers' selections, and teachers can place many of their students. *Teachers' long-term relationships with employers become a dependable hiring channel for employers, and thus a dependable career pathway for students.*

Finding Jobs for Youth Who Might Not Otherwise Be Hired

Do teachers help only students who would get jobs anyway? Although minorities and females are generally disadvantaged in the labor market, these groups are more likely to get their first jobs with the help of their high school, and these jobs are more likely to lead to career advancement than jobs obtained by other means (chapter 9). How does this happen?

One explanation may be that teachers' greater familiarity with students makes their ratings less biased than employer interviews. If prejudice is conceived as prejudging, prejudice is more likely to arise in an employer's fifteen-minute interview than in a teacher's judgment of a student's work over the course of one or more semesters of daily interaction. Teachers probably cannot escape societal biases, and some teachers report being initially put off by the student qualities that employers reject in interviews, such as hairstyles, T-shirt slogans, and dialect. Yet over the course of a school year, teachers come to see students' actual work capabilities.

However, how do teachers get employers to respond to their evaluations? Like any third party trying to make a transaction happen, *teachers sometimes act like brokers—getting buyers and sellers to modify their expectations to accommodate to reality.* Just as real estate brokers try to get both sellers and buyers to reduce their expectations so that a transaction will occur, some vocational teachers try to convince employers and students that they meet each other's needs, even if neither exactly matches the other's ideal.

Students who get jobs that they would not have gotten otherwise are the ultimate evidence of teachers' impact on employers' hiring decisions. Teachers often bring about this outcome by brokering— shaping the expectations of both students and employers. First, *teachers convince their students to have realistic expectations.* They tell students what pay to expect, what tasks they will be doing, how to act, what skills will improve their careers, and the timetables for advancement. Students do not know how to tell whether a job will offer valuable skill training and the possibility of later advancement, but teachers can direct youth to such jobs and tell them how to gain those benefits. Without teachers' advice, students would refuse many promising entry-level jobs or quit them soon after beginning.

Even more surprising, *teachers shape employers' expectations of students.* The teacher-broker can help employers to understand what students can and cannot do and how they can help their new hires progress. Teachers can tell employers to ignore their customary hiring criteria and rely on the more relevant information about job candidates that the teacher can give them.

Minority students and students with academic or personal difficulties sometimes have difficulty showing their value to employers, but vocational teachers provide an answer to this dilemma. They report that students' work-relevant performances in vocational classes provide alternative opportunities to signal labor market value on alternative dimensions of value besides academic skills. Relying on their reputation with employers, some vocational teachers encourage employers to overlook superficial appearances for more work-relevant personal qualities. Vocational teachers' evaluations give otherwise low-achieving students positive signals to take into the labor market.

For students with handicapping features or experiences, teacher brokering provides opportunities that the impersonal labor market cannot. Several teachers offer anecdotes that illustrate this function. An urban business teacher recalls:

> I called the bank and asked them to give [a teenage mother] a chance, because she was much more mature than the other students. . . . She had the desire and the motivation, and she could develop the skill level. . . . So, on that recommendation, they took her. They probably would not have [otherwise]. . . . She's received three promotions. She's the youngest loan officer in the history of that particular branch, and she's going back to school. . . . Employers know that you don't stick your neck out for people that you know are not going to work out.

In another case, the construction teacher at a suburban vocational school recalls a student with a speech impediment:

> If you had a job interview with him, [you're] not gonna hire this guy. But . . . he comes when he's supposed to . . . and if you [explain a task], he'll pick up anything. . . . I've already lined the kid up with a job, and I said, "You probably won't like this kid until after he's worked for you a month or two, but then you'll realize he'll probably be a lifelong employee." I'd hire the kid in a second, but I wouldn't have the first time I met him.

Similarly, teachers place students with limited English skills. An urban business school teacher tells employers to "forget testing. I've got Hispanic kids with poor English skills, they won't test out, but they show up every day, they're reliable. I know what you're looking for. I've got what you want. . . . I tell them the inside scoop."

Teachers even place students with learning disabilities. A suburban teacher reports: "I've had LD [learning disabled] students that maybe aren't gonna be tool-and-die makers or mold makers but they can definitely be trained to run a type of machine."

Some teacher-brokers convince employers to make a hire when they do not have a vacancy. An urban teacher recalls: "A year ago, I went to these people that I dealt with for many years . . . and I said, 'I know you don't need anybody right now, but you can't pass this person up.' They hired him, and they're very happy."

Sometimes teachers convince employers to hire females or minorities in jobs that have always been held by white males. One teacher gives the example of a young woman who did well in his sheet-metal class. When an employer was reluctant to consider her job application since he had never hired a female, the teacher reassured him that she was "as good as the last five males I sent you." The employer hired her. Without the teacher's recommendation, the young woman would not have been hired.

Although teachers usually try to serve employers' needs as employers state them, teacher brokering can go even further: *sometimes teachers tell employers whom to hire.* Employers are reluctant to give teachers authority to override their traditional hiring criteria. However, many employers realize the limitations of their established procedures, and if a trusted teacher is enthusiastic about a student, the employer may forgo procedures that do not work all that well anyway. Vocational teachers gain leverage because they can provide a trusted source of information that is not available through other screening methods. Trusted teachers offer numerous advantages over the ordinary labor market gamble. In the words of the teacher quoted earlier, they provide the "inside scoop."

These examples contradict a common conception. Getting jobs through contacts is often viewed as cronyism—as unmeritocratic and biased. However, minorities and females more often get jobs through school contacts than white males do. That there are so many minority, female, and low-achieving students who get better jobs through teacher contacts than they could get otherwise suggests that there is a less biased, meritocratic quality to contacts. Teachers sometimes use their employer linkages to convince employers to judge a candidate by using alternative criteria that are more work-relevant and less biased. Hiring based on contacts may sometimes be more meritocratic than using objective "merit" criteria.

Conclusions

Teachers are often thought of as operating in the closed world of the classroom (Lortie 1975), but in contrast to this view, teachers in other nations have formal responsibilities to help place their students in the labor market. Although American vocational teachers are not formally given this responsibility, we have discovered that some of them assume it informally. They know that employers have difficulty assessing new high school graduates and that, as teachers, they possess the very information that employers need.

Contrary to labor market models that ignore intermediaries, we find that some vocational teachers play a pivotal role in helping their students get jobs and in helping employers get useful information about youth. Some vocational teachers have made themselves inter-mediaries for conveying information between students and em-ployers, and some employers allow teachers to influence their hiring decisions, trusting them even to the extent of hiring teacher-recom-mended applicants they might not have considered otherwise.

Network theory has generally focused on the ways in which weak contacts help people get jobs (Granovetter 1995). Indeed, many teachers use *weak contacts.* Of the 110 vocational teachers in our study, 95 percent have casual employer contacts from jobs they held before teaching, 85 percent know the specific attributes that local employers value, 86 percent have made efforts to learn local employers' needs, and 82 percent believe that their references are of some value to em-ployers.

Some teachers have *strong contacts:* 30 percent still do summer jobs in their field, 32 percent have ten or more years of experience in that field, 38 percent say they have a good reputation with employers, and 31 percent prescreen students for specific employers. These teachers have strong relationships with employers, and they use these relation-ships to get jobs for deserving students. Although such strong con-tacts are not formally recognized and do not appear in teachers' job descriptions, many teachers improvise informal placement transac-tions that are similar to those in the more formal systems of Japan and Germany. In effect, teachers not only make contacts, but they also actively construct linkages, which they strengthen by conveying hard-to-assess, relevant, and trusted information to employers. Through these activities, teachers make their contacts into strong linkages that convince employers to hire the youths they recommend, even those applicants whom they might not have considered otherwise.

Japanese high schools have institutional charters for job placement similar to the institutional charters of prestigious colleges in the United States (Meyer and Rowan 1977). American high schools gener-ally lack such formal charters, but our results suggest that some American teachers build linkages that turn ordinary recommenda-tions into *trusted certifications* of students' quality. Teachers do not view youths' problems as merely due to their deficiencies or labor market rigidities. Teachers see employers' difficulties in trusting the information they get about young job applicants, as employers them-selves also report (chapter 6), and students' difficulties in knowing what behaviors employers value. In response, teachers take steps to provide both sides with the information they need in the context of trusted relationships.

These findings have policy implications. Since many work-bound students come from low-SES families, their families may have poor contacts with employers. Teachers' links can provide options that would otherwise be unavailable to these students. Research finds that students hired for "skill-relevant" jobs do considerably better in the labor market than other students (Grasso and Shea 1979), but research has not described how students obtain these skill-relevant jobs. It may be teacher contacts with employers that give students access to these jobs with higher wages and better earnings trajectories years later (chapter 9). Policy reformers have advocated expensive and cumbersome certification bureaucracies, but the informal initiatives that teachers describe are likely to be inexpensive and easily implemented.

Giving signals of value to these students contradicts a common stereotype in our society. Vocational students are often viewed as academic dummies and behavior problems, but like all stereotypes, these are partly wrong. Although vocational students have lower academic skills than college-track students on average, there is great variation in their academic skills, and some are higher-achieving than some college-track students. In addition, John Wirt and his colleagues (1989) find that some vocational courses increase academic skills more effectively than do general-track courses.

More important, academic achievement is not employers' highest priority, despite the speeches of top executives at top corporations (which rarely hire youths). Small businesses are the main employers of new high school graduates, and their highest priorities are work habits like attendance, responsibility, initiative, perseverance, and attention to quality, as national surveys show (NCEQW 1994). Vocational teachers are in a good position to evaluate and certify these attributes in their students.

These findings are also theoretically significant. Functionalist theory predicts a simple automatic responsiveness that rarely occurs. However, we do find support for the theory's assumptions that employers have functional needs that schools can meet and that schools will respond to those needs. Although functionalist theory is too complacent about expecting the social system to respond automatically, some teachers improvise responses to employers' information needs. These responses may be hard to see, idiosyncratic, and sporadic. Perhaps because of the functionalist assumption of automatic responsiveness, these teacher activities are not expected, encouraged, or even publicly recognized in schools.

Besides finding that some teachers create strong ties, we have also identified some properties of those ties, which resemble the social processes in the formal infrastructures of Japan and Germany. On their own, some vocational teachers enhance the signaling effectiveness of their recommendations by learning what information employers value and then conveying back to them information that is otherwise hard to get, relevant (through quasi-apprenticeship activities), and trusted. Teachers build trust by emphasizing their professional reputation and their history of transactions, prescreening, and making other sacrifices to preserve their reputation. In effect, these teachers turn ordinary recommendations into trusted certifications of students' quality by giving students signals that employers value and cannot easily assess in other ways.

These actions are certainly not automatic; many teachers do not take such actions. Yet it is amazing that so many individual teachers across unrelated schools take these informal initiatives, and that some local employers report that these relationships are a dependable source of good employees. Although these contacts affect fewer than 9 percent of work-bound students, they could have a greater influence if they were recognized and encouraged, and they could offer a valuable option to a higher percentage of work-bound students, or even to those who hold jobs while attending college, especially if college does not work out for them. Such findings pose an agenda for further research and for social policy.

Appendix: Research Strategy and Sample of 110 Vocational Teachers

Since vocational teachers are likely to be key agents in youths' transition from school to work, vocational teachers were studied, and vocational schools, which emphasize jobs more than comprehensive high schools do, were oversampled. The analysis is primarily qualitative, and it focuses on what vocational teachers do in ordinary schools. The generalizability of quantitative results cannot be certain.

We interviewed 110 vocational teachers in twelve public high schools across the Chicago metropolitan area, six in the city and six in the suburbs. Four are vocational high schools, which strongly emphasize job help; eight are comprehensive high schools with several substantial vocational programs. These are the same schools in which we surveyed more than two thousand students, as reported in chapter 3.

Eleven of these twelve schools are fairly typical in operation and resources. The six suburban schools have larger budgets than the city schools, but they do not emphasize vocational programs as much.

Three of the four vocational schools are urban, and none has a large budget for new equipment. The suburban vocational school is the only one with many programs and new equipment in most fields.

The four vocational high schools encourage vocational teachers to have contacts with employers to keep abreast of employers' current practices, but teachers are not expected to help students get jobs. In the comprehensive schools, vocational programs are not highly valued, and vocational teachers are not encouraged to contact employers. Instead, students are encouraged to have college plans. None of the vocational programs are very selective; all primarily enroll students with below-average achievement.

The six urban schools have substantial minority populations, ranging from 30 to 100 percent black. Although three of the suburban schools are mostly white and middle-class, the other three are not: one is mostly lower-middle-class white, and two have high proportions of low-income and minority students. Although no claims can be made about generalizability, these schools represent a wide spectrum.

We interviewed approximately one-quarter of each school's vocational teachers in business and trade-technical training. These fields are the two largest vocational programs in the United States, and they have positive occupational benefits (Arum and Shavit 1995). Focusing on teachers who taught seniors, we conducted one-hour interviews during school hours. Interviews were taped, transcribed, and coded into Factfinder, a computer-based qualitative data analysis program.

= Chapter 11 =

Theoretical Implications: Using Institutional Linkages to Signal and Enhance Youths' Capabilities

ALL SOCIETIES initiate young people into adulthood (Parsons 1959). They provide ways for youths to attain adult status and recognition of their productive value, and they give employers ways to know which individuals are ready to be productive. In simpler societies, youths are awarded adult status through initiation ceremonies that signal to all members of the society that they can meet tests of their survival skills and self-sufficiency.

In modern societies, such signals usually come through schools. Although policymakers recognize the need for schools to provide students with training in the competencies demanded to be productive in society, they rarely consider the need for schools to provide signals. Schools do not give students clear signals of employers' needs or of the payoffs for achievement. Nor do schools provide employers with clear signals about students' capacity to be productive adults in society. In our interviews, employers complained that a high school diploma does not ensure basic literacy, and their complaints are confirmed by examinations (NAEP 1990). As detailed in chapter 6, teachers give students vague statements about employers' needs (which students dismiss as self-serving platitudes), but no one provides students with authoritative information that grades will increase their earnings. Indeed, employers are not even aware of the relationship between grades and earnings.

This signaling function often occurs informally when youths manage to get signals from informal sources, such as neighbors, friends, and relatives. However, if youths want jobs in fields different from those in which their friends and relatives work, or if their friends and relatives are unemployed or lack influential contacts, schools may be their only source of signals.

This signaling function can be clearly seen in other nations. In Japan and Germany, work-bound students see that their school achievement is rewarded in the labor market, and employers see students' value through school-provided evaluations. These processes work in Japan and Germany because these nations have infrastructures that clearly communicate information about employers' hiring criteria to students and information about students' school achievements to employers. These infrastructures persuade employers to trust and value school information in their hiring decisions.

The United States lacks an infrastructure for giving employers dependable information about new high school graduates, and students believe (mostly correctly) that their school achievements are not known or valued by employers. As economic theory posits, American employers and students get information through ordinary market processes, but they are not certain whether the information is relevant or trustworthy. Employers do not trust the signals they get about students' value, and students do not trust the information they get about schools' relevance to future careers. This lack of trusted information discourages employers from hiring students and discourages students from exerting effort in school. However, we discovered that some teachers create informal linkages that help employers get trusted information and help students see school's relevance, and that these informal linkages are maintained through processes that resemble the formal infrastructures in other nations.

These findings raise new issues that are often ignored by customary theories about the youth labor market. Neoclassical economic theory warns that structures may hurt efficiency by limiting competition, but our findings suggest that linkage structures increase efficiency by providing better-quality information, even if they limit competition. Signaling theory says that employers and students need more information, but our research indicates that what they need is the right kind of information. Network theory focuses on the benefits of weak ties, but our research indicates that the youth labor market is helped by strong ties that ensure the dependability of information.

This chapter asks what kinds of information are needed to improve the youth labor market, and what kinds of social contacts provide the information that effectively signals students' value to employers and employers' needs to students. Selective colleges communicate clear incentives to students, but the communication of incentives and signals between employers and high school students is poor, according to our findings. We present a linkage model that describes how information may be effectively communicated between institutions. Just as James Coleman (1988) showed that individuals have greater capabilities in the context of preexisting ethnic ties, the linkage model indicates that strong ties can be created that lead to similar outcomes. Even if students have the same human capital, being in a school or classroom that is effectively linked to employers improves students' labor market outcomes and their incentive to achieve. We discover that Coleman's model describes the three conditions required to make effective linkages—information channels, normative sanctions, and reciprocity.

Finally, we consider the general properties of linkages by examining linkages in other contexts. Reviewing studies of select prep schools, a proprietary school, and job training programs, we find that linkages operate differently from what we might have supposed. Although linkages in our society usually help high-achieving students applying to selective colleges (chapter 3) and reinforce traditional biases, we find examples of linkages helping low-status individuals. Linkages can operate in non-elite schools, they can reduce discrimination, and they can improve programs for disadvantaged groups. The linkage model explains these surprising findings, extends traditional theories, and suggests new perspectives on the operation of contacts.

Why Common Sense Is Sometimes Wrong

It is often said that sociology is just common sense. This book's findings are remarkable because they indicate that common sense is sometimes wrong, and it interferes with our understanding on some issues. Much of what we consider common sense is based on our assumption that good information is easily available (Stigler 1961). When information is problematic, commonsense assumptions may be wrong, and individuals may take actions that do not appear rational to outside observers.

Labor market policies in the United States are based on five commonsense assumptions:

1. If employers need information about academic skills, they ask schools to provide it.

2. If employers hire based on interviews, it is because they have confidence in interviews.

3. Employers get good information through ordinary market processes.

4. Students know how to get jobs and do not need help applying for jobs.

5. Students see labor market incentives, so a lack of school effort indicates poor motivational capacity.

Our findings indicate that all of these commonsense assumptions are often wrong. First, although employers often complain about workers' academic skills, they do not use information available from schools—high school grades, test scores, and teacher recommendations. None of this information has any influence on which youths are hired, what their wages are, or what jobs they get right after high school (Griffin et al. 1981; Meyer and Wise 1982; Willis and Rosen 1979).

Second, employers may rely on interviews, but not because of their confidence in this hiring method. Some researchers have trumpeted their discovery that interviewers rely on superficial cues that are poor predictors of performance (Wanous 1992), but our study indicates that employers already know that. As one says: "Some of the few [applicants] that I thought would be outstanding, crashed and burned." Some employers explicitly complain about interviews: "An interview is a bad game. . . . If a person has any skill at all, in being deceptive or a good actor, you can learn next to nothing in an interview." Another observes that what some applicants "do best is interview." As we saw in chapter 6, employers rely on interviews, not because of their confidence in interviews, but because of their greater mistrust of everything else.

Third, although labor market policy assumes that employers want more information, we find that employers need better information. Our interviews suggest that researchers have underestimated employers' difficulty in getting trusted information. Employers are skeptical about the information they get from outside sources (schools, employers, tests, employment services).

Fourth, youths often do not know how to get jobs. Labor market policy seems to assume that the invisible hand takes care of this process. Employment services rarely help young people, however, and school counselors do not help youths search for jobs. Youths must figure out how to do it on their own, and they often make mistakes. Our employers report that youths go to great effort to arrange interviews, then undercut their own efforts. They arrive late, wear T-shirts with slogans like "Fuck you" or "Megadeath," wear earphones, are inattentive, bring babies, or have a friend help them fill out the application. One student who was eager for a downtown office job prepared for her interview by spending $140 on new clothes—a designer sweat suit! Obviously, commonsense information is not common throughout society. Youths often go to great efforts to get to job interviews, but poor information prevents them from getting the job, and they do not even realize why.

Fifth, youths who do not exert effort in school may not lack motivational capacity. Although teachers tell students about school's relevance to their future careers, students disregard these messages as self-serving and untrustworthy. We find that many students do not believe their school efforts have a future payoff, and the variation in this belief is strongly associated with which students exert effort in school. As we have seen, many students believe that school is irrelevant to their future career, and we find that their school efforts are determined not only by their internal motivation but also by their perceptions of school's future relevance.

Our view of labor markets is built on assumptions that appear to be common sense but are often untrue. Our assumptions are wrong, and the failures of these commonsense assumptions contribute to youths' work-entry problems.

Limitations of Customary Labor Market Models

Our findings raise doubts about traditional theories and about reforms based on these theories. Traditional theories assume that labor markets are improved by more competition, more information, and weak social ties. In the following sections, we examine each of these assumptions.

Do Labor Markets Need More Competition or Better Information?

Some people think that linkages hurt market efficiency. Neoclassical economic theory posits that competition improves efficiency—that increasing the number of jobs and applicants improves the match between them. Linkages that give advantages to certain schools (or certain employers) limit the number of applicants (or jobs), limit competition, and thus limit efficiency.

However, the theory assumes that adequate information is available. Larger applicant pools do not improve hiring outcomes if employers cannot assess applicants' quality. Our employers said that advertising brings in many more applicants, but that they have difficulty selecting among them and poor decisions often result (chapter

6). In contrast, even though linkages limit the number of applicants, they provide better and more trusted information, better selections, and thus improved efficiency. To exaggerate the contrast, employers end up hiring *random* students from unlinked schools and the *best* students from linked schools.

Linkages can improve efficiency by helping employers and students make better decisions. Employers report that trusted linkages at certain schools give them dependable information for making hiring decisions, and that this process is vastly better than relying on their own judgment in interviews. We also see that students who get jobs through linkages have better career advancement. Even though schools may have linkages with only a few employers, their students—including students with academic problems but good soft skills—get better jobs through these linkages. And even though employers may have linkages with only a few schools, hiring through school placements brings them youths who advance further than those hired through direct applications (chapter 9).

Ironically, while reducing the absolute number of applicants, linkages may increase the proportion of applicants whom employers can consider by providing new sources of information about desirable qualities that usually cannot be detected. Applicants who would normally be ignored because they have poor test scores and poor interviewing skills may have good soft skills that can be detected by employers only through recommendations from trusted teachers. Since employers care more about soft skills than test scores, linkages may put into contention more new applicants who are more appropriate for employers' needs. Thus, in a sense, linkages broaden the applicant pool by providing a way for employers to detect students' soft skills, which would not be considered otherwise.

Do Labor Markets Need More Information or Trusted Information?

The signaling model contends that information is costly, and that these costs prevent employers from obtaining as much information as they would like for making their decisions (Stigler 1961; Spence 1974). These costs of information lead to market inefficiencies. Thus, when national surveys find that employers rarely use teacher references, transcripts, and other high school information (Bishop 1993; Shapiro and Goertz 1998), researchers infer that employers want this information, but that it must be difficult to obtain. For example, noting that a major corporation has difficulty obtaining high school transcripts on applicants, John Bishop (1993) suggests that employers want more information and would be eager to use transcript information if they could get it.

Yet Robert Crain's (1984) survey of employers suggests that most employers are not eager to use this information from high schools, even though they would use transcript information from colleges. In our study, employers report that they ignore this potentially valuable information because they do not believe it is relevant or trustworthy. Signaling theory contends that employers need *more* information about applicants, but our employers complain that they get a great deal of information they do not use because they are not sure it is relevant and trustworthy. As it turns out, Bishop is right that employers should use this information, but employers do not realize that the information is relevant and trustworthy, so merely providing the information does not ensure that it is used.

Do Labor Markets Need Weak or Strong Ties?

Our findings also suggest problems with network models. Network theory contends that weak ties are better than strong ties because they give job seekers access to more information about possible job openings; strong ties, according to this view, only provides information from a few sources that have information similar to what job seekers already know. Research has shown that individuals with wide diversity of weak ties get better jobs than those who rely on strong ties (Granovetter 1995). Thus, weak ties are useful to job seekers (or recruiters) for providing leads about available jobs (or applicants). Of course, these leads may be questionable—they may be irrelevant or untrustworthy. That is not a serious problem. Before clinching the deal, job seekers and employers will verify these leads for themselves.

Although weak ties are good for opening up opportunities, they are not enough to "clinch the deal." For that, strong ties are needed. Because poor hiring decisions are costly, employers would like to get trustworthy information before making a hiring decision. Similarly, before taking a job offer, applicants would like to check out an employer's promises. Because they cannot provide trusted information, weak ties are not very useful for making hiring decisions or deciding to accept a job offer. To obtain trustworthy information, both parties need strong ties. As we have seen, a few employers and teachers do have strong ties with each other. These strong ties can provide information that is more readily available, trustworthy, and relevant to each other's needs than weak ties can provide.

How Social Context Can Increase Individuals' Value: Social Capital

Linkages have advantages over unstructured markets: they convey trusted, relevant information, and they create strong ties that improve hiring decisions. How does this happen? We need a model that explains how employers can overcome their mistrust and obtain useful information for assessing youths. The model must describe the conditions that allow employers to trust and value information about applicants' value from another institution that they normally mistrust (Useem 1986).

James Coleman (1988) provides a model for understanding how social context can enhance individuals' value, and our linkage model extends his ideas. Coleman (1988, S98) proposes that social capital, a property of the social context, can enhance individuals' value. Like physical capital or human capital, "social capital is productive, making possible the achievement of certain ends that . . . [otherwise] would not be possible. . . . Unlike other forms of capital, social capital inheres in the structure of the relations . . . among actors. It is not lodged either in the actors themselves or in physical implements of production." Thus, some aspects of social relations create social capital—a resource that enables people to achieve goals that they otherwise could not achieve.

Coleman identifies three forms of social capital: information channels, normative sanctions, and sense of obligation. He defines information channels as "the potential for information that inheres in social relations" (1988, S104). Normative sanctions are expectations that constrain certain self-interested actions but enable other actions. For example, norms that inhibit crime enable us to walk outside at night, and norms that inhibit cheating enable diamond merchants to cooperate in informal ways without expensive documentation or policing. Coleman defines the third form of social capital, a sense of obligation, as a form of "credit slip": "If A does something for B and trusts B to reciprocate in the future, this establishes an expectation in A and an obligation on the part of B" (S102).

Although Coleman illustrates these forms of social capital with a wide range of examples, most of them are taken from closed ethnic communities—Orthodox Jewish jewel merchants, the El Khalili market in Cairo, South Korean social networks, and religious private schools. Does social capital operate beyond such closed ethnic groups, and can it even be created anew? All three forms of social capital depend on a social structure with dependable, continuing interaction between all parties ("closure"). Thus, Coleman's model suggests the possibility that *social capital can be fostered by creating new social relations* with appropriate properties, and individuals' capabilities can be enhanced if they are placed in such a circumstance.

How Linkages Create Social Capital

We propose a linkage model that builds on Coleman's concept. We define linkages as repeated preferential transactions between institutions that enable individuals to make career transitions from one institution to another. Such repeated transactions resemble the preferential relationships in product markets when one firm becomes a dependable supplier to another (Scott 1991; Bradach and Eccles 1991; Eccles 1981). Linkages can be established between schools and employers, between schools and other schools, or between training programs and employers, as we illustrate later.

The linkage model contends that linkages can radically alter the labor market by transforming the nature of information. Linkages provide more information, but they also provide *better* information: they make it readily available, trusted, and relevant.

Unlike Coleman's examples in which the context comes automatically from ethnic ties (for example, the El Khalili market in Cairo), linkages are new creations, and they are often intentionally constructed to improve the quality of information. Linkages change the nature of information by creating a context that provides the three social preconditions for social capital: information channels, normative sanctions, and reciprocity.

By promising to be available at any time, linkages provide information channels through which information is easily accessed. Both parties expect linkages to continue into the future, and they can count on information being available.

Linkages provide normative sanctions by offering benefits to both parties: the implicit threat of their termination is a sanction that encourages normative compliance. Linkages do not require formal contracts or enforcement procedures; the sanction is the termination of the linkage itself. Each party fulfills the other's expectations in order to preserve the relationship. Although both parties are sometimes tempted by short-term gains to depart from expectations (for example, a teacher is tempted to help a likable but incompetent student), they resist these temptations because the temporary benefits of deviation are trivial in comparison with the long-term costs of destroying the linkage relationship.

Linkages create reciprocity when each party knows that the other feels a sense of obligation to reciprocate for favors bestowed through the relationship. Both parties are aware of an obligation to the other, and the other's reciprocal obligation. Trust is assured because both parties realize that the relationship is valuable to the other, and that they would lose more than they would gain if they departed from expectations.

Reciprocity arises automatically in closed ethnic communities, but it must be created in less cohesive networks in which the parties may not realize each other's sense of obligation. Even when one party feels a sense of obligation, information will not be used if the other does not realize that the other party feels that way. Ironically, nearly all teachers say they would not deceive employers because doing so would damage their reputation, but employers do not realize that teachers feel this way. Employers do not trust teachers' ratings unless they have ongoing relationships with them. The context of a trusted relationship is necessary to make employers realize that teachers have a sense of obligation to them.

It is striking how employers stress reciprocity. In our interviews, some employers say: "I want to know what teachers are getting from this relationship." At first, this seems like a strange statement, as if they are cynically asking to see evidence of selfishness in a profession that portrays itself as selfless. However, employers are simply stating a pre-condition for trust. They believe that trust comes from reciprocity. Teachers' ratings are credible only if employers can see that the context makes teachers obligated to them. If employers can see that teachers value the relationship, then they are confident that teachers are motivated to reciprocate and that the information they provide is relevant and trustworthy (Heimer 1992). If employers cannot see what teachers get from the relationship, then they are reluctant to trust teachers, even though teachers report that they try to give trustworthy information. Employers' confidence comes from the context, not the content.

Nor does confidence develop because of the personal qualities of the parties. Unlike moralistic models that see trustworthiness as a personal attribute of certain "honest" individuals, Coleman sees trust arising from the social context.

Thus, linkages are effective in providing useful information because they create a social context that provides information channels, normative sanctions, and reciprocity. Trust arises in a situation in which both parties are trustworthy because the context makes each readily available to satisfy the other's needs, because the context would make each party suffer if the relationship ended, and because the context makes both parties *realize* that the other party would suffer if the relationship ended. Trust is assured because these conditions reduce uncertainty (Heimer 1985); each party is reassured that the other wants to avoid disappointing them. Any deviation from expectations is a threat to the relationship and the benefits it offers, and both parties feel obligated to maintain their credibility and to serve the other's needs. Failure to do so for the sake of a temporary gain is inconceivable because of its long-term costs. But equally important, each party realizes that the context gives the other party a strong incentive to preserve the relationship. Thus, employers can trust that teachers are providing information that is relevant and trustworthy, and teachers can trust that employers will offer good jobs to their students, because each realizes that their relationship provides strong incentives for the other to act dependably.

The Japanese school-to-work transition is a prototype of such linkages. Long-term relationships between employers and certain high schools allow both parties to make commitments to each other because they expect these linkages to meet their needs. Employers expect high schools to offer a continuing information channel about their students, information about relevant student skills, and trusted information. In return, high schools expect employers to offer graduates relevant jobs of dependable quality every year (Rosenbaum and Kariya 1989). Teachers do not mislead employers to help likable individual students because the short-term benefits of doing so would have long-term costs in all future dealings with that employer. Under such linkages, neither teachers nor employers even contemplate actions that would undermine their long-term relationship and the benefits it will bring in the future.

Similarly, in our U.S. studies, employers report that they need hard-to-assess information, relevant information, and trusted information. A few employers have long-term ties with teachers that provide readily available information channels and relevant and trusted information. Because of their long-term relationship, these employers and teachers have a sense of obligation to each other and are motivated by a desire to continue making job placements in the future.

Linkages create a social context that permits information to be transmitted and used in ways that would otherwise not be possible. For instance, weak ties can convey objective information about attendance and grades but would not be trusted to convey subjective evaluations about hard-to-measure attributes like work-readiness and persistence. Within trusted linkages, however, teachers can convey their evaluations of students' effort, persistence, attention to quality, initiative, dependability—the attributes that employers value more highly than academics. Employers can trust that certain teachers will be candid about students' qualities because they know that these teachers want to continue making referrals in the future.

Most remarkably, these linkages allow employers to see the positive value of some students with obvious shortcomings. Teachers reported that they helped get jobs for students with poor academic records, learning disabilities, or language difficulties, and they did so by stressing other positive qualities of these students that employers valued but could not easily see for themselves. Linkages create a social context that allows employers to trust such subjective information about students who otherwise appear to be poor prospects. When teachers say, "You can trust me on this," linkages provide conditions that give employers reasons to do so.

The Limitations of More Information, Weak Ties, and Mediated Ties

If, as we have found, the primary problem in the youth labor market is not the amount of information but its relevance and trustworthiness, then current policy reforms are not addressing some of the key issues. In chapter 12, we focus on policy proposals in detail, but here we will mention the implications of our model for a few current policy reforms.

Reformers have advocated improving employment services by increasing the amount of information they convey. Employment services are not very successful, however, in helping people get good jobs (Osterman 1988, chapter 9). Consistent with the employment service's mission of providing "a highly automated, high-volume referral system," Bishop (1993) suggests the establishment of a creative computerized system that would combine tests, transcripts, and job-requirement and applicant-qualification listings to improve the effectiveness of employment service referrals. Test-based information might be effective if employers cared about academic skills, but academics is usually a fairly low priority for employers (NCEQW 1994). Moreover, the other information will not be very effective if employers and applicants do not trust it. If, as we have seen, employers mistrust most information about applicants, and applicants mistrust information about jobs, then even the most comprehensive computerized system will not be useful. Computers can do amazing things with information, but computers do not necessarily make information more trusted.

Similarly, contacts made through weak ties must be contrasted with linkages. Many reformers have advocated school-employer contacts that generally require little commitment and weak ties. Reformers hope that, when employers visit schools, offer field trips, donate equipment, or sponsor after-school programs, such contacts will help employers trust school evaluations and give students incentives to work in school. The results are often disappointing. A national study found that employers' school visits and donations are not correlated with their willingness to use school evaluations in hiring (Shapiro and Goertz 1998).

Moreover, third-party mediators may impede reciprocity. For instance, employment services, founded to promote job contacts, may actually weaken the effects of reciprocity in contacts. Unlike teachers, who get to know students very well over the school year and directly communicate with employers, employment service staff act as third-party mediators, collecting information about applicants from various sources (of uncertain and varying dependability) and passing this information on to employers, who may not trust the mediator. Even in the unlikely event that both steps constituted strong ties, the mediating role is likely to weaken the dependability of the information. Because employers cannot know whether the people who write references to the employment service are trustworthy, they mistrust information from employment services (chapter 6) and employment services do not lead to jobs with promising careers (chapter 9).

Similarly, although employee referrals provide trustworthy information to employers (Manwaring 1984), employers may have less trust in those referrals when they are mediated by third parties. Fernandez and Weinberg (1997, 887) found that employee referrals had significant effects on hiring in a bank even when mediated by a third-party personnel organization, but they speculated that the effect might have been stronger if the hiring process had not been mediated, and they proposed that it is important to study other settings that lack such mediators. The linkage model suggests that employers trust employee referrals because of the normative sanctions and social obligations between them and those employees, but third-party mediation may dilute these effects.

In contrast with reforms based on computer information systems, weak ties, or mediated ties, strong-ties linkages increase social capital and youths' value by making information be seen as relevant and trustworthy. Like Coleman's ethnic communities, linkages are a powerful force. They constrain behaviors, and they permit actors to trust each other. Just as merchants in the Cairo market could not imagine deceiving their colleagues because of the vast sanctions and possibility of exclusion from all future transactions, teachers would not even contemplate making recommendations that would undermine their long-term relationships with linked employers. The short-term benefit would have long-term costs for all their future dealings with that employer, and perhaps with many others. Moreover, linkages allow employers to realize that the context makes teachers dependable, so they can trust information that they otherwise would have mistrusted.

As social capital is created, remarkable benefits accrue to students. Students with the same human capital will have greater value if their social context is one in which strong linkages assure employers of the credibility of their teachers' ratings. Taking individuals with a certain amount of human capital out of an information-poor context and immersing them in a social context that effectively communicates their value to employers could vastly improve labor market outcomes for those individuals, even if their human capital does not change. For example, a student with mediocre grades in a poorly linked school cannot communicate her good work habits to employers, but if she is in a strongly linked school, her teachers can communicate her positive qualities in ways that employers can trust. Thus, after controlling for test scores, we found that school job placement has strong and significant benefits on youths' earnings (chapter 9). Moreover, such linkages can have feedback effects: by helping youths see incentives to exert effort in school, linkages may also motivate them to improve their achievement and human capital (chapter 3). If such processes are generalizable, then they offer a policy option with greater potential than many current weak-ties reforms.

Implications of Linkages

Although this book has focused on linkages between high schools and employers, linkages can also exist between other institutions. The next four sections describe how linkages work in other settings and reveal some of the general properties of linkages. Our analysis finds that linkages operate somewhat differently than we might have supposed. First, we find that linkages help not just high-status individuals, as we might expect, but also low-status individuals, including those who otherwise would lack signals of value. Second, Meyer and Rowan (1977) have described the "charters" (and associated linkages) in elite traditional schools, but we find that new non-elite schools can also have linkages. Third, far from being biased, linkages may actually reduce statistical discrimination, and we find examples of this. Fourth, we find that schools and training programs help individuals not only by increasing their human capital but also by providing trusted signals.

We discovered these general features of linkages by studying linkages in three radically different contexts: select prep schools, a new non-elite proprietary school, and job training programs.

Linkages and Meritocracy:
Select Preparatory Schools

First, in spite of the expectation that linkages may help only high-status individuals, we find that linkages can be most helpful to low-status individuals who otherwise would lack signals of value. A study of preparatory schools provides a remarkably rich description of the linkage process (Persell and Cookson 1985, 1986). Comparing sixteen select and thirty ordinary boarding schools, the study found that select schools have stronger relationships with elite colleges than other prep schools do: they are visited by more college admissions officers, and their staff visit far more colleges, especially the most selective colleges. Moreover, the select schools' college advisers have long tenures (fifteen years or more is usual) and "have close relationships with elite college admissions officers that are cemented through numerous face-to-face meetings each year" (122). At the other schools, college advisers often have short tenures (under three years) and no personal relationships with elite college admissions officers.

Although select schools' influence arises from personal ties, those ties are the result of the schools' conscious *institutional practices,* which encourage advisers to stay in their jobs. These linkages have strong benefits. Select schools have higher acceptance rates at selective colleges than other leading boarding schools do. Advisers at the select schools "can negotiate admissions cases with colleges," while other boarding schools cannot (121). Obviously, elite boarding schools allow "privileged members of society [to] transmit their advantages to their children" (126). This "transmission of privilege" model reflects a common belief that institutional linkages are largely corrupt, and that they create favoritism and reduce meritocratic selection. But ironically, several of the study's findings indicated that privilege is not the basis of these relationships.

In contrast with the privilege model, the linkage model helps explain some of the most interesting unexpected features of these findings. The linkage model suggests that select prep schools retain their influence with elite colleges by meeting their needs for hard-to-assess, dependable, and relevant information. Since elite colleges have increasingly stressed achievement (Lemann 1999), prep schools cannot merely rely on privilege; they must provide trusted information about students' achievement. Indeed, the linkage model conflicts with a "privilege" model in four ways, and the findings support the linkage model in each.

First, in contrast with the prediction of the privilege model that high-SES students will get the primary benefits, our linkage model suggests that the primary benefits of linkage accrue to students for whom ordinary signals are inadequate—low-SES students. Indeed, the Persell and Cookson (1985, 1986) study supports the linkage hypothesis.[1] Although select schools increase the elite college admission rates for all students compared to other schools, they confer a higher incremental benefit for low-SES students (see also Zweigenhaft and Domhoff 1991).

Second, in contrast with a prediction that high-test-score students reap the primary benefits, the benefits of attending select schools are even stronger for students with low test scores. Select-school advisers extensively document hard-to-measure achievements by interviewing "the entire faculty on each member of the senior class," recording and transcribing their comments, interviewing each senior, and writing a thorough letter with extensive corroborative details tailored to the specific achievements of each student (Persell and Cookson 1985, 123). As the linkage model predicts, the letter gives relevant, hard-to-assess information and stresses the distinctive needs of each college, including elusive qualities like "leadership" and "creativity." These efforts allow students from select schools to get recognition for those elusive qualities, which are not effectively communicated for students from other schools; as a result, students with low SAT scores benefit.

Third, in contrast with a prediction that select schools will stress parents' social or economic clout, the linkage model predicts that advisers at select schools gain their influence by providing colleges with dependable information about students' performance. "College advisers and admissions officers 'develop a relationship of trust,' so that colleges can evaluate the sources as well as the content of phone calls and letters." Advisers "have built up a track record with the private colleges over the years" by prescreening students and "present[ing] colleges with the most appropriate candidates." One adviser noted, "We don't sell damaged goods to the colleges" (Persell and Cookson 1985, 125). In contrast, prescreening is rare at other schools.

Fourth, in contrast with the prediction of the privilege model that advisers at select schools will defer to wealthy parents' influence, the linkage model suggests that these advisers cannot depart from achievement criteria to favor high-SES students if they do not want to lose credibility with selective colleges. Indeed, these advisers actively curtail family influence and express disdain for it.

While the children of certain big donors may be counseled with special care, in general the college advisers have *organizational concerns that are more important than the fate of a particular student.* Several select . . . school college advisers spoke with scorn about parents who see a rejection as the "first step in the negotiation." Such parents threaten to disrupt a delicate network of social relationships that link elite institutions over a considerable time span. (Persell and Cookson 1985, 124–25, emphasis added)

In an earlier era, advisers gained influence with colleges by referring to a student's family status or wealth (Baltzell 1958), but advisers at select schools now make their arguments on other grounds. Even these bastions of privilege retain their influence by responding to colleges' needs for information about students' achievement.

Do linkages in select schools create unfair advantages? The answer is complex. Most of these students, already from privileged backgrounds, have advisers who can give them special access and urge colleges to take "a chance on this one." Yet the grounds for "bargaining" are surprisingly meritocratic. Before reading this study, we might have assumed that elite schools simply send a note to Harvard saying, "This student has a wealthy father and good social graces," and perhaps fifty years ago that is what happened. However, by the 1980s these advisers had gained their bargaining power because they were performing a valuable service—reducing a college's risk of admitting students who could not handle its achievement demands. Advisers at select schools provide richer and more dependable information about their students' capabilities than colleges can get from advisers with unknown standards. They prescreen students to assess their suitability for the particular college. When an adviser says that a college would be "making a mistake" not to accept a student, such a comment is surely self-serving, but it is also a *warranty* that the student will work out. An adviser would not make that comment if he thought the student would fail and hurt his own effectiveness in future years.

A key feature of these linkages is the compelling sense of obligation in the relationship. Since these advisers consider their relationship to the colleges more important than the outcome for any one student, they do not jeopardize that relationship for a single student, and colleges can be confident that the adviser's highest priority is the college's interest. This may not be true for the advisers at other schools who rotate through the job every few years.

Ironically, unfairness arises because the process is more meritocratic for the students at select schools. Select schools confer the "privilege" of careful individual assessment, candid and informed advice, and effective presentation of each student's case by advisers with trusted standards. In contrast, about 25 percent of counselors and teachers from other schools "do little to help the applicants," reports James Wickenden, director of admissions at Princeton (quoted in Persell and Cookson 1985, 126). One counselor, he says, "prepared the same report for *all* applicants [and] made a xerox copy of the report with blank spaces left for the names of students." Perhaps the "privilege" of having trustworthy signals sent to colleges about a broad range of one's merits is a privilege that should be available to all students.[2]

Even for advisers at select schools, access is contingent on their meeting colleges' expectations for relevant, trusted information. "College advisors . . . seem quite aware . . . [that their] credibility influences how effectively they can work for their school in the future" (Persell and Cookson 1985, 124). Advisers give primacy to the colleges' own standards; in the process, they disappoint some wealthy parents, but they also help low-income students who test poorly, students whose merits are not signaled in the standard ways.

Linkages and Meritocracy: A Technical School

We might expect that only elite and traditional institutions have linkages (Meyer and Rowan 1977), but in fact we find that linkages can operate in relatively new, non-elite institutions, as illustrated by a case study of a large, private, postsecondary technical school (Mills 1977). Founded by a corporation to train workers for its own technical jobs, the school began to provide a wider range of training and became independent of the corporation. This school does not serve a selective student body; SAT scores are substantially below the national average. Also, unlike select preparatory schools, this school was founded only a few decades ago, so it needed to build connections and credibility with employers.

It did so through institutional linkages, and the school's efforts fit the conditions suggested by our linkage model. To ensure dependable types of training, the school surveyed the needs of potential employers, designed programs in areas of special need, and asked some employers to assist in the design of the relevant training programs and to serve on curriculum advisory committees to keep training up to current needs. To ensure program quality, school administrators meet with recruiters and alumni to get feedback on their programs' fit with changing industrial requirements. The school also offers faculty members sabbaticals in industry so they can catch up with changes in the field.

The placement office also assures employers of the dependable skills and quality of its students by counseling students to apply to appropriate employers and by preselecting students by interests and talents to meet with recruiters, to make the best use of recruiters' time. Moreover, employers with the best jobs are given extra help to identify the most capable students for their particular needs.[3]

For students, the placement office disseminates relevant information about interviewing techniques, résumé preparation, career self-appraisal, self-presentation at interviews, and typical recruiter questions. It critiques students' credentials, résumés, and cover letters, counsels them to apply for appropriate jobs, and identifies aspects of jobs that will appeal to their interests and abilities. As interviews are going on, the placement office learns of any difficulties students are having and counsels them in how to handle future interviews better. The amount of help given to students is similar to the individualistic attention that students get in select prep schools, even though most of the technical school students come from lower-middle-class backgrounds.

This example addresses two issues. First, it shows that linkage benefits are not limited to schools with elite status, like prep schools; they can also be conferred by less prestigious schools. Although the technical school and its students lack elite status, the school has created strong, successful linkages with major employers. Indeed, this school's success is clearly indicated by its high job placement rate—over 90 percent within ninety days of graduation every year from 1980 to 1988 (Roze and Curtis 1990). The rate dipped to 90 percent in the recession of 1982, and rose to over 95 percent in 1980, 1985, and 1988.

Second, this example shows that linkage benefits do not make selections less meritocratic. Previous research finds modest relationships between college grades and earnings in first jobs (Willis and Rosen 1979; Bishop 1988a, 1989). In contrast, the technical school's linkages have created a stronger emphasis on achievement. For this school's graduates, the correlation between grades and starting salaries was .94 in 1986 and higher the next year (Roze and Curtis 1990). Moreover, despite the large salary disadvantage that women and blacks usually experience, this school's female graduates received 3 percent higher starting salaries than men, while blacks received 97 percent of the starting salaries of whites (Roze and Curtis 1990, 51).

Although the school provides high-quality, specialized technical training, it does not rely only on that. The school devotes extensive efforts to developing linkages to improve the signals it transmits to employers. Employers know they can get a dependable supply of workers with dependable types and quality of training in specific areas. Students also learn how to present their merits effectively in interviews with employers, and they know that good performance in the school's programs ensures that they will get jobs of dependable types and quality.

Obviously, a single case may not be representative. Further research is needed to establish the incidence of linkages and their benefits at other such schools. However, this case does suggest that linkages can operate meritocratically in relatively unselective schools and that they can confer benefits.

Linkages and Discrimination

Linkages may seem to encourage favoritism and discrimination, but in fact they can *reduce* some forms of discrimination. The signaling model describes a world of statistical discrimination. Employers use easily available information to infer productivity. Such inferences are always imperfect, but if a signal reduces the chances of getting a bad employee by 10 percent, then employers will use that signal. If 95 percent of one group and 85 percent of a second group will be satisfactory, an employer will hire *no one* from the second group if they get enough group-one applicants. As Lester Thurow (1975, 172) notes: "The acceptable 85 percent of the individuals in group two suffer from statistical discrimination. They are not hired because of the objective characteristics of the group to which they belong, although they, themselves, are satisfactory." Statistical discrimination can occur without prejudiced attitudes. But it is still discrimination, and it has an impact on all members of a group.

The distinction between statistical discrimination and prejudice is important. The reluctance of some black employers to hire black youths from housing projects is due not to racial bias but to statistical discrimination: a perception that housing project residents have higher rates of problem behaviors. These perceptions may be incorrect. But, if they are correct, then employer hiring behavior will not be changed by changing their attitudes.

However, their behavior can be changed by better information. If hiring bias is caused by prejudice, then policy can reduce this bias only by changing employers' attitudes or behavior. In contrast, if hiring bias is caused by statistical discrimination, policy can persuade employers to abandon their reliance on statistical discrimination merely by giving them new, less biased selection criteria that are better predictors of productivity. Thus, employers who use tests to screen applicants are sometimes *more* likely to hire blacks than other employers are (Neckerman and Kirschenman 1991; Moss and Tilly 2000). Even if tests are biased against blacks, they introduce *less* racial bias than the subjective judgments employers would use in their absence.

Linkages can reduce statistical discrimination by giving employers better information about applicants than they can get otherwise. If linkages convey more performance-based information about an applicant than the crude categories that appear on job applications (such as age, sex, race), employers can abandon their reliance on statistical discrimination.

Research cites many examples. For instance, Mark Granovetter (1985) found that linkages between rehabilitation counselors and employers can reduce employers' discrimination against disabled job applicants. Employers can discover which disabled applicants can perform their jobs. Similarly, trusted linkages have permitted local employment agencies to overcome employers' biases against black applicants in Brooklyn (Kasinitz and Rosenberg 1996) and in Detroit, as described in the next section.

Although some employers try to narrow their applicant pool by prescreening on college grades, college placement staff can sometimes convince linked employers to hire a student below their usual grade standards if the placement staff vouch for other personal qualities in the student (Kariya and Rosenbaum 1995). Similarly, college co-op programs sometimes convince employers to hire students who they might not have hired otherwise because they show capabilities at work that are not evident in their school records (Kariya and Rosenbaum 1995). Select prep schools' linkages give colleges information about students' qualities that is not apparent in their test scores, to the particular benefit of low-SES students. A technical institute's linkages eliminated the gender gap in salaries and reduced the racial gap.

Our research has shown similar processes at work in high schools. Vocational teachers' linkages can convince employers to hire women and blacks for jobs that employers thought could only be done by white males, such as machining or electronics. When a sheet-metal teacher reported that a female student had done well in his class, his recommendation persuaded an employer to overlook his prejudices and hire her. Without this recommendation, she would not have been hired.

Indeed, we found that high school students with limited English proficiency, learning disabilities, or handicaps got jobs through teachers' linkages. Students with such disabilities would usually never get past an employment interview, but teachers inform employers of other desirable attributes in these students that are less visible but more important to them. These examples illustrate the theoretical point that linkages can overcome statistical discrimination by providing detailed, performance-based knowledge about candidates. Although we do not know how often such incidents happen, our analyses of HSB national survey data indicate that females and blacks get jobs through school placement more often than white males do, and that this method leads to jobs that lead to higher pay nine years later (chapter 9).

Of course, some teachers are prejudiced. In our interviews, some teachers express negative stereotypes about blacks and females. But even these prejudiced teachers feel a professional obligation to see the positive attributes of all their students, and over the course of a whole school year these prejudiced teachers may see student performances that challenge their prejudices. In contrast, employers' stereotypes are not likely to be contradicted in fifteen-minute interviews. Teachers may be biased, but they are likely to be less biased than employers.

By providing trustworthy information to employers, linkages can reduce statistical discrimination. Linkages may not always be unbiased, but by providing better firsthand information about individuals, they can contradict employers' uninformed stereotypes.

Signaling Human Capital: Job Training Programs

Human capital is the usual focus of schools and training programs, but signals are also important. Although youth labor market problems may arise in part from poor human capital (see Farkas 1996; Jencks and Phillips 1998), our model contends that information difficulties may also be responsible. If students' human capital improves but employers cannot detect that improvement, no benefit will occur. Even if students' human capital is not altered, providing employers with hard-to-get, relevant, and trusted information about them will improve the students' employment prospects.

Evaluations of various training programs have shown mixed success. The Wisconsin Youth Apprenticeship Program in Printing led to increased employment and earnings compared to co-op programs (Orr 1996). Students admitted to the New York Career Magnet Program through a lottery selection received higher starting wages after graduation than students not admitted to the program (Crain 1997). By contrast, the Manufacturing Technology Partnership Program led to improved employment, wages, and hours worked in some comparisons but not in others (Hollenbeck 1996). When a review of these studies asserts that apprenticeship programs "have not yielded clear results," that conclusion may seem inevitable given the great variation in school-to-work activities from one place to another (Urquiola, Stern, et al. 1997, 202). However, our model suggests that program effectiveness depends not just on training but on signals, which are generally ignored in this literature.

Perhaps we seem to be exaggerating the importance of "signals." Getting good information is nice, but surely it is no substitute for good training. That is what the British thought when they set up the expensive Youth Training Scheme (YTS) to give apprenticeship training to youths. They found that the program worked, but not because it provided training. Indeed, program *success* predicted labor market *failure!* Youths who successfully completed the program were more likely to be labor market failures than were program dropouts. Looking more closely, it was found that employers used the program to identify promising workers; once they had identified these workers, employers immediately shifted them to real jobs rather than wait for them to complete their apprenticeship (Cappelli and Rogowsky 1993). Apparently, information about youths is sometimes more important than training.

Similar results can be seen in high school co-op programs in the United States. Youths get earnings payoffs from co-op only if they get jobs with the same firm where they did their co-op program (Stern and Stevens 1992). If youths gain human capital from co-op, only their immediate employers know about it. Co-op programs seem to have payoffs because they provide an easy way for employers to get information about youths' capabilities, information they cannot get otherwise. But co-op programs do not give other employers any signals of youths' value.

Indeed, the importance of signals is most dramatically indicated by programs that seem to offer good training but actually hurt participants by the signals they convey. Several evaluation studies find that the graduates of job training programs have about the same earnings and employment rates as control groups who get no training (Basi and Ashenfelter 1986; Barnow 1987; Burghardt et al. 1992). Indeed, in some evaluations, graduates actually have *lower* earnings than control groups (Bloom et al. 1992; Cave and Doolittle 1991). A likely interpretation is that the job training programs may offer good training, but they also confer negative signals. Since these programs admit only people with troubled work histories, they confer a stigma that reduces employers' willingness to hire program participants.

However, while many job training programs stigmatize participants, Focus/Hope, a Detroit-based job training program serving low-income blacks, explicitly addresses the signaling problem with stringent entrance and completion requirements. This program admits only low-income people who have difficulty getting jobs, so like other job training programs, it implicitly stigmatizes participants. However, Focus/Hope offsets this initial stigma by certifying that all participants have a high school diploma (or GED) and no drug problems (referring others to GED and drug rehabilitation programs). Moreover, by requiring near-perfect attendance, instilling good work habits, and demanding strong skills before graduation, the program certifies that its graduates have met high standards and will be good workers. As a result, Focus/Hope has become a preferred provider of highly paid, skilled workers in the auto industry.

A study of Brooklyn employers found that most "jobs were filled via social networks that exclude local residents . . . [and] local employers considered . . . [local] residents undesirable employees" (Kasinitz and Rosenberg 1996, 180). This study illustrates that a person's home address can become a signal for statistical discrimination. However, as a side issue, the authors mention at the very end of their paper that a local development corporation (LDC) builds relationships with local employers, screens local residents, and has had success in getting them jobs. "The main reason that employers were willing to give them a chance in the first place was that the employers trusted the LDC and took their reference seriously" (194). The authors make this observation almost in passing, but the linkage model and the various studies reviewed in this chapter suggest that linkage between employers and such community institutions is a promising method for overcoming statistical discrimination and providing disadvantaged people with signals of value.

Thus, policymakers should shift their efforts from simply building human capital to finding ways to signal it, both by using better signals (Bishop 1989, 1993; Rosenbaum 1989a, 1989b) and by creating social contexts in which relevant and trusted information can be conveyed. The next chapter considers the implications of the linkage model for improving policymakers' understanding of youths' problems and for improving policy.

═ Chapter 12 ═

Policy Implications: Career
Paths for the Forgotten Half

ESPITE enormous changes in employment circumstances and
college opportunities over the past several decades, young
people continue to have work-entry problems. Although a
strong labor market reduces unemployment, a strong labor market
does not last forever, solve employers' skill shortages, or give unskilled youths good jobs, particularly if they lack the soft skills that
employers do not try to provide through training.

We explored the theoretical implications of our findings in chapter
11, and here we examine their policy implications. This chapter has
four goals: to show that policy has viewed work-entry problems too
narrowly; to show that current practices have led students to misperceive their incentives; to show how linkage practices, such as those
used in other nations for conveying incentives, could address work-
entry difficulties in the United States; and to recommend specific
ways to improve American practices.

First, we present evidence that policy has viewed work-entry problems too narrowly. In focusing on college goals, not job goals, policies
have been overly concerned with academic deficiencies rather than
other deficiencies. They have put too much emphasis on internal motivation rather than external incentives. As a result, policies underestimate how many students are work-bound, they do not help some
students develop soft skills, and they do not help many students prepare realistically for their careers.

Second, we discover that students seriously misperceive their incentives, and that these misperceptions are encouraged by societal
practices. Employer hiring practices and college open-admissions
practices give students the false impression that there are no incentives for high school effort, but incentives do exist. Our research finds
that although students' high school achievements do not necessarily

improve *short-term* outcomes (early pay and enrollment to open-admissions colleges), they have large effects on *long-term* outcomes nine years after high school. Unfortunately, since long-term payoffs are harder to perceive than short-term ones, students do not perceive their long-term incentives, but they do see the lack of short-term incentives. The challenge for policy is not to create incentives, because they already exist, but rather to make long-term incentives more visible.

Third, we show that linkage practices like those used in other nations for conveying incentives could address the difficulties encountered by American youths when they try to enter the work world. The United States already uses co-op and tech-prep reforms to help high schools make contacts with employers and colleges. However, problems sometimes arise in tech-prep and co-op reforms, and our model suggests procedures to make the contacts in these programs more effective.

Fourth, we reexamine our findings about teacher-employer relationships in the United States, and we consider their implications for improving the ways in which youths join the workforce or enroll in college. We describe how these relationships are created, and we recommend ways to improve current reforms.

This chapter reviews the findings from prior chapters to identify how they could help policymakers better understand youths' problems. We then suggest improvements to current reforms and propose some new reforms.

The Narrow Focus of Current Policies

Focusing on College, but Ignoring Jobs

Without any public decision to do so, American high schools have quietly and unofficially adopted a policy of encouraging all students to attend college—what I have called the "college-for-all" policy (chapter 3; see also Rosenbaum 1998a). High school guidance counselors, who used to be gatekeepers, now encourage *all* students to attend college, regardless of their past records, and they do not warn students if their chances of success in college are poor (chapter 4).

The new policy has had an impact across the nation. Barbara Schneider and David Stevenson (1999) have noted the change in students' postsecondary plans and called them *The Ambitious Generation.* However, although 71 percent of American seniors in 1982 expected to earn a college degree (A.A. or higher), many of them were disappointed. As we saw in chapter 3, fewer than 38 percent of seniors who planned to get a college degree actually did so in the ten years following graduation, and fewer than 14 percent of seniors with poor high school grades completed a degree. For this 14 percent, open admissions was an extremely helpful second chance. However, an 86 percent failure rate suggests that the college-for-all approach is usually an unrealistic policy for students with poor grades. Such students need to be told how hard they must work to overcome these odds, and they need to have fallback options.

These findings have at least five important policy implications. First, many "college-bound" students are really work-bound. Many students who plan college degrees are almost certain to drop out of college. It is highly predictable which college-bound students will enter the labor market with a high school diploma as their highest degree (often with no college credits), although they did not plan or prepare to do so.

Second, many students in college are not college students. Indeed, 40 percent of college students report taking remedial courses (NCES 1999), many students report taking three or more remedial courses, and, since some students do not realize that their courses are remedial, the actual numbers may be much higher (Deil and Rosenbaum 2000). Remedial courses usually give no college credits, and the higher the number of remedial courses a student takes, the greater the chances that student will drop out of college (Deil and Rosenbaum 2000). Students are taking courses in college buildings, but they are not college courses. They are paying college tuition to take remedial courses—high school–level courses that confer no college credits. Students expect that a two-year degree will take two years, but this is unlikely when they need to take remedial courses.

Third, even after entering college, many students are unclear about requirements. Community colleges do a good job of spreading information about their open-admissions policies, but they do not disseminate information about remedial courses, dropout rates, or the requirements for taking college credit courses. So as not to discourage students, some community colleges avoid telling them that they are in remedial courses, or that their courses are not conferring college credit, even after they have taken several such courses (Deil and Rosenbaum 2000).

Fourth, although the labor market requires higher skills than in the past, many good jobs do not require college skills. There has been a large increase in the need for *high school*–level skills—math, reading, and writing skills at a ninth- to tenth-grade level, yet "close to 50% of all 17-year-olds cannot read or do math at a level needed to get a job in a modern automobile plant" (Murnane and Levy 1996, 35). We need to improve youths' skills, but the skills that are needed can be provided in high school. Students do not need to go to college to obtain these skills.

Fifth, postponing college may be a desirable option for some students. Many students enter college when they are older, often after several years of work. More than half of the students in two-year colleges are older than twenty-four, and about one-quarter of them are over thirty-five (NCES 1999, table 216). Their age and employment may give them the experience to make better course choices, the maturity to be more disciplined students, skills that will help them pass some courses, and perhaps even employer-paid tuition benefits. As noted, high school graduates with low grades who are unprepared for college have an 86 percent chance of dropping out (often with zero credits). For these students, postponing college might improve their chances of benefiting from it later.

Although counselors' college-for-all focus hurts many students, they have good intentions. They do not want to discourage students or to close off their options too early. But by withholding information about the requirements for college-credit classes, counselors prevent students from knowing what high school efforts would prepare them for real college courses. Without such information, students are also unable to see incentives to make an effort in high school, to know their realistic chances of getting some college credits, and to know how much time and tuition it will take before they start getting college credits. Counselors should give students information about the requirements for college-credit classes, their likely prospects, and what high school efforts would prepare them for college.

Counselors should also give students information about backup options—good, well-paid careers that do not require college. Such jobs do exist, in a wide variety of fields: construction, trades, clerical, administrative, technicians, printing, graphics, financial services, and social services. Unfortunately, guidance counselors rarely know about such jobs and their requirements (chapter 4), so they will need training in this area. Alternatively, other staff could provide this information to students. Some vocational teachers already help some students whose academic achievement is poor to get jobs with career potential (chapter 10), so their role could be expanded.

The college-for-all focus prevents students from seeing that they must make an effort in high school if they are going to get some benefit from college, that college enrollment is not helpful to all students, that some jobs offer good career prospects, that high school can help students meet the requirements for better jobs, and that delayed college entry may improve their chances of benefiting from the experience.

Focusing on Academics, but Ignoring Soft Skills

Work-entry reforms have focused too narrowly on academics. Although employers value academic skills, they rate "soft skills," like motivation and social skills, as their greatest need, and as far more important than academic skills (Shapiro and Iannozzi 1999; Moss and Tilly 2000). In the interviews we conducted, employers stress attendance, deportment, dependability, initiative, and ability to work with others.

Moreover, youths must learn soft skills before entering the labor market. Although employers sometimes provide training in academic or technical skills, they do not provide training in soft skills. If workers lack these skills, if they are undependable, unmotivated, or prone to conflicts, employers do not train them—they fire them. Employers do not believe that they know how to train employees in soft skills (Miller and Rosenbaum 1996). Similarly, most job training programs focus on academic or job skills, and the few programs that try to teach motivation find that it is difficult, expensive, and very time-consuming (Herr, Wagner, and Halpern 1996). If students do not learn soft skills before entering the labor market, they probably will not be given a chance to learn them later.

High school is the last institution that all students attend, so it is the logical place for students to learn how to exert effort, if they have not done so already. Yet students believe that there is no reason to exert effort in high school. As we have seen, almost 40 percent of high school seniors believe that school effort has little relevance for their future careers (chapter 3). Even many college-bound students believe that high school efforts are not important and that, because of open admissions, they can enter college no matter how badly they do in high school, and that they can wait until college to exert effort (see also Steinberg 1996).

Again we discover a strange discrepancy between societal practices and societal needs. While high schools focus on academic skills, they are failing to develop soft skills, which employers value much more than academics and which must be learned before entering the labor market. Many employers report that some new workers are absent or late to work several days in the first week on the job, do poor-quality work, and talk back to supervisors. Students have learned that they can get away with these behaviors in high school, so they are surprised when employers fire them. High schools must help students learn the soft skills that employers require.

Focusing on Internal Motivation, but Ignoring External Incentives

Policy discussions often focus too narrowly on students' lack of internal motivation as the cause of their problems with school. We urge students to work harder, we try to increase their motivation by redesigning curricula, and we blame teachers for not making students more motivated. We even give up on students, assuming that they are incapable of working hard.

However, we cannot expect students to exert effort if they do not see incentives. Our policies rarely provide incentives or make them visible to students. Although researchers discover incentives by doing statistical analyses of which kinds of effort and achievement lead to later payoffs, students do not possess long-term longitudinal data, and they cannot do these statistics. To judge from students' unrealistic college goals and their failure to see the future relevance of their high school achievement, it seems that students are often unaware of the incentives that our research has discovered.

If we want students to perceive incentives, we need to provide some mechanism to make this happen. What is missing from current practices is a mechanism for creating and conveying signals that tell students the value of their present actions in achieving desirable career goals. Other countries produce such signals with linkage mechanisms, which have a great impact on students' attitudes and behaviors.

The German system provides a clear mechanism that makes the relationship between school performance and career outcomes totally obvious to students (Hamilton and Hurrelmann 1994). Non-college-bound students know that apprenticeships lead to respected occupations, and that school grades affect selection into apprenticeships. Similarly, in Japan, non-college-bound students know that high school grades are signals of their chances of getting good jobs. Students can look at their grades and infer how well they are doing and the quality of whatever job they are likely to get. They can see well in advance that their achievement is too low for their plans, and they know that they must increase their efforts or lower their plans.

In contrast, the United States does not provide incentives or clear career payoffs for the high school efforts of many students. Open-admissions policies tell students that they can attend college even with poor grades and test scores—even a D average is good enough.

Similarly, employer hiring practices ignore students' high school records (Crain 1984), and nothing in students' high school records—not grades, test scores, or attendance records—has any relationship to employment or earnings right after high school (Griffin, Kalleberg, and Alexander 1981; Bishop 1989; see also chapter 9). Employers assign new high school graduates to a few undemanding entry-level jobs at low pay until they see how youths do in their workplace (chapter 5). These employer practices tell students that there are no incentives for high school efforts.

Thus, unlike German or Japanese students, many American students have no sense that their school achievements matter for their college or job plans. Students do not know whether their goals are realistic, whether they should work harder to attain their goals, or what actions they can take to improve their chances of attaining their goals. While American policy focuses narrowly on students' motivation and makes moral appeals to students to work harder in school, employer practices and college open-admissions practices fail to offer students payoffs for school achievement. If we want our students to be motivated in high school, we must show them incentives for school effort.

Making Policies More Effective

Showing Students the Relevance of High School Evaluations

Students are unlikely to exert effort in high school if they do not see incentives. American students' belief in the irrelevance of high school is not just their individual perception. This belief arises because American society lacks any mechanism to authorize high schools to produce signals of students' value. American reformers do not try to create any mechanism because of three common assumption:

1. The Japanese and German systems cannot be replicated in the United States.

2. High school behaviors are irrelevant to career success.

3. High schools cannot help students get good jobs.

However, all three assumptions are contradicted by strong evidence.

Contrary to the assumption that the Japanese and German systems would not work in the United States, the United States in fact already has such a system, but only for some students. For students who aspire to selective colleges, the College Board has spelled out a college admission procedure that creates signals of students' value. As a result, all students who aspire to selective colleges know that their grades and test scores (SAT or ACT) determine admissions outcomes. In addition, the PSAT informs students well in advance of how they are doing and what postsecondary goals may be realistic. These students can assess their chances because our society has institutionalized a common, agreed-upon procedure for admissions to selective colleges, and the College Board and the SAT/ACT provide institutional mechanisms for defining those procedures.

The United States stratifies incentives. We provide clear incentives to students who aspire to selective colleges, but we do not provide incentives for other students. We give our best students signals for planning their careers and communicating their value to selective colleges, but we do not give other students signals that would predict their career outcomes. This is dismaying. We give clear incentives to students who do well in high school, but none at all to lower-achieving students.

Another common assumption is that high school behaviors are irrelevant to later success. American high schools give students many evaluations, but no one thinks that these evaluations have any value after high school (unless students aspire to selective colleges). Indeed, hiring and open-admissions practices make high school evaluations irrelevant to outcomes right after high school. However, we found that even though high school grades are not related to *short-term* outcomes (college admissions or earnings right after high school), they are strongly related to *long-term* outcomes at age twenty-eight. Although many employers think that nothing that happens in high school is relevant to the workplace, the qualities that lead to better grades (academic achievement, attendance, discipline, and social skills) also make young people more successful at work. High school grades predict students' ultimate educational attainment and earnings (even after many controls). A rise of one letter grade (from C to B) is associated with a 12 percent earnings gain.[1]

Grades are not the only determinant of later attainment. We also find that other high school behaviors have similar effects. Students' soft skills in high school—their attendance, deportment, social skills, and leadership—also affect earnings and educational attainments (chapter 8). Although employers do not realize it when they hire youths, school behaviors are strong predictors of youths' later earnings at age twenty-eight. Some vocational teachers have used their knowledge of work demands to help their students develop appropriate work habits and social skills, and they convey trusted evaluations of these behaviors to some employers (chapter 10). Unfortunately, other students and other employers do not realize that high school behaviors predict how well students will do at work.

The third assumption is that high schools cannot help students get good jobs. We discovered that high schools are in fact helping some students get jobs. They do not help only students who are already favored in the labor market; females and minorities are more likely to get school help than white males. In addition, we find that students who get jobs with the help of their school have better career trajectories. They have 17 percent higher earnings at age twenty-eight than students who got jobs through direct applications, and their earnings are even higher than those of students who got jobs through family contacts (chapter 9). Obviously, high schools can help students get good jobs.

In some respects, American society works like Japan's. In both nations, students with better high school achievement are more likely to get a college degree and higher earnings. The main difference is that Japanese students can look at their grades and have some clear idea of their career prospects and whether they need to work harder to attain their goals, but *the American practice is to keep students in the dark.* No one—not employers, not students, and not most teachers— seems to realize that high school grades predict how well students will do in the labor market. Some guidance counselors suspect that grades are a pretty good predictor of whether students will get any benefit from college, but they withhold such information to preserve the high expectations of students with low grades. Thus, although students know their grades, they do not realize that grades predict career outcomes, so they do not realize that low grades mean that they should be working harder to prepare themselves to attain their goals. Although counselors may be trying to protect students' self-esteem, keeping students in the dark is not a kindness; it deprives them of incentives to get the skills they need to attain their goals.

Improving the Quality of Contacts

The challenge for policy is not creating the right incentives, but rather making the current incentives more visible. Incentives exist, but they are not seen. Contacts are a good way to convey incentives. Many reformers have concluded that youths' prospects would be improved by helping high schools make contacts with employers and colleges. Two major types of reforms are based on contacts: tech-prep and co-op. These reforms are very promising, but they are often ineffective at conveying information about incentives or about students' value.

Tech-prep programs create contacts between high schools and community college programs in specific occupational fields, such as health care and technology. Tech-prep is consistent with economic theory, and even critics of other approaches are impressed with the tech-prep idea (Donahoe and Tienda 2000). By 1990 there were more than 120 tech-prep programs in thirty-three states and the Carl Perkins Act included funds to encourage further implementation of this model (Bailey and Merritt 1993). These programs organize the high school curriculum in the junior and senior years to meet directly the prerequisites for certain occupational programs in community colleges, and some even give college credits. Ideally, tech-prep makes a seamless transition between high school and the first course in community college. High school graduates in these programs are fully prepared to take college courses.

The ideal tech-prep program should reduce some of our concerns about the college-for-all approach by synchronizing high school courses with college programs. Mastery of high school courses is supposed to meet the prerequisites for college courses, and performance in high school courses should provide clear information to students about how well prepared they are for college. If students do poorly in a high school course, they get clear information about a problem that they must repair before they go to college. Tech-prep programs that synchronize high school and college in very strong linkages will address many of the problems that usually arise with a college-for-all approach.

Unfortunately, tech-prep programs do not always fulfill these conditions. Research finds that in many tech-prep programs, students enter college unprepared for college-credit courses, high schools do not give students clear signals of what colleges demand or how well they meet college requirements, and colleges give their own tests because they do not trust high school evaluations (Orfield and Paul 1994). In actual practice, these programs are often poorly synchronized and fail to convey effective signals of college demands or student preparation.

Tech-prep programs could be improved by providing more effective and trusted signals of college requirements and students' readiness. Such signals help students to see incentives for appropriate achievement and to know whether they are prepared for college-level courses.

Youth apprenticeship and cooperative learning (co-op) programs create contacts between high schools and employers. They attempt to coordinate learning at school and in the workplace. Both programs try to help students learn academic skills, job skills, and soft skills. Youth apprenticeships are more structured and usually include close supervision and coursework synchronized with the job experience. However, they are very expensive. Apprenticeships are extensively used in Germany, but few American employers are willing to pay for them, and only a few thousand students are in youth apprenticeships in the entire United States.

Co-op is sometimes viewed as an inexpensive youth apprenticeship. It is widely practiced across most American high schools: about 8 percent of American high school juniors and seniors are in co-op programs (GAO 1991). In most co-op programs, students are released from some classes so that they can get experience at their co-op jobs, which are supposed to provide more training than average jobs.

In practice, co-op programs have had two kinds of problems. First, if the jobs are not carefully screened, they may be ordinary "youth jobs" that provide little or no training for skilled jobs (Hamilton and Hurrelmann 1994).

Second, co-op leads to earnings benefits for students, but only if students take jobs in the same company where they did the co-op program. Research finds that students get no earnings benefit if they take a job in another company (Stern and Stevens 1992). While students who complete German apprenticeships get a generalized signal of value that is trusted by all employers (Hamilton 1989; Prais 1995; Soskice 1994), students who complete a co-op experience do not get such a signal. Co-op has problems in providing relevant, trusted signals that are valued by other employers.

Tech-prep and co-op are promising ideas. They indicate that contacts can improve the transitions from high school to college or work. However, these programs could be improved by providing more effective signaling. They must convey trusted signals of students' readiness for college and signals of job requirements.

Creating Linkage Mechanisms to Convey Relevant and Trusted Signals of Value

To improve the transition to college and work, the United States must implement procedures that provide signals of students' value that are relevant and trusted by employers and colleges. To be relevant, evaluations must be valued for both job applications and college admissions, and they must assess both academic skills and soft skills. To be trusted, evaluations must be candid, and they must be conveyed in a trusted context.

Surprisingly, U.S. high schools are further along in providing such information than is generally realized. High schools give evaluations and have employer contacts, and these evaluations and contacts predict career outcomes. Unfortunately, no one realizes this, and information is not always effectively communicated. We propose several policy actions to improve information and to improve the use of information.

Improving the Transition to College To improve the transition to college, tech-prep programs can develop tests that convey trusted signals of students' readiness for college courses. Colleges already give tests to determine whether students will take college-credit or remedial courses, but various colleges use different tests. Students can shop around for colleges with easier tests, and high schools do not know what standards are expected. This creates serious problems. There should be uniformity across all colleges in a state so that students can transfer from community colleges to four-year colleges. At a minimum, all colleges in a state should adopt the same test.

Currently, remedial placement tests are not available to high schools. Colleges should make these tests available to high schools. They would inform high school students of how prepared they are for college courses and give them both an incentive to work harder and information for guiding their career plans.

New Jersey community colleges have recently been considering adopting the same placement test across the state. In addition, some New Jersey high schools have administered the college placement test to assess students' readiness for college-level courses. Students take such tests of academic proficiency anyway after they arrive at college. But taking the tests in high school would give them signals of whether they are prepared for college-level classes and what actions they should be taking while they are still in high school.

Pretests of college readiness help students assess how realistic college is for them and what they must do, not merely to enter college but to enter college-credit classes and get some benefit from college. Some students will discover achievement deficiencies that they need to repair. Unlike the students in our study who had unrealistic plans, New Jersey students who take this test in high school will know whether they will be in college-credit or remedial courses when they get to college.

Pretests will give some students important information about their chances of succeeding in college. While preparing for college, they will also make backup plans and get job preparation. Shielding students from this information is not a kindness; it prevents them from seeing their real situation and condemns them to enter the labor market with no job skills and without the benefit of school job placement help. In particular, students who lack basic ninth-grade skills and face several years of noncredit remedial courses may decide that a job is a better option than college. That decision will save them from wasting time and tuition on noncredit remedial courses with high dropout rates. For some students, a good job is a better alternative, especially if high schools help them get it.

Improving the Transition to Employment   Providing good information to improve the transition to employment is a more complex challenge. There are at least three steps, however, that high schools can take to improve students' access to promising jobs.

First, high schools can work with employers to help them see grades as relevant and dependable signals of students' readiness for work. Contrary to employers' beliefs about the irrelevance of school, we have shown that high school evaluations predict success in the work world. High school grades strongly affect earnings, even after controlling for achievement test scores (chapter 8). If employers realized this, they could benefit from this already available information, and they could convey clearer incentives to students to keep their grades up. If students realized this, they would see actions they could take in high school to improve their career success.

Second, high schools can provide new signals of soft skills, qualities like attendance, discipline, motivation, sociability, and leadership, which predict students' later earnings (chapter 8). Just as some teachers already evaluate soft skills for employers in informal contacts, schools could devise new evaluations so that valuable signals of the soft skills of all students could be conveyed to employers.

Indeed, in response to an article urging such reforms (Rosenbaum 1989a), some American high schools have created new "employability" ratings. According to reports from one high school, local employers see these ratings as relevant to their hiring needs, students see these ratings as making their school behaviors relevant to job outcomes, and teachers believe that these ratings have improved students' motivation. Indeed, teachers were initially reluctant to do these ratings but have found them so useful in motivating students that they have increased the number of times they give "employability" ratings (from two to six times a year).

Some critics argue that high schools should not respond to employers' needs (Bowles and Gintis 1976). However, many of the traits that employers need in their workers are attributes that youths will need in all realms of life—attendance, punctuality, cooperation, persistence, attention to quality, initiative, and responsibility. These are the qualities that go into the employability ratings at the school just cited. Research needs to examine how high schools can make such ratings trustworthy, how they can help motivate students to improve their soft skills, and to what extent employers would use them.

Third, high schools need to have trusted relationships with employers. Information is more likely to be used if it is conveyed in a trusted relationship, and our studies indicate that trusted relationships can and do exist. This finding was perhaps the greatest surprise in our research. Some vocational teachers have trusted relationships with employers; they take actions to create these relationships; and these relationships allow them to get jobs for students who have good soft skills, even those with poor academic achievement, limited English proficiency, learning disabilities, or other problems (chapter 10). These linkages are rare in our studies, as they are in the national study, in which fewer than 9 percent of seniors get jobs with the help of their school. However, these linkages provide a way for students who do poorly in academics or who have weak interviewing skills to get recognition for hard-to-detect soft skills. These linkages also give employers information that they need but cannot get in other ways. Employers report that these relationships help them make better hiring decisions (chapter 6).

The national survey also indicates that high school assistance in finding jobs serves students who have difficulties in the labor market—females and minorities are more likely to get school job help than white males. Moreover, students assisted by their school in getting a job have better career trajectories. They have 17 percent higher earnings nine years after high school than students who got jobs through direct application. The task for school reforms is to find ways to encourage these relationships and make them more generally available across many teachers in a school.

Teachers and employers report that trust is essential to make these job placements work. Urging that all parties build trusting relationships may sound moralistic, but it is not. Some mundane actions can develop trust in relationships. Teachers build trust by their experience in the trade, their track record of placements, their prescreening, and their candor.

Moreover, employers (and to a lesser extent teachers) indicate that the key to developing trust in employer-teacher linkages is to make it apparent that each party is getting some clear benefits from the relationship. This condition, which we term reciprocity, reassures each party that the other is seriously committed to maintaining the relationship in order to keep getting that benefit. Employers must see that teachers value the relationship. If schools reward teachers for placing students in good jobs, employers will trust teachers to convey dependable information. Similarly, in order to trust employers to give students good jobs, teachers must see that employers value the relationship as a way to meet their skill needs.

The meaning of reciprocity can be clarified by examples of its absence. Reciprocity may be the missing ingredient in some co-op programs in which employers and school staff are not motivated to serve each other. In our interviews, some employers confess that public relations is the only reason they are in a co-op program; they have no intention of hiring co-op students. On the other side, some co-op coordinators admit that principals have pressured them to place *all* applicants, including unmotivated students whom they feel would get little from the program and would sour employers on their future evaluations and their other students. In such a situation, there is no reciprocity. Teachers are rewarded by principals for placing all students, including inappropriate ones; employers are rewarded by the public relations benefits, even if they offer no training or job access. Without reciprocity, these weak ties do not create trust, a mutual sense of obligation, or social capital.

Such co-op arrangements illustrate what Grubb (1996) has called "low-quality equilibrium"—everyone is satisfied in this relationship, but it provides only minimal benefits to each party. Employers get poor workers, and in turn, they offer bad jobs and poor employment prospects. The lack of reciprocity explains these low-quality relationships. Both parties see their primary rewards coming from outside third parties, not from each other or from the relationship itself.

To achieve a "high-quality equilibrium," both parties must place higher demands on the relationship, make greater sacrifices for it, and see that the other party cares about those rewards and feels obligated to maintain the relationship. Under such conditions, both parties would see incentives to improve the quality of their contribution. For instance, if freed from administrative pressure, teachers might try to please employers so that they could provide better employment help to their students. Reciprocity would encourage them to shift the relationship from low-quality to high-quality.

Unfortunately, policy is now moving in the wrong direction. Perpetuating the college-for-all myth, schools are deemphasizing employers' needs, reducing vocational education, and retiring vocational teachers who have employer contacts. These are terrible losses. Besides the instructional value of vocational education for teaching academic skills in applied tasks (Stern et al. 1995; Grubb 1995b), we have found that vocational teachers provide schools with valuable employer contacts that are especially helpful in providing incentives and real job payoffs to students who are unlikely to benefit from college. We have also found that vocational teachers use their knowledge of work demands to teach work habits and social skills in their classes, and that their work histories and contacts make their claims credible.

Declining enrollments are often blamed for the cutbacks in vocational programs, but it is also true that parents and students are avoiding vocational programs because schools encourage all students to attend college, even if they have poor prospects. Indeed, it is sad to see school systems dismantling vocational programs and bragging that they send large numbers of students to college but avoiding any mention of the large number of students who must take remedial courses in college and who drop out with no college credits.[2]

In sum, in order for tech-prep, co-op, or other linkage programs to be effective, these programs must convey relevant and trusted signals of value. Evaluations will be trusted if they are offered in a context in which each party sees that the other is seriously committed to maintaining the relationship. This is not a terribly restrictive condition. High schools, employers, and colleges all have vested interests that can be satisfied by a strong relationship.

But they also have some competing concerns, and those must be recognized and addressed. Thus, high school staff must not be pressured to give college-for-all advice. They must be given time and recognition for placing students in good jobs. They must also be encouraged to give candid information to students.

Although high schools may be reluctant to provide information that lowers students' postsecondary plans, failure to inform students about the remedial courses they will have to take in college is a cruel deception. Providing clear criteria and assessment tests may help students see both the need to try harder to prepare for college demands and the payoffs for these efforts, whether in college or in a job.

Similarly, while most employers are reluctant to trust school information, a few employers already recognize that school contacts are a source of valuable information that creates incentives for students and provides good information for their own hiring decisions. Other employers would be surprised and impressed to learn that some employers use school contacts. Even when they get many applicants, these employers have complained about the difficulty of hiring youths with the right motivation and social skills, and they would value relevant and trusted information about applicants.

Why should teachers, colleges, and employers invest time and effort to develop trusted relationships for conveying trusted signals of students' value? The current low-quality equilibrium is easy and requires low investment, so it seems to be a comfortable solution. However, no one is really happy with that solution. There is an alternative, some parties are already using it and benefiting from it, and there are steps that can be taken to remedy these concerns. Policymakers can tell all parties how to shift from low- to high-quality equilibrium and inform them of the benefits of doing so.

Conclusions

By ignoring goals beside college, ignoring soft skills, and ignoring long-term incentives, policy on the school-to-work transition for American youths misleads them about societal needs and payoffs. Indeed, employer hiring practices and college open-admissions practices prevent students from seeing the incentives for high school effort. There actually are long-term payoffs to good grades and soft skills in high school, but no one sees them. We must develop a mechanism to make these incentives visible and to convey signals that tell students the value of their high school actions in achieving desirable career goals. If employers and colleges want students to exert more effort in high school, they must help high schools develop relevant and trustworthy evaluations, and they must develop relationships that reinforce trust. Tech-prep and co-op can do it, but they often do not. These programs can be improved. Other nations have developed ways to encourage trusted relationships, and some U.S. schools have begun such reforms. We must find ways to introduce these reforms to more American high schools to make them more effective.

Many practical steps can be taken. State and local policymakers can help counselors and teachers learn about the factors that predict college dropout and the jobs with good career prospects that do not require college. There actually are long-term payoffs to good grades and soft skills in high school, and policymakers can help school staff to see them.

High schools must develop evaluations that tell students what actions they can take in high school to improve their future careers. If employers and colleges want students to exert more effort in high school, they must help high schools develop relevant and trustworthy evaluations, and they must develop relationships that will reinforce trust.

College tests for remedial courses should be made uniform across all colleges and made available to high school students so that they can assess how prepared they are for college courses.

Tech-prep and co-op reforms can help, but these programs can also be improved to provide relevant and trusted signals of students' value.

The importance of soft skills reinforces the value of vocational courses, which are good ways to teach soft skills. Deemphasizing work-bound students' needs and dismantling vocational education are disservices to students, and a college-for-all policy is a poor justification.

Vocational teachers who have trusted contacts with employers are a valuable resource, not only to vocational students but also to other students. Indeed, these teachers can help college-bound students with low grades form fallback plans. High schools should recruit and retain teachers with experience and contacts in the work world (see Guarino et al. 2000).

Finally, high schools should reward teachers for placing students in good jobs. If employers know that teachers are rewarded for making good placements, they will trust teachers to try to maintain their relationship and to give candid student evaluations.

This approach is not easy, but that should not be surprising. If it were easy, it would already have been done. What is encouraging, however, is that the underlying conditions are already present for accomplishing such reforms. Colleges and the labor market actually do reward grades and soft skills, and some individual teachers and employers have made informal contacts through which they convey trusted information. The key is to get institutional actors to recognize the benefits of these linkages and to produce linkage mechanisms that will create and convey relevant and trusted signals of student value. Current tech-prep, co-op, and other linkage activities are the right kinds of approaches, but these contacts must be made more trustworthy if they are to be effective.

= Notes =

Chapter 1

1. Among males age thirty-five to thirty-nine, the percentage of workers with short job tenure (less than five years) is 40 percent in the United States, but only 28 percent in Germany, 24 percent in the Netherlands, 22 percent in France, and 17 percent in Japan (OECD 1993, tables 4.3, 4.4).

2. Although only 10 percent of Japanese employers have special relations with schools, they are the larger firms, they hire about half (49.6 percent) of all the work-bound graduates from each school, and they offer the most desirable jobs (those with more training, security, and advancement). As a result, these employers have a large impact on each school's graduates.

3. Some Japanese teachers note that this constraint does help them resist pressures from influential parents. If they succumb to parent pressure and nominate students with substandard grades, employers will ignore their nomination and possibly stop offering jobs to their school in future years. Indeed, analyses find that social class background has very little influence on the jobs that youths get after high school (see Kariya and Rosenbaum 1988; Rosenbaum and Kariya 1989).

Chapter 2

1. This chapter extends the work of James Rosenbaum, Takehiko Kariya, Rick Settersten, and Tony Maier (1990) and James Rosenbaum and Karen A. Nelson (1994).

2. This difference in the experiences of high school graduates in the United States and Japan is not due to any greater selectivity in Japan. Indeed, a higher proportion of youth graduate from high school in Japan (about 95 percent) than in the United States (about 73 percent), and the enrollment rate in colleges and postsecondary schools is virtually the same in Japan and the United States. Indeed, if, as human capital theory assumes, low-achieving youth have more work-entry problems, American high school graduation is more selective because of its higher dropout rate, and it excludes a greater proportion of problem youth than in Japan. Indeed, if

dropouts had been considered in the these analyses, the United States would have even greater work-entry problems, while Japan's rate would increase only slightly.

3. Of course, other barriers to employment may also operate, including lack of transportation; discrimination on the basis of age, sex, or race; and insufficient training or experience (Hills and Reubens 1983).

4. Not surprisingly, these practices have counterparts in students' behaviors. In the general track, the program that does not even pretend to offer specific preparation for jobs, students are particularly disengaged and classes tend to have more than their share of effort and discipline problems. John Combs and William Cooley (1968) found that nearly three-quarters of high school dropouts were in the general track at the time they left school. Delos Kelly (1974) found that, even after controlling for sex and social class, non-college-track students are more likely to report drinking alcohol, smoking cigarettes, skipping school, stealing, vandalizing, and gang fighting (see also Rosenbaum 1980a; Stinchcombe 1965; Polk and Schafer 1972; Oakes 1985). Of course, it is hard to separate the effects of weak incentives from selection effects that put people into this track.

5. The same constraint would apply if teachers were tempted to favor students from influential families. In fact, such bias rarely if ever occurs. Social background has very little influence on entry-level jobs. Employer contracts provide strong institutional controls to keep selections meritocratic (Rosenbaum and Kariya 1989).

6. Japanese high schools do not have distinct guidance counselors. College and job placements are handled by teachers.

Chapter 3

1. College degrees are considered to be an associate's or higher degree (*Digest of Education Statistics* 1998, table 9).

2. While a prior version of this paper used students' reports of their educational attainment, this chapter uses a variable based on transcript information. This variable is likely to be more accurate than students' reports, and it indicates slightly lower attainments.

3. Somewhat similar beliefs have been shown to influence students' achievements (Mickelson 1990), but since achievement is influenced by many factors besides motivation, this study has chosen to focus on the determinants of effort (for an excellent overview, see Steinberg 1996).

4. The data in these analyses are for the class of 1982, so that we can analyze long-term follow-up outcomes. Analyses of the class of 1992 (NELS) indicate a big increase over a decade, consistent with contentions of Schneider and Stevenson (1999). Unfortunately, the class of 1992 data do not allow long-term follow-up of outcomes.

5. Signithia Fordham and John Ogbu's prediction was also not supported in analyses by Philip J. Cook and Jens Ludwig (1997) and James Ainsworth-Darnell and Douglas Downey (1998).

6. Since one would not be concerned about the disappointment of very high plans, analyses were also run using recoded versions of plans and attainments, in which values higher than a B.A. degree were recoded to be the same as BA = 16. This recode does not alter results very much, so those results are not reported.

7. What determines grades? Samuel Bowles and Herbert Gintis (1976) have suggested that grades have noncognitive components, an idea that is not supported in some other studies (Bills 1983; Rosenbaum and Kariya 1989, 1991). Chapter 8 pursues this question in greater detail. Logit analyses were also run to see the determinants of which high school graduates got an A.A. degree or higher versus high school graduates who got less than an A.A. Using the same independent variables, the results lead to virtually the same conclusions as the above linear regression: grades, test scores, and homework all have significant influences, with grades having the largest influence. Grades have an even larger influence than test scores in explaining disappointed plans. Similar findings occur in explaining who attained a B.A. degree or higher, and the grade influence is even greater. These tables are not reported because the results are virtually the same as those reported here.

8. Youth who did not complete high school are removed from this analysis, so the constant represents all youth with a high school diploma but no college degree. Note that the MALoGPA coefficient is not significant, and only twenty-two (4 percent) M.A. students had low high school grades. Extending our original published paper (Rosenbaum 1998a), David Boesel and Eric Fredland (1999) have also traced the growth in students' educational plans since 1972, and they have shown that over 600,000 students leave four-year colleges without graduating, and four-year noncompleters tend to earn the same or less than comparable individuals from two-year colleges.

9. Thomas Kane and Cecilia Rouse (1995) showed only the average benefits of courses, so it is hard to know whether all courses offer economic value, whether courses have economic value for all students (including students with prior academic deficiencies), and whether their value is contingent on their current jobs. If the benefits accrue only to students who take vocational courses in particular fields, as W. Norton Grubb (1995a, 1996) suggests, then high school vocational courses might provide similar benefits. It is also possible that isolated college credits have economic value because individuals seek specific job-relevant courses, perhaps because of a job they already hold or one they know is available. Employers in some fields (tool and die, machining, and so on) require employees to take a few specific college courses, but not to attain a certificate or degree (Rosenbaum and Binder 1997).

10. W. Norton Grubb's inference is supported by our finding that "no transcript" students have even lower high school grades than students with zero college credits.

11. One-year certificates are not college degrees, and their economic value varies greatly. Including one-year certificates slightly improves the ratios—48.5 percent of 1982 seniors planning to get a certificate or degree succeeded in doing so over the next ten years.

Chapter 4

1. This chapter is based on a paper by James Rosenbaum, Shazia Miller, and Melinda Krei (1996).

Chapter 5

1. This chapter is based on a paper by James Rosenbaum and Amy Binder (1997).

2. Berg (1971, 94) notes that measures of job performance are more dubious for white-collar jobs, and that findings for professional and managerial work suffer even more from this problem.

3. Three employers did not directly answer our question: "Do you often find that high school graduates do not have the reading and math skills to work here?" One answered the question by discussing his applicants' poor vocational skills; one responded with information about his English-as-a-second-language program; and the third said that he had not noticed. All three of these ambiguous responses were coded as employer claims that basic academic skills are not lacking in their workers and thus are included in the subsample of sixteen noncomplainers.

Chapter 6

1. This chapter is an expanded version of a paper by Shazia Miller and James Rosenbaum (1997).

Chapter 7

1. This chapter is based on an unpublished maunscript by James Rosenbaum and Shazia Miller (1997).

2. It should be noted that while some employers said that they initiated this type of outreach in order to start relationships with the schools that would help them get workers, others described their outreach as straight altruism—a gift offered to help students.

Chapter 8

1. This chapter is based on an unpublished manuscript by James Rosenbaum, Stephanie DeLuca, and Shazia Miller (2000).

2. Since more cases were lost for 1991 earnings, analyses of this outcome have only 6,243 individuals. Because missing data reduced the size of the sample, we reran the primary regressions substituting the mean for missing values, but the pattern of results did not change substantially.

3. We also ran analyses including dummies for missing values of the non-cognitive variables, but only one came close to significance in any analysis (discipline). For simplicity, these variables are omitted here.

4. The NELS two-year follow-up does not allow sufficient time to judge ultimate educational attainment.

5. Our finding that 35.8 percent do more than five hours of homework per week is similar to other national findings that 33 percent do this much homework (NAEP 1985). In contrast, 57 percent of Japanese high school seniors did this much homework in 1979 (Rosenbaum and Kariya 1991).

Chapter 9

1. This chapter is an expansion of a unpublished paper by James Rosenbaum, Kevin Roy, and Takehiko Kariya (1995) and a paper by James Rosenbaum, Stephanie DeLuca, Shazia Miller, and Kevin Roy (1999).

2. The analyses use the restricted release 1992 file and use students who answered the 1982 and 1992 surveys. Analyses are factor-weighted accordingly. This chapter is a revised version of two earlier papers (Rosenbaum and Roy 1995, 1996).

3. About 10 percent offered no answer to this question. Because of the way students might have interpreted the question, we suspect that this group got their jobs primarily through direct methods, and these students are in the constant for the earnings analyses.

4. We might be tempted to use multinomial logistic analysis for these analyses, since these job search strategies seem to be a coherent choice set. College graduates from well-connected families can certainly choose among their job search strategies, but high school graduates' job strategy choices are often determined by others, not themselves. In multinomial logistic analysis, Hoffman and Duncan (1988, 419) remind us,

> the assumption of independence is critical. . . . If, for example, there is a change in the characteristics of any other alternative in the choice set, this property requires that the [other] two probabilities must adjust precisely in order to preserve their initial ratio. This is equivalent to assuming that the percentage change in each probability is equal, a response pattern that may be an unwarranted and inappropriate restriction. For example, the possibility that one choice probability might be more greatly affected by such a change is thereby excluded.

If one alternative is removed, it is assumed that the choices of the others increase proportionally. For example, a person's travel destinations (Boston, Miami, Los Angeles) might have a certain set of probabilities, and the others would increase proportionately if one destination were removed.

However, that assumption does not apply when outcomes are structurally constrained. School help is probably not offered as a choice to all students (chapter 10, this volume), and low-income youth (who are over-represented among work-bound students) may get no job contacts from relatives (Wilson 1996). Therefore, excluding one of the other alternatives would not proportionately increase the use of school or relatives' help. Multinomial logistic analysis requires assumptions that seem inappropriate to these phenomena.

Although multinomial analysis does not seem appropriate, separate logistic analyses are not without problems as well, for the results of one job contact are not totally independent of those of the others. For comparison, we ran multinomial logistic analyses, and these analyses found similar, but not identical, results. Females totally matched our results; females are significantly more likely to get school and employment service help and less likely to get relatives' help in the short and long multinomial models. Blacks confirmed the results for school and relatives' help and had no effects for the other two (as in the simple logistic analyses). Socioeconomic status was significant in affecting employment service in both the short and long models (but had no other significant influences), and Hispanic and track variables were never significant. The main departure was test scores, which affected help from relatives, friends, and employment services (each time negatively), but not school placement. With the exception of the last finding, the multinomial results generally confirm the results of the single logistic analyses. The finding that relatives, friends, and employment services are "anti-meritocratic" is intriguing, but we are dubious about the assumptions required by multinomial analysis.

5.   It is commonly assumed that even if employers do not know test scores, they can infer ability in other ways during a job interview. This is contradicted by interviews with employers. Employers report that they are often misled by applicants' performances during interviews (chapter 6). Moreover, teachers also report that students who are shy and unimpressive in interviews may have the most promise as employees in many jobs (chapter 10).

Chapter 10

1.   This chapter extends some sections of a paper by James Rosenbaum and Stephanie Jones (2000).

2.   This question was near the end of the survey and was not asked of all teachers. Fifty-eight percent of the teachers in the sample (forty of sixty-nine) and 66 percent of teachers in vocational schools (twenty-five of thirty-eight) said they could place three-quarters or more of their stu-

dents in good jobs that would use their skills. The labor market was even weaker in the city, yet many urban teachers were as confident as suburban teachers about their ability to place students.

Chapter 11

1. Grouping SES and SAT scores into thirds, the authors found that among high-SAT students, select schools raised admission rates slightly more for low-SES than for high-SES students, compared to other leading boarding schools—27.8 percent versus 24.3 percent. Among students with low test scores, the SES difference was much greater—a 66.7 percent gain for low-SES students versus a 22.6 percent gain for high-SES students. That is, admission rates for low-SES students were 33 percent at nonselect schools and 55 percent at select schools; admission rates for high-SES students were 53 percent at nonselect schools and 65 percent at select schools (Persell and Cookson 1985, table 4).

2. Persell and Cookson (1985) did not study whether elite colleges stress family wealth in their own decisions, nor were they able to see whether advisers avoid discussing family wealth in their confidential discussions. Yet colleges probably do not need to rely on select schools to identify wealthy students, even if they rely on select schools to identify ability and other personal qualities.

3. Consistent with the need for dependable skills and quality in justifying linkages, Maryalice Burke (1984) reports that an M.B.A. program screened students to fit employers' expectations for specialty, quality, and likelihood of accepting a job offer. Many colleges and graduate schools devote more resources to admissions than to job placement, but both the technical school and the M.B.A. program spend roughly equal resources and efforts on both.

Chapter 12

1. Each unit of grades indicates a half-grade (for example, from mostly Cs to mostly Bs and Cs), and a half-grade increase raises earnings by 6.4 percent (chapters 8 and 9). See also Miller (1998), who finds an 11 percent gain for men and a 23 percent gain for women who lack college degrees (after fewer controls).

2. Many students drop out of college with no job preparation because many vocational programs require that remedial courses be completed before students are admitted to college vocational programs.

References

Ainsworth-Darnell, James, and Douglas Downey. 1998. "Assessing Racial/ Ethnic Differences in School Performance." *American Sociological Review* 63 (4, August): 536–53.

Alexander, Karl L., Martha Cook, and Edward L. McDill. 1978. "Curriculum Tracking and Educational Stratification." *American Sociological Review* 43(1): 7–66.

Althauser, Robert, and Arne Kalleberg. 1981. "Firms, Occupations and the Structure of Labor Markets." In *Sociological Perspectives on Labor Markets,* edited by Ivar Berg. New York: Academic Press.

Altonji, Joseph G., and Charles Pierret. 1995. "Employer Learning and Statistical Discrimination." Working paper. Chicago: Northwestern University, Institute for Policy Research.

Alwin, Duane F., and Robert M. Hauser. 1975. "The Decomposition of Effects in Path Analysis." *American Sociological Review* 40: 37–47.

Amano, Ikuo. 1982. "Koto Gakko no Shinro Bunka to Sono Kiteiyouin" (Selection Functions of High Schools and Their Determinants). Paper submitted to Toyota Foundation.

———. 1984. "Koto Gakko no Shokugyo Shido to Seito no Shinro Keisei (1)" (Vocational Guidance and Students' Career in High School [1]). *Bulletin of Department of Education of Tokyo University* 23.

Andrisani, Paul J. 1973. "An Empirical Analysis of the Dual Labor Market Theory." Ph.D. diss., Ohio State University.

———. 1976. "Discrimination, Segmentation, and Upward Mobility: A Longitudinal Approach to the Dual Labor Market Theory." Paper presented at the joint meeting of the American Economic Association and the Econometric Society, Atlantic City, N.J. (1976).

Armor, David J. 1971. *The American School Counselor.* New York: Russell Sage Foundation.

Arnow, Philip 1968. *The Transition from School to Work.* Princeton, N.J.: Woodrow Wilson School.

Arrow, Kenneth J. 1973. "Information and Economic Behavior." Chapter 11 in *Collected Papers of Kenneth J. Arrow,* vol. 4. 1984. Cambridge, Mass.: Belknap Press.

Arum, Richard, and Yossi Shavit. 1995. "Secondary Vocational Education and the Transition from School to Work." *Sociology of Education* 68: 187–204.

Arvey, Richard D., and James E. Campion. 1982. "The Employment Interview: A Summary and Review of Recent Research." *Personal Psychology* 35: 281–322.

Arvey, Richard D., and Robert H. Faley. 1988. *Fairness in Selecting Employees.* Reading, Mass.: Addison-Wesley.

Attewell, Paul. 1987. "The Deskilling Controversy." *Work and Occupations* 14: 323–46.

———. 1992. "Skill and Occupational Changes in U.S. Manufacturing." In *Technology and the Future of Work,* edited by Paul S. Adler. New York: Oxford University Press.

Bailey, Thomas. 1994. "Barriers to Employer Participation in School-to-Work Programs." Paper presented at a seminar, "Employer Participation in School-to-Work Transition Programs," Brookings Institution, Washington, D.C. (May 4).

Bailey, Thomas, and Donna Merritt. 1993. "The School-to-Work Transition Project." New York: Manpower Demonstration Research Corporation.

Baltzell, E. Digby. 1958. *An American Business Aristocracy.* New York: Macmillan.

Barnow, Burt S. 1987. "The Impact of CETA Programs on Earnings: A Review of Literature." *Journal of Human Resources* 22(Spring): 157–93.

Baron, James N. 1984. "Organizational Perspectives on Stratification." *Annual Review of Sociology,* 10: 37–69.

Baron, James N., and William Bielby. 1980. "Bringing the Firms Back In." *American Sociological Review* 45: 737–65.

Barrett, Gerald V., and Robert L. Depinet. 1991. "A Reconsideration of Testing for Competence Rather Than for Intelligence." *American Psychologist* 46: 1012–24.

Basi, Laurie, and Orley Ashenfelter. 1986. "The Effect of Direct Job Creation and Training Programs on Low-skilled Workers." In *Fighting Poverty: What Works and What Doesn't,* edited by Sheldon H. Danziger and Daniel H. Weinberg. Cambridge, Mass.: Harvard University Press.

Baxter, Milton B., and Jerry L. Young. 1982. "What Do Employers Expect from High School Graduates?" *NASSP Bulletin* 66, no. 458: 93–98.

Becker, Gary. 1964. *Human Capital.* New York: National Bureau of Economic Research.

Bellak, Alvin O. 1984. "Specific Job Evaluation Systems: The Hay Guide Chart-Profile Method." In *The Handbook of Wage and Salary Administration,* edited by Milton Rock. New York: McGraw-Hill.

Ben-Porath, Yoram. 1980. "The F-Connection: Families, Friends, and Firms in the Organization of Exchange." *Population and Development Review* 6(1): 1–30.

Berg, Ivar. 1971. *Education and Jobs: The Great Training Robbery.* Boston: Beacon Press.

Berryman, Susan E. 1992. "Apprenticeship as a Paradigm for Learning." In *Youth Apprenticeship in America: Guidelines for Building an Effective System,* edited by James E. Rosenbaum. Washington, D.C.: William T. Grant Foundation Commission on Work, Family, and Citizenship.

Berryman, Susan E., and Thomas R. Bailey. 1992. *The Double Helix: Education and the Economy.* New York: Teachers College Press.

Betsey, Charles L., Robinson G. Hollister, and Mary R. Papageorgiou, eds. 1985. *Youth Employment and Training Programs: The YEDPA Years.* Washington, D.C.: National Academy Press.

Bills, David. 1983. "Social Reproduction and the Bowles-Gintis Thesis of a Correspondence Between School and Work Settings." In *Research in Sociology of Education and Socialization*, vol. 4, edited by Alan C. Kerckhoff. Greenwich, Conn.: JAI Press.

———. 1988. "Educational Credentials and Hiring Decisions: What Employers Look for in Entry-level Employees." *Research in Social Stratification and Mobility*, 7: 71–97.

———. 1992. "A Survey of Employer Surveys: What We Know About Labor Markets from Talking with Bosses." *Research in Social Stratification and Mobility*, 11: 3–31.

Birman, Beatrice F., and Gary Natriello. 1978. "Perspectives in Absenteeism in High School." *Journal of Research and Development in Education*, 11: 29–38.

Bishop, John. 1987a. "Information Externalities and the Social Payoff to Academic Achievement." Working Paper 8706. Ithaca, N.Y.: Center for Advanced Human Resource Studies, Cornell University.

———. 1987b. "The Recognition and Reward of Employee Performance." *Journal of Labor Economics* 4(5): 71–86.

———. 1988a. "Why High School Students Learn So Little and What Can Be Done About It." Working Paper 88–01. Ithaca, N.Y.: New York State School of Industrial and Labor Relations, Cornell University.

———. 1988b. "Vocational Education for At-risk Youth: How Can It Be Made More Effective?" Working Paper 88–11. Ithaca, N.Y.: New York State School of Industrial and Labor Relations, Cornell University.

———. 1989. "Why the Apathy in American High Schools?" *Educational Researcher* 18(1): 6–13.

———. 1992. "Workforce Preparedness." Working Paper 92–03. Ithaca, N.Y.: School of Industrial and Labor Relations, Cornell University.

———. 1993. "Improving Job Matches in the U.S. Labor Market." In *Brookings Papers in Economic Activity: Microeconomics*, edited by Martin N. Bailey. Washington, D.C.: Brookings Institution.

Bishop, John, Arthur Blakemore, and Stuart Low. 1985. *High School Graduates in the Labor Market: A Comparison of the Class of 1972 and 1980.* Columbus: National Center for Research in Vocational Education, Ohio State University.

Blau, Peter, and Otis D. Duncan. 1967. *The American Occupational Structure.* New York: Wiley.

Blaug, Mark. 1976. "The Empirical Status of Human Capital Theory: A Slightly Jaundiced Survey." *Journal of Economic Literature* 14(3): 827–55.

———. 1985. "Where Are We Now in the Economics of Education?" *Economics of Education Review* 4(1): 17–28.

Bloom, Howard S., Larry Laurence Orr, George Cave, Sam H. Bell, and Fred Doolittle. 1992. *The National JTPA Study: Title II-A Impacts on Earnings and Employment at Eighteen Months.* Bethesda, Md.: Abt Associates.

Boesel, David. 1994. *BLS Survey of Employer-Provided Formal Training*. Washington: U.S. Department of Labor, Bureau of Labor Statistics (September 23).

Boesel, David, and Eric Fredland. 1999. *College for All: Is There Too Much Emphasis on Getting a 4-Year College Degree?* Washington.: U.S. Department of Education.

Boesel, David, Lisa Hudson, Sharon Deich, and Charles Masten. 1994. *Participation in and Quality of Vocational Education*, vol. 2, *National Assessment of Vocational Education*. Washington: U.S. Department of Education.

Borman, Katherine M. 1991. *The First "Real" Job: A Study of Young Workers*. Albany, N.Y.: State University of New York Press.

Borman, Katherine M., and Michael C. Hopkins. 1987. "Leaving School for Work." In *Research in the Sociology of Education and Socialization*, edited by Alan C. Kerckhoff. Greenwich, Conn.: JAI Press.

Borus, Michael E. 1984. *Youth and the Labor Market*. Kalamazoo, Mich.: W. E. Upjohn Institute.

Bossert, Steven T. 1979. *Tasks and Social Relationships in Classrooms*. New York: Cambridge University Press.

Bowles, Samuel, and Herbert Gintis. 1972. "IQ in the U.S. Class Structure." *Social Policy*, vol. 3. Reprinted in *The New Assault on Equality*, edited by Alan Gartner. New York: Harper and Row.

———. 1976. *Schooling in Capitalist America: Educational Reform and the Contradictions of Economic Life*. New York: Basic Books.

Bradach, Jeffrey L., and Robert G. Eccles. 1991. "Price, Authority and Trust." *Annual Review of Sociology* 15: 97–118.

Bridges, William, and Wayne Villemez. 1986. "Informal Hiring and Income in the Labor Market." *American Sociological Review* 51(August): 574–82.

Brint, Stephen, and Jerome Karabel. 1989. *The Diverted Dream: Community College and the Promise of Educational Opportunity in America*. New York: Oxford University Press.

Brinton, Mary. 1993. *Women and the Economic Miracle*. Berkeley: University of California Press.

Buchmann, Marlis. 1989 *The Script of Life in Modern Society: Entry into Adulthood in a Changing World*. Chicago: University of Chicago Press.

Bullock, Peter. 1972. *Aspiration Versus Opportunity: "Career" in the Inner City*. Ann Arbor: Institute of Labor and Industrial Relations, University of Michigan.

Burghardt, John, Ann Rangarajan, Anne Gordon, and Ellen Kisker. 1992. *Evaluation of the Minority Female Single Parent Demonstration*. New York: Rockefeller Foundation.

Burke, Maryalice A. 1984. "Becoming an M.B.A." Ph.D. diss., Northwestern University.

Cain, Glen G. 1976. "The Challenge of Segmented Labor Market Theories to Orthodox Theory: A Survey." *Journal of Economic Literature* 14(4): 1215–57.

Campbell, Paul, Karen S. Basinger, Mary Dauner, and Marie Parks. 1986. *Outcomes of Vocational Education for Women, Minorities, the Handicapped, and the Poor*. Columbus: National Center for Research in Vocational Education, Ohio State University.

Cantor, Leonard. 1989. *Vocational Education and Training in the Developed World: A Comparative Study.* New York: Routledge.

Cappelli, Peter. 1991. "Are Skill Requirements Rising?" Working paper. Philadelphia: National Center on the Educational Quality of the Workforce (EQW), University of Pennsylvania.

———. 1992. "Is the 'Skills Gap' Really About Attitudes?" Philadelphia: National Center on the Educational Quality of the Workforce, University of Pennsylvania.

Cappelli, Peter, and Nikolai Rogowsky. 1993. "Skill Demands, Changing Work Organization, and Performance." Philadelphia: National Center on the Educational Quality of the Workforce, University of Pennsylvania.

Carline, Derek. 1985. *Labour Economics.* New York: Longman Group.

Cave, George, and Fred Doolittle. 1991. *Assessing Jobstart: Interim Impacts of a Program for School Dropouts.* New York: Manpower Demonstration Research Corporation.

CED (Committee for Economic Development). 1985. *Investing in Our Children: Business and the Public Schools.* New York: CED.

Chabot, Richard B., and Antoine Garibaldi. 1982. "In-school Alternatives to Suspension: A Description of Ten School District Programs." *Urban Review* 14: 317–36.

Cicourel, Aaron V., and John I. Kitsuse. 1963. *The Educational Decisionmakers.* Indianapolis: Bobbs-Merrill.

Clark, Burton. 1960. "The 'Cooling Out' Function in Higher Education." *American Journal of Sociology* 65: 569–76.

———. 1985. "The High School and the Universities: What Went Wrong in America." *Phi Delta Kappan* 66: 391–97, 472–75.

Coleman, James S. 1974. *Youths: Transition to Adulthood.* Chicago: University of Chicago Press.

———. 1988. "Social Capital in the Creation of Human Capital." *American Journal of Sociology* 94: S95–120.

———. 1994. "Social Capital, Human Capital, and Investment in Youth." In *Youth Unemployment and Society,* edited by Anne C. Petersen and Jeylan T. Mortimer. Cambridge: Cambridge University Press.

Collins, Randall. 1971. "Functional and Conflict Theories of Educational Stratification." *American Sociological Review* 36: 1002–19.

———. 1974. "Where Are Educational Requirements for Employment Highest?" *Sociology of Education* 47: 419–42.

———. 1975. *Conflict Sociology: Toward an Explanatory Science.* New York: Academic Press.

———. 1979. *The Credential Society.* New York: Academic Press.

Combs, John, and William W. Cooley. 1968. "Dropouts: In High School and After School." *American Educational Research Journal* 5: 343–63.

Cook, Philip J., and Jens Ludwig. 1997. "Weighing the Burden of 'Acting White': Are There Race Differences in Attitudes Toward Education?" *Journal of Policy Analysis and Management* 16(2): 256–78.

Crain, Robert. 1984. "The Quality of American High School Graduates: What

Personnel Officers Say and Do." Baltimore: Center for the Study of Schools, Johns Hopkins University.

————. 1997. *The Effects of Magnet Education on High Schools and Their Graduates.* Berkeley: National Center for Research in Vocational Education, University of California.

Crohn, Robert L. 1983. *Technological Literacy in the Workplace.* Portland, Oreg.: Northwest Regional Educational Laboratory.

Crosswhite, Fred J. 1984. "Second Study of Mathematics: Summary Report, United States." Unpublished paper. Urbana, Ill.: U.S. National Coordinating Center.

Cummings, William K. 1979. *Changes in the Japanese University: A Comparative Perspective.* New York: Praeger.

————. 1980. *Education and Equality in Japan.* Princeton, N.J.: Princeton University Press.

————. 1986. *Educational Policies in Crisis.* New York: Praeger.

Cusick, Philip A. 1983. *Inside High School: The Student's World.* New York: Longman Group.

Dalton, Melville. 1951. "Informal Factors in Career Achievement."*American Journal of Sociology* 56: 407–45.

————. 1959. *Men Who Manage.* New York: Wiley.

D'Amico, Ronald, and Timothy Brown. 1982. "Patterns of Labor Mobility in a Dual Economy: The Case of Semi-skilled and Unskilled Workers." *Social Science Research* 11: 153–75.

D'Amico, Ronald, and Nan Maxwell. 1990. *Black-White Employment Differences During the School-to-Work Transition: An Explanation for Between- and Within-Race Differences.* Palo Alto, Calif.: SRI International.

Daymont, Thomas N., and Russell W. Rumberger. 1982. "Job Training in the Schools." In *Job Training for Youth: The Contributions of the United States Employment Development System,* edited by Richard Taylor, Harold Rosen, and Fred Pratzner. Columbus: National Center for Research in Vocational Education, Ohio State University.

Deil, Regina, and James E. Rosenbaum. 2000. "Unintended Consequences of Stigma-free Remediation." Paper presented to the meeting of the American Sociological Association, Washington (August).

DeLany, Brian. 1991. "Allocation, Choice, and Stratification Within High Schools: How the Sorting Machine Copes." *American Journal of Education* 99(2, February): 181–207

DeLeonibus, Nancy. 1978. "Absenteeism: The Perpetual Problem." *The Practitioner* 5: 13.

DeLuca, Stefanie Ann. 2001. "Comparisons of Students' Self-Reports and Teachers' Reports." Unpublished paper. Evanston, Ill.: Institute for Policy Research, Northwestern University.

DeLuca, Stefanie Ann, and James E. Rosenbaum. Forthcoming. "Individual Agency and the Life Course: Do Low-SES Students Get Less Long-Term Payoff for Their School Efforts?" *Sociological Focus.*

Diamond, Daniel E. 1970. "Industry Hiring Requirements and the Employment of Disadvantaged Groups." Working paper. New York: New York University School of Commerce.

Dickens, William T., and Kevin Lang. 1985. "A Test of Dual Labor Market Theory." *American Economic Review* 75: 792–805.

DiMaggio, Paul J., and Walter W. Powell. 1991. *The New Institutionalism in Organizational Analysis.* Chicago: University of Chicago Press.

DiPrete, Thomas A. 1981. *Discipline and Order in American High Schools.* Chicago: National Opinion Research Center.

Doeringer, Peter, and Michael J. Piore. 1971. *Internal Labor Markets and Manpower Analysis.* Lexington, Mass.: Lexington Books.

Donahoe, Debra, and Marta Tienda. 2000. "The Transition from School to Work: Is There a Crisis? What Can Be Done?" In *Securing the Future,* edited by Sheldon Danziger and Jane Waldfogel. New York: Russell Sage Foundation.

Dore, Ronald. 1976. *The Diploma Disease.* Berkeley: University of California Press.

———. 1983. "Goodwill and the Spirit of Market Capitalism." *British Journal of Sociology* 34: 459–82.

Dore, Ronald, and Mari Sako. 1988. *Vocational Education and Training in Japan.* Tokyo: Center for Japanese and Comparative Industrial Research, Imperial College.

Dougherty, Kevin J. 1994. *The Contradictory College.* Albany: State University of New York Press.

Dunham, Daniel B. 1980. "The American Experience in the Transition from Vocational Schools to Work." ERIC ED186725. Paper presented to the International Symposium on Problems of Transition from Technical and Vocational Schools to Work, Berlin (1980).

Dunlop, John T. 1957. "The Task of Contemporary Wage Theory." In *New Concepts in Wage Discrimination,* edited by George W. Taylor and Fred C. Pierson. New York: McGraw-Hill.

Durkheim, Emile. 1956 [1912]. *Education and Sociology.* New York: The Free Press.

Eccles, Robert. 1981. "The Quasi-firm in the Construction Industry." *Journal of Economic Behavior and Organization* 2: 335–57.

Elder, Glen H., Jr. 1980. "Adolescence in Historical Perspective." In *Handbook of Adolescent Psychology.* New York: Wiley.

England, Paula, and George Farkas, eds. 1986. "Economic and Sociological Views of Industries, Firms, and Jobs" In *Industries, Firms, and Jobs,* edited by George Farkas and Paula England. New York: Plenum.

Ericksen, Eugene, and William Yancey. 1980. "The Locus of Strong Ties." Unpublished paper. Philadelphia: Temple University.

Erickson, Frederick. 1975. "Gatekeeping and the Melting Pot: Interaction in Counseling Encounters." *Harvard Educational Review* 45(1): 44–70.

Etzioni, Amitai. 1988. *The Moral Dimension: Towards a New Economics.* New York: Free Press.

Eurich, Nell P. 1985. *Corporate Classrooms: The Learning Business.* Princeton, N.J.: Carnegie Foundation for the Advancement of Teaching.

Faia, Michael A. 1981. "Selection by Certification: A Neglected Variable in Stratification Research." *American Journal of Sociology* 86(5): 1093–1111.

Faist, Thomas. 1992. "Social Citizenship and the Transformation from School to Work Among Immigrant Minorities." Ph.D. diss., New School for Social Research.

Fallows, James. 1989. *More Like Us.* Boston: Houghton Mifflin.

Farkas, George. 1996. *Human Capital or Cultural Capital?* New York: Aldine de Gruyter.

Farkas, George, Paula England, and Margaret Barton 1986. "Structural Effects on Wages." In *Industries, Firms, and Jobs,* edited by George Farkas and Paula England. New York: Plenum.

Farkas, George, Robert P. Grobe, Daniel Sheehan, and Yuan Shuan. 1990. "Cultural Resources and School Success: Gender, Ethnicity, and Poverty Groups Within an Urban School District." *American Sociological Review* 55: 127–42.

Farrar, Elinore, and Anthony Cipollone. 1988. *The Business Community and School Reform: The Boston Compact at Five Years.* Unpublished paper (March).

Fernandez, Roberto, and Nancy Weinberg. 1997. "Sifting and Sorting: Personal Contacts and Hiring in a Retail Bank" *American Sociological Review* 62(6): 883–902.

Ford, Michael E., and Michael S. Tisak. 1983. "A Further Search for Social Intelligence." *Journal of Educational Psychology* 75: 196–206.

Fordham, Signithia, and John Ogbu. 1986. "Black Students' School Success: Coping with the Burden of 'Acting White.'" *Urban Review* 18(3): 176–206.

Friedland, Roger, and Robert R. Alford. 1991. "Bringing Society Back In: Symbols, Practices, and Institutional Contradictions." In *The New Institutionalism in Organizational Analysis,* edited by Paul J. DiMaggio and Walter W. Powell. Chicago: University of Chicago Press.

Gamoran, Adam. 1994. *The Impact of Academic Coursework on Labor Market Outcomes for Youth Who Do Not Attend College: A Research Review.* Washington, D.C.: National Assessment of Vocational Education.

Garbin, Alan P. 1970. *Worker Adjustment Problems of Youth in Transition from High School to Work.* Columbus: Center for Vocational Education, Ohio State University.

General Accounting Office. 1991. *Transition from School to Work.* Washington: GAO.

Ginzberg, Eli. 1971. *Career Guidance: Who Needs It, Who Provides It, and Who Can Improve It.* New York: McGraw-Hill.

Goffman, Erving. 1952. "Cooling the Mark Out: Some Aspects of Adaptation to Failure." *Psychiatry* 15(November): 451–63.

Goodlad, John I. 1984. *A Place Called School.* New York: McGraw-Hill.

Gordon, David M., ed. 1971. *Problems in Political Economy: An Urban Perspective.* Lexington, Mass.: D. C. Heath.

———. 1972. *Theories of Poverty and Underemployment.* Lexington, Mass.: Lexington Books.

Granick, David 1973. "Differences in Educational Selectivity and Managerial Behavior in Large Companies: France and Britain." *Comparative Education Review* (October): 350–61.

Granovetter, Mark. 1973. "The Strength of Weak Ties." *American Journal of Sociology* 78(May): 1360–80.

———. 1981. "Toward a Sociological Theory of Income Differences." In *Sociological Perspectives on Labor Markets*, edited by Ivar Berg. New York: Academic Press.

———. 1985. "Economic Action and Social Structure: The Problem of Embeddedness." *American Journal of Sociology*, 91: 481–510.

———. 1995. *Getting a Job: A Study of Contacts and Careers*. 2nd ed. Chicago: University of Chicago Press. Originally published in 1974.

Grasso, John T. 1972. "The Contributions of Vocational Education, Training, and Work Experience to the Early Career Achievements of Young Men." Ph.D. diss., Ohio State University.

Grasso, John T., and John R. Shea. 1979. *Vocational Education and Training: Impact on Youth: A Technical Report for the Carnegie Council on Policy Studies in Higher Education*. New York: Carnegie Foundation for the Advancement of Teaching.

Grieco, Margaret. 1987. *Keeping It in the Family: Social Networks and Employment Chance*. London: Tavistock Publications.

Griffin, Larry J., Arne L. Kalleberg, and Karl L. Alexander. 1981. "Determinants of Early Labor Market Entry and Attainment: A Study of Labor Market Segmentation." *Sociology of Education* 54: 206–21.

Grubb, W. Norton. 1989. "Dropouts, Spells of Time, and Credits in Postsecondary Education." *Economics of Education Review* 8(1):49–67.

———. 1992. "Postsecondary Education and the Sub-baccalaureate Labor Market." *Economics of Education Review* 11(3): 225–48.

———. 1993. "The Varied Economic Returns of Postsecondary Education." *Journal of Human Resources* 28(2): 265–82.

———. 1995a. "Response to Comment." *Journal of Human Resources* 30(1): 222–28.

———. 1995b. *Education Through Occupations in American High Schools*, vol. 1. New York: Teachers College Press.

———. 1996. *Working in the Middle*. San Francisco: Jossey-Bass.

Grubb, W. Norton, and Judy Kalman. 1994. "Relearning to Earn." *American Journal of Education* 103(November): 54–93.

Guarino, Cassandra M., Dominic Brewer, and Anders Hove. 2000. *Who's Teaching, and Who Will Teach, Vocation Education?* Berkeley, Calif.: National Center for Research in Vocational Education.

Haaken, Janice, and Joyce Korschgen. 1988. "Adolescents and Conceptions of Social Relations in the Workplace." *Adolescence* 23(89): 1–14.

Hamilton, Stephen F. 1986. "Excellence and the Transition from School to Work." *Phi Delta Kappan* (November): 239–42.

———. 1987. "Apprenticeship as a Transition to Adulthood in West Germany." *American Journal of Education* (February): 314–45.

———. 1990. *Apprenticeship for Adulthood: Preparing Youth for the Future*. New York: Free Press.

Hamilton Steve, and Klaus Hurrelmann. 1994. "The School-to-Career Transition in Germany and the United States." *Teachers College Record* 96(2, Winter): 329–44.

Harhoff, Dieter, and Thomas Kane. 1994. "Financing Apprenticeship Training." Working Paper 4557. Cambridge, Mass.: National Bureau of Economic Research.

Hazler, Richard J., and Lowell D. Latto. 1987. "Employers' Opinions on the Attitudes and Skills of High School Graduates." *Journal of Employment Counseling* 24(3, September): 130–36.

Heckman, James J. 1994. "Is Job Training Oversold?" *Public Interest* (Spring): 91–115.

Heimer, Carol A. 1985. "Organizational and Individual Control of Career Development in Engineering Project Work." In *Organization Theory and Project Management*, edited by Arthur L. Stinchcombe and Carol A. Heimer. Bergen: Norwegian University Press.

———. 1992. "Doing Your Job and Helping Your Friends: Universalistic Norms About Obligations to Particular Others in Networks." In *Networks and Organizations*, edited by Nitin Nohria and Robert G. Eccles. Boston: Harvard Business School Press.

Heinz, Walter H. 1986. "The Transition from School to Work in Crisis: Coping with Threatening Unemployment." Paper presented at the annual meeting of the American Educational Research Association, San Francisco (April 1986).

———. 1999. *From Education to Work.* Cambridge: Cambridge University Press.

Herget, Hermann. 1986. "The Transition of Young People into Employment After Completion of Apprenticeship in the 'Dual System.'" Paper presented at the meeting of International Experts in Vocational Education and Training, Bonn (March 7).

Herr, Toby, Suzanne Wagner, and Robert Halpern. 1996. "Making the Shoe Fit." Project Match. Unpublished paper. Chicago: Erikson Institute.

Herrnstein, Richard J., and Charles Murray. 1994. *The Bell Curve.* New York: Free Press.

Hess, Laura E., Anne C. Petersen, and Jeylan T. Mortimer. 1994. "Youth, Unemployment, and Marginality." In *Youth Unemployment and Society*, edited by Anne C. Petersen and Jeylan T. Mortimer. Cambridge: Cambridge University Press.

Heyns, Barbara. 1974. "Social Selection and Stratification Within Schools." *American Journal of Sociology* 79(6): 1434–51.

Hida, D. 1982. "Nihon no Koukousei to Shuushoku" (Japanese High School Students and Entry into the Labor Force). In *Koukousei* (High School Students), edited by H. Iwaki and H. Mimizuka. *Gendai no Esupuri 195.* Tokyo: Shibundou.

Hill, Robert B., and Regina Nixon. 1984. *Youth Employment in American Industry.* New Brunswick, N.J.: Transaction Books.

Hills, Stephen M., and Beatrice G. Reubens. 1983. "Youth Employment in the United States." In *Youth at Work: An International Survey*, edited by Beatrice Reubens. Totowa, N.J.: Rowman & Allanheld Publishers.

Hodson, Robert, and Robert L. Kaufman. 1982. "Economic Dualism: A Critical Review." *American Sociological Review* 47: 727–39.

Hoffman, Saul, and Greg J. Duncan. 1988. "Multinomial Logit Discrete-Choice Models in Demography." *Demography* 25(3): 415–27.

Hogan, David P., and Nan M. Astone. 1986. "The Transition to Adulthood." *Annual Review of Sociology* 12: 109–30.

Hollenbeck, David. 1996. *An Evaluation of the Manufacturing Technology Partnership Program.* Kalamazoo, Mich.: Upjohn Institute.

Hollingsworth, Ellen Jane, Henry S. Lufler, and William H. Clune. 1984. *School Discipline: Order and Autonomy.* New York: Praeger.

Holsinger, David B., and Roberto M. Fernandez. 1987. "School to Work Transition Profiles." *Sociology and Social Research* 71(3): 211–20.

Holzer, Harry. 1988. "Search Methods Used by Unemployed Youth." *Journal of Labor Economics* 6: 1–12.

———. 1996. *What Employers Want: Job Prospects for Less-Educated Workers.* New York: Russell Sage Foundation.

Hotchkiss, Lawrence, and Lawrence E. Dorsten. 1987. "Curriculum Effects on Early Post-High School Outcomes." In *Research in the Sociology of Education and Socialization,* 7th ed., edited by Alan C. Kerckhoff. Greenwich, Conn.: JAI Press.

Howe, Harold. 1988. *The Forgotten Half.* New York: William T. Grant Foundation.

Hunter, John E., and Robert F. Hunter. 1984. "Validity and Utility of Alternative Predictors of Job Performance." *Psychological Bulletin* 96(1): 72–98.

Inoue, Ken. 1986. "Manpower and Development in Japan." In *Finding Work: Cross-National Perspectives on Employment and Training,* edited by Ray Rist. London: Falmer Press.

Iwanaga, M. 1984. "Jakunen Rodo Shijo no Soshikika to Gakko" (The Organization of the Youth Labor Market and School). *Journal of Educational Sociology* [Tokyo] 38.

Jacobs, Jerry. 1989. *Revolving Doors.* Stanford, Calif.: Stanford University Press.

Jencks, Christopher, Mary Corcoran, Susan Bartlett, James Crouse, David Eaglesfield, Kent McClelland, Peter Mueser, Michael Olneck, Joseph Schwartz, Sherry Ward, and Jill Williams. 1979. *Who Gets Ahead?* New York: Basic Books.

Jencks, Christopher, and James Crouse. 1982. "Aptitude Versus Achievement: Should We Replace the SAT?" *The Public Interest* 33: 21–35.

Jencks, Christopher, and Meredith Phillips, eds. 1998. *The Black-White Test Score Gap.* Washington, D.C.: Brookings.

Jencks, Christopher L., Marshall Smith, Henry Acland, Mary Jo Bane, David K. Cohen, Herbert Gintis, Barbara Heyns, and Stephan Michaelson. 1972. *Inequality.* New York: Basic Books.

Jepperson, Ronald L. 1991. "Institutional Isomorphism and Collective Rationality in Organizational Fields." In *The New Institutionalism in Organizational Analysis,* edited by Paul J. DiMaggio and Walter W. Powell. Chicago: University of Chicago Press.

Jobs for the Future. 1993. *Improving the School-to-Work Transition: A Chicago Perspective.* Boston: Jobs for the Future.

Johnson, James, and John G. Backman. 1973. *The Transition from High School to Work*. Ann Arbor: Institute for Social Research, University of Michigan.

Jones, Stephanie A., and James E. Rosenbaum. 1995. "Vocational Teachers' Linkages as Quasi-apprenticeships." Paper presented at the annual meeting of the American Educational Research Association, San Francisco (April).

Kaestle, Carl, and Mavis A. Vinovskis. 1978. "From Fireside to Factory: School Entry and School Learning in Nineteenth-century Massachusetts." In *Transitions: The Family and the Life Course in Historical Perspective*, edited by Tamara K. Hareven. New York: Academic Press.

Kahl, Joseph. 1953. *The American Class Structure*. New York: Holt.

Kamens, David. 1977. "Organizational and Institutional Socialization in Education." In *Research in Sociology of Education and Socialization*, edited by Alan C. Kerckhoff. Greenwich, Conn.: JAI Press.

Kandel, Denise, and Gerald Lesser. 1972. *Youth in Two Worlds: The United States and Denmark*. New York: Jossey-Bass.

Kane, Thomas, and Cecilia E. Rouse. 1995. "Labor-Market Returns to Two- and Four-Year Colleges." *American Economic Review* 85(3): 600–14.

Kang, Suk, and John Bishop. 1986. "The Effect of Curriculum on Labor Market Success." *Journal of Industrial Teacher Education* (Spring): 133–48.

Kanter, Rosabeth M. 1977. *Men and Women of the Corporation*. New York: Basic Books.

Karabel, Jerome. 1972. "Community Colleges and Social Stratification." *Harvard Educational Review* 42: 521–62.

———. 1986. "Community Colleges and Social Stratification in the 1980s." In *The Community College and Its Critics*, edited by Stephen Zwerling. San Francisco: Jossey-Bass.

Kariya, Takehiko. 1985. "Institutional Networks Between Schools and Employers and Delegated Occupational Selection to Schools: A Sociological Study of the Transition from High School to Work in Japan." Ph.D. diss., Northwestern University.

Kariya, Takehiko, and James E. Rosenbaum. 1987. "Self-selection in a Japanese Junior High School." *Sociology of Education* 60(3): 168–80.

———. 1988. "Selection Criteria in the High School to Work Transition: Results from the High School and Beyond Surveys in the U.S. and Japan." Paper presented at the annual meeting of the American Sociological Association, Atlanta (August 1988).

———. 1995. "Institutional Linkages Between Education and Work as Quasi-internal Labor Markets." *Research in Social Stratification and Mobility* 14: 99–134.

Kasinitz, Philip, and Jan Rosenberg. 1996. "Missing the Connection: Social Isolation and Employment on the Brooklyn Waterfront." *Social Problems* 43: 180–96.

Katz, Lawrence. 1986. "Efficiency Wage Theories." In *Macroeconomic Annual*. Cambridge, Mass.: National Bureau of Economic Research.

Kaufman, Jacob K., and Carl J. Schaefer. 1967. *The Role of the Secondary School in the Preparation of Youth for Employment*. University Park: Institute for Research on Human Resources, Pennsylvania State University.

Kelly, Delos H. 1974. "Track Position and Delinquent Involvement." *Sociology and Social Research* 58: 380–86.

Kerckhoff, Alan C., and Lorine Bell. 1998. "Hidden Capital: Vocational Credential and Attainment in the U.S." *Sociology of Education* 71(2): 152–74.

Kerckhoff, Alan C., and Richard T. Campbell. 1977. "Black-White Differences in the Educational Attainment Process." *Sociology of Education* 50: 15–27.

Kett, Joseph F. 1977. *Rites of Passage: Adolescence in America, 1790 to the Present.* New York: Basic Books.

Kirschenman, Joleen, Philip Moss, and Chris Tilly. 1995. "Employer Screening Methods and Racial Exclusion." Working Paper 77. New York: Russell Sage Foundation (October).

Kirschenman, Joleen, and Kathryn M. Neckerman. 1991. "'We'd Love to Hire Them, but . . .': The Meaning of Race for Employers." In *The Urban Underclass,* edited by Christopher Jencks and Paul Peterson. Washington, D.C.: Brookings Institution.

Kohn, Melvin. 1979. *Class and Conformity: A Study in Values.* 2nd ed. Chicago: University of Chicago Press.

———. 1997. *Class and Conformity.* Chicago: University of Chicago Press.

Kohn, Melvin, and Carmine Schooler. 1983. *Work and Personality.* Norwood, N.J.: Ablex.

Kozeki, Burt, and Nan J. Entwistle. 1984. "Identifying Dimensions of School Motivation in Britain and Hungary." *British Journal of Educational Psychology* 54: 306–19.

Krei, Melinda, and James E. Rosenbaum. 1998. "Analyses of the High School and Beyond Teacher Survey." Unpublished paper. Evanston, Ill.: Institute for Policy Research, Northwestern University.

Labaree, David F. 1988. *The Making of an American High School.* New Haven, Conn.: Yale University Press.

Lah, David. 1983. *Longer-term Impacts of Pre-employment Services on the Employment and Earnings of Disadvantaged Youth: A Project of the Private Sector Initiatives Demonstration of Public/Private Ventures.* ERIC Document Reproduction Service ED 245 000. Philadelphia: Public/Private Ventures.

Lambert, Nadine M., and Richard C. Nicoll. 1977. "Conceptual Model for Non-intellectual Behavior and Its Relationship to Early Reading Achievement." *Journal of Educational Psychology* 69: 481–90.

Lawrence, Barbara S. 1987. "An Organizational Theory of Age Effects." In *Research in the Sociology of Organizations,* edited by Samuel Bacharach and Nancy DiTomaso. Greenwich, Conn.: JAI Press.

Layard, Richard. 1982. "Youth Unemployment in Britain and the United States Compared." In *The Youth Labor Market Problem,* edited by Richard B. Freeman and David A. Wise. Chicago: University of Chicago Press.

Lazear, Edward. 1979. "Why Is There Mandatory Retirement?" *Journal of Political Economy* 87(6): 1261–84.

Lazerson, Marvin, and W. Norton Grubb. 1974. *American Education and Vocationalism.* New York: Teachers College Press.

Lemann, Nicholas. 1999. *The Big Test : The Secret History of the American Meritocracy.* New York: Farrar, Straus and Giroux.

Lerman, Robert, and Hillard Pouncy. 1990. "The Compelling Case for Youth Apprenticeships." *The Public Interest* 101: 62–77.

Lester, Richard A. 1954. *Hiring Practices and Labor Competition.* Princeton, N.J.: Industrial Relations Section, Princeton University.

Levin, Henry, and Richard Rumberger. 1987. "Educational Requirements for New Technologies." *Educational Policy* 1: 333–54.

Lewis, Darrell R., James C. Hearn, and Eric E. Zilbert. 1993. "Efficiencies and Equity Effects of Vocationally Focused Postsecondary Education." *Sociology of Education* 66(3): 188–205.

Lin, Nan, Walter Ensel, and John Vaughn. 1981. "Social Resources and Strength of Ties." *American Sociological Review* 46: 393–405.

Lortie, Dan. 1975. *School Teacher: A Sociological Study.* Chicago: University of Chicago Press.

Lynch, Lisa M. 1989. "The Youth Labor Market in the Eighties: Determinants of Reemployment Probabilities for Young Men and Women." *Review of Economics and Statistics* 71(1): 37–45.

Lynn, Irene, and Joan Wills. 1994. *School-Work-Transition: Lessons on Recruiting and Sustaining Employer Involvement.* Washington, D.C.: Institute for Educational Leadership.

Macaulay, Stewart. 1963. "Non-contractual Relations in Business: A Preliminary Study." *American Sociological Review* 28(1): 55–67.

MacLeod, Jay. 1987. *Ain't No Makin' It.* Boulder, Colo.: Westview Press.

Malm, Theodore F. 1954. "Recruiting Patterns and the Functioning of Labor Markets." *Industrial and Labor Relations Review* 7(4): 507–25.

Manski, Charles F. 1989. "Schooling as Experimentation." *Economics of Education Review* 8(4): 305–12.

Manwaring, Tony. 1984. "The Extended Internal Labour Market." *Cambridge Journal of Economics* 8: 161–87.

Manwaring, Tony, and Stephen Wood. 1984. "Recruitment and the Recession." *International Journal of Social Economics* 11: 49–63.

Mayer, Karl U., and Walter Muller. 1986. "The State and the Structure of the Life Course." In *Human Development and the Life Course,* edited by Aage B. Sørensen, Fred E. Weinert, and Lonnie R. Sherrod. Hillsdale, N.J.: Erlbaum Associates.

McPartland, James M., and Edward L. McDill. 1977. *Violence in Schools.* Lexington, Mass.: Heath Lexington.

Meyer, John. 1971. *The Expansion of the Autonomy of Youth: Responses of the Secondary School to the Problems of Order in the 1960s.* Stanford, Calif.: Department of Sociology, Stanford University.

———. 1977. "The Effects of Education as an Institution." *American Journal of Sociology* 83: 55–77.

Meyer, John W., and Brian Rowan. 1977. "Institutionalized Organizations: Formal Structure as Myth and Ceremony." *American Journal of Sociology* 83: 340–63.

Meyer, Robert. 1982. "An Economic Analysis of High School Vocational Education." In *The Federal Role in Vocational Education,* Special Report 39. Washington: National Commission for Employment Policy, U.S. Government Printing Office.

————. 1984. "The Transition from School to Work: The Experiences of Blacks and Whites." *Research in Labor Economics 6.* Greenwich, Conn.: JAI Press.

Meyer, Robert H., and D. A. Wise. 1982. "High School Preparation and Early Labor Force Experience." In *The Youth Labor Market Problem,* edited by Richard B. Freeman and D. A. Wise. Chicago: University of Chicago Press.

Mickelson, Roslyn. 1990. "The Attitude-Achievement Paradox Among Black Adolescents." *Sociology of Education* 63(January): 44–61.

Mickelson, Roslyn, and Matthew R. Walker. 1997. "Will Reforming School-to-Work Education Resolve Employer Dissatisfaction with Entry-level Workers?" Paper presented at the meeting of the American Sociological Association, Toronto (August).

Miller, Shazia R. 1998. "Shortcut: High School Grades as a Signal of Human Capital." *Educational Evaluation and Policy Analysis* 20(4): 299–311.

Miller, Shazia, and James E. Rosenbaum. 1996. "Social Infrastructure and Employers' Use of Information." Paper presented at the annual meeting of the American Sociological Association, New York (August 1996). Working Paper, Center for Urban Affairs and Policy Research, Northwestern University.

————. 1997. "Hiring in a Hobbesian World: Social Infrastructure and Employers' Use of Information." *Work and Occupations* 24(4, November): 498–523.

————. 1998. "What Do Grades Mean?" Institute for Policy Research. Unpublished paper. Evanston, Ill.: Northwestern University.

Mills, Virginia. 1977. "From School to Work: Matching Graduates to Careers." Paper presented at the conference "Labor Market Intermediaries," sponsored by the National Commission for Manpower Policy, Washington, D.C. (November 1977).

Ministry of Labor. 1981–83. *Shokugyou Antei Gyoumu Toukei* (Statistics on Employment Stability). Tokyo: Ministry of Labor.

Modell, John, Frank Furstenberg Jr., and Thomas Hershberg. 1976. "Social Change and Transitions to Adulthood in Historical Perspective." *Journal of Family History* 1: 7–31.

Moss, Philip, and Chris Tilly. 1996. "'Soft' Skills and Race." *Work and Occupations* 23(3, August): 252–76.

————. 2000. *Stories Employers Tell: Race, Skill, and Hiring in America.* New York: Russell Sage Foundation.

Murnane, Richard J., and Frank Levy. 1996. *Teaching the New Basic Skills: Principles for Educating Children to Thrive in a Changing Economy.* New York: Free Press.

Murnane, Richard J., John B. Willett, and Frank Levy. 1995. "The Growing Importance of Cognitive Skills in Wage Determination." *Review of Economics and Statistics* 77(2, May): 251–66.

NAEP (National Assessment of Educational Progress). 1985. *The Reading Report Card.* Princeton, N.J.: Educational Testing Service.

————. 1990. *Learning to Read in Our Nation's Schools.* Washington: U.S. Government Printing Office.

Nardone, Thomas. 1987. "Decline in Youth Population Does Not Lead to Lower Jobless Rates." *Monthly Labor Review* [research summaries] (June): 37–41.

NAS (National Academy of Sciences). 1984. *High Schools and the Changing Workplace: The Employers' View.* Washington, D.C.: National Academy Press.

National Research Council. 1989. *Fairness in Employment Testing: Validity Generalization, Minority Issues, and the General Aptitude Test Battery.* Washington, D.C.: National Academy Press.

NCEE (National Center on Education and the Economy), National Commission on Excellence in Education. 1983. *A Nation at Risk.* Washington: U.S. Government Printing Office (April).

————. 1990. *America's Choice: High Skills or Low Wages!* Rochester, N.Y.: NCEE.

NCEQW (National Center on the Educational Quality in the Workforce). 1994. "The EQW National Employer Survey: First Findings." Issue 10. Philadelphia: University of Pennsylvania.

NCES (National Center for Education Statistics). 1983. *High School and Beyond: 1980 Senior Cohort First Follow-up (1982): Data File User's Manual.* Chicago: National Opinion Research Center.

————. 1992. *Digest of Educational Statistics.* Washington: U.S. Government Printing Office.

————. 1993. *The Condition of Education.* Washington: U.S. Government Printing Office.

————. 1995. *Remedial Education at Higher Education Institutions.* Washington: U.S. Government Printing Office.

————. 1997a. *Digest of Educational Statistics.* Washington: U.S. Government Printing Office.

————. 1997b. *Youth Indicators: Trends in Well-being of American Youth.* Washington: Office of Educational Research and Improvement, U.S. Department of Education.

————. 1999. *Digest of Educational Statistics.* Washington: U.S. Government Printing Office.

Neckerman, Kathryn M., and Joleen Kirschenman. 1991. "Hiring Strategies, Racial Bias, and Inner-city Workers." *Social Problems* 38: 801–15.

Nelson-Rowe, Shan. 1991. "Corporation Schooling and the Labor Market at GE." *History of Education Quarterly* 31: 27–46.

Neubauser, Antonia. 1986. "Industry/Education Partnerships: Meeting the Needs of the 1980s." In *Becoming a Worker*, edited by Katherine M. Borman and John Reisman. Norwood, N.J.: Ablex.

Neugarten, Bernice L., and Gunhilde O. Hagestad. 1976. "Age and the Life Course." In *Handbook of Aging and the Social Sciences*, edited by Robert H. Binstock and Elaine Shanas. New York: Van Nostrand Reinhold.

Newitt, Jane. 1987. "Will the Baby Bust Work?" *American Demographics* 33–35(September): 1–63.

NLS72 1972 (National Longitudinal Survey of the Class of 1972). 1972. Washington: U.S. Department of Education.

Nolfi, George J. 1978. *Experiences of Recent High School Graduates.* Lexington, Mass.: Lexington Books.

NSK (Nihon Seishounen Kenkyuujo). 1984. *Gakkoukyouiku to Sono Kouka* (Education and Its Effects). Tokyo: NKS.

Oakes, Jeannie. 1985. *Keeping Track.* New Haven, Conn.: Yale University Press.

OECD (Organization for Economic Cooperation and Development). 1993. *Employment Outlook.* Paris: OECD.

Olneck, Michael R., and David B. Bills. 1980. "What Makes Sammy Run?: A Empirical Assessment of the Bowles-Gintis Correspondence." *American Journal of Education* (November): 27–61.

Orfield, Gary. 1984. *The Chicago Study of Access and Choice in Higher Education.* ERIC ED 248 929. Chicago: Committee on Public Policy, University of Chicago.

———. 1997. "Going to Work: Weak Preparation, Little Help." In *Advances in Educational Policy,* vol. 3, edited by Kenneth K. Wong. Greenwich, Conn.: JAI Press.

Orfield, Gary, and Faith G. Paul. 1994. *High Hopes, Long Odds: A Major Report on Hoosier Teens and the American Dream.* Indianapolis: Indiana Youth Institute.

Ornstein, Michael. 1976. *Entry into the American Labor Force.* New York: Academic Press.

Orr, Marie. 1996. *Wisconsin Youth Apprenticeship Program.* Boston: Jobs for the Future.

Osterman, Paul. 1980. *Getting Started: The Youth Labor Market.* Cambridge, Mass.: MIT Press.

———. 1988. *Employment Futures.* New York: Oxford University Press.

———. 1994. "Strategies for Involving Employers in School to Work Programs." Paper presented at the Brookings Institution conference, Washington, D.C. (May).

———. 1995. "Skill, Training, and Work Organization in American Establishments." *Industrial Relations* 34(2): 125–46.

Parcel, Toby. 1987. "Theories of the Labor Market and the Employment of Youth." In *Research in Sociology of Education and Socialization,* vol. 7, edited by Alan C. Kerckhoff. Greenwich, Conn.: JAI Press.

Parker, Jeffrey G., and Steven R. Asher. 1987. "Peer Relations and Later Personal Adjustment: Are Lower Accepted Children at Risk?" *Psychological Bulletin* 102: 357–89.

Parnes, Herbert S., and Andrew I. Kohen. 1975. "Occupational Information and Labor Market Status: The Case of Young Men." *Journal of Human Resources* 10(1): 44–55.

Parsons, Talcott. 1959. "The School Class as a Social System: Some of Its Functions in American Society." *Harvard Educational Review* 29(4): 297–318.

Paul, Faith. 1997. "Negotiated Identities and Academic Program Choice." In *Advances in Educational Policy,* vol. 3, edited by Kenneth K. Wong. Greenwich, Conn.: JAI Press.

Pauly, Edward, Hilary Kopp, and Joshua Haimson. 1995. *Homegrown Lessons: Innovative Programs Linking School and Work.* San Francisco: Jossey-Bass.

Persell, Caroline, and Peter Cookson. 1985. "Chartering and Bartering: Elite Education and Social Reproduction." *Social Problems* 33(2, December): 114–29.

———. 1986. *Preparing for Power.* New York: Basic Books.

Polk, Kenneth, and Walter E. Schafer, eds. 1972. *Schools and Delinquency.* Englewood Cliffs, N.J.: Prentice-Hall.

Porter, James N. 1974. "Race, Socialization, and Mobility in Educational and Early Occupational Attainment." *American Sociological Review* 39(June): 303–16.

Powell, Arthur G., Eleanor Farrar, and David K. Cohen. 1985. *The Shopping Mall High School.* Boston: Houghton Mifflin.

Prais, S.J. 1995. *Productivity, Education and Training: An International Perspective.* Cambridge, U.K.: Cambridge University Press.

Raffe, David. 1981. "Education, Employment, and the Youth Opportunities Programme: Some Sociological Perspectives." *Oxford Review of Education* 7(3): 211–22.

Raider, Holly J., and Ronald S. Burt. 1996. "Boundaryless Careers and Social Capital." In *Boundaryless Careers,* edited by Michael Arthur and Denise Rousseau. Oxford: Oxford University Press.

Rau, William, and Ann Durand. 2000. "The Academic Ethic and College Grades." *Sociology of Education* 73(January): 19–38.

Ray, Carol A., and Roslyn A. Mickelson. 1993. "Restructuring Students for Restructured Work." *Sociology of Education* 66: 1–20.

Rees, Albert. 1986. "An Essay on Youth Joblessness." *Journal of Economic Literature* 24: 613–28.

Resnick, Lauren B., and John G. Wirt. 1996. "The Changing Workplace." In *Linking School and Work: Roles for Standards and Assessment,* edited by Lauren B. Resnick and John G. Wirt. San Francisco: Jossey-Bass.

Reubens, Beatrice G. 1974. "Foreign and American Experiences with the Youth Transition." In *From School to Work,* edited by Eli Ginzberg. Washington, D.C.: National Commission on Manpower Policy.

Rhodes, Samuel R. 1983. "Age-Related Differences in Work Attitudes and Behavior: A Review and Conceptual Analysis." *Psychological Bulletin* 93(2): 328–67.

Riley, Maltilde W., Marilyn Johnson, and Anne Foner. 1972. *Aging and Society,* vol. 3, *A Sociology of Age Stratification.* New York: Russell Sage Foundation.

Riley, Maltilde W., and John Waring. 1976. "Age and Aging." In *Contemporary Social Problems,* 4th ed., edited by Robert K. Merton and Richard Nisbet. New York: Harcourt, Brace & Jovanovich.

Robinson, John P., Phillip R. Shaver, and Larence S. Wrightsman. 1991. *Measures of Personality and Social Psychological Attitudes.* San Diego, Calif.: Academic Press.

Rose, Lowell C., and Alec M. Gallup. 1999. "Phi Delta Kappa/Gallup Poll of the Public's Attitudes Toward the Public Schools." *Phi Delta Kappan* (September): 41–56.

Rosen, Sherwin. 1982. "Authority, Control, and the Distribution of Earnings." *Bell Journal of Economics* 13(2): 328–67.

Rosenbaum, James E. 1975. "The Stratification of Socialization Processes." *American Sociological Review* 40(1): 48–54.

———. 1976. *Making Inequality: The Hidden Curriculum of High School Tracking.* New York: Wiley.

———. 1978. "The Structure of Opportunity in School." *Social Forces* 57: 236–56.

———. 1980a. "Social Implications of Educational Grouping." In *Annual Review of Research in Education,* edited by David C. Berliner. Itasca, Ill.: American Educational Research Association.

———. 1980b. "Track Misperceptions and Frustrated College Plans: An Analysis of the Effects of Tracks and Track Perceptions in the National Longitudinal Survey." *Sociology of Education* 53(April): 74–88.

———. 1984. *Career Mobility in a Corporate Hierarchy.* New York: Academic Press.

———. 1986. "Institutional Career Structures and the Social Construction of Ability." In *Handbook of Theory and Research for the Sociology of Education,* edited by John Richardson. Westport, Conn.: Greenwood Press.

———. 1989. *Empowering Schools and Teachers: A New Link to Jobs for the Non-College-Bound.* Report to the U.S. Department of Labor, Commission on Workforce Quality and Labor Market Efficiency.

———. 1989a. "What If Good Jobs Depended on Good Grades?" *American Educator* 13(4, Winter): 10–43.

———. 1989b. "Organizational Career Systems and Employee Misperceptions." In *Handbook of Career Theory,* edited by Michael Arthur, Douglas T. Hall, and Barbara Lawrence. New York: Cambridge University Press.

———. 1992. *Youth Apprenticeship in America.* New York: W. T. Grant Foundation.

———. 1996a. "Policy Uses of Research on the High School-to-Work Transition." *Sociology of Education* (Summer): 102–22.

———. 1996b. "Schools and the World of Work." in *The Urban Crisis: Linking Research to Action,* edited by Burton A. Weisbrod and James C. Worthy. Evanston, Ill.: Northwestern University Press.

———. 1996c. "Analyses of College Plans of Students in the Vocational Track in the High School and Beyond." Unpublished paper. Evanston, Ill.: Institute for Policy Research, Northwestern University.

———. 1998a. "College-for-All: Do Students Understand What College Demands?" *Social Psychology of Education* 2(1): 55–80.

———. 1998b. "Should Low-achieving High School Graduates Attend College?" Unpublished paper. Evanston, Ill.: Northwestern Institute for Policy Research.

———. 1999. "Institutional Networks and Informal Strategies for Improving Work Entry for Youth." In *Education and Work in a Comparative Perspective,* edited by Walter Heinz. Cambridge: Cambridge University Press.

Rosenbaum, James E., and Amy Binder. 1997. "Do Employers Really Need More Educated Youth?" *Sociology of Education* 70: 68–85.

Rosenbaum, James, Stefanie DeLuca, and Shazia Miller. 2000. "Do Noncognitive Behaviors Affect School Grades and Life Outcomes?" Paper Presented at the Annual Meeting of the American Sociological Association, Washington D.C. (August 2000).

Rosenbaum, James E., Stefanie DeLuca, Shazia Miller, and Kevin Roy. 1999. "Pathways Into Work: Short and Long-term Effects of Personal and Institutional Ties." *Sociology of Education* 72(3, July): 179–96.

Rosenbaum, James E., and Stephanie Jones. 1995. "Creating Linkages in the High-School-to-Work Transition: Vocational Teachers' Networks." In *Restructuring Schools: Promises, Practices, and Policies*, edited by Maureen Hallinan. New York: Plenum.

———. 2000. "Interactions Between High Schools and Labor Markets." In *Handbook of Sociology of Education*, edited by Maureen Hallinan. New York: Plenum.

Rosenbaum, James E., and Takehiko Kariya. 1989. "From High School to Work: Market and Institutional Mechanisms in Japan." *American Journal of Sociology* 94(6, May): 1334–65.

———. 1991. "Do School Achievements Affect the Early Jobs of High School Graduates in the United States and Japan?" *Sociology of Education* 64(April): 78–95.

Rosenbaum, James E., Takehiko Kariya, Rick Settersten, and Tony Maier. 1990. "Market and Network Theories of the Transition from High School to Work: Their Application to Industrialized Societies." *Annual Review of Sociology* 16: 263–99.

Rosenbaum, James E., and Shazia S. Miller. 1997. "Ships Passing in the Night: When Do Beneficial Transactions Occur?" Paper Presented at the Annual Meeting of the American Sociological Association, Toronto (August 1997).

———. 1998. "The Earnings Payoff to College Degrees for Youths with Poor High School Achievement." Unpublished paper. Evanston, Ill.: Institute for Policy Research, Northwestern University.

Rosenbaum, James E., Shazia Miller, and Melinda Krei. 1996. "Gatekeeping in an Era of More Open Gates." *American Journal of Education* 104(August): 257–79.

———. 1997. "What Role Should Counselors Have?" In *Advances in Educational Policy*, vol. 3, edited by Kenneth K. Wong. Greenwich, Conn.: JAI Press.

Rosenbaum, James E., Shazia Miller, and Kevin Roy. 1996. "Long-term Effects of High School Grades and Job Placements." Paper presented at the annual meeting of the American Sociological Association, New York (August 1996).

Rosenbaum, James E., and Karen A. Nelson. 1994. "The Influence of Perceived Articulation on Students' School Effort." Paper presented at the annual meeting of the American Educational Research Association, New Orleans (April 4, 1994).

Rosenbaum, James E., and Kevin Roy. 1995. "Long-term Effects of High School Grades and Job Placements." Paper presented at the annual meeting of the American Sociological Association, New York (August 1995).

———. 1996. "Trajectories for Success in the Transition from School to Work." Paper presented at the annual meeting of the American Educational Research Association, New York (April 8, 1996).

Rosenbaum, James E., Kevin Roy, and Takehiko Kariya. 1995. "Do High Schools Help Some Students Enter the Labor Market?" Paper presented at the annual meeting of the American Sociological Association, Washington (August 1995).

Rosenthal, Rachel, and James Hearn. 1982. "Sex Differences in the Significance of Economic Resources for Choosing and Attending a College." In *The Undergraduate Women,* edited by Pamela Perun. Lexington, Mass.: Lexington Books.

Roze, Marie, and Mary Curtis. 1990. "Alumni Survey." Unpublished report from the (unidentified) technical school (May 1990).

Ryder, Norman B. 1965. "The Cohort as a Concept in the Study of Social Change." *American Sociological Review* 30: 843–61.

SCANS (Secretary's Commission on Achieving Necessary Skills). 1991. *What Work Requires of Schools: A SCANS Report for America 2000.* Washington: U.S. Department of Labor.

Schafer, Walter E., and Carol Olexa. 1971. *Tracking and Opportunity.* Scranton, Penn.: Chandler.

Schneider, Barbara, and David Stevenson. 1999. *The Ambitious Generation.* New Haven, Conn.: Yale University Press.

Scott, John. 1991. "Networks of Corporate Power." *Annual Review of Sociology* 15: 181–203.

Sedlak, Michael W., Christopher W. Wheeler, Diane C. Pullin, and Phillip A. Cusick. 1986. *Selling Students Short.* New York: Teachers College Press.

Seeley, Daniel S. 1984. "Educational Partnership and the Dilemmas of School Reform." *Phi Delta Kappan* 65(6): 383–88.

Sewell, William H. 1971. "Inequality of Opportunity for Higher Education." *American Sociological Review* 36: 793–809.

Sewell, William H., and Robert Hauser. 1975. *Education, Occupation, and Earnings.* New York: Academic.

Shaiken, Harley. 1984. *Work Transformed.* Lexington, Mass.: Lexington Books.

Shapiro, Daniel, and Margaret Goertz. 1998. "Connecting Work and School." Paper presented at the meeting of the American Educational Research Association, San Diego (April).

Shapiro, Daniel, and Maria Iannozzi. 1999. *The Benefits to Bridging Work and School: Results of the 1997 National Employer Survey.* Philadelphia: National Center for Postsecondary Education, University of Pennsylvania.

Shavit, Yossi, and Walter Muller. 1998. *From School to Work.* Oxford: Clarendon Press.

Shouse, Roger, Barbara Schneider, and Stephen Plank. 1992. "Teacher Assessments of Student Effort: Effects of Student Characteristics and School Type." *Educational Policy* 6: 266–88.

Sizer, Theodore R. 1984. *Horace's Compromise: The Dilemma of the American High School.* Boston: Houghton Mifflin.

Smigel, Edwin O. 1965. *The Wall Street Lawyer.* New York: Free Press.

Smith, Gene M. 1967. "Personality Correlates of Academic Performance in Three Dissimilar Populations." Proceedings of the seventy-seventh annual convention of the American Psychological Association.

Sørensen, Aage. 1977. "The Structure of Inequality and the Process of Attainment." *American Sociological Review* 42(6): 965–78.

Soskice, David. 1994. "Reconciling Markets and Institution: The German Apprenticeship System." In *Training and the Private Sector: International Comparisons,* edited by Lisa M. Lynch. Chicago: University of Chicago Press.

Spence, A. Michael. 1974. *Market Signaling: Informational Transfer in Hiring and Related Screening Processes.* Cambridge, Mass.: Harvard University Press.

Spenner, Kenneth. 1995. "Technological Change, Skill Requirements, and Education." In *The New Modern Times,* edited by David Bills. Albany: State University of New York Press.

Spenner, Kenneth, and Luther B. Otto. 1982. *Career Lines and Careers.* Lexington, Mass.: Lexington Books.

Spring, Joel. 1986. "Business and the Schools: The New Partnerships." In *Becoming a Worker,* edited by Katherine M. Borman and John Reisman. Norwood, N.J.: Ablex.

Squires, Gregory D. 1979. *Education and Jobs: The Imbalancing of the Social Machinery.* New Brunswick, N.J.: Transaction Books.

Steinberg, Lawrence. 1996. *Beyond the Classroom.* New York: Simon & Schuster.

Stern, David, Neal Finkelstein, James Stone, John Latting, and Carolyn Dornsife. 1995. *School to Work: Research on Programs in the United States.* Washington, D.C., and London: Falmer Press.

Stern, David, Marylyn Raby, and Charles Dayton. 1992. *Career Academies: Partnerships for Reconstructing American High Schools.* San Francisco: Jossey-Bass.

Stern, David, and David Stevens. 1992. "Analysis of Unemployment Insurance Data on the Relationship Between High School Cooperative Education and Subsequent Employment." Paper prepared for the National Assessment of Vocational Education. Berkeley: School of Education, University of California.

Stern, David, and Daniel A. Wagner. 1999. *International Perspectives on the School to Work Transition.* Cresskill, N.J.: Hampton Press.

Stevenson, Harold W., and James W. Stigler. 1992. *The Learning Gap: Why Our Schools Are Failing and What We Can Learn from Japanese and Chinese Education.* New York: Summit.

Stigler, George J. 1961. "The Economics of Information." *Journal of Political Economy* 69: 213–25.

Stinchcombe, Arthur L. 1965. *Rebellion in a High School.* Chicago: Quadrangle.

———. 1985. "Contracts as Hierarchical Documents." In *Organization Theory and Project Management,* edited by Arthur L. Stinchcombe and Carol A. Heimer. Bergen: Norwegian University Press.

Stolzenberg, Ross M. 1975. "Occupation, Markets, and Wages." *American Sociological Review* 40: 298–321.

Tessler, R., and R. Sushelsky. 1978. "Effects of Eye Contact and Social Status on the Perception of a Job Applicant in an Employment Interviewing Situation." *Journal of Vocational Behavior* 13: 338–47.

Thompson, Scott, and David Stanard. 1975. "Student Attendance and Absenteeism." *The Practitioner* 1: 1–12.

Thurow, Lester. 1975. *Generating Inequality.* New York: Basic Books.

Timpane, Michael. 1984. "Business Has Rediscovered the Public Schools." *Phi Delta Kappan* 65(6): 389–92.

Tolbert, Charles. 1982. "Industrial Segmentation and Men's Career Mobility." *American Sociological Review* 47 (August): 457–77.

Trow, Martin. 1961. "The Second Transformation of American Secondary Education." *International Journal of Comparative Sociology* 2: 144–65.

Turner, Ralph. 1960. "Modes of Social Ascent Through Education: Sponsored and Contest Mobility." *American Sociological Review* 25: 855–67.

U.S. Bureau of Education, Department of the Interior. 1916. "Vocational Secondary Education." Washington: U.S. Government Printing Office.

U.S. Department of Education. 1987. *Japanese Education Today.* Washington: U.S. Government Printing Office.

Urquiola, Miguel, David Stern, Ilana Horn, Carolyn Dornsife, Bernadette Chi, Lea Williams, Donna Merritt, Katherine Hughes, and Thomas Bailey. 1997. *School to Work, College, and Career.* Berkeley: National Center for Research in Vocational Education, University of California.

Useem, Elizabeth. 1986. *Low-Tech Education in a High-Tech World: Corporations and Classrooms in the New Information Society.* New York: Free Press.

Useem, Elizabeth L., and Michael Useem. 1974. *The Education Establishment.* Englewood Cliffs, N.J.: Prentice-Hall.

———. 1992. "Middle Schools and Math Groups." *Sociology of Education* 65: 263–79.

Useem, Michael. 1979. "The Social Organization of the American Business Elite and Participation of Corporation Directors in the Governance of American Institutions." *American Sociological Review* 44: 553–72.

Veum, Jonathan R., and Andrea B. Weiss. 1993. "Education and the Work Histories of Young Adults." *Monthly Labor Review* 116(4): 11–20.

Waldman, David A., and Bruce J. Avolio. 1986. "A Meta-analysis of Age Differences in Job Performance." *Journal of Applied Psychology* 71(1): 33–38.

Wanous, John P. 1992. *Organizational Entry: Recruitment, Selection, Orientation, and Socialization of Newcomers.* 2nd ed. Reading, Mass.: Addison-Wesley.

Wegener, Bernd. 1991. "Job Mobility and Social Ties." *American Sociological Review* 56(February): 60–71.

Wentzel, Kathryn R. 1991. "Social Competence at School: Relation Between Social Responsibility and Academic Achievement." *Review of Educational Research* 61: 1, 1–24.

Wentzel, Kathryn R., Daniel A. Weinberger, Martin E. Ford, and S. Shirley Feldman. 1990. "Academic Achievement in Preadolescence: The Role of Motivational, Affective, and Self-regulatory Processes." *Journal of Applied Developmental Psychology* 11: 179–93.

West, Michael, and Peggy Newton. 1983. *The Transition from School to Work.* New York: Nichols.

Wielgosz, John B., and Susan Carpenter. 1987. "The Effectiveness of Alternative Methods of Searching for Jobs and Finding Them: An Exploratory Analysis of the Data Bearing Upon the Ways of Coping with Joblessness." *The American Journal of Economics and Sociology* 46(April): 151–64.

Williamson, Oliver E. 1975. *Markets and Hierarchies: Analysis and Antitrust Implications.* New York: Free Press.

———. 1981. "The Economics of Organization: The Transaction-Cost Approach." *American Journal of Sociology* 87(November): 548–77.

Willis, Paul. 1977. *Learning to Labor.* New York: Columbia University Press.

Willis, Robert, and Sherwin Rosen. 1979. "Education and Self-selection." *Journal of Political Economy* 87(5, pt. 2): 527–36.

Wilms, Wellford W. 1984. "Vocational Education and Job Success: The Employer's View." *Phi Delta Kappan* (January): 347–50.

Wilson, Bruce L., and Gretchen B. Rossman. 1993. *Mandating Academic Excellence: High School Responses to State Curriculum Reform.* New York: Teachers College Press.

Wilson, William Julius. 1996. *When Work Disappears.* New York: Vintage.

Wirt, John G., Lana D. Muraskin, David A. Goodwin, and Robert H. Meyer. 1989. *National Assessment of Vocational Education.* Washington: U.S. Department of Education.

Witte, James, and Arnie L. Kalleberg. 1994. "Determinants and Consequences of Fit Between Vocational Education and Employment in Germany." In *School-to-Work: What Does Research Say About It?*, edited by Nevser Stacey. Washington: U.S. Office of Education.

Zemsky, Robert. 1994. "What Employers Want." Philadelphia: National Center on the Educational Quality of the Workforce, University of Pennsylvania.

Zucker, Lynn G. 1986. "Production of Trust: Institutional Sources of Economic Structure 1980–1920." In *Research in Organizational Behavior,* 8th ed., edited by Barry M. Staw and Lawrence L. Cummings. Greenwich, Conn.: JAI Press.

Zucker, Lynn G., and Carolyn Rosenstein. 1981. "Taxonomies of Institutional Structure: Dual Economy Reconsidered." *American Sociological Review* 46: 869–84.

Zweigenhaft, Richard, and William Domhoff. 1991. *Blacks in the White Establishment?* New Haven, Conn.: Yale University Press.

= Index =

Boldface numbers refer to figures and tables.

Coleman, J., 243, 248
college admissions testing, 272, 289*n*1
College Board, 272–73
college-bound students: back-up plans, 83, 84, 282; high school relevance, 59–62, 269; motivation of, 41; readiness testing, 276–77, 280, 281. *See also* students' perceptions of college
college credit completion, 76–79
college curriculum tracks, 90. *See also* curriculum tracks
college degree attainment and earnings payoff, 75–76
college-for-all norm: and counseling strategies, 99–101, 103; and educational attainment, 1–2; explanation, 56–57; opportunity costs of, 80–81; policy considerations, 81–84, 266–69
colleges and universities: charters, 232; enrollment, 55; graduation rates, 67–68, 266–67; linkages, 49–50, 255–58, 261; noncognitive behavior of applicants, 170–71. *See also* community colleges
Colleges of Further Education (Britain), 48
Collins, R., 26, 111
Combs, J., 284*n*4
community colleges: dropout rates, 56, 57; enrollment, 55; graduation rates, 67–68, 104, 266–67; growth of, 89; nondisclosure of student performance information, 267; open-admissions policies, 64–65, 89, 99–101, 104; opportunity costs of attending, 79–80; as recruitment source, 154; as "second chance" institution, 64–65; and students' perceptions of high school relevance, 60; transfer rate to four-year colleges, 104
contacts. *See* job contacts analysis
contest mobility norm, 90, 99
Cook, P., 285*n*5

Cookson, P., 256, 289*n*2
Cooley, W., 284*n*4
"cooling out," 55–56, 91, 102–3
co-op programs, 229, 263, 274–75, 279
counselors: employers' view of, 126–27, 157–59; in preparatory schools, 255–58; time pressures of, 41; in vocational schools, 259
counselors' influence on college plans: historical perspective, 88–89; methodology, 92, 104–5; research considerations, 89–92; role, 92–98, 103–4, 105, 106–7, 268; strategies, 91, 98–103
Crain, R., 39, 247
credential inflation, 142
credentialism, 25–26, 36–37, 67
Crohn, R., 135
cultural differences, 15–16, 143
curriculum tracks: and academic skills, 238; and educational attainment, 69–71, **73**, 74; and future earnings, 205–6, 207, **208**; and job contacts, 198–99, 201; signaling theory, 37–38; and student behavior, 284*n*4. *See also* vocational programs

data sources: grades and earnings payoff, 112; hiring criteria, 8–9, 29, 136; job contacts analysis, 195–96, 197, 198–99; noncognitive skills, 173; student behavior, 10, 28, 176–77; students' perception of college, 59; vocational education and earnings payoff, 220
DeLany, B., 91
Diamond, D., 39, 136
diploma, importance of, 36–37
disabled students, 235, 261
disadvantaged youths, 197, 204
discipline, of students, 28, 185, 187, 191–92
discrimination: and educational attainment, 74; hiring procedures, 150–51; and linkages, 260–62;